DOCUMENTARY SOURCES IN ANCIENT NEAR EASTERN AND GRECO-ROMAN ECONOMIC HISTORY
METHODOLOGY AND PRACTICE

edited by

Heather D. Baker and Michael Jursa

Oxbow Books
Oxford & Philadelphia

Published in the United Kingdom in 2014 by
OXBOW BOOKS
10 Hythe Bridge Street, Oxford OX1 2EW

and in the United States by
OXBOW BOOKS
908 Darby Road, Havertown, PA 19083

© Oxbow Books and the individual contributors 2014

Hardback Edition: ISBN 978-1-78297-651-6
Digital Edition: ISBN 978-1-78297-759-9

A CIP record for this book is available from the British Library

Library of Congress Cataloging-in-Publication Data

Documentary sources in ancient Near Eastern and Greco-Roman economic history : methodology and
practice / edited by Heather D. Baker and Michael Jursa.
     pages cm.
 Includes bibliographical references and index.
 ISBN 978-1-78297-758-2
 1. Economic history--To 500. 2. Babylonia--Economic conditions. 3. Rome--Economic conditions--30
B.C.-476 A.D. 4. Rome--Economic conditions--510-30 B.C. 5. Egypt--Economic conditions--332 B.C.-640
A.D. I. Baker, Heather D. II. Jursa, Michael.
 HC31.D63 2014
 330.935'5--dc23
                     2014027157

Printed in the United Kingdom by Short Run Press, Exeter

For a complete list of Oxbow titles, please contact:

UNITED KINGDOM
Oxbow Books
Telephone (01865) 241249, Fax (01865) 794449
Email: oxbow@oxbowbooks.com
www.oxbowbooks.com

UNITED STATES OF AMERICA
Oxbow Books
Telephone (800) 791-9354, Fax (610) 853-9146
Email: queries@casemateacademic.com
www.casemateacademic.com/oxbow

Oxbow Books is part of the Casemate Group

Cover details: P.Vindob. G 2119 Recto (Papyrus, Hermupolis, 6th/7th century AD): SPP III2 97. Receipt for
the payment of rents as share of an inheritance. SPP III2 97. © Österreichische Nationalbibliothek,
Papyrussammlung. BM 77394 (Cuneiform tablet, Babylon, 494 BC): H.D. Baker, The Archive of the Nappāḫu
Family. Vienna, 2004, p. 401, no. 66a. Promissory note for silver with temple prebend as security. © H.D.
Baker and the Institut für Orientalistik, Universität Wien.

Table of Contents

PRICES IN THE ANCIENT MEDITERRANEAN AND NEAR EAST

Preface

This volume comprises the proceedings of an interdisciplinary conference held in Vienna in 2008 to mark the final phase of the START Project "The Economic History of Babylonia in the First Millennium BC" funded by the Fonds zur Förderung der wissenschaftlichen Forschung (Austrian Science Fund). The preparation of this book has benefitted from the assistance of a number of individuals, to whom the editors owe their grateful thanks. With exemplary care and efficiency, Daniela Niedermayer and Georg Tanzler took care of the preliminary formatting of most of the contributions, and we thank Judith Pfitzner for preparing one article and especially for her work on compiling the Index. We are also greatly indebted to Emmanuelle Salgues and Elvira Wakelnig, who translated the articles by Dominique Charpin and Sven Tost from their respective original French and German. Finally, we thank Julie Gardiner and her colleagues at Oxbow Books for accepting this volume and seeing it through to publication.

Heather D. Baker and Michael Jursa
Vienna, October 2013

Contributors

Heather D. Baker (Vienna University)

Dominique Charpin (Paris)

Jan Gerrit Dercksen (Leiden University)

Michael Jursa (Vienna University)

Dennis Kehoe (Tulane University)

Myrto Malouta (Oxford University)

Reinhard Pirngruber (VU University Amsterdam)

Dominic Rathbone (King's College London)

Sitta von Reden (Albert-Ludwigs-Universität, Freiburg im Breisgau)

R. J. van der Spek (VU University Amsterdam)

Sven Tost (Vienna University)

Caroline Waerzeggers (VU University Amsterdam)

1

Introduction

Michael Jursa

This collection of papers is the result of a conference in Vienna in 2008 that brought together scholars of different periods of Mesopotamian history and classicists working on Greco-Roman sources. The conference was held under the auspices of the START project 'The Economic History of Babylonia in the First Millennium BC' which was directed by M. Jursa at the University of Vienna between 2002 and 2009. Correspondingly, the objective of the conference was to explore the potential of interdisciplinary approaches to ancient economic history on a methodological and a factual level, a research programme that has since led to the establishment of a joint project of classicists, papyrologists, Islamic historians and Assyriologists exploring aspects of ancient administrative history.[1] In fact, similar agenda are being pursued also elsewhere, e.g., by the 'Legal Documents in Ancient Societies' group.[2]

The Vienna conference aimed not only at establishing a dialogue between different academic fields that might eventually broaden the protagonists' perspective as they pursued their respective interests; it was also intended – as this volume intends – to address methodological points of contact in the study of Ancient Near Eastern and Greco-Roman documentary sources, and to investigate the potential commensurability of the results of such investigations. More specifically, the conference's agenda was informed by the – admittedly very old – question of whether it should be accepted, following in the footsteps of Moses Finley, that the basic structure of the Ancient Mesopotamian economies, in which institutional households and redistributive bureaucracies played an important role, precludes making useful comparisons with the economic systems of the Greco-Roman world, in which such institutions generally

---

[1] http://imperiumofficium.univie.ac.at/ (accessed 22.8.2013).

[2] http://www.ldas-conf.com/ (accessed 22.8.2013). See now Faraguna 2013, where some issues related to ancient archival documentation from the Ancient Near East and the Greco-Roman world that are at stake also in the present volume are explored.

did not have an important function.[3] While this position continues to be held in the field of Greco-Roman history, it is – increasingly, it would seem – at odds with the perception of Assyriologists that the nature of the Mesopotamian economies is not captured sufficiently by the institutional household model which informed Finley's thesis. Nowadays a much more important role is ascribed to the economic agency and the economic interdependence (on the basis of commercial exchange) of individuals and nuclear households. The papers presented by Charpin and especially Dercksen in this volume can serve as an example for the state of research on the first half of the second millennium BC.[4] A 'modernist' or 'formalist' view of the Mesopotamian economy is especially prevalent among the specialists in the Mesopotamian Iron age, where, as can now be demonstrated, from the sixth century BC at least, a strongly monetized economy experienced phases of noticeable aggregate and per capita growth on the strength of agricultural intensification and efficient institutions, which include fairly well performing commodity markets and, at least in part and for some time, also factor markets.[5] Incidentally, at the same time some students of the Greco-Roman economy have turned against what used to be minimalist or primitivist readings of the evidence, emphasizing the remarkable performance especially of the Roman economy, and seeing evidence for economic growth that is structurally not dissimilar (albeit happening on a much larger scale) from the model that can be posited for the economic development in Mesopotamia's imperial phase of the Iron Age.[6] However, while the 'formalist' reading of the Mesopotamian economy of the first millennium BC can be supported not only by a rich body of qualitative information extracted from thousands of economic documents, but also by an irregular, but still quite abundant flow of quantifiable data (see, e.g., the contributions of van der Spek, Pirngruber and Jursa in this volume), such data are largely lacking for much of Greco-Roman antiquity – and archaeological data, which can serve as a proxy for textual data, is quite often ambiguous.[7] It comes thus as no surprise that opinions on the Roman (and Greek) economy still differ widely and that a reviewer might state that a book on "The Roman Market Economy" did "a good job of persuading me that there was really nothing resembling an integrated Roman market economy",[8] that "there are no ancient statistics" and that "as Finley insisted, the crucial point is that the Romans simply did

---

[3]   See below the contribution by Jursa, notes 5–7.

[4]   For a nuanced view of the data from the third millennium BC, which lend themselves best to the traditional 'household model,' see Garfinkle 2012.

[5]   Van der Spek *et al.* (forthcoming).

[6]   See, e.g., Morris *et al.* 2007, Bresson (2014) and Jongman (2014).

[7]   As can be shown by the divergent interpretations of the huge amphora mound (Monte Testaccio) outside Rome as evidence for long-distance trade in olive oil or for state-controlled distribution: e.g., Thonemann 2013, 10–11 (to which Jongman (2014) can be added).

[8]   While, according to Rathbone 2007, 719, "the main stimulus to economic development in Roman Egypt came from the Roman creation of a peaceful and open Mediterranean market, and the boom in demand caused by empire-wide urbanization."

not conceive of their "economic" activity (buying, selling, lending) in what we would think of as economic terms at all."[9]

The specific contribution of this volume, beyond the methodological level, lies in its offering a point of comparison that may cause the Greco-Roman data to appear in a new light. Ancient Near Eastern data, once they are demonstrated to be commensurable with corresponding Greco-Roman information, can serve as proxy-data to compensate for the lack of data on the Greco-Roman side (providing this comparison is done with some control over the different cultural settings, obviously). Two examples: it may potentially be conceded that Romans, or perhaps some Romans, thought about their economy "not in terms of commerce, contracts and profits, but obligations, benefits, and reciprocity," rendering this a "moral economy"[10] – but Ancient Near Eastern data can show that this is quite probably a misleading contrast in that, for instance, "a characterization of Old Assyrian merchants as profit-driven private entrepreneurs is correct, but ignores the all-permeating influence of religious, legal, and other institutions into which the trade and the traders (as in other periods and places) were embedded" (Dercksen, this volume): the market is evidently as culturally embedded as any other institution of socio-economic life. While this is perhaps by now a commonplace among economic historians and economic anthropologists,[11] it is satisfying to note that the Old Assyrian evidence as discussed by Dercksen contains, if not the Assyrian equivalent of the lost work *De opibus gentium* by a putative Roman Adam Smith,[12] then at least explicit textual data that refer to the Assyrian merchants' awareness of the economic rules of the socio-economic environment in which they operated. A second example: the mere fact that Rathbone, van der Spek and von Reden are able to make a meaningful comparison between grain prices in Seleucid Babylonia, Ptolemaic Egypt and Rome is a remarkable first, especially as the robust Babylonian data lend considerable additional weight to the argument: "We seem to be dealing with a world where regional factors of production and consumption set normal ranges of grain prices but there was sufficient overarching market integration to link these ranges in patterns of fairly stable relationships" (Rathbone, this volume): a conclusion not easily squared with a Finleyite view of the Mediterranean economy.

Two papers present the extraordinarily rich information from Middle Bronze-Age Mesopotamia. Drawing on evocative anecdotal information and quantitative data alike, Dercksen presents a nuanced picture of Old Assyrian trade and the workings of the embedded markets he posits, and of the institutions that governed their functioning.[13] Charpin offers a survey of the even more vast and more variegated, but also more

---

[9] All quotes from Thonemann 2013.

[10] All quotes from Thonemann 2013.

[11] In direct opposition to Polanyi's view of the market, in fact. This is relevant because Polanyi is still frequently invoked with respect to the Ancient Near East (Dale 2013), but it does not seem that there is still much to be gained here.

[12] Who, according to Thonemann 2013, 11, is literally inconceivable.

[13] Note that a recent systematic survey of the structure of the documentary record which Dercksen uses can be found in Veenhof 2013.

dispersed Old Babylonian corpus. This is a background article to an ongoing project directed by Charpin that aims at building an online database of Old Babylonian texts (http://www.archibab.fr/). The article explores some of the aspects of the corpus that are of relevance for economic history, e.g., institutional record-keeping, accounting and the forecasting of institutional resources, all of which was done in a controlled and rational manner. There are structural parallels here to the estate accounts from Roman Egypt studied, e.g., in Rathbone 1991: the implications of such functional parallels in accounting systems for the reconstruction of their socio-economic setting have yet to be explored.

Three papers pursue an explicitly methodological interest. Kehoe brings the approach of New Institutional Economics to bear on legal and economic data relating to agrarian conditions in the Roman Empire. This institutional approach – which implicitly informs Dercksen's contribution too – is demonstrably also fruitful for Ancient Near Eastern studies (Jursa 2013) and can be expected to elicit a considerable degree of interest. While Kehoe draws on recent developments in economics and economic history, Waerzeggers finds her inspiration in the social sciences. Exploring the possibility of applying Social Network Analysis to ancient data – in this case, Late Babylonian private archives, – she introduces into Assyriological discourse a potent methodology that is certain to be taken up elsewhere in the field. The prosopographical data offered by the vast Mesopotamian tablet archives from the late third millennium, the first half of the second millennium and from the seventh and sixth century BC are well-suited for a quantifying analysis of this kind.[14] There is significant potential for dialogue between Ancient Near Eastern Studies and Papyrology here, as can be shown by a comparison of Waerzeggers' work (or of the studies cited in note 14) with, e.g., the work of Ruffini (2008) on Byzantine Egypt (see Kehoe 2013, 13–14). By drawing on both archaeological and textual data for the study of house sizes and their implications for household structure in first millennium BC Babylonia, and by attempting quantification on the basis of this information, Baker demonstrates not only that such an approach is possible on the basis of the information that can be culled from the tablet archives of the period and from the archaeological record, but that it is in fact the only way to overcome the inherent bias of any single type of source material we possess. By correlating dwelling sizes and textual data bearing on the size of households, the resulting investigation is also a contribution to the comparative study of living standards and social status in antiquity as well as an important corrective to the tendency in the study of urban demography to adopt all too simplified models for calculating population densities.

The remaining papers address some core issues of the economic history of the Iron Age and the Eastern Mediterranean world of Late Antiquity. Tost offers a nuanced reading of the evidence for money use in the Egyptian countryside from the fifth to the eighth century, i.e., from Late Antiquity to the early Islamic period. The

---

[14]   See now also, for instance, Brumfield 2013 and Bamman *et al.* 2013

documentary record does not support the thesis of a lesser degree of penetration of money into the rural economy in comparison to exchange in urban contexts, thus supporting at least one aspect of Banaji's view of Late Antique economic development (Banaji 2007). The paper argues against considering Egypt, and thus Egyptian evidence, of Late Antiquity as in any way exceptional in comparison to the rest of the Roman empire. This point has also been emphasized by others, e.g., Rathbone (2007, 698–699), while for Finley (1992, 98), at least for conditions in the countryside, Egypt was still "extreme and untypical." The value of using Egyptian data for extrapolations valid for the Empire as a whole is apparent also in Malouta's paper on the evidence for water-lifting devices in Roman Egypt (see also Malouta and Wilson 2013), in that the Finleyite vision of a Greco-Roman economy hamstrung by static productivity levels and the absence of technological development is implicitly under review here. Another aspect of the same vision, viz., the fundamental difference between the Mesopotamian economy and the economy of the Greco-Roman world, is addressed by the implications of Jursa's contribution. Summarizing some of the main results of the START Project, this paper demonstrates that the Babylonian economy in the sixth century experienced sustained economic growth through agrarian and commercial expansion within the context of an increasing monetization of exchange. It is argued that structurally, this stage of economic development in Mesopotamia displays many points of similarity with later Greco-Roman economies which at the same time distinguish it from the (alleged) continuum of 'the' Mesopotamian economy from the Early to the Late Bronze Age. In this sense the paper can be seen to set the stage for Pirngruber's paper and for the joint contribution of van der Spek, von Reden and Rathbone. Drawing on what is probably the best, or at least the most coherent, source on commodity prices from all of Antiquity, viz. the Babylonian Astronomical Diaries, Pirngruber studies the impact of natural catastrophes, in this case, locust plagues, on the commodity market in Babylonia,[15] demonstrating thereby the high volatility of this market under the influence of exogenous shocks. Van der Spek investigates the same sources for his study of grain prices in Seleucid and Parthian Babylonia, van Reden studies the corresponding information from Ptolemaic Egypt (which is less abundant), and Rathbone assembles what is known about grain prices from other parts of the Mediterranean world. The result is "a unified analysis of grain prices over this long period [the last three centuries BC] in the broad area of the ancient Mediterranean and Near Eastern world" (Rathbone, this volume). As stated above, they argue that there was a certain degree of overarching market integration in the Mediterranean basin and adjacent areas in this period.

---

[15]   See now also Pirngruber 2012.

REFERENCES

Bamman, D., Anderson, A. and Smith, N. A. (2013) Inferring Social Rank in an Old Assyrian Trade Network. In: *arXiv:1303.2873v1 [cs.CY] 12 Mar 2013* (http://arxiv.org/pdf/1303.2873v1.pdf; accessed 22.8.2013)

Banaji, J. (2007) *Agrarian Change in Late Antiquity. Gold, Labour, and Aristocratic Dominance.* Revised edition, Oxford: Oxford University Press.

Bresson, A. (2014) Capitalism and the Ancient Greek Economy. In L. Neal (ed.), *The Cambridge History of Capitalism. Vol. 1: The Rise of Capitalism*, 43–74. Cambridge: Cambridge University Press.

Brumfield, S. (2013) *Imperial Methods: Using Text Mining and Social Network Analysis to Detect Regional Strategies in the Akkadian Empire.* PhD dissertation, UCLA.

Dale, G. (2013) 'Marketless Trading in Hammurabi's Time': A Re-appraisal. *Journal of the Economic and Social History of the Orient* 56, 159–188.

Faraguna, M. (ed.) (2013) *Archives and Archival Documents in Ancient Societies. Trieste 30 September-1 October 2011* (Legal Documents in Ancient Societies IV). Trieste: Edizioni Università di Trieste.

Finley, M. (1992) *The Ancient Economy.* London: Penguin Books.

Garfinkle, S. J. (2012) *Entrepreneurs and Enterprise in Early Mesopotamia. A Study of Three Archives from the Third Dynasty of Ur (2112-2004 BCE).* Bethesda, MD: CDL Press.

Jongman, W. (2014) The Reconstruction of the Roman Economy. In L. Neal (ed.), *The Cambridge History of Capitalism. Vol. 1: The Rise of Capitalism*, 75–100. Cambridge: Cambridge University Press.

Jursa, M. (2013) L'economia babilonese nel sesto secolo a.C.: crescita economica in un contesto imperiale. *Studi Storici* 54/2, 247–266.

Kehoe, D. (2013) Archives and Archival Documents in Ancient Societies: Introduction. In Faraguna 2013, 11–19.

Malouta, M. and Wilson, A. I. (2013) Mechanical Irrigation: Water-Lifting Devices in the Archaeological Evidence and the Egyptian Papyri. In A. K. Bowman and A. I. Wilson (eds) *The Agricultural Economy*, 275–307 (Oxford Studies in the Roman Economy). Oxford: Oxford University Press.

Morris, I., Saller, R.P. and Scheidel, W. (2007) Introduction. In W. Scheidel, I. Morris and R. Saller (eds), *The Cambridge Economic History of the Greco-Roman World*, 1–12. Cambridge: Cambridge University Press.

Pirngruber, R. (2012) *The Impact of Empire on Market Prices in Babylon in the Late Achaemenid and Seleucid periods, ca. 400-140 B.C.* PhD Dissertation, VU Amsterdam.

Rathbone, D. (1991) *Economic Rationalism and Rural Society in Third-Century A.D. Egypt. The Heroninos Archive and the Appianus Estate.* Cambridge: Cambridge University Press.

Rathbone, D. (2007) Roman Egypt. In W. Scheidel, I. Morris and R. Saller (eds), *The Cambridge Economic History of the Greco-Roman World*, 698–719. Cambridge: Cambridge University Press.

Ruffini, G. R. (2008) *Social Networks in Byzantine Egypt.* Cambridge: Cambridge University Press.

Thonemann, P. (2013) Who made the amphora mountain? *Times Literary Supplement August 9 2013*, 10–11.

van der Spek, R. J., van Leeuwen, B. and van Zanden, J. L. (eds) (forthcoming), *A History of Market Performance from Ancient Babylonia to the Modern World* (Routledge Explorations in Economic History) London: Routledge.

Veenhof, K. (2013) The Archives of Old Assyrian Traders: their Nature, Functions and Use. In Faraguna 2013, 27–61.

2

House Size and Household Structure: Quantitative Data in the Study of Babylonian Urban Living Conditions[1]

Heather D. Baker

INTRODUCTION

The aim of this paper is to examine the relationship between dwelling size, household structure and social status in urban Babylonia during the first millennium BC. For this period we have a wealth of complex data on dwelling size that, properly contextualised, can contribute significant insights to the wider debate concerning living space in antiquity. In contrast to comparable studies for other parts of the ancient world, which have relied on archaeological evidence alone, the dataset for Babylonia at this period is supplemented by a sizable corpus of textually-documented urban property sizes. However, matching the written and archaeological evidence is, as we shall see, no straightforward matter. One of my tasks here will be to evaluate the problems and pitfalls in the hope of determining how we might make the best use of the available data.

The relationship between dwelling size and household size is of interest for a number of reasons. Although the present paper is not primarily concerned with methods of

[1] Much of the research on which this article is based was conducted during the period 2004–2008 within the framework of the START Project led by M. Jursa at the University of Vienna and funded by the FWF (Austrian Science Fund). The article was completed under the auspices of the project 'Royal Institutional Households in First Millennium BC Mesopotamia' led by the author since March 2009 and funded by the FWF (grant S10802–G18) as part of the National Research Network 'Imperium and Officium: Comparative Studies in Ancient Bureaucracy and Officialdom'.

estimating urban populations, nevertheless the findings presented here are of some relevance because demographic studies in archaeological research normally rely on some method of determining occupation densities, for example by using a multiplier such as the number of households per hectare, or the number of persons per hectare.[2] The application of such methods in a Mesopotamian context have been discussed by Postgate, based on case studies from the Early Dynastic and Old Babylonian periods.[3] It should be noted that for 1st millennium BC Babylonia there is barely a single excavated urban settlement for which the total area of occupation can be reliably estimated, at least within a historically meaningful timeframe.[4] In spite of the problems posed by this lack of accurate information on the extent of urban occupation, there remain other aspects of urban demography that can be usefully addressed based on the study of living space. For example, the data on the size of houses (and of urban properties in general, including unbuilt land) provide a means of detecting changes in living densities over time and space.[5]

As the fundamental unit of social organisation, the household and any discernible variation in its size and composition are issues of central importance for the study of Babylonian society. Dwelling size, including degrees of variability across time and space, may serve as an indicator of social status, prosperity and degrees of relative equality/ inequality. House size has been discussed as a possible means of studying standards of living in other parts of the ancient world,[6] but the rich Babylonian data have not yet been investigated from this perspective, although in some cases it is possible to identify significant changes over the very long term. For example, it is clear that there was a significant increase in dwelling size between the Old Babylonian period (earlier 2nd millennium BC) and the Neo-Babylonian period, as well as a much bigger range of attested dwelling sizes, suggesting 'an unprecedented degree of social inequality' in the first millennium BC.[7] The topic is therefore central to the study of urban living conditions in Babylonia, especially the question of how far dwelling size and household structure varied according to social status and other parameters. Thus Babylonian household demography is a topic worthy of study in its own right, since the evidence available to us offers an opportunity to examine trajectories of social change and development over the very long term. A nuanced appreciation of the relationship between the physical dwelling and the household may also help us to refine the framework for interpreting the excavated remains of domestic architecture, both within the Mesopotamian region and beyond.

---

[2] E.g. Naroll 1962, based on prehistoric settlements. In a recent study of the Roman economy Bowman and Wilson 2009, 57–8 expressed a preference for methods based on population densities per hectare, or on the number of dwellings per settlement, over those based on the floor area of houses.

[3] Postgate 1994.

[4] Uruk is something of an exception: the Seleucid occupation is estimated at c. 300 hectares, and the early Parthian occupation at least 200 hectares (Finkbeiner 1991, 213).

[5] See Baker 2009, 93–4 on unbuilt urban land as an indicator of urban living densities, and on variability in occupation densities between different city districts in Hellenistic Uruk.

[6] See, e.g., Morris 2005 on housing as an indicator of living standards in ancient Greece.

[7] Baker 2011, 541.

THE SOURCES

Since this study depends on the judicious integration of the textual and archaeological sources for Babylonian housing, a brief introduction to both is in order. As to the written sources, comprising cuneiform tablets written in the Babylonian dialect of the Akkadian language, the most important documents are those recording the transfer of urban properties through sale, exchange, inheritance and dowry-giving. Since these tablets were intended to serve as proof of ownership, they typically include the most complete property descriptions of all document types. The most detailed examples give the following categories of information: area; property type; location (city district, city); dimensions of each side plus details of adjacent properties and their owners as well as any adjacent topographical features; price. In addition we are told the names and ancestry of the parties involved, as well as the witnesses, scribe, place and date.[8] Given this considerable amount of detailed information, the tablets constitute a valuable resource for studying the physical characteristics of the urban properties thus described and for relating the resulting findings to the wider socio-economic context. In terms of their chronological range, the relevant cuneiform tablets are not evenly spread over the first millennium BC. Like other document categories, they predominantly come from the 7th century through to the earlier 5th century, with a smaller number dating to the later Achaemenid period. The Hellenistic period is also well represented by the Uruk corpus, with a much smaller number of relevant tablets from Babylon, and a very small number from other settlements.

The archaeological evidence I shall be discussing consists of some 46 excavated Neo-Babylonian houses.[9] Residential areas of the Neo-Babylonian/Achaemenid period have been excavated at Babylon (Merkes), Ur and Uruk, but there are some reasons for believing that those at Babylon and Ur are rather atypical (in so far as they appear to represent high-status quarters). For the Hellenistic era we have a certain amount of continuity in the use of some of the Merkes houses at Babylon, but other residential parts of the city remain unexplored. Virtually nothing has been excavated of the residential sectors of Hellenistic Uruk,[10] and it is here especially that the textual data come into their own; without them, we would know virtually nothing about the conditions of urban living. Finally, it should be noted that Neo-Babylonian houses with upper storeys are only rarely attested, therefore for the sake of the figures and the discussion presented below,[11] I shall assume that we are dealing with single-storey structures.

---

[8]   For a specimen tablet see Baker 2009, 90.

[9]   See Miglus 1999, 307–14 (catalogue), pls. 89–100 (plans).

[10]   See Kose 1998, 380, fig. 232 for the small area of Seleucid-era housing uncovered in square U/V 18.

[11]   In my view the textual record confirms the conclusion that Miglus 1999, 204–5 arrived at based on the archaeological evidence. Even when upper storeys (or lofts) are attested, it cannot be assumed that their presence doubled the amount of available roofed space, since we could just as easily be dealing with smaller and/or more ephemeral structures built on the roof. For further discussion see Baker forthcoming.

DWELLING SIZE: SOME CONSIDERATIONS

So far I have deliberately used the word 'dwelling' in preference to 'house,' because in the Mesopotamian textual record a 'house' need not necessarily equate to a complete house of the kind typically recovered through excavation; this issue will be addressed in greater detail below. Dwelling size had, potentially, a profound effect on the quality of life of the inhabitants, but on its own it tells us little about the domestic lives of the householders. Ideally, we need to know not only the amount of available domestic space, but also its social and functional allocations, as well as the size and composition of the co-resident group. We need to understand how living space was apportioned among members of the household, as well as how it was used, including not only the stable functions that might be assigned to specific rooms or areas, but also changes in use throughout the course of the day, or with the seasons.[12]

Another related question is the relationship between house size and the number of inhabitants: does a larger house imply a correspondingly larger household,[13] or is the relationship more complex than that? That is, did larger houses have different modes of spatial organisation and use that were not linked solely to the presence of a larger household? It has been suggested, for example, that the largest and most complex Neo-Babylonian 'houses' actually served as both the residences and the bureaux of high administrative officials.[14] If this is correct then we should expect such a residence to accommodate not only the official's own family, but also some other household members, such as subordinates and slaves, as well as providing space for conducting official duties and receiving visitors. Even if some of the subordinates and slaves resided elsewhere, their daily activities would still have required space within the residence. In any case, it is clear that with increasing house size come greater possibilities for allocating specific functions to different rooms/sectors and also for separating different individuals or groups within the household, whether on a temporary or a long-standing basis. Very likely, then, we are dealing with both a larger resident household and a greater degree of complexity in spatial organization.

In general, the inclusion (or not) of family slaves within the household remains pretty much an unknown quantity since data on numbers of slaves per household, and especially on their modes of residence, are hard to come by. It is clear that wealthier Babylonian families owned considerably larger numbers of slaves than middle-income families (and the poorest citizens would have owned none at all).[15] However, these

---

[12]   As attested in the traditional housing of the Middle East; see, e.g., Ragette 2003, 84–5 on horizontal and vertical nomadism.

[13]   Wallace-Hadrill 1994, 92–3 notes the tendency of wealthy families to live in larger households, citing larger numbers of children and servants as possible factors.

[14]   Baker 2011, 541.

[15]   The number of slaves owned at any one time by middle-ranking temple personnel, such as the Nappāḫu family of Babylon, was rather small (Baker 2004, 70–3). However, the addition of only 2–3 slaves to a simple family unit of c. 5 persons would of course make a significant difference in terms of household size. Although I have characterised these middle-ranking temple prebendaries

slaves might well have been dispersed among the multiple residences which wealthy city-dwellers typically owned, and some of them might even have been based in other cities. Occasionally the textual sources attest to slaves living independently of the family they served, in rented accommodation. On present evidence, then, the various possible scenarios cannot be quantified and the lack of reliable information on the numbers of slaves and their place of residence is a serious impediment to estimating household size, especially in the case of middle and higher income families.

Another important issue which affects any study of urban populations is the question of how representative are the available data on house size. The problems of extrapolating from relatively small areas of excavated housing have confronted other scholars, especially those interested in estimating urban populations.[16] These difficulties also hinder our ability to investigate intra-site variability in house size and household structure: for example, it seems likely that poorer/low-status dwellings would have been particularly concentrated at the urban margins and that they are under-represented since excavators have typically focused on the centres of urban settlements. The textual data can to some extent make up for the relatively small samples of excavated housing available for study. However, it should be borne in mind that the written data too may not be entirely representative. We have to reckon with structural biases in the dataset, such as the fact that rental contracts hardly ever give the size of the house, therefore the kinds of houses occupied by people who did not have the means to buy their own house will not normally be represented in the house size dataset drawn from the cuneiform tablets.[17] Or at least, if such houses are represented, they will not be readily identifiable as rental properties, since houses attested in sale documents cannot normally be matched up with the houses that are the subject of rental contracts.[18]

HOUSE SIZE DATA: THE MESOPOTAMIAN BACKGROUND

For the first millennium BC, textually attested Babylonian 'houses' of known size are much more numerous than the actual excavated examples, therefore they form a

---

as 'middle income' families in order to distinguish them from the extremely wealthy entrepreneurial families such as the Egibis of Babylon (Wunsch 1993; 2000), nevertheless, the cost of slave ownership was very high and it has been characterised as 'an elite concern only' (Jursa 2010, 744). The tablet Dar. 379, an inheritance division document from the Egibi archive, lists over 100 slaves who were to be divided between the three sons of Itti-Marduk-balāṭu.

[16] E.g. Postgate 1994.

[17] It seems reasonable to assume that the majority of tenants were of rather lower status and means, compared with those who owned their own dwellings. However, there were certainly exceptions to this, with known house owners renting additional houses, in some cases clearly to further their business interests.

[18] A rare exception from the Nappāḫu family archive is discussed below; see note to Table 2.3, case 1.

Table 2.1 Textually-attested house sizes, 3rd and 2nd millennia BC (data from Van de Mieroop 1999, 261-262) (dates follow Radner and Robson 2011, xxix).

Period	Textually-attested 'house' size range
Fara (c. 2500 BC)	42–72 m²
pre-Sargonic Lagash (c. 2700–2350 BC)	18–63 m²
Sargonic (c. 2350–2200 BC)	24–66 m²
Ur III (c. 2100–2000 BC)	36–366 m²
Old Babylonian (c. 2000–1600 BC)	2.45–144 m² (Ur) 6–120 m² (Kutalla)

substantial addition to the dataset.[19] However, matching the two is not straightforward, since it has often been noted by Mesopotamian scholars that textually-attested house plots tend to be substantially smaller than their excavated counterparts. Van de Mieroop, for example, provides the following figures for the third and second millennia BC in Mesopotamia (Table 2.1).

When we compare some of these data with the excavation evidence, we find that several of the excavated houses at Fara and Abu Salabikh measured over 400 m²,[20] that is, almost ten times larger than the houses at the lower end of the textually-attested size range. Similarly, all of the textually attested Old Babylonian houses fall below the average excavated house size,[21] though there is a substantial overlap between the two size ranges.[22] The excavated houses of the earlier 2nd millennium BC range in size from 8.5 m² to 700 m², with an average size of 152 m² and a median of 110 m².[23]

---

[19]   This dataset will be presented and discussed in full in Baker forthcoming.

[20]   Postgate 1992, 89.

[21]   Though note that the Old Babylonian documents refer only to roofed space, therefore one must add an adjustment for the area occupied by walls in order to make a direct comparison between the textually attested size data and the excavated houses of known size; see below for further details.

[22]   Concerning the reduction in (excavated) house size between the late Early Dynastic and Old Babylonian period, Postgate (1992, 90) remarks: "it is tempting to see the differences as reflecting a shift in the residential structure of society, involving changes in the size and/or complexity of households". He cites an Old Babylonian text from Kish listing the members of individual households and notes that it contains no examples of 'multiple family households' (Postgate 1992, 93, text 5.3), which would fit rather well with the smaller average house size at this period.

[23]   Based on the data presented by Miglus 1999, 329–31, table 12. My figures take into account all 138 instances where a total house area is given, including a few which are restored or represent minimum areas.

The reason for this discrepancy is clear, as Van de Mieroop and others have noted:[24] the sale documents which routinely mention 'house' size are often dealing only with parts of houses – individual rooms, or suites of rooms – rather than with complete houses. On the other hand, the area of an excavated house is typically measured by its external perimeter, in so far as that can be determined.[25] Thanks to these structural differences between the two categories of evidence, archaeological and textual, the prevalence of what are actually only parts of houses among the sale (and related) documents drives down the average size of the textually-documented properties when compared with their excavated counterparts. This same point was stressed by Charpin recently in his study of the large merchants' houses at Old Babylonian Larsa, where he noted that the tablets document realities which have yet to be identified in excavation.[26] A recent preliminary study of the Neo-Babylonian data confirmed that this phenomenon, long noted for the 3rd and 2nd millennia BC, holds true also for the 1st millennium: textually attested house sizes are on average considerably smaller than their excavated counterparts.[27]

When whole houses *are* attested in the written sources, the context often involves surveying and describing inherited properties rather than sold ones, as noted by Van de Mieroop based on data from the Ur III and Old Babylonian periods.[28] Again, the same principle can be detected in the first millennium data. This is owed to the tendency to retain whole houses within the family whenever possible, with the result that complete houses were rarely the subject of sale, except in cases of persistent or severe hardship. On the other hand, complete houses could be passed on via inheritance, and their size in their 'intact' state may well not be documented in such cases since it was not directly relevant to the transaction, although the original size is sometimes documented in (or can be reconstructed from) subsequent inheritance division documents. A proper understanding of the house size data and the conditions under which house size was documented (or not) therefore requires close attention to contemporary record-keeping practices and modes of property transmission. At the lowest end of the textually-documented size range, it is generally clear that we are dealing with only small parts of larger dwellings, since the properties in question are so small that they cannot possibly have functioned as viable houses.[29] However,

---

[24] Van de Mieroop 1999, 264 (citing an observation made by Diakonoff in 1973).

[25] In cases where there are no immediate neighbours this is done by tracing the outer walls of the house. When adjacent dwellings shared one or more party walls, one dwelling is distinguished from the next using other criteria, such as the integrity of architectural units and the presence or absence of doorways.

[26] Charpin 2003, 320.

[27] Baker 2004, 57–9; a more detailed study based on a considerably bigger dataset will be published in Baker forthcoming.

[28] Van de Mieroop 1999, 263.

[29] For example, a tablet from Hellenistic Uruk mentions a 'house' measuring 5.25 m², clearly the equivalent of a small room (BiMes 24 26, dated 230 BC). Similarly, Van de Mieroop refers to an Old Babylonian 'house' measuring 3.36 m² in a tablet from Tell Sifr.

with larger textually-attested dwellings it may be difficult – if not impossible – to determine whether we are dealing with an 'intact' house or a part of a still larger one, since even quite large houses were sometimes subject to division, depending on the family circumstances.[30]

In investigating long-term trends in house sizes we have also to be sensitive to changes in the nature of the sources. For example, when comparing the written data on Old Babylonian and Neo-Babylonian houses, we have to bear in mind the different conventions for surveying and describing houses. Whereas Old Babylonian house sizes take into account only roofed space (é.dù.a), the Neo-Babylonian documents give the total area of the plot, that is, including walls and the courtyard.[31] Thus if we compare an Old Babylonian textually-attested house with a Neo-Babylonian one of the same size, the latter would have less roofed space since its total area included also the walls. Another factor to consider when integrating the written and archaeological data over the longer term is that Neo-Babylonian house walls were typically thicker than their Old Babylonian counterparts – Miglus has determined that c. 50% of the Neo-Babylonian house area was occupied by walls, compared with c. 30–40% in the Old Babylonian period.[32] The presence or absence of party walls is another factor to be borne in mind: in areas of smaller and more densely occupied Neo-Babylonian housing, valuable building space was saved by the use of party walls.[33]

HOUSE FORM IN RELATION TO HOUSEHOLD STRUCTURE AND MODES OF INHERITANCE

The average simple ('nuclear') family, generally assumed to consist of c. 5 individuals (parents plus children),[34] could be supplemented by the addition of one or more members of the extended family (e.g. unmarried sister, widowed mother),[35] as well as by the presence of one or more slaves (see above). Residence was virilocal, and instances of adult sons living in the same household as their father would have been relatively few.[36] Where adult brothers occupied the same house ('frérèche'), they presumably did so as heads of their own households and thus their combined families would in

---

[30]   For an example of a large house divided between four heirs see the case study of YOS 6 114, discussed in Baker in press (b) as well as below (note to Table 2.3, case 6).

[31]   Baker 2004, 57. Neo-Babylonian land survey and property description conventions are treated in detail in Baker 2011.

[32]   Miglus 1999, 184.

[33]   For example, party walls are found in the housing associated with the Eanna temple at Uruk, but not in the Merkes district of Babylon; for plans see Miglus 1999, pls. 87 and 93.

[34]   See, e.g., Bowman and Wilson 2009, 58 (citing 4.5–5 people for a nuclear family unit).

[35]   Attested scenarios include, e.g., a household comprising a widowed male, his two young sons, his widowed mother, and his two unmarried sisters (Baker 2010, 185).

[36]   See Gehlken 2005, 103 for the finding that around half of Neo-Babylonian temple personnel worked alongside their father for up to five years. Gehlken (p. 103) also revises downward the age of marriage for Babylonian males, to c. 20 years (from 29, as proposed by Roth).

theory number approximately 10 (2 brothers) or 15 (3 brothers). Textual references to more than three brothers sharing the same house are very rare, and even in those cases – which invariably involve a division of inheritance – it is by no means clear that we are dealing with actual living arrangements which would be maintained for any length of time: in practice, brothers often 'fissioned' to form their own households.

At this period various measures were taken to help prevent the family estate from being depleted through repeated inheritance division. Most notably, the oldest son received a double share in the father's property and any brothers shared the remainder between them equally.[37] Formal

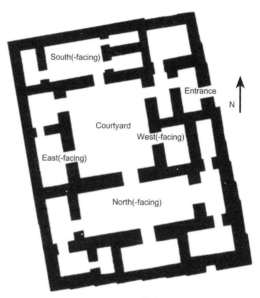

Fig. 2.1 House I, Babylon, Merkes

division of the inherited property could be postponed, with property (especially rural estates) being administered jointly by the heirs. Daughters had no actual right of inheritance but received a share of the paternal estate in the form of dowry; however, only a minority of dowries included a house (or a part of a house).[38] Despite these various measures to mitigate the negative effects of repeated division, much depended ultimately on the size of the inherited estate and on the number of surviving male heirs who were to share it.

The typical Babylonian house of the first millennium BC consisted of a central courtyard surrounded by suites of rooms on all four sides (although occasionally rooms on only three, or even two sides are attested). It had a single entrance from the exterior, usually opening onto a vestibule suite which was configured so as to prevent direct visual access to the house's interior. The central courtyard (*tarbaṣu*) was typically surrounded on all four sides by rooms or suites known in the contemporary written sources as *bīt iltāni*, *bīt šūti*, *bīt amurri* or *bīt šadî*, that is, 'north/south/west/east(-facing) suite' respectively. House I from Babylon, Merkes, can be taken as a 'classic' Neo-Babylonian house layout; its plan is reproduced in fig. 2.1, with the different sectors labelled according to their names.[39]

This type of house corresponds rather closely in its basic features to what Nevett

---

[37] Oelsner, Wells and Wunsch 2003, 938; Wunsch 2012, 20 n. 27.

[38] Roth 1991–93, 26 n. 109.

[39] For a detailed study of the spatial organisation of the Neo-Babylonian house and the correlation of the Babylonian terminology with the excavated ground plans see Baker in press (b) and Baker forthcoming.

Table 2.2 Disposition of space in House I, Babylon, Merkes

Babylon, Merkes, House I—disposition of space					
total area	745 m²				
walls		348 m²			
usable area		397 m²			
courtyard			100 m²		
roofed space			297 m²		
north(-facing) suite				169 m²	8 rooms
south(-facing) suite				50 m²	4 rooms
entrance suite				38 m²	3 rooms
east(-facing) suite				35 m²	2 rooms
west(-facing) suite				5 m²	1 room

has termed in a Greek context the 'single entrance, courtyard house'.[40] This form is found throughout large parts of the eastern Mediterranean region and the Near East in antiquity and it is also traditional in much of the Middle East.[41] The type, although widespread, nevertheless admits of considerable variation, even within Mesopotamia: the typical Old Babylonian house, for example, shared similar basic features with the Neo-Babylonian house but its layout still differed significantly in certain crucial respects.[42] In order to get a better idea of the disposition of domestic space during the Neo-Babylonian period we can break down the total area of our 'archetype', Merkes House I, as shown in Table 2.2.

In this particular case, if it had been necessary to apportion self-contained architectural units within House I to different individuals or family groups, then the possibilities would have been limited to three sectors: the north(-facing) suite (NFS), the south(-facing) suite (SFS), and the east(-facing) suite (EFS). The entrance suite clearly had to be available for use by all occupants, and archaeological evidence suggests that the west(-facing) suite, in this case a small single room, was a typical location for

---

[40]   Nevett 1995, 373.

[41]   See, e.g., Bianca 2000, 77 who writes of 'major cellular units which were grouped around a central distribution space or a courtyard'. Numerous examples from across the region are illustrated in Ragette 2003.

[42]   Baker 2011, 547.

the kitchen.[43] In the case of shared occupation by members of an extended family household, it is clear that the NFS would have been occupied by the head of the household. It is interesting to note that the NFS occupied almost exactly twice as much roofed space as the SFS and EFS combined. The sizes of the respective suites would conform nicely to a hypothetical scenario whereby an older son inherited a double share in the house (the NFS) and one or two younger brothers of his occupied the remainder (the SFS and the EFS). This correspondence may be fortuitous, but it certainly reminds us of the kind of situation that features repeatedly in the contemporary documents.

Though the 'single entrance, courtyard house' was the dominant form in Babylonia, we also have to reckon with other kinds of house design and to consider their implications. For the Old Babylonian period a different type of house has been identified, namely, the 'linear house,' with rooms on two or three sides of a courtyard (or in some cases simply a row of rooms without any adjacent courtyard at all), in contrast to the 'square house' with rooms on all four sides.[44] Based on this distinction and on the textual evidence for the division of houses through inheritance and subsequent adjustments, Stone suggested that the linear houses accommodated nuclear families while the square houses were associated with extended families.[45] This is supported by her study of the ownership history and physical transformation of House I in the TA sounding at Nippur: what was originally a courtyard house inherited by four brothers was soon transformed in such a way that only one of the brothers remained in possession of a linear house comprising three rooms, the remainder of the original house having been acquired by neighbours. This is not to say that all linear houses were necessarily formed out of what had originally been courtyard houses: some were no doubt planned and built from scratch, perhaps in situations where the availability of land for building was an issue. In fact, there is also evidence for the converse process, that is, for linear houses being combined in order to form a larger house. For example, Gruber and Roaf suggest that the Old Babylonian house plan depicted on tablet BM 86394 was a sketch suggesting how two such linear houses, each formed out of two '3(or 4)-room row-houses', could be combined into a single dwelling made up of four rows of rooms.[46]

Linear houses have also been found at other sites apart from Nippur, such as Old Babylonian Ur.[47] The more simple linear house forms, those without any courtyard, have no counterpart among the excavated Neo-Babylonian houses. This raises the

---

[43] See Baker in press (b).

[44] Stone 1981, 26.

[45] Stone 1981, 29.

[46] Gruber and Roaf 2012; their contribution is an appendix to Gruber 2012, which contains further detailed discussion of tablet BM 86394.

[47] For illustrations see Miglus 1999, pl. 6; Gruber and Roaf 2012, 194–5, figs. 6–9. See also Brusasco 1999–2000, 20–26, who divides the more simple Ur houses into single room/court buildings (fig. 1.6), buildings without courtyard (fig. 1.7), buildings with rooms on one side of the courtyard (fig. 1.8), and buildings with rooms on two sides of the courtyard (figs. 1.9–1.11).

question of whether the known house types of the first millennium BC are representative of the entire spectrum of housing types, or whether – as in the Old Babylonian period – there would also have been simpler forms which have not yet been recovered because they lay beyond the areas that have been excavated. Since housing located in the outer areas of Neo-Babylonian sites has rarely been investigated,[48] and the total amount of housing uncovered is not great, this clearly remains a possibility that cannot be discounted. Thus, while it may be assumed that most textually-documented 'houses' which are smaller than the smallest attested size for a viable courtyard house represent parts of such houses (individual rooms or suites of rooms),[49] it remains possible that some of them were actually independent small dwellings.[50]

In the case of the linear houses, it is clear that they were generally unsuitable for further subdivision for the purpose of shared occupation by members of an extended family, and as Stone supposed, they must have been occupied by simple family households. This was normally the case also with the houses at Late Bronze Age (13th–12th century BC) Emar: upon inheritance, individual houses were not normally divided up but rather separate houses were distributed among the heirs.[51] The oldest son, as head of the family, was typically assigned the 'main/large house' (*bītu rabû*), while other siblings received smaller, secondary houses. Instances of heirs having to share the same house were relatively rare,[52] and in common with the linear houses of the Old Babylonian period, the Emar houses could not easily be divided into self-contained suites. Furthermore, they were relatively small, with an average roofed living space of 43 m².[53]

DWELLING SIZE ACROSS THE SOCIAL SPECTRUM

In this section I present a synchronic study of dwelling size in urban Babylonia in the first millennium BC. Given the multiplicity of possible residence scenarios and the problem of determining their relative prevalence, it is difficult (if not impossible) to extrapolate the 'typical' amount of domestic space available to the average simple family household. It seems more productive therefore to establish a series of benchmark sizes, based on textual and/or archaeological evidence that associates dwellings of known size with particular individuals/families or with members of a particular social class. The selected data are summarised in Table 2.3, with further explanation and references given in the accompanying notes below.

---

[48]   The Neo-Babylonian houses excavated in the WC sounding at the southern tip of Nippur, near to the city wall, are an exception to this (Gibson *et al.* 1983; discussed also by Baker 2010).

[49]   The smallest excavated courtyard houses measured c. 90 m² and 95 m² (Baker 2004, 62); see also Table 2.3, case 2 and notes ad loc.

[50]   See also the remarks below referring to Table 2.3, case 1.

[51]   Mori 2003, 35–9.

[52]   Mori 2003, 38.

[53]   McClellan 1997, 45.

Table 2.3 *Dwelling size across the social spectrum*

case	dwelling category	details of dwelling category	area
1	minimal living suite (part of house)	house shared as member(s) of extended family (or as tenant)	c. 73.50 m^2
2	small house (excavated)	smallest excavated courtyard house	c. 90 m^2
3	small house (textually attested)	*širku* ('temple oblate'), Uruk, c. 555 BC	c. 120 m^2
4	slightly bigger house	middle-ranking temple personnel within temple precinct (excavated houses, Eanna & Esagila)	c. 240 m^2
5	average house	average excavated house size (all sites)	c. 417 m^2
6	double courtyard house	textually attested example from Uruk, 555 BC	c. 784 m^2 (441 + 343)
7	large house (three courtyards)	e.g. Babylon, Merkes, House III	c. 1,475 m^2
8	official residences/bureaux	e.g. Achaemenid Residence, Abu Qubur; house 'al-Bayati', Babylon	c. 2,000 m^2
9	local governor's palace	e.g. 'Palace of Bel-šalṭi-Nannar', Ur	c. 5,743 m^2
10	royal palace	Babylon, Südburg	c. 43,840 m^2

Explanatory notes to Table 2.3

1. The 'minimal living suite' is a self-contained architectural unit within the typical Neo-Babylonian courtyard house. Such suites can be equated with those known in the contemporary written sources as *bīt iltāni*, *bīt šūti*, *bīt amurri* or *bīt šadî* (see above). There are documented instances of such suites being assigned to individuals for residence, and occasionally their sizes are mentioned. Owners/occupants of such suites include women (as dowry recipients or as widows), and also (albeit rarely) tenants in rental situations. An example is a 5-reed (c. 61 m^2) south(-facing) suite (*bīt šūti*) received by a woman from Borsippa as part of her dowry in 494 BC and then rented out by her to a third party (see Baker 2010, 186). A similar scenario may lie behind the case of a house in the Šuanna district of Babylon which was purchased by Iddin-Nabû of the Nappāḫu family and then rented out (see Baker 2004, 47–9, section 5.2, with schematic reconstructions). In this case the 'house', measuring c. 62 m^2, was not explicitly described by one of the aforementioned Babylonian terms for a 'suite', but given its size it is likely to have formed one part of a larger courtyard house. The adjacent owners were apparently not related either to the owner, Iddin-Nabû, or to the tenant, Nabû-lū-salim. Alternatively, if the assumption that this 'house' formed part of a larger, courtyard house is incorrect, then we are dealing with an entirely different type of housing, of a linear or even possibly an agglutinating character, that has not yet been recovered through excavation.

Some of the people attested as owning or occupying suites of this kind no doubt headed their own simple family household, but others (e.g. widows) may have had the suite to themselves. For further details and discussion see Baker 2010, 185–7 and Baker in press (b).

2. The smallest excavated Neo-Babylonian courtyard house is House C at Nippur, measuring 90 m^2 (TA, level V), according to Miglus 1999, 341, table 27. This house expanded considerably in levels IV and III (see Miglus 1999, pl. 97, figs. 431–433). The next smallest house is House d6 at Uruk, with an area of 95 m^2 (Miglus 1999, 341, table 27 and pl. 94, fig. 418). Both of these houses had four rooms, in addition to the courtyard.

3. The average size of the dwellings of the temple oblates (*širkus*) at Uruk is based on the administrative document OIP 122 169 (555 BC) which lists residences assigned to them; the areas of 18 dwellings are preserved in the tablet. See Baker forthcoming for detailed discussion, and on the status of the *širkus* see Kleber 2011. It may be assumed that the temple oblates listed here were typically heads of simple family households.

4. The data for houses occupied by the middle-ranking temple personnel are based on the houses excavated to the west and southwest of Eanna in Uruk, together with the two houses excavated within the ziggurat precinct Etemenanki at Babylon (data taken from Miglus 1999, 341, table 27; for discussion see Baker 2011, 543). The attribution of these houses to this category of personnel is based on (a) the private family archives of temple prebendaries excavated in one of the houses associated with the Eanna temple (see Kessler 1991); (b) inscriptional evidence for temple prebendaries living within the Esagila precinct at Babylon.[54]

5. Average house size here is based on all excavated Neo-Babylonian houses (from all sites) whose sizes are known or can be reconstructed (Miglus 1999, 307–14, with size data p. 341, table 27). The average size of the houses in Babylon, Merkes, is somewhat higher, at 538 m^2.

6. This example involves a double courtyard house described in the inheritance division tablet YOS 6 114 (Uruk, 555 BC). The house, which comprised a main sector (*bītu rabû*) and a secondary outer sector (*tarbaṣu bābānû*) measuring 441 m^2 and 343 m^2 respectively, was apportioned between three brothers and their paternal uncle. It is clear that the deceased father and his brother (the uncle of the other three heirs) had previously owned the house without any formal division: this was no doubt unnecessary because the house comprised two self-contained sectors, each of them equivalent to a typical courtyard house of the day. For preliminary remarks see Baker 2010, 188; for a more detailed discussion of this case see Baker in press (b); an edition of the tablet can be found in Baker forthcoming.

7. This category comprises the two largest excavated residential houses of the period: House III at Babylon, Merkes (1475 m^2) and House 1 at Ur (1490 m^2); see Miglus 1999, 341, table 27.

8. Official residence/bureaux: it has been suggested that these residences served to accommodate a high official and his family as well as his administrative department, implying a greater complexity of spatial organisation compared with 'regular' domestic dwellings (Baker 2011, 540).

9. Only one Neo-Babylonian building has so far been excavated that can plausibly be identified as the palace of a local governor: the so-called 'Palace of Bel-šalṭi-Nannar' at Ur (Woolley

---

[54] An inscription of king Neriglissar refers to cultic personnel of Esagila (the main temple of Marduk at Babylon) living within the enclosure wall of the temple (CT 36 Pl. 19, ii 9–11 // VAB 4 216, ii 8–10); for further discussion and commentary on this passage see Baker in press (a).

and Mallowan 1962, 41–3 and plan pl. 70). The building was formerly interpreted as the Egipar, residence of Nabonidus's daughter Bel-šalṭi-Nannar (now read En-nigaldi-Nanna), which was rebuilt for her when she was consecrated as *entu*-priestess. This can now be ruled out and it is more likely that the building housed the local governor (Weadock 1975, 112–14).

10. The Südburg ('South Palace') in Babylon, built originally by Nabopolassar, rebuilt and extended by his son Nebuchadnezzar II; see the excavation report of Koldewey 1931. The palace has been reconstructed by Iraqi archaeologists.

CONCLUSIONS

This paper has explored the methodological issues involved in making use of the rich data on house size from Babylonia. Analysis of these data should ideally take into account contextual information, including the following: domestic spatial organisation and its relationship with architectural forms; modes of property transmission, especially inheritance practice; record-keeping practices; conventions for measuring and describing houses, and socio-historical data on the family and household, including prosopographical study of specific case studies. Given the massive variation in attested Babylonian house sizes in the first millennium BC, with excavated examples ranging from c. 90 m² to very nearly 1500 m², it seems unsound to isolate one 'typical' house size/type as representative. I have tried instead to illustrate the range of housing across the social spectrum, associating different size brackets with particular residence scenarios where possible, and with particular sectors of the population. This approach is intended to encompass the known range of variation and to provide a more nuanced frame of reference for the comparative study of dwelling sizes, especially as an indicator of relative living standards. Finally, it should be noted that we cannot be certain that either the excavated houses or the textually attested ones are fully representative of the actual range, especially since the urban margins are generally under-explored and the sizes of rental properties were not usually written down.

REFERENCES

Baker, H. D. (2004) *The Archive of the Nappāḫu Family* (Archiv für Orientforschung Beiheft 30). Vienna: Institut für Orientalistik der Universität Wien.

Baker, H. D. (2009) A waste of space? Unbuilt land in the Babylonian cities of the first millennium BC. *Iraq* 71, 89–98.

Baker, H. D. (2010) The social dimensions of Babylonian domestic architecture in the Neo-Babylonian and Achaemenid periods. In J. Curtis and S. Simpson (eds), *The World of Achaemenid Persia-History, Art and Society in Iran and the Ancient Near East*, 179–194. London: IB Tauris.

Baker, H. D. (2011) From street altar to palace: reading the built environment of urban Babylonia. In Radner and Robson (eds), 533–552.

Baker, H. D. (in press a) Beyond planning: how the Babylonian city was formed. In C. Wunsch (ed.), *The Neo-Babylonian Workshop of the 53rd RAI. City Administration in Neo-Babylonian Times* (Babel und Bibel). Winona Lake, IN: Eisenbrauns.

Baker, H. D. (in press b) Family structure, household cycle and the social use of domestic space in urban Babylonia. In M. Müller (ed.), *Household Studies in Complex Societies. (Micro) Archaeological and Textual Approaches* (Oriental Institute Seminars 10). Chicago: The Oriental Institute of the University of Chicago.

Baker, H. D. (forthcoming) *The Urban Landscape in First Millennium BC Babylonia.*

Bianca, S. (2000) *Urban Form in the Arab World – Past and Present.* London: Thames & Hudson.

Bowman, A. and Wilson, A. (2009) Quantifying the Roman economy: integration, growth, decline? In A. Bowman and A. Wilson (eds), *Quantifying the Roman Economy: Methods and Problems*, 3–84 (Oxford Studies on the Roman Economy). Oxford: Oxford University Press.

Brusasco, P. (1999–2000). Family archives and the social use of space in Old Babylonian houses at Ur. *Mesopotamia* 34–35, 3–173.

Charpin, D. (2003) La politique immobilière des marchands de Larsa à la lumière des découvertes épigraphiques de 1987 et 1989. In J.-L. Huot (ed.), *Larsa, travaux de 1987 et 1989*, 311–322 (Bibliothèque Archéologique et Historique 165). Beirut: IFAPO.

Finkbeiner, U. (1991) 5.8 Seleukidisch-parthische Zeit. In U. Finkbeiner, *Uruk, Kampagne 35-37, 1982-1984, die archäologische Oberflächenuntersuchung*, 211–214 (Ausgrabungen in Uruk-Warka, Endberichte 4). Mainz am Rhein: von Zabern.

Gehlken, E. (2005) Childhood and youth, work and old age in Babylonia – a statistical analysis. In H. D. Baker and M. Jursa (eds), *Approaching the Babylonian Economy. Proceedings of the START-Project Symposium Held in Vienna, 1-3 July 2004*, 89–120 (Alter Orient und Altes Testament 330). Münster: Ugarit-Verlag.

Gibson, M., Zettler, R. L. and Armstrong, J. A. (1983) The southern corner of Nippur: excavations during the 14th and 15th seasons. *Sumer* 39, 170–190.

Gruber, M. (2012) KA2 GIBIL – ein altbabylonischer Hausteilungsplan? In H. D. Baker, K. Kaniuth and A. Otto (eds), *Stories of Long Ago. Festschrift für Michael D. Roaf*, 177–191 (Alter Orient und Altes Testament 397). Münster: Ugarit-Verlag.

Gruber, M. and Roaf, M. (2012) Addendum. Converting the barber's room into a staircase: home improvements in Old Babylonian Sippar. In H. D. Baker, K. Kaniuth and A. Otto (eds), *Stories of Long Ago. Festschrift für Michael D. Roaf*, 191–205 (Alter Orient und Altes Testament 397). Münster: Ugarit-Verlag.

Jursa, M. *et al.* (2010) *Aspects of the Economic History of Babylonia in the First Millennium BC. Economic Geography, Economic Mentalities, Agriculture, the Use of Money and the Problem of Economic Growth* (Alter Orient und Altes Testament 377). Münster: Ugarit-Verlag.

Kessler, K. (1991) *Urkunden aus Privathäusern - Die Wohnhäuser Westlich des Eanna-Tempelbereichs I* (Ausgrabungen in Uruk-Warka, Endberichte 8). Mainz am Rhein: Von Zabern.

Kleber, K. (2011) Neither slave nor truly free: the status of the dependents of Babylonian temple households. In L. Culbertson (ed.), *Slaves and Households in the Near East*, 101–111 (Oriental Institute Seminars 7). Chicago: The Oriental Institute of the University of Chicago.

Koldewey, R. (1931) *Die Königsburgen von Babylon, 1. Teil: Die Südburg* (Ausgrabungen der Deutschen Orient-Gesellschaft in Babylon 5). Leipzig: Hinrichs.

Kose, A. (1998) *Uruk: Architektur IV, von der Seleukiden- bis zur Sasanidenzeit* (Ausgrabungen in Uruk-Warka, Endberichte 17). Mainz am Rhein: Von Zabern.

McClellan, T. L. (1997) Houses and households in North Syria during the Late Bronze Age. In C. Castel *et al.* (eds), *Les maisons dans la Syrie antique du IIIe millénaire aux débuts de l'Islam. Pratiques et représentation de l'espace domestique. Actes du Colloque International, Damas 27-30 Juin 1992*, 29–59 (Bibliothèque Archéologique et Historique 150). Beirut: IFAPO.

Miglus, P. A. (1999) *Städtische Wohnarchitektur in Babylonien und Assyrien* (Baghdader Forschungen 22). Mainz am Rhein: Von Zabern.

Mori, L. (2003) *Reconstructing the Emar Landscape* (Quaderni di Geografica Storica 6). Rome: Casa Editrice Università degli Studi di Roma La Sapienza.

Morris, I. (2005) Archaeology, standards of living, and Greek economic history. In J. G. Manning and I. Morris (eds), *The Ancient Economy: Evidence and Models*, 91–126. Stanford: Stanford University Press.

Naroll, R. (1962) Floor area and settlement population. *American Antiquity* 27, 587–589.

Nevett, L.C. (1995) Gender relations in the Classical Greek household: the archaeological evidence. *Annual of the British School at Athens* 90, 363–381.

Oelsner, J., Wells, B. and Wunsch, C. (2003) Mesopotamia: Neo-Babylonian Period. In R. Westbrook (ed.), *A History of Ancient Near Eastern Law*, 911–974. Leiden: Brill.

Postgate, J. N. (1992) *Early Mesopotamia. Society and Economy at the Dawn of History*. London and New York: Routledge.

Postgate, J. N. (1994) How Many Sumerians Per Hectare? – Probing the Anatomy of an Early City. *Cambridge Archaeological Journal* 4/1, 47–65.

Radner, K. and Robson, E. (2011) Introduction. In K. Radner and E. Robson (eds), *The Oxford Handbook of Cuneiform Culture*, xxvii–xxxii. Oxford: Oxford University Press.

Ragette, F. (2003) *Traditional Domestic Architecture of the Arab Region*. Sharjah: American University of Sharjah.

Roth, M. T. (1991–93) The Neo-Babylonian Widow. *Journal of Cuneiform Studies* 43–45, 1–26.

Stone, E. C. (1981) Texts, Architecture and Ethnographic Analogy: Patterns of Residence in Old Babylonian Nippur. *Iraq* 43, 19–33.

Van de Mieroop, M. (1999) Thoughts on Urban Real Estate in Ancient Mesopotamia. In M. Hudson and B. A. Levine (eds), *Urbanization and Land Ownership in the Ancient Near East*, 253–287 (Peabody Museum Bulletin 7). Cambridge: Peabody Museum of Archaeology and Ethnology, Harvard University.

Wallace-Hadrill, A. (1994) *Houses and Society in Pompeii and Herculaneum*. Princeton: Princeton University Press.

Weadock, P. N. (1975) The Giparu at Ur. *Iraq* 37/2, 101–128.

Woolley, L. and Mallowan, M. E. L. (1962) *Ur Excavations, IX. The Neo-Babylonian and Persian Periods*. London: British Museum & the University Museum, University of Pennsylvania.

Wunsch, C. (1993) *Die Urkunden des babylonischen Geschäftsmannes Iddin-Marduk. Zum Handel mit Naturalien im 6. Jahrhundert v. Chr.* (Cuneiform Monographs 3a-b). Groningen: STYX.

Wunsch, C. (2000) *Das Egibi Archive 1. Die Felder und Gärten* (Cuneiform Monographs 20a-b). Groningen: STYX.

Wunsch, C. (2012) Legal narrative in Neo-Babylonian trial documents. Text reconstruction, Interpretation, and Assyriological method. In K.-P. Adam, F. Avemarie, N. Wazana and D. Felsch (eds), *Law and Narrative in the Bible and in Neighbouring Ancient Cultures*, 3–34. Tübingen: Mohr Siebeck.

3

The Historian and the Old Babylonian Archives[1]

Dominique Charpin

"There is no such thing as an ordinary inscription,
only an ordinary way of looking at it"
                                            Jean Sauvaget

Published Old Babylonian archives constitute a considerable collection of texts, the number of which, until now and to my knowledge, has not been specified in any publication. On 1st January 2008 the project entitled "ARCHIBAB" (Archives babyloniennes, XXe–XVIIe siècles) was launched.[1] Among its objectives is assembling the entire corpus of Old Babylonian archival documents into a digital database. The first phase has consisted of creating a bibliography, which has yielded a figure of 29,228 fully published texts.[2] This means that, for a period of four centuries, there is an

---

[1] This study was undertaken within the framework of the "ARCHIBAB (Archives babyloniennes, XXe–XVIIe siècles) project," financed in 2008–2010 by ANR (Agence Nationale de la Recherche) under the rubric "Corpus et outils de la recherche en sciences humaines et sociales". I would like to thank Antoine Jacquet for his valuable contribution to this project as well as several members of the group "Mondes mésopotamiens" of the UMR 7192, Lucile Barberon, Lionel Marti, and Hervé Reculeau, who also contributed to this project.

For a political rather than economic approach, using the royal correspondence in particular, see Charpin 2012.

This project begins in the same year that marks the end, after six years, of the START project, "*The Economic History of Babylonia in the First Millennium BC,*" directed by M. Jursa. I take this as an auspicious sign, considering the significant accomplishments of the Viennese group.

[2] This figure, established 30/10/2008, is subject to a slight increase. It consists of texts published in full. Texts that have only been subject to citation (however long) were not included, nor were those described in various catalogues such as those of the British Museum and Yale (Figulla 1961; Sigrist *et al.* 1996; Sigrist *et al.* 2006; Beckman 1995; Beckman 2000).

average of 70 texts for each year, or one text for every five days. To be sure, the significance of such an average is questionable when certain decades are practically undocumented, while others are abundantly so.[3] This number nevertheless gives an idea of the abundance of documentation available for this period of Mesopotamian history.[4] While this figure may appear low compared to the Ur III period (for which, according to the BDTNS, there are over 86,000 texts for a period of one century),[5] and without indulging in "academic prejudice," it should be noted that Old Babylonian archives are more diverse and richer than what is extant from the previous century, the bulk of which consists of short accounting documents.[6] The number of letters and legal documents in the Old Babylonian archives is, by contrast, much greater, and the geographical distribution of the archives is much broader.

I would like to use the occasion of this symposium to present an overview of Old Babylonian archives and how the ARCHIBAB program was designed to tackle them. By way of illustration from this large collection, I have chosen three specific examples to discuss:

1) The richest set of archives, both in terms of number and quality, found in the palace of Mari and dated to the 18th century BCE
2) A type of text: the loan document
3) And a historical event: the "real estate boom" at Larsa in the half-century spanning the years 1840 to 1790

Quantitative ("*sérielle*") history, best represented in France by historians such as P. Chaunu and E. Le Roy Ladurie, was in fashion when I was still a student. Today this methodology is considered outdated. However, I believe it deserves to be explored and developed. Assyriologists have amply demonstrated the importance of taking quantitative information mentioned in the texts into account in their work.[7] The problem remains that we must be able to determine the exact nature of the texts that have been handed down to us, in order to know how representative are these samples that were produced by the accident of excavation (whether illicit or controlled).

---

[3] It is noteworthy that the average of one text every five days corresponds to that of the archives of the house of Ur-Utu at Tell ed-Dêr: see Tanret 2004, 35.

[4] Studies of Mesopotamian archives from various periods are found in the work edited by Brosius 2003. Earlier work on the topic, found in the volume edited by Veenhof 1986, continues to be relevant.

[5] http://bdts.filol.csic.es/about_uk.php.

[6] If we take into account the number of lines, the Old Babylonian corpus is larger than that of Ur III, from a strictly numerical standpoint.

[7] I am thinking in particular of the work done by G. Visicato on Presargonic Fara.

1. OLD BABYLONIAN ARCHIVES AND THE "ARCHIBAB" PROJECT[8]

We begin with a brief introduction to Old Babylonian archives and to the conception of ARCHIBAB, according to the archives' varying characteristics. Some preliminary results of the project will then be presented.

1.1 State of the question

It is my intention to present here the archives, not only by stressing their qualitative aspects, as is commonly done, but also by taking into account their quantitative features.

1.1.1 RICH AND ABUNDANT ARCHIVES

During the Old Babylonian period, 2000–1600 BCE,[9] the Ancient Near East experienced great cultural unity, despite encountering periods of political fragmentation, before and after the years of domination by the kingdom of Babylon under Hammu-rabi and his successor.[10] The use of writing developed considerably during these four centuries, providing us with a significant number of archives. These come no longer solely from large institutions, such as palaces and temples, as is largely the case during the third millennium. The first half of the second millennium yields numerous family archives from the houses of individuals – a clear innovation. The fact that cuneiform tablets were, almost exclusively, the writing medium, explains the large number of texts preserved. In the first millennium, the competing presence of papyrus and leather led to the gradual drying up of texts preserved as tablets.[11]

The ARCHIBAB project is dedicated to archival documents. It thus excludes the other two large corpora of the period: the so-called "literary" texts, stemming from the scholarly tradition and primarily known from school copies; and the "royal inscriptions," commemorative texts celebrating the achievements of the sovereigns. These two text categories have long been the object of study by specialists. They are in the process, moreover, of being assembled into an adequate corpus.[12] Archival documents, meanwhile, have been relatively neglected, despite their crucial significance to the study of social, economic, cultural, and political life.

---

[8]   This first section replicates certain parts of the ARCHIBAB project report submitted to the ANR, now online (www.digitorient.com/?p=168). Results from after January 2008 have also been incorporated.

[9]   Until a consensus is reached on the absolute chronology, the ARCHIBAB project uses the so-called "middle" chronology (Hammu-rabi: 1792–1750 BCE).

[10]   For a recent synthesis, see Charpin, Edzard and Stol 2004.

[11]   See Jursa 2005, 1 (16,000 published documents, spanning the period from the end of the 8th century to 331 BCE).

[12]   For "literary" texts in the Sumerian language, see the ETCSL site. The Akkadian language corpus is being assembled by M. Streck and N. Wasserman (http://www.seal.uni-leipzig.de/). For royal inscriptions, see the corpus edited by Frayne 1990 and most recently Charpin 2006.

From a typological point of view, the documents can be divided into two broad categories: those that were intended to be preserved and those that were of limited temporal value. The first category includes property titles: sale contracts (fields, orchards, houses, and slaves), descriptions of inheritance, as well as documents establishing the status of people and their property (marriage, adoption, and manumission). The documents deemed without long-term value or effect include: letters intended for practically instantaneous long distance communication, accounting documents, and short-term contracts (loans, hires, and rentals). The study of Old Babylonian archives has led to the conclusion that such documents were sorted out from time to time,[13] based on a two-fold phenomenon observed in the family archives. First, the documents that were meant to be preserved go back as far as two centuries and more,[14] as illustrated, for example, by the archives of Ur-Utu from Tell ed-Dêr.[15] Second, the closer one gets to the end date of the archive, the more the documents become varied in content, the short-term texts not having been sorted out.[16] It is important to emphasise, moreover, another difference between family archives and those of large institutions, such as the temple and palace: the span of time covered by this last group (large institutions) is noticeably shorter. This is because, for the most part, they contain only short-term documents, which were sorted out on a regular basis. It may be possible to attribute this to the vicissitudes of political life.[17] The abundance of family archives, which distinguishes second-millennium Mesopotamia from previous centuries, can be explained by two wholly independent factors.[18] The first is that the archaeological situation is such that levels of habitation prior to the second millennium have rarely been excavated, accounting for the lack of "private" archives for these periods.[19] The second is associated with the considerable expansion of the use of writing that took place in the first centuries of the second millennium.[20] This led to a much broader geographical distribution of texts than that found for the third millennium, as well as a considerable number of archives.[21]

With these archives it is possible to write on every aspect of Babylonian history.

---

[13] For a general overview, see the proceedings of the colloquium "Les phénomènes de fin d'archives en Mésopotamie" (Joannès 1995).

[14] See my study on "Transmission des titres de propriété et constitution des archives privées en Babylonie ancienne" (Charpin 1986). A revised version of this contribution appears as Chapter 4 in Charpin 2010a.

[15] See Van Lerberghe and Voet 1991, in anticipation of Tanret, Janssen and Dekiere forthcoming.

[16] This is attested, for example, in the archives of the family of Dadâ at Isin; for now see Charpin 2000a, 200f. For the occurrence of several expired documents preserved in the Ur-Utu archives, see Tanret 2008.

[17] See Charpin, Edzard and Stol 2004, 55f.

[18] Stone 2002.

[19] Ur III Nippur seems to be an exception, but see van Driel 1994.

[20] See my book Charpin 2008a and the revised English edition Charpin 2010b.

[21] M. Jursa calculated that 132 Neo-Babylonian archives have been found (Jursa 2005). We are not yet able to provide an approximate number for the Old Babylonian period; it will be one of the results of the ARCHIBAB project.

While social and economic history takes the foreground, they also shed light on the history of religious and cultural institutions, as well as on political events. And while, in matters concerning the economy and society, these documents are mostly relevant to the elite – since the poor did not have archives –, certain processes of impoverishment within the upper echelons of society are, nevertheless, perceivable. Families were forced to borrow money on a regular basis and eventually sell their inheritance to more fortunate neighbours. Sovereigns intervened from time to time, especially at their accession, but also in periods of economic crises. By proclaiming *mîšarum* edicts, they cancelled arrears owed to the palace, as well as debts between individuals.[22] The merchants' archives allow us to understand long distance trade (towards the Arab-Persian Gulf or Anatolia), as well as local exchange, subjects which have often been neglected by scholars. Using these archives one can, likewise, write on the history of families and households; one can also reconstruct genealogies, inheritance procedure, and the status of women, among others.

1.1.2 RESEARCH DIFFICULTIES
The vast potential wealth of the Old Babylonian archives remains under-exploited owing to an absence of adequate tools for their study. Texts from controlled excavations have been, for the most part, satisfactorily published in monographs and collections,[23] even if the pace of publication has not always proceeded as quickly as one would hope.[24] Most disconcerting, however, is the presence of the thousands of texts obtained from illicit excavations over the past century and a half, which have then been dispersed into public and private collections: access to their content is often difficult. The attendant problems are multiple. The absence of editions and the scattered state of the archives I would stress as the most daunting.

For the most part, texts have been published as hand-copies. At best, these publications include a catalogue (often very succinct) and indices (generally limited to personal, geographical, topographical, and divine names). When these are available, they are often outdated. Moreover, collections are often published as they are, containing texts from vastly different periods and genres. It is not uncommon, furthermore, that an Assyriologist who publishes a collection containing Old Babylonian texts is not a specialist in Old Babylonian archives, and that his or her understanding of the texts suffers from a lack of familiarity with this type of source.

---

[22] For more details regarding this situation see below, § 2.2.

[23] See my annotated bibliography in Charpin, Edzard and Stol 2004, 403–80, and the appendix below.

[24] It is unfortunate that only 55 letters from the hundreds of Old Babylonian texts found at Tell Asmar in the 1930s have so far been published, and only 150 texts out of some 3,000 discovered at Tell Harmal, and that the bulk of the archives unearthed at Tell ed-Dêr in 1975, Terqa since 1975, and Tell Leilan in 1985–87, remain unedited. On the other hand, we can rejoice at the speed with which the 210 texts found in 2000–2002 at Chagar-Bazar were published by D. Lacambre and A. Millet Albà (cf. Tunca and Baghdo 2008). The publication of the Mari archives began 70 years ago and continues at the average rate of 100–200 new texts each year.

A recent example of this are the two volumes of Old Babylonian texts from the Horn collection,[25] an American collection containing primarily late third-millennium texts (Third Dynasty of Ur), along with which the editor has published early second-millennium texts (more than 300) in a way unsatisfactory to a specialist of the period.[26]

Assyriology functions, as a result of the phenomena observed above, in a world of personal index-cards, where individuals must spend considerable time creating and indexing their own corpus of transcriptions. This problem is clearly exacerbated over time, leading to a loss of interest in this kind of research that could otherwise be so rich a resource for the study of the economic and social life of the period. The urgency of a collective effort is, thus, clear to all involved.

Another problem is linked to the way in which these collections have been assembled. The existence of illegal excavations cannot be sufficiently deplored. Not only are these morally and legally condemnable, but their scientific ramifications are appalling. The antiquities market functions in such a way that the groupings in which documents are originally found are often dispersed: the components of the archives of one family are thus scattered among many different collections.[27] Thus, the archives of a creditor named Ibni-Amurrum had to be reconstituted from tablets in the Louvre, Yale, and the Horn Collection.[28] There are many such examples. It is evident that there is little purpose in studying isolated documents. And it is only when texts of these types are incorporated into the corpus to which they belong that they acquire their full meaning.

1.1.3 THE PRESENT CORPUS

It would be difficult to begin with anything other than the Mari archives, the traditional corpus of which is found in the *Archives Royales de Mari*, begun after the Second World War and currently comprising 30 volumes. For the most part, the texts are reproduced in *facsimile* (copies and/or photos), edited (transcriptions and translations), and annotated. The *ARM* series was complemented with *MARI* (8 volumes that appeared from 1981 to 1997), as well as with the new collection of *Florilegium Marianum* (10 volumes since 1992).

Otherwise, the only "living" Old Babylonian corpus is characterised by one particular genre: the letter. This corpus can be found in the series *Altbabylonische Briefe*, from the University of Leiden (14 volumes appeared between 1964 and 2006; the translations are in German for 9 volumes and in English for the other 5, including the last 4). The corpus presently includes 2,762 letters. The pragmatism of the series' founder, F. R. Kraus, led him to sequence the volumes according to the location of the tablets, in order to facilitate their collation, and with the objective of producing the best edition

---

[25] Sigrist 1990; 2003.

[26] See my review of *AUCT* 4 (Charpin 1993) and my review article of *AUCT* 5 (Charpin 2005a).

[27] Not to mention the "sorting" that sometimes occurs when the tablets that are in bad shape are eliminated before the sale so as not to diminish the value of the lot...

[28] See Charpin 2000a, in particular 198f. and 206–10, to be supplemented by Charpin 2005a, 412.

possible. The focus of the project was first and foremost philological, to the extent that *AbB* does not even include an index of proper names. The downside of this approach is that it isolates the letters from non-epistolary archival documents to which they are related (only the most recent volumes provide prosopographical indications to help the reader situate the letters in their archival context). Letters, moreover, rarely indicate the location and date of composition. It is often only in relation to these other documents that the letters' location in space and time can be determined, something that is significant for the study of dialect. Lastly, to this day the series has yet to be completed. The result being that it is impossible to quickly and easily have access to all of the letters written by the kings of Babylon between 1880 and 1595, or, even more limitedly, to the letters authored by Hammu-rabi. This situation constitutes a clear hindrance to research on institutions and on political, economic, and social life.

The other corpora of edited material are quite old and have long since ceased. The principal one is the six-volume *Hammurabis Gesetz*, the last of which appeared in 1923. This work has the inconvenience of providing only translations without transcriptions.

Other projects have been announced but have not yet been realised. These have usually focused on a particular type of text, such as the lawsuit collection announced by E. Dombradi, meant to replace M. Schorr's volume from 1913.[29] The disadvantage of such a corpus is that it isolates the documents from their archival context, leading to a strictly typological approach through which many elements of the texts find little elucidation. The archives from an Isin family are a good illustration of the situation: a lawsuit pitted two family members against each other, a situation which is inexplicable without knowing that the two brothers were in exile at the time. This fact can only be determined from other documents from their archives.[30]

Many existing research tools are outdated, moreover. Such is the case with the *Répertoire géographique des textes cunéiformes* III, dedicated to Old Babylonian texts, published in 1980 and never updated. A complete revision of the volume is very much in order. Indeed the corpus has increased by 12,000 texts since 1980, from slightly fewer than 17,000 to more than 29,000...

To date, the only database dedicated to Old Babylonian texts is the Old Babylonian Text Corpus (OBTC), available on the internet.[31] Created and maintained by a group of Czech researchers, it focuses exclusively on the philology and palaeography of Old Babylonian Akkadian texts of all genres.[32] The objectives of ARCHIBAB, however, are very different and will in no way compete with OBTC.

---

[29]   Schorr 1913. See Dombradi 1996.

[30]   Charpin 2000b, especially 77f., nos. 36f.

[31]   http://www.klinopis.cz/.

[32]   Its value is more pedagogical than scientific investigation, as evidenced, for example, by the fact that the palaeography is based on published copies.

1.2 The ARCHIBAB project

A good project is one designed to be carried out in stages. It is thus necessary to determine what the essential needs are, on the one hand, and what can be reasonably completed at a later date, on the other. The ARCHIBAB project was conceived with these concerns in mind. It is also based on the idea that a project of this sort must be carried out by a small and carefully assembled research team, which is also open to the outside scientific community on both the European and the international level – the number of Old Babylonian specialists in countries where Assyriology is studied, being, admittedly, somewhat limited.

The project, then, is composed of three parts: a general guide and bibliography, a digital database, and a series of monographs.

1.2.1 GENERAL GUIDE AND BIBLIOGRAPHY

In 2005, E. Frahm (Yale University) and M. Jursa created a new series entitled GMTR, *Guides to the Mesopotamian Textual Records*. The purpose of this series is to create a guide to facilitate the utilisation of the hundreds of thousands of cuneiform documents from all periods. The first volume in the series is devoted to Neo-Babylonian documents.[33] The editors of the series have asked me to be in charge of the volume on Old Babylonian archives.[34] The resulting monograph will present the main types of documents (form, content, etc.) as well as principal text groups, arranged by city.

We thereby intend to create a bibliography. A need for one has been long felt. J. Renger announced over thirty years ago a "Bibliographie der altbabylonischen Rechts- und Verwaltungsurkunden," with specifications of geographical origin and references or attributions of the texts to the different archives.[35] This project, unfortunately, never saw the light of day, and the need for it is now felt more than ever. It should, furthermore, be accessible in two ways, both in book form and online. Prepared by A. Jacquet, it will have the advantage of serving as an annotated bibliography. The online bibliography will be searchable using multiple criteria and will be updated regularly.

1.2.2. THE DIGITAL DATABASE

A prototype of the structure of the database was established in January–February 2008 and, in March, was presented in Paris to a group of experts at a round-table, consisting of Old Babylonian specialists and colleagues with long experience of online databases. Based on their recommendations, a definitive version of the structure was created, needing only minor modifications.[36]

---

[33] Jursa 2005.

[34] Provisionally entitled *Old Babylonian Archival Documents; Letters, Legal Records and Administrative Texts.*

[35] Renger 1977, 28.

[36] This database was created with the program "4D." It functions in Unicode, eliminating the longstanding problems associated with diacritical signs. I will not go into details of the design of the database at present.

1.2.2.1 THE BIBLIOGRAPHY

The first table is dedicated to the BIBLIOGRAPHIE (bibliography). Each publication (book, article, etc.) is entered, no matter what kind: copies, editions, commentaries.[37] If the publication is available on the internet, a link is established (URL), which allows for its immediate access.[38] Various ways of searching are possible: name of author(s) of the publication; title (partial if necessary); abbreviation of the review or collection; volume, and year. All combinations are possible. One of the riches of Assyriology, as an academic field, is its production of numerous and thorough reviews, often appearing years after the book. While several bibliographical works make these available – such as the *Keilschriftbibliographie* published in *Orientalia* or the *Register Assyriologie* published by *Archiv für Orientforschung* – their consultation remains tedious, leading to their limited use. ARCHIBAB provides instant access to all reviews of a given work, as well as to its corresponding review articles.

1.2.2.2 THE TEXTS: CATALOGUE

The next step will consist of gathering the complete text corpus. This table ("TEXTES") is, primarily, a catalogue containing the various kinds of descriptive elements, the selection of which, retained for presentation, represent the questions ARCHIBAB hopes to address. It is vital not to forget the lessons learned from the fancies of the 1970s, when computerising information in a "neutral" manner was thought possible, and that it would allow for answering unforeseen questions *a posteriori*. The ARCHIBAB database was thus conceived, in the first instance, to follow a historical line of questioning, even though other uses are doubtless possible.

The selected descriptive elements are the following:

- **Support du texte (textual medium)**: Provides information relative to the medium of the text: collection, nature of the medium (tablet and/or envelope, label, etc.), museum number, acquisition or find-spot (grid number, locus and level, if the text is from a documented excavation), dimensions, etc. In addition, the digital database was conceived in such a way that it is able to deal with joins, in the case of texts reconstructed from multiple fragments (which can be spread across multiple collections).[39]

- **Publications**: Copy and/or photo, transcription, translation, and commentary. The copy and the edition are most often found in different publications, although several combinations are possible. The digital database has no limitations in this regard: a link is established with all corresponding entries in the BIBLIOGRAPHIE table. The

---

[37] This is not an *exhaustive* bibliography of Old Babylonian studies. Its focus is on archival texts and is necessarily selective.

[38] Providing the work station from which it is consulted has the appropriate subscriptions, if the link is to limited-access sites such as JSTOR.

[39] This is infrequent, but see for example AbB, 14 9 (AO 4318 from the Louvre, "virtually" joined to L. 10934 from Istanbul).

copies and/or photos are registered in the database,[40] *with source citation*, allowing for the analysis of the external characteristics of the documents (format, layout of the text, etc.).

- **Référence-clé (reference key)**: A single unit comprising a unique identifier of the text, which can itself be designated in several ways: as a museum number, a copy, or as different editions. The database is arranged in such a way that it will allow for a text to be retrieved in all possible manners: AO 2704 (museum number), TCL 1 1 (copy), VAB 6 37 (first edition) or AbB 14 1 (most recent edition).[41] Thus, a reference key, chosen when the data is entered, must be established (if only for sorting the lists) and, in general, should correspond to the latest edition of the text (in this case AbB 14 1). This reference can easily be altered at a later point in time, since the links between the tables is stabilised by the assignment of an arbitrary and invisible number which is assigned by the program and cannot be modified.

- **Résumé (summary)**: Free of input parameters, this should allow for quickly apprehending the basics of the document.

- **Type (text type)**: Sale, rental, adoption, or marriage, among others. Contrary to the summary, the typology must be scrupulously defined. Determining a precise typology (with a list of key words) has been one of the primary aims of this project.

- **Objet(s) (object(s))**: Child/adult/slave, field/orchard/house/prebend, and boat/door, among others. The purpose of distinguishing text type from object is to allow for the rapid assembly of documents dealing with slaves, houses, and so on. One may thus indicate as many objects as necessary.

- **Date**: Day/month/king/year. One difficulty is that every reign has successive "year names" for each sovereign, the chronological order of which is not always known.[42] Attributing a numbered date (conventional if necessary) allows for documents to be sorted chronologically. The program will also manage eponym dates (an Upper Mesopotamian practice).

- *Lieu de découverte et lieu de redaction (find spot and place of composition)*: A distinction particularly relevant for letters, although not exclusively. This is also relevant, for example, to receipts composed in Babylon, preserved in the merchants' archives from Sippar.[43] It is apposite, moreover, to instances of people moving: the archives of a certain Amurrum-šemi were found in a house in Nippur, though a study

---

[40] Access to certain visual documentation on the internet will only be possible observing proper legal norms.

[41] This will allow the user to find one's way easily through the multiple re-editions of Mari texts, for example *ARM* 14 26 (edition with copy in TCM 1 26) = *LAPO* 18 995 (translation) = FM 8 18 (with photo in *FM* 8 p. 73).

[42] The benefits of dating by regnal year number, practiced in Babylonia from the second half of the second millennium, are obvious; recourse to a list of year names is not necessary for the dating of the document. We must not forget the inconvenience of this practice: if the number is broken, the date is forever lost, whereas a year formula that covers several lines leaves a greater possibility for identification.

[43] Charpin 1982, especially p. 38.

of diplomatics has shown that most of these texts were written in places other than Nippur.[44] Unfortunately, two-thirds of the texts come from undocumented excavations, illegal or ancient, where the finds were mostly not registered.[45] In such cases, determining the place of composition can be tricky. It must be noted that, apart from rare exceptions, letters contain no indication of date or place of composition. In addition, and unlike in the Neo-Babylonian period, contracts never indicate their place of composition. A date allows for the delineation of a geographical region, where a specific king exercised power at the time of the text's composition (which can be very limited in periods of political fragmentation). Such a specification requires a preserved date and a known and attributed "year name" formula, which does not always exist. Also of possible use is the oath, which often (but not always) includes the name of the city deity and king. Lastly, topographical indications, onomastic data, and other such elements, can limit the extent of the problem, but do not always solve it. This is also the case with texts unearthed by looters on sites where controlled excavations have taken place. In some instances the looters have preceded the archeologists;[46] in others they have followed.[47] Needless to say, looters have also excavated sites that were never subjected to controlled excavation.[48] The task is, furthermore, much more difficult for the Old Babylonian period than it is for the Neo-Sumerian and Neo-Babylonian periods, because the number of sites that have yielded texts is much higher (more than fifty).[49] Our process will allow us to establish a coefficient of uncertainty for suggested locations.[50]

- **Archives**: Determining to which archive a text belongs. This is a continuation of the process of determining the place of composition, described above. Even with controlled excavations, precise indications for the provenance of a tablet are often missing, whether because the information was never registered or later lost.[51] Long experience allows the scholar to reconstruct archival groups as they were likely discovered by looters and later dispersed as they were sold. The term "dossiers/files" would seem

---

[44]   Charpin 1989, 109–12.

[45]   This figure is applicable if we exclude the archives from Mari. See the details in the appendix to this contribution.

[46]   The British museum texts from Kisurra were acquired in 1898–99 (Goddeeris 2002, 94), while the German excavations began in 1903.

[47]   This unfortunately took place at Meskene/Emar after the excavations of J.-Cl. Margueron in 1976. On the other hand, contrary to Dalley *et al.* 2005, 3, the pillage of Larsa predates, rather than postdates, Parrot's 1933 excavations (cf. Charpin 2007, 148).

[48]   Lagaba is such an example; see Charpin, Edzard and Stol 2004, 432 (add now the texts copied in OECT 15).

[49]   See bibliography in Charpin, Edzard and Stol 2004, 407–80, where the sources are presented according to 9 zones, as well as the appendix of the current article where they are quantified.

[50]   Following the model of *The Helsinki Atlas of the Near East* (Parpola and Porter 2001) and its treatment of Neo-Assyrian toponyms.

[51]   Here we can cite the cases of Kisurra and Babylon, where many of the tags, which were attached to tablets during the excavations of the Deutsche Orient Gesellschaft, were later lost. For Babylon, see Pedersén 1998; also Pedersén 2005.

more suitable for such groupings than "archives," since doubts remain as to the exact boundaries of these artificial sets – product of scholarly research that has relied heavily on prosopographical analysis. Such adjustments usually appear in the reviews of major series of edited texts.[52] Henceforth, all of these preliminary endeavours should be collected and completed.

Thanks to this catalogue, we will be able to call up, for example, the list of all of the house sale texts from Larsa under Rîm-Sîn, effortlessly (by crossing the fields **type**, **objet** (object), **lieu** (place) and **date**. Similarly, all of the adoption records may be sorted chronologically, and all of the documents from the family archives of Balmunamhe may be sorted chronologically or by type (text type). This represents a significant transformation of research conditions.

1.2.2.3 THE TEXTS: TRANSCRIPTIONS

Gradually, the database will incorporate a complete transcription and translation of each and every text.[53] Transliterations may be entered line by line in a separate search field, which is linked to the TEXTES field, and the reconstructed text becomes visible in each TEXTES window. A coding system makes it possible to identify different parts of the text. For a land sale contract, for example, the following are indicated: the definition of property sold, survey, price, oath, and date, among others. This will enable precise inquiries such as: Which oaths were found in the Larsa contracts during the time of Hammu-rabi? And what were the blessing formulas in the letters found at Ur?

The collation of all of the originals is the ideal long-term outcome. In the meantime, we must accept an intermediate stage during which we will give clear preference to pragmatism rather than perfectionism. For now, the actions identified as pressing are twofold:
- Incorporating texts from text series published within the last 20 years or so and containing texts in facsimile (copy) only. These include: OECT 15 [2005; 381 texts]; VS 29 [2002; 132 texts]; OECT 13 [1991; 291 texts]; BBVOT 1 [1989; 176 texts]; SAOC 44 [1987; 97 texts]. These five series alone contain over 1,000 texts. Corrected transcriptions of recent and reasonably well-edited texts will also be incorporated, such as: Edubba 1 [1992; 24 texts] and 7 [2000; 136 texts], AUCT 4 [1990; 101 texts] and 5 [2003; 276 texts], etc., more than 500 texts altogether. And, gradually, we will be able to go back further in time and complete the series: YOS 12 [1979; 560 texts], YOS 13 [1972; 538 texts], YOS 14 [1978; 351 texts], etc.
- Incorporating published, isolated, and dispersed texts from compilations including *Festschrifts*, conference proceedings, and journals of difficult access. Priority will be

---

[52] See, for example, the review of YOS 13 by Stol 1973; of YOS 14 by Charpin 1979; of YOS 12 by Charpin 1981; of Stone 1987 by Charpin 1989 and 1990; or of VS 29 by van Koppen 2003/4 and by Charpin 2005c. The indications relative to archaeological context from the recently excavated tablets from Sippar (Abu Habbah), published in *Edubba* 7, are also faulty (cf. Charpin 2005b, 152–63).

[53] A summary will be sufficient for certain types of documents (especially for accounting records).

given to publications that do not contain editions (tablet copies only), or that are very old.

1.2.2.4 THE TEXTS: INDICES

The contents of the texts will then be indexed: Personal names, divine names, geographical names, and vocabulary (especially titles). When possible, indexing will occur directly after entering the transcription of the text.[54]

The recent book on local power in Mesopotamia during the Old Babylonian by A. Seri[55] is a good illustration of the present situation. The book contains a chapter on the "mayor" (*rabiânum*), where one would have hoped to find a list of all of the *rabiânum* attested in Old Babylonian documents, arranged by place and date. The author admits that the dispersed condition of the sources, and the difficulty in accessing them, discouraged her from this task.[56] Such a tool will clearly be indispensable to the scholarly community.

The project has been conceived in a way that will make the database ready to use before its completion.[57] Its priority will be to establish a complete catalogue of Old Babylonian documents.

1.2.3. A SERIES OF MONOGRAPHS

Launching a new project that will take many years to complete is not enough: the enthusiasm injected into the research presumes, likewise, the production of examples of what has been achieved, illustrating the spirit with which this effort has been undertaken and as preview of the results to come. In this vein, three well-defined corpora will be published in monograph form, within the next three years. I have already begun work on this project, and have submitted it to the ANR, where it has received the necessary funding. The unity of these three sets is based on chronology; all date to the last third of the reign of Samsu-iluna, the son and successor of Hammu-rabi (1749–1712). These three publications will gather the texts known in a dispersed manner, and will be completed by several dozen unedited ones.

Archibab 1: The daily life of a domain in Babylonia (based on the archives of Alammuš-nâṣir from Damrum)
This book will be an edition and study of some 100 texts, from a northern Babylonian

---

[54]   It may come as a surprise that we intend to enter these in a semi-manual fashion. The idea of an automatic prosopography seems, at present, dubious to me. A system of index cards is still necessary to note useful information. Without this semi-manual entry system, the results will be disconcertingly poor (much in the way current attempts at automatic lemmatisation have been).

[55]   Seri 2005.

[56]   "Despite my attempts to be thorough in compiling data, I am aware of the fact that some attestations could have escaped my notice. One cannot but wait eagerly for the completion of the Old Babylonian electronic corpus, because such a valuable tool will prevent omissions and make the gathering of information easier" (p. 2). I have included a fair amount of the most obvious missing ones in my review article (Charpin 2007, 167–82).

[57]   Indeed, one of the advantages of a digital database is its flexibility.

city near Kiš, which we have identified as Damrum (HI.GAR[ki]). The texts were discovered at the beginning of the twentieth century. They include a dozen letters that are in Yale (AbB 9), one in the Vatican museum (IB 197), a few texts from the Louvre (TCL 17 and BBVOT 1), and the largest group of 55 unedited tablets in Chicago, which I transcribed and photographed in May 2006.[58] These archives are significant on several levels. The majority of the texts are letters written by Alammuš-nâṣir to different people, and in particular to a certain Nabi-Šamaš. The latter was the manager of the estate to whom Alammuš-nâṣir habitually gave oral instructions. However, when Alammuš-nâṣir had to leave for a few weeks on a trip to Sippar, he communicated his instructions to him by means of writing. Allusions to missives sent, which appear in many of the letters, allow for the chronological classification of the correspondence, a very rare occurrence. This thereby constitutes an unparalleled corpus of documents, presenting a picture of the management of an estate down to its most concrete details.[59] Such details include milling, shearing, basket making (and the manufacture of many other reed objects), brick moulding, compensation of daily labourers, and the treatment of slaves. Important questions, such as what was the role of money and grain in economic transactions, or what was the application of the code of Hammu-rabi, find unanticipated answers here.[60] These letters have been able to be located chronologically thanks to the 40-plus administrative documents that come from the same archive and are dated to years 19 and 20 of Samsu-iluna's reign.

Archibab 2: An Isin neighbourhood from the Old Babylonian period
This set of archives was purchased in the 1920s, in part by the Louvre and in part by the Nies Babylonian Collection of Yale University. Some of the texts have since been published; I have been charged with publishing the rest.[61] The most interesting group concerns three generations of a family (the last member of which was Dadâ son of Kubbulum), who over 56 years were prebend-holders.[62] These texts represent a typical example of the increasingly varied nature of archival documents toward the end of the archive-period. In addition to property titles (mostly prebend purchases) there are letters, loans, and different rental contracts, including for fields and plough teams.

Archibab 3: The nakkamtum storehouse of the Ebabbar in Sippar.
This set of texts deals with the operations of a storehouse (*nakkamtum*) of the temple of Šamaš in Sippar during the final third of Samsu-iluna's reign. The majority of the

---

[58] I would like to thank W. Farber, curator of the Oriental Institute Collection, for letting me complete this work under optimal conditions.

[59] The lexical riches of these letters have provided many examples cited in the CAD.

[60] See the letter A 3529, cited in translation by Roth 1995, 6.

[61] I would like to thank B. André-Salvini, head of the department/general curator of the Antiquités Orientales of the Louvre, and B. Foster, curator of the Yale Babylonian Collection, as well as U. Kasten, the associate curator, who let me work on these tablets.

[62] See my study Charpin 2000a, 200f.

documents are unedited and housed at the Musée départemental des Antiquités in Rouen, to which the abbé de Genouillac donated his personal collection. I have studied and photographed these with the collaboration of J.-M. Durand. It is quite likely that these tablets come from the excavations undertaken by Scheil at Abu Habbah in 1893. They may have been given to Genouillac by the Sultan as a reward for his work at Kiš (in 1911/12), as was common practice during the Ottoman Empire.[63] These texts provide material for the study of the administrative organisation of the Šamaš temple in Sippar-Yahrurum. The documents mostly deal with livestock – big and small (shearing of sheep, grain rations, registry of losses, etc.) – related to offerings made to the gods.

Other works
The work done on the electronic corpus will doubtless lead to the composition of other monographs. We are anticipating publications of collaborative volumes resulting from the preparation of the corpus in the *Archibab* series.

1.2.4 PERSPECTIVES
The reconstitution of these archives is an absolute imperative for these texts – preserved, as they are, in such great numbers – to do full justice to their value as usable historical documents. The digital database under construction will give direct access to the documents for all who are interested in Old Babylonian history. This will be useful not only to philologists, but also to historians (economic, social, political, and of religion), lawyers, and archaeologists. In this way we hope to contribute to the decompartmentalisation of Assyriology, a field that, by not developing the appropriate tools, has too often erected the walls of its own confinement.

2. THREE CASE STUDIES

I would like to devote the second half of this contribution to the description of three specific examples that illustrate how a quantitative approach to historical documents leads to interesting results for the study of Old Babylonian history. First we will look at the largest group of Old Babylonian texts obtained from controlled excavations, namely, those found in the palace of Mari. Then we will examine a particular type of text, i.e. loan documents, whose chronological distribution can, indirectly, help us identify periods of crisis. We will end with the particularly interesting case of the real estate "boom" at Larsa, during the first half of the reign of Rîm-Sîn.

---

[63] This conclusion is confirmed by the presence of a tablet belonging to this same group, found in the collection of the EPHE, assembled by Scheil himself (Durand 1981, 77, HE 484). The presence of another text in the museum of Geneva is more difficult to explain (Birot 1969, 43).

2.1 The archives from the Mari palace

We will begin by looking at the archives discovered in the Mari palace by A. Parrot between 1934 and 1939.

2.1.1 PRESENTATION OF THE ARCHIVES

These archives are an excellent example of a *"large corpus of documentary evidence."* The total number of texts remains uncertain, because the catalogue established by M. Birot and J.-M. Durand[64] recorded both tablets and fragments. Hundreds of joins have been made since, however, reducing the number of texts, some reconstituted from as many as five or six fragments. If we take into account the number of fragments that have not yet been joined, the texts amount to about 13,000 out of a generally given inventory number of 20,000. At present, a little over 8,000 texts have been published in full,[65] representing approximately 60% of the total. This is the largest number of archives ever found in a single building. The palace at Nineveh, in comparison, has only produced (not counting the texts belonging to the library) about 6,000 archival documents.[66]

The typological distribution of the texts is interesting.[67] It includes three categories: epistolary, legal, and accounting documents.
- Letters have, since the beginning, attracted the most attention. They represent more than 2,500 documents,[68] or approximately one third of the 8,000 published texts.
- The legal documents are few in number.[69] This can be explained by the fact that the archives are palatial and contracts are usually found in family archives. Most of these legal texts, moreover, form part of individual and family archives, which were most likely not originally kept in the palace. Their presence there may, in some instances, represent cases of confiscation.
- The accounting documents represent the largest portion of the archives. The term "administrative documents," moreover, which is often applied to them, is not entirely correct, since a good number of letters also deal with administrative matters.

2.1.2 THE REPRESENTATIVENESS OF THE SAMPLES

Having described the richness of the Mari archives, the problem remains of what the

---

[64] Cf. Birot 1978, 343.

[65] This number is reliable to within a few digits (8,085 on 18 June 2008); it was produced by the ARCHIBAB database from the bibliographical records entered at the beginning of the project. The texts in question are those that are *fully* published; the texts that have only been the object of citation (even long ones) have not been counted. This number corresponds to archival documents only. The other categories of texts from Mari ("literary" texts, royal inscriptions, etc) are very limited in number.

[66] See the statistics compiled by Parpola 1986, 228.

[67] For a presentation of the collected archives, see Charpin and Ziegler 2003, 1–27, complemented by Charpin 2008c.

[68] 2,536 on 5 June 2008.

[69] See most recently my contribution on "Les formulaires juridiques des contrats de Mari à l'époque amorrite: entre tradition babylonienne et innovation" (Charpin 2010c).

texts that have come down to us represent. The nature and scope of the sample available to us should not be ignored when making use of the economic information contained therein.

2.1.2.1. WHAT THE BABYLONIANS LEFT BEHIND

What was found in the Mari palace is composed of what the Babylonians left there before they destroyed it. And at the heart of the archives, we appreciate two sets of circumstances. First, certain groups of tablets were not touched by the Babylonians. This is the case for many of the accounting documents, especially the hundreds of "king's meals" texts found in open jars in Room 5 of the palace. These probably fell from the storey above.[70] It also appears that the archives from the women's quarter stayed intact. These were found in Rooms 52 and 110 and include accounting texts and letters to the queen mother and to Zimrî-Lîm's wives.[71] In addition to this, Room 24 appears to have housed the archives of Iddin-Numušda, otherwise known as Iddiyatum, chief of the merchants.

Second, another part of the archives was, however, sorted out. This is especially true of the royal correspondence and is clear from a series of tags found in Room 115.[72] A date between the 28th and 30th of month vii of the 32nd year of Hammu-rabi (1761) is written on the reverse. The obverse indicates the contents: "Tablet basket/box (=letters) of the servants of Samsî-Addu" (one example), or "tablet basket/box (=letters) of the servants of Zimrî-Lîm" (six examples). This shows that, doubtless by relying on pre-existing classifications, the Babylonians put the archives of the chancellery in containers which they stored in Room 115. A fragment of a tag, however, and probably belonging to one of the chests that was taken away, was found next to the palace gate. It thus appears that the seven tags found correspond to seven cases that, for whatever reason, were not taken out of the palace.[73] The conclusion to be drawn from this is clear: a portion of the original archives was no longer present in the ruins of the Mari palace, most likely because it was taken to Babylon. This conclusion is corroborated by internal analysis of the correspondence.[74]

A third situation is represented by the "dead archives." These texts were already discarded in antiquity and include the several hundred tablets from the reigns of kings

---

[70] Charpin 2001b, 29.

[71] Charpin 1995, 39; this article is available at www.digitorient.com/?attachment_id=112.

[72] Charpin 1995.

[73] I have calculated the weight and number of tablets stored in this kind of case. One case could hold 450 letters, totalling 45 kg. An example of such a tablet-box was found at Tell ed-Dêr in the house of Ur-Utu, the chief lamentation priest (Tanret 2008). It contained 207 tablets arranged in four layers. The actual container, which was probably made out of reed, has disappeared, but the tablets took up a space of 36 × 24 cm, the chest being about 20 cm deep. It was sturdy enough to carry 23 kg, the weight of the 207 tablets found. My theoretical calculations for the Mari cases, which were done before Tanret's study, are exactly double, an amount that does not seem improbable to me.

[74] See Durand 1997, 28.

Yahdun-Lîm and Sûmû-Yamam, found under the last occupation level of the palace, particularly in the area of Rooms 133 to 142. They were used as backfill during the construction carried out at the beginning of Yasmah-Addu's reign. Some of the accounting archives from the time of Yasmah-Addu are of the same status. These are the several dozen oil expenditure records, found in Room 116, on a bench specifically intended to support jars of oil.[75]

2.1.2.2 THREE SAMPLES OF ACCOUNTING DOCUMENTS

In order to determine the value of the accounting document samples that are available to us, I will present three examples of texts recording internal expenditure from the Mari palace. These deal with sheep/goats, oil, and grain.

The first group contains 153 tablets describing incomes and expenditures of sheep. These date to the first three months of Zimrî-Lîm's reign, from 24–ix to 16–xii.[76] Eleven tablets record incomes of sheep in the care of Dabi'um, the animal fattener.[77] 137 tablets contain accounts of sheep expenditures for different occasions: the king's table (viz., for the consumption of the king and his entourage); oracular consultation; sacrifices and various rituals; presents to the royal family, dignitaries, and foreign envoys. Almost all of these tablets were sealed by the diviner Asqûdum.[78] Altogether, the small tablets account for 979 animals.[79] ARM 7 224 provides us with a summary of these expenditures, doubtless established at the end of the year.[80] 1,294 sheep were thus expended under the responsibility of Asqûdum. This shows that over 150 texts were written in less than three months. Using this total to calculate a number for the 13 years of Zimrî-Lîm's reign shows that we should have 8,000 tablets for this type of transaction alone. Around 5,200 sheep were expended every year, or 67,600 for the total reign. A more detailed study of royal expenditures compared against the husbandry activity of the entire kingdom is very much in order.[81]

A second example is found in the oil expenditure records. A particularly interesting group of these was found in Room 79 of the palace.[82] This group is composed of small

---

[75]   Charpin 1984; 1987.

[76]   See Charpin and Ziegler 2003, 172f.

[77]   Lafont 1984, 277–8.

[78]   Lafont 1984, 231–51.

[79]   Because of an absence of interest in the quantitative aspect of the file, this total has not been calculated until now. I totalled the tablets from the list in Lafont 1984, 232–3. I counted 22 sheep in ARM 23 264 (the total is broken but should be some 30 animals); in ARM 23 233 I counted 3, but there must be more; the total in ARM 23 496 is missing.

[80]   Unlike the other texts in this lot, the record is not dated. See collations of the text in *MARI 2*, p. 92. The total from ARM 7 224 probably corresponds to the total of expenditures since Zimrî-Lîm's arrival in Mari. It exceeds by 315 units the total resulting from the small accounts, which means that we do not have all of these.

[81]   One should look at the figures from the *sugâgûtum* texts, recently published by Marti 2008.

[82]   Duponchel 1997. Although it was not pointed out in this study, two accounts of oil, from Room 79 had already been published. The tablets are long ration lists:

- The tablet known as AB: Birot 1953a; Birot 1953b; Birot 1955: A name list of oil rations distributed

documents – recording oil expenditures over a period of three months during Zimrî-
Lîm's first regnal year – along with three corresponding monthly account summaries.
It must be pointed out that jars were found in the adjoining Rooms 79 and 80 (as well
as in nearby Room 78). These were likely used to store the oil that was redistributed.
The rations were delivered in a regular manner to several specific groups: "the palace"
(*ekallum*), i.e., the women from the harem (350 to 382 women) along with the 15 guards;
254 men, the Bedouin guard of Mari and Ṣuprum, which was supervised by Ka'ala-AN;
51 servants of the apartments (*ša temenni*); 19 porters of the royal palanquin (*ša nubalim*);
and 16 guards who originated from Nuruggûm. We thus have 397 people from the
harem and 340 servants attached to the king, making a total of 737 people who received
oil rations every month. In addition to this, oil was irregularly distributed for such
purposes as offerings to the gods, lamps, vehicle maintenance, and for the care of
various people, among others. The tablet group found in Room 79 contains 106
individual accounts and 3 account summaries for a period of three months. If we
extrapolate from this information, we should have 5,700 such texts for the entire reign
of Zimrî-Lîm. From a quantitative point of view, the monthly sum of the expenditures
is more than 5 gur (about 600 litres),[83] amounting to 7,200 litres a year. We can compare
this total with the one from a later document, ARM 22 276, an account of outgoing
sesame over a period of 28 months (from ix/ZL 2 to xii/ZL 4), under the responsibility
of Mukannišum. The document is a clearing of accounts (*nipiṣ nikkassî*), which took
place in the *bît têrtim* of the palace gate, under the control of three administrators,
on 2/v/ZL 5, four months after the period discussed. The general total of expenditures
is 283 *ugar* of sesame, which corresponds more or less to 283 gur of oil.[84] The average
consumption for this period is therefore 1,212 litres of oil per month, which is double

to the men of the Bedouin guard of Mari and Ṣuprum, under the responsibility of Ka'ala-AN; to the
apartment servants (*ša temenni*); to the porters of the royal palanquin (*ša nubalim*); and to the guards
who originate from Nuruggûm (date: 30/xi/ZL 1 [Kahat]). The contents of this list reappear in the
account summary FM 3 95 1 "6";
   - Tablet known as C: Birot 1956, re-edited with joins as FM 4 3: A name list of oil rations distributed
to the 382 women and 15 doormen of the harem (date 1/xi/ZL 1 [Kahat]). The contents of this list
reappear in the account summary FM 3 95: 38'–42' (30/xi/Zl 1 = Kahat), but the lines are almost
entirely broken and the reconstructions in FM 3 need to be revised (cf. Ziegler 1999, 23).
   Also note that tablet FM 3 66 was already published by Birot 1972, 132f. (copy and transliteration).
   A similar tablet (T.340), but discovered under the floor of Room 142, was recently published by
Chambon 2008; it probably dates to the month iii/ZL 2 (*Ah Purattim*). It differs in that it is an account
of expenditures both of oil and tallow. Lastly, unedited accounts of oil from Rooms 69 and 74, dating
to the "Kahat" year, were cited by Birot 1972, 133. These illustrate once again the problem of the
"disorder" of the archives found in the palace, due, in part, to registration errors that occurred at
the time of discovery of the archives (Charpin and Durand 1986, 147 and, more recently, Lacambre
1997, 93 n. 6). A clearer picture of the situation will be possible only when all of the documentation
has been published.
   [83]   The number in FM 3 60: 64 is broken, but partially legible on the photo. In FM 3 95: 1' shows
at least 3 gur, but the number is also broken.
   [84]   The relationship between the quantity of oil produced and the amount of sesame necessary
for its production is 10 %, as demonstrated by Chambon 2008 (cf. n. 82).

what we calculated above from the small texts, from the beginning of Zimrî-Lîm's reign. This is also consonant with the development of palatial consumption between these two periods.[85]

The two cases just presented are analogous; the documentation is (almost) complete, covers a short period of time, and was under the authority of "bureaux" in charge of accounting for sheep expenditures and the distribution of oil rations respectively.[86] The fact that both cases date to the beginning of Zimrî-Lîm's reign suggests that these were discarded documents. However, the excavation procedures of 1934–39 were not sophisticated enough to recognise this. The "bureaux" managed the internal everyday expenditures of the palace. They dealt with commodities such as grain, oil, wool, animals, alcoholic beverages, copper, and bronze.[87] If we extrapolate the results obtained above, then each bureau would have produced around 7,000 tablets during the reign of Zimrî-Lîm. The number of these bureaux is unknown, but we can estimate that there were at least six. This leads to the conclusion that the internal accounting of expenditures yielded 42,000 tablets, begging the question: why have these not reached us? One explanation is the practice of recycling tablets. After having composed account summaries, the scribes no longer needed to store the small accounts and they recycled the clay to make new tablets.[88]

A third group of tablets, recording grain expenditures destined for the "meal of the king" (*naptan šarrim*),[89] differs from the cases described above. These accounts were recorded daily by two female scribes attached to the palace kitchens.[90] Account summaries were drawn up at the end of every month. These texts were first studied on a lexical level, contributing to the study of food and diet.[91] We were also able to draw conclusions about royal sociability, since the king invited distinguished guests but also certain soldiers to his table.[92] If we estimate that one tablet was written per day,[93] then we should have a total of 4,700 texts, excluding account summaries. What

---

[85] N. Ziegler was able to calculate that the number of women in the harem (350 at the beginning of Zimrî-Lîm's reign) was double in Year 6 of Zimrî-Lîm (Ziegler 1999, 18).

[86] This notion of "bureau" is undoubtedly a modern simplification, as was shown by Chambon 2008. Nonetheless, it appears that the head of the sheep "bureau" was the diviner Asqûdum (cf. the presence of his seal and the account summary *ARM* 7 224: 14), whereas the head of the oil "bureau" was Šubnalû (*FM* 3, p. 205 based on *FM* 3 60, 65–6).

[87] Here, too, we are dealing with small tablets and large account summaries. See the study by Lacambre 1997.

[88] For an overview see Faivre 1995. For a concrete example from the reign of Yahdun-Lîm, see Charpin and Ziegler 2003, 36, end of note 49 (jar from square E).

[89] It must be noted that such texts are in no way particular to Mari. For similar texts dating to the reign of Rîm-Sîn of Larsa, see Beckman 1995, 2 n. 14. Such texts were also present in the homes of notables (*naptan awîlim* "meal of the man"): cf. Charpin 2003, 314.

[90] For these two women, see Ziegler 1999, 91f. and 106.

[91] See Bottéro 1957, 256–68; Birot 1960, 274–295; Burke 1963; Birot 1964; Durand 1983, 166–80.

[92] See Lafont 1985.

[93] There are several cases where we have two tablets written for the same day. These were probably written for the morning and evening meals (cf. Sasson 1982, 328).

has come into our possession, however, is far short of this number. Once the sequence of Zimrî-Lîm year names was established,[94] we organised the texts into chronological order and realised that these accounted for a large part of his reign, with several periods for which there were no texts. The intervals simply correspond to times when the king was absent from the palace. We were thereby able to establish the periods of time when the king was on campaign.[95]

There were, to be sure, accounting documents other than the ones recording daily expenditures, such as inventories of precious crockery.[96] In addition, a separate accounting was kept for gifts received and given during the king's travels. The records were brought back to the palace upon the king's return. These small accounting documents have allowed us to reconstruct the king's military campaigns. The documents are important for reducing the risk of distortion prominent in the interpretation of commemorative inscriptions. They allow for a more precise reconstruction of the king's itinerary.[97]

2.1.2.3 THE MIKSUM-TAX COLLECTION

Tax collection registers provide a good indicator of economic activity for all periods. While account summaries dealing with this activity were not found in the Mari palace, another group of documents is noteworthy. These are not accounting documents but letters, which have contributed significantly to the study of economic history. One group of 45 letters, for example, discusses the collection of the *miksum*, contributing to the discussion of Euphrates trade. These short notes were written by Numušda-nahrari, an official posted at Terqa, 75 km upstream from Mari.[98] The messages are addressed to Iddiyatum, the "chief of the merchants" of Mari. They specify whether or not the contents of a boat had been subjected to a tax known as *miksum*, which was levied on commodities going to market.[99] The following are two examples:[100]

> "Say to Iddiyatum: thus (speaks) Numušda-nahrari. Six shekels of silver were levied as *miksum*-tax on Sumuqân-išar's oil cargo: let (him) pass! 24/iii."

> "Say to Iddiyatum: thus (speaks) Numušda-nahrari. There is a cargo belonging to Summân which has not been inspected nor subjected to the *miksum*-levy: impose the *miksum*-levy! 25/iv."

---

[94]   See most recently Charpin and Ziegler 2003, 257–62.

[95]   See Charpin and Ziegler 2003, 195 n. 204; 199 n. 249; 201 n. 269 and 275; 207 n. 343; 235 n. 612; 240 n. 676.

[96]   Guichard 2005.

[97]   Villard 1986; Villard 1992; Charpin 1994.

[98]   See Durand 2000, nos. 862–905.

[99]   See Michel 1996. We also have tablets which record levied sheep as the *miksum*-tax of the Suteans during the reign of Yahdun-Lîm (cf. Charpin 2001b, 23–7).

[100]   *ARM* 13 91 (= *LAPO* 18 871) et *ARM* 13 95 (= *LAPO* 18 875).

These short notes cover the period of nine months from 2/ix to 28/v of the following year.[101] We should therefore be in possession of 800 such documents for the entire reign of Zimrî-Lîm. The lingering question is whether the extrapolation of such samples can be used to calculate the volume of river-borne commercial activity. Such an endeavour may be premature.

2.1.3. FORECASTS AND VERIFICATION

C. Wilcke has suggested that writing developed more to allow for "accounting forecasts"[102] than for the more commonly believed purpose of *a posteriori* verification or control. This is particularly clear in the Ur III period. In the case of the Mari palace archives,[103] most of the accounting documents record expenditures.[104] It must be pointed out, however, that once a list of rations was established, it served to make forecasts for the next distribution. A particularly clear example of this occurs in a list of rations for the harem women. The scribe erased the date of the tablet and re-dated it to the following month.[105] The record was reused because the ration distribution did not change from one month to the next. This illustrates the difficulty of drawing a clear line of demarcation between these two purposes.

The letters of Yasîm-Sûmû, the "minister of finance/chief accountant" (*šandabakkum*) reveal clear economic forecasts.[106] We do not have the corresponding texts, however, because his archives have yet to be found. We only have the letters he wrote to Zimrî-Lîm.[107] Yasîm-Sûmû played a role in decisions concerning the calendar, the key element in accounting control and in making forecasts.[108]

The question that arises, then, is whether or not account verification took place. J. Sasson has not found evidence of this in the records concerning the "king's meals."[109] He explained the frequent discrepancies between the daily records and summary accounts by assuming that it was often difficult for the scribes to find the original records, and that in such cases they would feel little hesitation in fabricating data, to the point of re-writing fake "originals". I must admit that I find this explanation difficult to accept. J. Sasson is insistent on the fact that the "king's meals" tablets were found in five different rooms: Rooms 5, 69, 79, 110, 111 (we can also add 160). We know, however, that there was some confusion during the excavation. In 1934, more than 13,000 documents were found by Parrot, who was excavating with 300 workmen and only one area supervisor, one photographer, and an interpreter (no epigrapher).

---

[101] Zimrî-Lîm year 12 and 13; see Charpin and Ziegler 2003, 235 n. 612.

[102] Wilcke 1970, 166.

[103] See Ziegler 2001.

[104] We do not have accounting records of commodities *coming into* the palace. These may be in a part of the palace that has not been excavated, the area of the "Nergal gate" (cf. Durand 1987, 48).

[105] Ziegler 1999, 23.

[106] See Maul 1997.

[107] See especially the letter *ARM* 13 35 = *LAPO* 18 858.

[108] Charpin and Durand 2004.

[109] Sasson 1982.

Moreover, the distribution of the tablets during the excavation represents the final state of things and not necessarily what prevailed some years earlier. In fact, we know of several cases where the scribe composed an account statement with a group of tablets before him, as evidenced by a document concerning the collection of arrears.[110] Yet, while the explanation given by J. Sasson is not entirely convincing, it is also difficult to contest. In a recent study of two account summaries of oil expenditures (T. 340 and ARM 22 276), G. Chambon came to a similar conclusion; he was struck by the precision of the totals and suspected that the scribe performed *a posteriori* calculations.

The "census" (*têbibtum*) texts clearly fit into the "(accounting) forecast" category. These are lists of men of fighting age, established locally and then compiled at three provincial capitals (Mari, Terqa, and Saggarâtum). They were then recopied onto large tablets that were sent to the capital.[111] From these lists, the king could know how many men were available for future military campaigns. We know that these lists were kept with great care in the palace, in sealed chests,[112] and that great care was involved in their consultation.[113] We thus have concrete proof that these texts were used. Certain documents compare the actual number of men mobilised with the theoretical number of men expected;[114] in some instances the absentee rate is 60 %! It clear, then, that these "forecast" documents were used as instruments for verification.

2.2 Debt: an indicator of economic activity?

"Loans" are the most frequent type of legal documents.[115] The principal question relevant to them is what information they provide regarding economic activity.[116] Their chronological organisation is, therefore, *a priori* a crucial tool for analysis. One must be cautious when looking at the samples that have come into our possession. Usually the tablet kept by the creditor was destroyed when the debt had been settled. The loan documents we have must therefore represent debts which had never been repaid. My study, which focuses mainly on the reigns of Hammu-rabi and Samsu-iluna, shows that the level of loan documents increased as a date scheduled for debt remission by royal decree (*mîšarum*) approached.[117] The loan documents cancelled by these edicts, although no longer of any value, were often kept by the creditor instead of being destroyed. This allows us to see that the remission of debt, decided by the sovereign,

---

[110] Charpin 2008b (cf. Charpin 2007, 149).

[111] These lists were studied by A. Millet Albà 2001.

[112] See the tablet-basket labels published in Charpin 2001b, 16–18.

[113] See the letters ARM 10 82 (= *LAPO* 18 1205) and ARM 13 14 (= *LAPO* 17 652), glossed in Charpin 2001b, 14f.

[114] See *ARM* 23 428 and 429, with comments by D. Soubeyran (see Bardet *et al.* 1984, 358–368). The historical context is now better understood: see Charpin and Ziegler 2003, 224 n. 499.

[115] Unfortunately, the book by Skaist 1994 does not provide numbers for the corpus that is the object of his study.

[116] Van de Mieroop 2002.

[117] Charpin 2000a.

was a welcome occasion. Even if the majority of the loans were incurred in the months preceding the *mîšarum*, it also appears that loans could go unpaid and date back several years.

In the time since the aforementioned study was published, several new elements have come to light that substantiate its general conclusion. Newly published collections of tablets as well as unedited texts confirm the existence of this phenomenon, possibly for periods beyond what I limited myself to as essential. These collections include:
- The publication of a group of tablets from Sippar concerning the application of the *mîšarum* during Samsu-iluna year 8.[118] These have the advantage of having been found in a well-defined archeological context.
- Unedited texts from Tell Egraineh.[119] These form a group of 31 loan documents dating to the end of Ammi-ditana's reign, apparently cancelled following the *mîšarum* proclaimed at the accession of Ammi-ṣaduqa. This group illustrates how the temple was affected by these measures in the same way "private" creditors were.[120]
- Information from unedited texts from the archives of Ur-Utu found at Tell ed-Dêr. This attests to the application of the *mîšarum* at the accession of Ammi-ṣaduqa.[121]
- A recent article looking at the loan documents from the reign of Samsu-iluna, including unedited texts known from catalogues of the British Museum and Yale.[122] While the corpus has quadrupled, from 130 to 560 texts, the chronological distribution remains identical. There is an element of comfort to this, showing, as it does, that even with a relatively limited sample, we were able to obtain dependable results.

Stemming from how the documents were preserved, the chronological distribution of loan contracts reflects the actual situation only in an indirect manner. The number of loans not repaid increases with the approach of a *mîšarum*, because these debts were cancelled by the king. However, the king must have proclaimed a *mîšarum* because an economic catastrophe prevented the poorest from paying their debts.[123]

2.3 The real estate boom under Rîm-Sîn

Unfortunately, the great majority of published Old Babylonian texts from Larsa have come from the illicit excavations of the early 20th century. Looking at the chronological distribution of the corpus of urban land sales, one is struck by an anomaly:

---

[118] Al-Rawi and Dalley 2000; see my remarks on the subject in Charpin 2005b, especially pp. 154–157, which clarifies and complements my previous observations in Charpin 2001a.

[119] Kessler 1997/98; see my note on the subject (Charpin 2001a).

[120] Contrary to what was stated by Richardson 2002, 231: "a *mîšarum* would have no authority to remit loans issued under temple authority".

[121] Van Lerberghe 2003, especially p. 72f. and fig. 4.3 (p. 63). The author gives the impression (pp. 72–3) that there is a *direct* link between the economic situation and the number of loans, without taking into account that we have no knowledge of the number of loans, only the number of loans *not reimbursed*; the formulation on p. 75, on the other hand, is correct.

[122] Suurmeijer 2006/7.

[123] One of the clearest economic crises is the one that led Samsu-iluna to proclaim a *mîšarum* in the 28th year of his reign: see Charpin, Edzard and Stol 2004, 359 n. 1875.

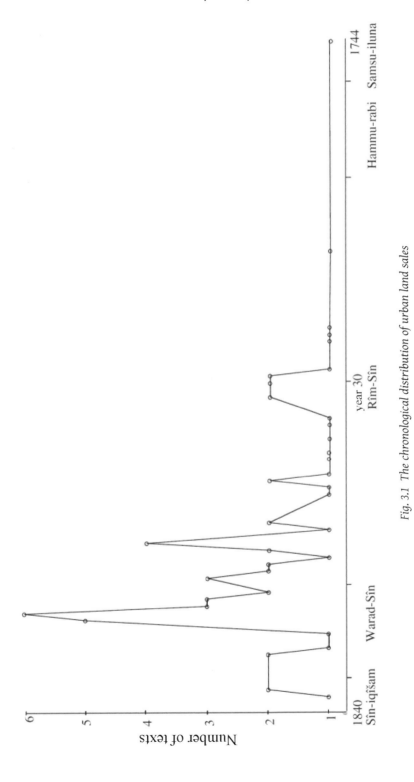

Fig. 3.1 The chronological distribution of urban land sales

The graph (fig. 3.1) above shows the distribution over a century, from 1840 (accession of Sîn-iqîšam) to 1744 (Samsu-iluna Year 6). The number of property purchases in Larsa is very high under Sîn-iqîšam, Warad-Sîn (with its peak during Year 9) and in the first part of Rîm-Sîn's reign. It subsequently becomes considerably lower: 92% of the contracts pre-date the 32nd year of Rîm-Sîn. There are no indications of judicial changes, however, neither during the middle of Rîm-Sîn's reign, nor at the time of the Hammu-rabi's Babylonian conquest (1763). This phenomenon has long remained unexplained. The number of contracts, more than 60, is large enough to rule out coincidence. The sample, coming from several archives, is significant. The work done on the site of Larsa from 1985 to 1989 has thus led me to venture an explanation.[124]

Archaeological research has shown that the entire northern part of the *tell* was occupied by large houses (from 500 m² to more than 1,000 m²), standing in the middle of vacant plots, which we assume were gardens. These reveal an aspect of Mesopotamian urbanism very different from that uncovered by excavations at Ur, Nippur, and at smaller sites such as Šaduppûm or Harrâdum, characterised by small, closely-packed houses. In this neighbourhood of Larsa, by contrast, we are dealing with "small palaces" of a sort, where the members of the elite reproduced, on a reduced scale, the palatial constructions of the period.[125]

In light of these archaeological finds, it has been possible to take another look at the documents unearthed by looters from this quarter in the beginning of the 20th century. And we have deduced that over a period of a few decades members of several prominent families systematically bought land parcels adjoining the lots they owned. When the head of the family died, the heirs divided, among other property, the large house, which was what the father had presumably erected on the large parcel of land he had pieced together. The chronological evolution of Larsa's real estate activities thus becomes clear: the upsurge in lot purchases came to a sudden halt in the middle of Rîm-Sîn's reign, because the available parcels in Larsa's "residential" quarter had been purchased and amassed into larger lots for larger houses. These families of notables experienced a period of rapid economic growth during the reign of Warad-Sîn and the first half of Rîm-Sîn's. The construction of a beautiful "mansion" was the *social* symbol of their achievement. This is reinforced by the fact that the contracts do not reveal *economic* activity related to real estate investment.

3. CONCLUSION

These three cases were presented here because they represent particularly clear examples of both the wealth and limits of the Old Babylonian documentation from which we will write new pages of the economic and social history of Mesopotamia in the first half of the second millennium BCE. Much remains to be done to this end, and it is the ARCHIBAB project's ambition to contribute to this endeavour.

---

[124]   Here I summarise the conclusions of my previous study (Charpin 2003).

[125]   Battini and Calvet 2003.

I know not how to end this article other than by drawing attention to the disastrous effects the damage of the illicit excavations in Iraq since 1991 will have on the continuation of this research. I admit to not being an Assyriologist who rejoices over having new and additional tablets. Taking these out of context largely deprives them of potential value for those interested in economic history. It takes a particularly stubborn philologist not to understand this fact...

4. APPENDIX: OLD BABYLONIAN TEXTS FROM CONTROLLED EXCAVATIONS

I have tried to indicate the number of Old Babylonian archival texts that have come from controlled excavations.[126] These represent about half of the total (as many as 29,228). The situations vary, however. We know very little about the archaeological context in which the archives were found for many excavations that took place prior to 1914 (in some cases for later ones as well...). In these cases, the only advantage we have over texts unearthed by illicit excavations is that the provenance is assured.[127] I have thus only included texts that come from what I refer to as "documented excavations." Not only are these from controlled sites, but they were registered with a minimum of care. The total amounts to slightly higher than 15,000.

It must be pointed out that the Mari archives distort the statistics because of their great number (more than 8,000 published texts). Setting these aside, we see that of the 21,000 published texts, only 7,000 are from documented excavations. Two thirds of the archival texts published to date (apart from Mari), from both controlled and illicit excavations, are therefore lacking an archaeological context. This reveals the difficulty of the task at hand.

N.B. The following list refers to the bibliography of Charpin, Edzard and Stol 2004, 403–480. Certain sites are not included (such as Lagaba, Ṣupur-Šubula, etc.) because the texts come from illicit excavations. The + sign precedes entries which are not in the aforementioned bibliography.

1. The Sumerian south

      1.1. Ur (tell Muqqayair): 1,059
      1.2. Uruk (Warka): 564
      1.3. Larsa (tell Senkereh): 141
      1.4. Lagaš
            – Lagaš (al-Hiba): 6
            – Girsu (Tello): 18

---

[126] Here, I take up again the geographical distribution of the bibliography found in Charpin, Edzard and Stol 2004, 403–80, where I did not include the number of texts. Naturally, the numbers here are approximate: they only take into account published texts.

[127] Unfortunately, these are often dispersed over several collections. The texts excavated at Nippur in the 19th century provide a good example of this, where the tablets are located in Istanbul, Philadelphia and Jena.

1.5. Kutalla (tell Sifr): 106
Total for the 6 sites: 1,894

2. THE CENTRE
  2.1. Nippur (Nuffar)
    The texts from the end of the 19th century excavations are devoid of any archaeological context (and sometimes not identified as such in the museum collections).
      – since 1948: 507
  2.2. Isin (Išān Baḥrīat): 128
  2.3. Kisurra (Abu Hatab): 212
  2.4. Adab (Bismaya): 71
  Total for the 4 sites: 918

3. THE NORTH
  3.1. Babylon: 112

    3.2. Kiš: unfortunately the texts excavated by the French in 1911–12 (90 texts from archives found in PRAK 1 and 2, preserved in Istanbul [*siglum* Ki] or in the Louvre) or from the Anglo-American excavations between the two wars (Chicago/Oxford) were published without any reference to context (various articles by Langdon; OECT 13 and 15). We cannot reconstitute these archives, therefore the texts were not included.
  3.3. Sippar
      – Sippar-Yahrurum (Abu Habbah): 93
      – Sippar-Amnânum (Tell ed-Dēr): 436
    Many towns for which we were able to establish a provenance are only known from archival texts which come from illicit excavations: Dilbat, Lagaba, etc.
  Total for the 4 sites: 641

4. THE DIYALA BASIN
  4.2. Ešnunna (Tell Asmar): 55
  4.3. Nêrebtum (Ishchali): 135
  4.4. Tutub (Khafajah): 111
  4.5. Šaduppûm (Tell Harmal): 143
  4.6. Uzarlulu (Dhib'ai): 5
    4.+ Tulul Khattab: 36
  4.9.1. Mê-Turan (Tell Ḥaddad and Tell es-Sib): 169
  Total for the 7 sites: 654

5. Susa and Elam

5.1. Suse (Shush): 826

6. Upper Mesopotamia

6.1. Nineveh: 7
6.2. Šušarra (Shemshāra): 246
6.+ Nuzi (Yorghan Tepe): 1
6.3. Qaṭṭarâ (Tell Rimah): 335
6.3.1 Tell Taya (= Zamiyatum?): 1
6.4. Tell Hawa (= Razamâ of Yussân?): 1
6.6. Šehnâ/Šubat-Enlil (Tell Leilan): 335
6.8. Chagar Bazar (Ašnakkum): 334
Total for the 8 sites: 1,260

7. The Middle-Euphrates

7.1. Tell Shishin: 7
7.2. Harrâdum (Khirbet ed-Diniye): 116
7.3. Mari (Tell Hariri): 8,085
7.4. Terqa (Tell Ashara): 13
7.5. Tuttul (Tell Bi'a): 379
7.6. Imâr/Emar (Meskene): 1
Total for the 6 sites: 8,601

8. Western Syria

8.1. Alalah (Tell Atchana): 268
8.2. Ebla (Tell Mardikh): 2
Total for the 2 sites: 270

9. Palestine

9.1. Haṣor: 1
9.2. Hebron: 1

Total for all sites: 15,066

Afterword

My French contribution has been translated by E. Salgues and revised by H. Baker; my gratitude goes to both of them. I have left my text (and the statistics it contains) as submitted in November 2008, only updating the bibliography when necessary. The French version can be downloaded at http://www.digitorient.com/?p=190.[128]

BIBLIOGRAPHICAL ABBREVIATIONS

Abbreviations generally follow CAD and *Archiv für Orientforschung* 48/49 pp. 311ff. Note furthermore the following sigla and abbreviations:

BDTNS   Database of Neo-Sumerian Texts (http://bdts.filol.csic.es/, accessed August 2010).
ETCSL   Electronic Text Corpus of Sumerian Literature (http://etcsl.orinst.ox.ac.uk/, accessed August 2010)
OBTC   Old Babylonian Text Corpus (http://www.klinopis.cz/, accessed August 2010)
OECT 15   see Dalley *et al.* 2005
SEAL   Sources of Early Akkadian Literature (http://www.seal.uni-leipzig.de/, accessed August 2010)

REFERENCES

Al-Rawi, F. N. H. and Dalley, S. (2000) *Old Babylonian Texts from Private Houses at Abu Habbah, Ancient Sippir. Baghdad University Excavations* (Edubba 7). London: NABU Publications.

Battini, L. and Calvet, Y. (2003) Construction royale, construction privée: la maison B 59 de Larsa. *Iraq* 65, 131–141.

Bardet, G., Joannès, F., Lafont, B., Soubeyran, D. and Villard, P. (1984) *Archives administratives de Mari I* (Archives Royales de Mari 23). Paris: Éditions Recherche sur les Civilisations.

Beckman, G. (1995) *Old Babylonian Archival Texts in the Nies Babylonian Collection. Catalogue of the Babylonian Collections at Yale 2*. Bethesda, MD: CDL Press.

Beckman, G. (2000) *Old Babylonian Archival Texts in the Yale Babylonian Collection. Catalogue of the Babylonian Collections at Yale 4*. Bethesda, MD: CDL Press.

---

[128] The reader will find supplementary information in:

Charpin, D. (2010 [2011]) Les nouvelles technologies au service de l'historien de la Mésopotamie: le projet "ARCHIBAB." *Comptes rendus de l'Académie des Inscriptions et Belles Lettres* 2010 [2011], 1381–1394.

Charpin, D. (in press) The Assyriologist and the Computer: the "Archibab" Project. *Hebrew Bible and Ancient Israel* 4 (due 2014).

Jacquet, A. (2013) Family Archives in Mesopotamia during the Old Babylonian Period. In M. Faraguna (ed.), *Legal Documents in Ancient Societies IV. Archives and Archival Documents in Ancient Societies. Trieste 30 September-1 October 2011*, 63–85. Trieste: Edizioni Università di Trieste.

Birot, M. (1953a) Trois textes économiques de Mari (I). *Revue d'Assyriologie* 47, 121–130.

Birot, M. (1953b) Trois textes économiques de Mari (I). *Revue d'Assyriologie* 47, 161–174.

Birot, M. (1955) Trois textes économiques de Mari (II). *Revue d'Assyriologie* 49, 15–31.

Birot, M. (1956) Textes économiques de Mari (IV). *Revue d'Assyriologie* 50, 57–72.

Birot, M. (1960) *Textes administratifs de la salle 5 du palais* (Archives Royales de Mari 9). Paris: P. Geuthner.

Birot, M. (1964) *Textes administratifs de la salle 5 du palais (2° partie)* (Archives Royales de Mari 12). Paris: P. Geuthner.

Birot, M. (1969) *Tablettes économiques et administratives d'époque babylonienne ancienne conservées au Musée d'art et d'histoire de Genève*. Paris: P. Geuthner.

Birot, M. (1972) Simaḫlânê, roi de Kurda. *Revue d'Assyriologie* 66, 131–139.

Birot, M. (1978) Données nouvelles sur la chronologie du règne de Zimri-Lim. *Syria* 55, 333–343.

Bottéro, J. (1957) *Textes économiques et administratifs* (Archives Royales de Mari 7). Paris: P. Geuthner.

Brosius, M. (ed.) (2003) *Ancient Archives and Archival Traditions. Concepts of Record Keeping in the Ancient World*. Oxford: Oxford University Press.

Burke, M. L. (1963) *Textes administratifs de la salle 111 du palais* (Archives Royales de Mari 11). Paris: P. Geuthner.

Chambon, G. (2008) Un nouveau récapitulatif sur la gestion de l'huile à Mari. In D. Bonatz, R. M. Czichon and F. J. Kreppner (eds) *Fundstellen. Gesammelte Schriften zur Archäologie und Geschichte Altvorderasiens ad honorem Hartmut Kühne*, 283–297. Wiesbaden: Harrassowitz.

Charpin, D. (1979) Review of YOS 14. *Bibliotheca Orientalis* 36, 188–200.

Charpin, D. (1981) Review of YOS 12. *Bibliotheca Orientalis* 38, 517–547.

Charpin, D. (1982) Marchands du palais et marchands du temple à la fin de la I° dynastie de Babylone. *Journal Asiatique* 270, 25–65 [accessible at www.digitorient.com/?p=98].

Charpin, D. (1984) Nouveaux documents du bureau de l'huile à l'époque assyrienne. *MARI* 3, 83–126.

Charpin, D. (1986) Transmission des titres de propriété et constitution des archives privées en Babylonie ancienne. In Veenhof (ed.), 121–140.

Charpin, D. (1987) Nouveaux documents du bureau de l'huile (suite). *MARI* 5, 597–599.

Charpin, D. (1989) Un quartier de Nippur et le problème des écoles à l'époque paléo-babylonienne. *Revue d'Assyriologie* 83, 97–112.

Charpin, D. (1990) Un quartier de Nippur et le problème des écoles à l'époque paléo-babylonienne (suite). *Revue d'Assyriologie* 84, 1–16.

Charpin, D. (1993) Review of AUCT 4. *Revue d'Assyriologie* 87, 185–187.

Charpin, D. (1994) Une campagne de Yahdun-Lîm en Haute-Mésopotamie. In D. Charpin and J.-M. Durand (eds) *Florilegium Marianum II: recueil d'études à la mémoire de Maurice Birot*, 177–200 (Mémoires de N.A.B.U. 3). Paris: SEPOA.

Charpin, D. (1995) La fin des archives dans le palais de Mari. *Revue d'Assyriologie* 89, 29–40.

Charpin, D. (2000a) Les prêteurs et le palais: les édits de *mîšarum* des rois de Babylone et leurs traces dans les archives privées. In A. C. V. M. Bongenaar (ed.) *Interdependency of Institutions and Private Entrepreneurs. MOS Studies 2. Proceedings of the Second MOS Symposium (Leiden 1998)*, 185–211 (PIHANS 87). Leiden: Nederlands Historisch-Archaeologisch Instituut te Istanbul.

Charpin, D. (2000b) Lettres et procès paléo-babyloniens. In F. Joannès (ed.) *Rendre la justice en Mésopotamie*, 69–111. Paris [accessible at www.digitorient.com/?attachment_id=114]

Charpin, D. (2001a) Les prêteurs et le palais (suite). *Nouvelles Assyriologiques Brèves et Utilitaires* 2001/51.

Charpin, D. (2001b) L'archivage des tablettes dans le palais de Mari: nouvelles données. In W. H. van Soldt, J. G. Dercksen, N. J. C. Kouwenberg and Th. J. H. Krispijn (eds) *Veenhof Anniversary Volume. Studies Presented to Klaas R. Veenhof on the Occasion of his Sixty-Fifth Birthday*, 13–30 (PIHANS 89). Leiden: Nederlands Historisch-Archaeologisch Instituut te Istanbul.

Charpin, D. (2003) La politique immobilière des marchands de Larsa à la lumière des découvertes épigraphiques de 1987 et 1989. In J.-L. Huot (ed.) *Larsa, travaux de 1987 et 1989*, 311–322 (Bibliothèque archéologique et historique 165). Beirut: Institut français d'archéologie du Proche-Orient (available at www.digitorient.com/?attachment_id=91).

Charpin, D. (2005a) Données nouvelles sur la vie économique et sociale de l'époque paléo-babylonienne. *Orientalia* 74, 409–421.

Charpin, D. (2005b) Économie et société à Sippar et en Babylonie du nord à l'époque paléo-babylonienne. *Revue d'Assyriologie* 99, 133–176.

Charpin, D. (2005c) Review of VS 29. *Revue d'Assyriologie* 99, 133–152.

Charpin, D. (2006) Les inscriptions royales suméro-akkadiennes d'époque paléo-babyloniennes. *Revue d'Assyriologie* 100, 131–160.

Charpin, D. (2007) Chroniques bibliographiques 10. Économie, société et institutions paléo-babyloniennes: nouvelles sources, nouvelles approches. *Revue d'Assyriologie* 101, 147–182.

Charpin, D. (2008a) *Lire et écrire à Babylone*. Paris: Presses universitaires de France.

Charpin, D. (2008b) Archivage et classification: un récapitulatif de créances à Mari sous Zimrî-Lîm. In R. D. Biggs, J. Myers and M. T. Roth (eds) *Proceedings of the 51st Rencontre Assyriologique Internationale held at the Oriental Institute of the University of Chicago July 18-22, 2005*, 1–13 (SAOC 62). Chicago: Oriental Institute.

Charpin, D. (2008c) "Tell Hariri - Mari (Textes) ... II. Les archives". In L. Pirot *et al.* (eds) *Dictionnaire de la Bible*, Supplément vol. 14, fasc. 77–78 (Taršiš–Tell Hariri), col. 233–248. Paris: Letouzey & Ané.

Charpin, D. (2010a) *Writing, Law and Kingship: Essays on Old Babylonian Mesopotamia*. Chicago: University of Chicago Press.

Charpin, D. (2010b) *Reading and Writing in Babylon*. Cambridge, MA: Harvard University Press.

Charpin, D. (2010c) Formulaires des contrats de Mari à l'époque amorrite: entre tradition babylonienne et innovation. In S. Démare-Lafont and A. Lemaire (eds) *Trois millénaires de formulaires juridiques*, 13–42 (Hautes Études Orientales 48). Geneva: Droz.

Charpin, D. (2012) L'exercice du pouvoir par les rois de la Ière dynastie de Babylone: problèmes de méthode. In G. Wilhelm (ed.) *Organization, Representation, and Symbols of Power in the Ancient Near East. Proceedings of the 54ᵗʰ Rencontre Assyriologique at Würzburg, 20-25 July 2008*, 21–32. Winona Lake, IN: Eisenbrauns.

Charpin, D. and Durand, J.-M. (1986) apud J. Margueron, Quelques remarques concernant les archives retrouvées dans le palais de Mari. In Veenhof (ed.), 141–152.

Charpin, D. and Durand, J.-M. (2004) Yasîm-Sûmû et les noms d'années de Zimrî-Lîm. *Nouvelles Assyriologiques Brèves et Utilitaires* 2004/76.

Charpin, D., Edzard, D. O. and Stol, M. (2004) *Mesopotamien: Die altbabylonische Zeit* (Orbis Biblicus et Orientalis 160/4). Fribourg/Göttingen: Academic Press/Vandenhoeck & Ruprecht.

Charpin, D. and Ziegler, N. (2003) *Florilegium Marianum V. Mari et le Proche-Orient à l'époque amorrite: essai d'histoire politique*. Paris: SEPOA.

Dalley, S., Robson, E. and Breckwoldt, T. (2005) *Old Babylonian Texts in the Ashmolean Museum, mainly from Larsa, Sippir, Kish, and Lagaba* (Oxford Editions of Cuneiform Texts 15). Oxford: Oxford University Press.

Dombradi, E. (1996) *Die Darstellung des Rechtsaustrags in den altbabylonischen Prozessurkunden* (Freiburger Altorientalische Studien 20/1). Stuttgart: Franz Steiner Verlag.

van Driel, G. (1994) Private or Not-so-private: Nippur Ur III Files. In H. Gasche, M. Tanret, C. Janssen and A. Degraeve (eds) *Cinquante-deux réflexions sur le Proche-Orient ancien offertes en hommage à Léon De Meyer*, 181–195 (Mesopotamian History and Environment, Occasional Publications 2). Leuven: Peeters.

Duponchel, D. (1997) Les comptes d'huile du palais de Mari datés de l'année de Kahat. In D. Charpin and J.-M. Durand (eds) *Florilegium Marianum III: Recueil d'études à la mémoire de Marie-Thérèse Barrelet*, 201–262. Paris: SEPOA.

Durand, J.-M. (1981) *Documents cunéiformes de la IVe Section de l'Ecole pratique des Hautes études. Tome I: Catalogue et copies cunéiforme* (Hautes Études Orientales 14). Paris: Droz.

Durand, J.-M. (1983) *Textes administratifs des salles 134 et 160 du palais de Mari* (Archives Royales de Mari 21). Paris: P. Geuthner.

Durand, J.-M. (1987) L'organisation de l'espace dans le palais de Mari. In E. Lévy (ed.) *Le système palatial en Orient, en Grèce et à Rome. Actes du Colloque de Strasbourg, 19-22 juin 1985*, 39–110 (Travaux du Centre de recherche sur le Proche-Orient et la Grèce antiques 9). Strasbourg: Brill.

Durand, J.-M. (1997) *Les Documents épistolaires du palais de Mari, Vol. I* (Littératures anciennes du Proche-Orient 16). Paris: les Éditions du Cerf.

Durand, J.-M. (2000) *Les Documents épistolaires du palais de Mari, Vol. III* (Littératures anciennes du Proche-Orient 18). Paris: les Éditions du Cerf.

Faivre, X. (1995) Le recyclage des tablettes cunéiformes. *Revue d'Assyriologie* 89, 57–66.

Figulla, H. H. (1961) *Catalogue of the Babylonian tablets in the British Museum, Volume I*. London: British Museum.

Frayne, D. R. (1990) *Old Babylonian Period (2003-1595 BC)* (Royal Inscriptions of Mesopotamia, Early Periods 4). Toronto: University of Toronto Press.

Goddeeris, A. (2002) An adoption document from the Kisurra collection in the British Museum. In C. Wunsch (ed.) *Mining the Archives. Festschrift for Christopher Walker on the Occasion of His 60th Birthday*, 93–98 (Babylonische Archive 1). Dresden: ISLET.

Guichard, M. (2005) *La Vaisselle de luxe des rois de Mari* (Archives Royales de Mari 31). Paris: Éditions Recherche sur les Civilisations.

Joannès, F. (ed.) (1995) Les phénomènes de fin d'archives en Mésopotamie. *Revue d'Assyriologie* 89, 1–147.

Jursa, M. (2005) *Neo-Babylonian Legal and Administrative Documents. Typology, Contents and Archives* (Guides to the Mesopotamian Textual Record 1). Münster: Ugarit-Verlag.

Kessler, K. (1997/98) Das spätaltbabylonische Tempelarchiv vom Tell Egraineh. *Archiv für Orientforschung* 44/45, 131–133.

van Koppen, F. (2003/4) Review of VS 29. *Archiv für Orientforschung* 50, 379–392.

Lacambre, D. (1997) La gestion du bronze dans le palais de Mari: collations et joints à ARMT XXII. In D. Charpin and J.-M. Durand (eds) *Florilegium Marianum III: Recueil d'études à la mémoire de Marie-Thérèse Barrelet*, 91–123. Paris: SEPOA.

Lafont, B. (1984) Chapter 3 (texts nos. 246–427). In Bardet *et al.*, 227–326.

Lafont, B. (1985) Le ṣâbum du roi de Mari au temps de Yasmah-Addu. In J.-M. Durand and J. R. Kupper (eds) *Miscellanea Babylonica. Mélanges Offerts à Maurice Birot*, 161–179. Paris: Éditions Recherche sur les Civilisations.

Marti, L. (2008) *Florilegium Marianum X. Nomades et sédentaires à Mari: la perception de la taxe-sugâgûtum*. Paris: SEPOA.

Maul, S. M. (1997) Zwischen Sparmaßnahme und Revolte... Die Aktivitäten des Iasīm-Sūmû, des šandabakkum von Mari. *MARI* 8, 755–774.

Michel, C. (1996) Le commerce dans les textes de Mari. In J.-M. Durand (ed.), *Amurru 1. Mari, Ébla et les Hourrites: dix ans de travaux*, 385–426. Paris: Éditions recherche sur les civilisations.

Millet Albà, A. (2001) *La population du royaume de Mari à l'époque du roi Zimrî-Lîm d'après les archives du palais de Mari*. EPHE. Unpublished PhD thesis, Paris.

Oppenheim, A. L. (1967) *Letters from Mesopotamia*. Chicago/London: University of Chicago Press.

Parpola, S. (1986) The royal archives of Nineveh. In Veenhof (ed.), 223–236.

Parpola, S. and Porter, M. (2001) *The Helsinki Atlas of the Near East in the Neo-Assyrian Period*. Chebeague Island, ME/Helsinki: Casco Bay Assyriological Institute/The Neo-Assyrian Text Corpus Project.

Pedersén, O. (1998) Zu den altbabylonischen Archiven aus Babylon. *Altorientalische Forschungen* 25, 328–338.

Pedersén, O. (2005) *Archive und Bibliotheken in Babylon. Die Tontafeln der Grabung Robert Koldeweys 1899–1917* (Abhandlungen der Deutschen Orient-Gesellschaft 25). Saarwellingen: SDV.

Renger, J. (1977) Cooperation internationale – Berlin. *Akkadica* 5, 26–28.

Richardson, S. (2002) Ewe Should Be So Lucky. In: C. Wunsch (ed.) *Mining the Archives. Festschrift for Christopher Walker on the Occasion of His 60th Birthday*, 229–244 (Babylonische Archive 1). Dresden: ISLET.

Roth, M. (1995) *Law Collections from Mesopotamia and Asia Minor* (SBL Writings from the Ancient World Series 6). Atlanta, GA: Scholars Press.

Sasson, J. M. (1982) Accounting discrepancies in the Mari NÌ.GUB [NÍG.DU] texts. In G. van Driel *et al.* (eds) *Zikir šumim. Assyriological Studies Presented to F.R. Kraus*, 326–341. Leiden: Brill.

Schorr, M. (1913) *Urkunden des Altbabylonischen Zivil- und Prozessrechts* (Vorderasiatische Bibliothek 5). Leipzig: Hinrichs.

Seri, A. (2005) *Local Power in Old Babylonian Mesopotamia*. London: Equinox.

Sigrist, M. (1990) *Old Babylonian Account Texts in the Horn Archaeological Museum* (Andrews University Cuneiform Texts 4). Berrien Springs, MI: Andrews University Press.

Sigrist, M. (2003) *Old Babylonian Account Texts in the Horn Archaeological Museum* (Andrews University Cuneiform Texts 5). Berrien Springs, MI: Andrews University Press.

Sigrist, M., Figulla, H. H. and Walker, C. B. F. (1996) *Catalogue of the Babylonian tablets in the British Museum. Volume II*. London: British Museum Press.

Sigrist, M., Zadok, R. and Walker, C. B. F. (2006) *Catalogue of the Babylonian Tablets in the British Museum. Volume III*. London: British Museum Press.

Skaist, A. (1994) *The Old Babylonian Loan Contract. Its History and Geography. Bar-Ilan Studies in Near Eastern Languages and Culture*. Ramat Gan: Bar-Ilan University Press.

Stol, M. (1973) Review of YOS 13. *Journal of Cuneiform Studies* 25, 215–233.

Stone, E. (1987) *Nippur Neighborhoods* (Studies in Ancient Oriental Civilization 44). Chicago: Oriental Institute of the University of Chicago.

Stone, E. (2002) The Ur III–Old Babylonian Transition: an Archaeological Perspective. *Iraq* 64, 79–84.

Suurmeijer, G. (2006/7) Loans and Edicts. A Quantitative Analysis of the Temporal Distribution of Loan Documents and Royal Edicts under the Reign of Samsu-iluna. *Jaarbericht Ex Oriente Lux* 40, 104–119.

Tanret, M. (2004) The Works and the Days ... On Scribal Activity in Old Babylonian Sippar-Amnānum. *Revue d'Assyriologie* 98, 33–62.

Tanret, M. (2008) Find the Tablet-box... New Aspects of Archive-Keeping in Old Babylonian Sippar-Amnānum. In R. van der Spek (ed.) *Studies in Ancient Near Eastern World View and Society Presented to Marten Stol*, 131–147. Bethesda, MD: CDL Press.

Tanret, M., Janssen, C. and Dekiere, L. (forthcoming) *Chains of Transmission: a search through Ur-Utu's property titles* (Mesopotamian History and Environment, Memoirs 2). Ghent: University of Ghent.

Tunca, Ö. and Baghdo, A. (eds) (2008) *Chagar Bazar (Syrie) III. Les trouvailles épigraphiques et sigillographiques du chantier I (2000-2002)* (A.P.H.A.O., Publications de la Mission archéologique de l'Université de Liège en Syrie). Louvain: Peeters.

Van de Mieroop, M. (2002) Credit as a Facilitator of Exchange in Old Babylonian Mesopotamia. In M. Hudson and M. Van de Mieroop (eds) *Debt and Economic Renewal in the Ancient Near East*, 163–173 (International Scholars Conference on Ancient Near Eastern Economies 3). Bethesda, MD: CDL Press.

Van Lerberghe, K. (2003) Private and Public: The Ur-Utu Archive at Sippar-Amnānum (Tell ed-Dēr). In M. Brosius (ed.), 59–77.

Van Lerberghe, K. and Voet, G. (1991) On 'Quasi-Hüllentafeln'. *Northern Akkad Project Reports* 6, 3–8.

Veenhof, K. R. (ed.) (1986) *Cuneiform Archives and Libraries. Papers read at the 30e Rencontre Assyriologique Internationale, Leiden, 4-8 July 1983* (PIHANS 57). Leiden: Nederlands Historisch-Archaeologisch Instituut te Istanbul.

Villard, P. (1986) Un roi de Mari à Ugarit. *Ugarit-Forschungen* 18, 387–412.

Villard, P. (1992) Le déplacement des trésors royaux d'après les archives royales de Mari. In D. Charpin and F. Joannès (eds) *La circulation des biens, des personnes et des idées dans le Proche-Orient ancien*, 195–205 (CRRAI 38). Paris: Éditions Recherche sur les Civilisations.

Wilcke, C. (1970) Review of Oppenheim 1967. *Zeitschrift für Assyriologie* 60, 165–167.

Ziegler, N. (1999) *Florilegium Marianum IV. Le Harem de Zimrî-Lîm. La population féminine des palais d'après les archives royales de Mari*. Paris: SEPOA.

Ziegler, N. (2001) Gestion et contrôle d'après les archives du palais de Mari (XVIIIᵉ siècle av. J.-C.). *Ktèma* 26, 63–72.

4

The Old Assyrian Trade and its Participants

Jan Gerrit Dercksen

The well-documented trade in Anatolia by merchants from the city-state of Assur represents an important episode in the economic history of Mesopotamia. The colony at ancient Kanesh (north-east of Kayseri) existed for over two hundred years (Level II: c. < 1935–1835, Level Ib: c. 1800–1720 BC). That more than 20,000 texts written by or on behalf of these merchants have been excavated should not obscure the fact that most of this evidence comes from a period of some 50 years during the 19th century BC, shortly before the destruction of Level II. Moreover, the great majority of texts have been found at Kültepe/Kanesh in Central Anatolia. The bias of the sources is, therefore, towards the trade in Anatolia, with reference to the situation in Assur or other places only as far as it concerns this trade.

This article deals with the merchants and their trading practices. A discussion of the prices and markets of the main objects of trade is followed by an analysis of the strategies regarding buying and selling and collecting outstanding debts. It ends with a study of the evidence for the costs of living and labour costs.

1. THE CULTURAL SETTING

A characterization of Old Assyrian merchants as profit-driven private entrepreneurs is correct, but ignores the all-permeating influence of religious, legal, and other institutions into which the trade and the traders (as in other periods and places) were embedded. The political and legal institutions have been the object of recent studies and need not be discussed here in detail.[1] Suffice it to recall that the policy of the city-state was directed at actively sponsoring the trade as its main political and

---

[1] Larsen 1976; Veenhof 2003b; Dercksen 2004; Veenhof 2008a.

economic goal, and thereby reducing the transaction costs, while also levying taxes on that trade. It did so in various ways: by concluding treaties with rulers in whose territories at least 37 Assyrian types of commercial organization (*kārum* 'colony' and *wabartum* 'trading post') were established; by empowering these settlements; by giving the eponym of Assur (*līmum*) and his office, the City Hall, a role in crucial aspects of trade; by expanding the legal framework to act upon trade-specific situations; and by creating a system of long-term joint-stock investments called *naruqqum*.

Old Assyrian (OA) society centred around the concepts of honour and dignity, a shame society. Violation of the accepted norms would bring shame on the transgressor and could ultimately lead to his isolation from society. In this respect, OA society does not differ from the rest of Mesopotamian civilization.[2] The socially acceptable Assyrian merchant was an *awīlum* 'gentleman', the opposite of which was a *lā awīlum*. Apart from being reliable and trustworthy, the main quality of a 'gentleman' was the ability and willingness to grant favours (*gamālum*) and help people in need. This was not unique to OA society.[3]

A typical example of a favour is contained in the letter TTC 18: "This is what Išme-Aššur said, speak to Imdilum: Before you left you asked from me a textile. In front of Šu-Hubur you said: 'Give me a *kutānum* and as soon as I arrive (in Kanesh) I will send you the equivalent out of my own money, and I will do you a favour.' You have not sent me the equivalent out of your own money. If you are my brother, do me a favour! I am a man of favour(s), I will do you a favour (in return). Send me my *tadmiqtum* with the very first envoy! I bought a house. (It will be) as if you made me a present."[4] Išme-Aššur had given a textile to Imdilum in Assur for which the latter would send an appropriate amount of money in payment. This type of sale was called a *tadmiqtum*. Despite Imdilum having made his promise before a respected merchant, he had not yet sent the money. However, the sender of the reminder letter remains keen on maintaining a good relationship with Imdilum, and he stresses his ability to grant a favour. His motivation appears from line 24. Although it will be his own money, he assures Imdilum that he will be as glad as if he had given it to him as a present. In general, the (future) beneficiaries take great care to stress their gratitude.[5] The favours to be done in Assur primarily consisted of buying merchandise before money sent from Kanesh had arrived, which amounts to granting an interest-free loan. According

---

[2]   Van der Toorn 2004, 499.

[3]   See Nakata 1971.

[4]   (1) *um-ma iš-ma-a-šur-ma* (2) *a-na im-dí-lim* (3) *qí-bi-ma i-na pá-ni* (4) *wa-ṣa-i-kà : a-ta-ma* (5) túg *té-ri-ša-ni* igi *šu-hu-bur* (5) [*um-m*]*a a-ta-ma* (7) [*ku*]-*ta-nam : dí-na-ma* (8) [*i-n*]*a e-ra-bi-a-ma* (9) [*me*]-*eh-ra-tim* (10) [*i*]-*na ra-mì-ni-a* (11) [*ú*]-*šé-ba-lá-ku-ma* (12) *a-ga-mì-il₅-kà* (13) *me-eh-ra-tim* (14) *i-na ra-mì-ni-kà* (15) *ú-lá tù-uš-té-bi-lam* (16) *šu-ma a-hi a-ta* (17) *gi-im-lá-ni* (18) *a-wi-il₅ gi-mì-lim* (19) *a-na-ku : a-ga-mì-il₅-kà* (20) *ta-ad-mì-iq-tí* (21) *i-na pá-ni-im-ma* (22) *a-li-ki-im* (23) *šé-bi-lam* (24) *bé-ta-am áš-am* (25) *ki-ma ša ta-qí-iš-šu-ni.*

[5]   AKT 3, 85:21–23: "I shall be happy as if you gave me 1 talent of silver; and I am a man of favour(s), I will do you a favour". Or in the words of Pūšu-kēn according to I 577: "In your presence it is (merely) an offering, but for me it is a great favour. And I am able to listen to your word."

to VS 26, 74 (cf. TC 3, 43), an anonymous merchant ordered his representatives in Assur to buy tin before the silver had arrived as a favour. But if that was impossible, they should borrow money against interest to make the purchases, but only for one month at the most. In Anatolia a favour could consist of selling goods for another person, as in TTC 18. Both in Anatolia and in Assur, granting a favour could also amount to being lenient to a debtor by rescheduling his debt or ignoring some of the interest due. What began as an opportunity to grant a favour, such as selling a few textiles as a *tadmiqtum* for a relative or friend, often became a burden and could even end in a lawsuit.

The OA epistolary style reflects the great value attached to respectful behaviour. The opening sentences of OA letters differ from Old Babylonian (OB) ones in that the first name to be mentioned is not necessarily that of the addressee but of the person of higher status, whether addressee or sender. Letters frequently contain expressions of politeness and respect by stressing actual or imagined family ties, such as *abī attā bēlī attā* "you are my father, you are my lord" (with many variations). Common violations of the code of conduct consisted of talking disparagingly of another person or acting in a way that would harm him. A merchant could also be shamed for making a loss, whether as a result of his own misjudgement or of circumstances beyond his control.

Although OA letters lack the pious wishes imploring divine protection that are a common element in the addresses of OB letters, religion played a major role in the lives of the merchants and their families. Expenditure is recorded on various occasions for sheep for offerings and for gifts (*niqi'um* 'offering') sent to others on the occasion of a trip to Assur, the birth of a child, a wedding or a religious festival. The idea of reaching a destination due to divine protection is expressed for instance in a letter sent by Aššur-idī to his son Aššur-nādā.[6] A recurring topic among family members is the danger of divine anger, which can be expressed by ominous signs like illnesses and often results from unkept promises and ignored warnings. For example, Šalim-ahum (in Assur) urges Pūšu-kēn to send him gold because the demons are haunting him.[7]

Sharing one's meal with others was a sign of hospitality and friendship and this extends to the custom of feeding workers. Parties were held with other Assyrians and occasionally with Anatolian magnates or colleagues. Inevitably alcohol abuse occurred

---

[6] TC 1, 18: (8) *i-na u₄-mì-im ša a-kà-ri-im* (9) ᵈ*a-šùr ú-ša-lu-mu-kà-ma* (10) *té-ru-bu*, "The day divine Aššur lets you safely enter the colony". See also Kt n/k 1192: (27) ... *i-na ma-tí : a-šùr* (28) *ù i-lí a-bi-a : ú-ša-lu-mu-kà-ma* (29) *i-nu-mì : ník-ka-sí : ta-du-nu* ... (34) ... *a-dí a-šùr ú-ša-lu-mu-kà-ma* (35) *ník-ka-sí : ta-du-nu*, "When Aššur and the god of my father protect you (on your way to Assur), when you present the accounts (the silver will be deducted). ... Until Aššur protects you (on your way to Assur) and you present the accounts".

[7] TC 2, 2 (Šalim-ahum to Pūšu-kēn): (29) ... 1/3 *ma-na* kù.gi (30) *ú* 1 *ma-na* kù.gi *pá-ša-lam i-pá-nim-ma* (31) *šé-bi₄-lam ú-tù-ku ú-ša-ah-du-ru-ni*, "Send me one-third mina of gold and 1 mina of *pašallum* gold as soon as possible. The demons are frightening me."

and formed a matter of grave concern,[8] and warnings "not to give oneself to drinking (lit. to the cup)" (*ana kāsim ramakka lā taddan*, WAG 48–1462:22–23), were necessary. Too much drink could result in a romantic advance, such as giving a fine textile to a girl for which the boy had to collect the money later.[9] It might, however, also lead to situations where all precautions were forgotten.[10] According to a difficult letter, a drunken Anatolian caused Aššur-malik to worry:

> "Here, Luhrahšu, being drunk, said to the general: 'You will see what I can do to a merchant who travels (or: what the merchant has done during the journey).' When the general told me these words, I said: 'If he really said it, I shall send to the Elders (in Assur) and they will spread word as far as is necessary.' But the general replied: 'My son, do not write at all.' He then brought forth the cup of Aššur and Šamaš to oblige me, and he drank to me up to ten times."[11]

Dishonour was brought upon another person by putting him to shame (*ba"ušum*) in the circle of merchants in Assur or in the colony. A person's reputation was also damaged through gossip and slander,[12] when a merchant did not use his services,[13] or

---

[8] Kt c/k 284 (unp. Ankara; to Alahum from Aššur-imittī): (28) *mì-[š]u : ša li-ba-kà* (29) *lam-na-ni* [k]b-*áp-kà-ma* (30) *la kb-pí : a-šùr li-ṭù-ul* (31) *u₄-mì a-na ší-ik-ri-im* (32) ʾù'-*lá a-li-ku*, "Why are you angry with me? Is your silver not my silver? By Aššur! I certainly did not go for a drink on that day". This text and other unpublished texts from the house of Alahum (Kt c/k) will be published by the author shortly. I thank the excavator of Kültepe, Prof. F. Kulakoğlu, for entrusting these documents to me for publication.

[9] TC 3, 61 (Inib-Ištar to Ṣilli-Adad): (3) 1/3 *ma-na kb ší-im ku-ší-tim* (4) *ša i-ší-ik-ri-kà a-na* dumu. mí (5) *i-ku-pí-a ta-dí-nu-ma tam-ší-ú* (6) *ša-áš-qí-il₅*, "Collect the 20 shekels of silver, the price of the *kušitum*, which you gave to the daughter of Ikuppiya in your beer and forgot about."

[10] CCT 4, 7b (to Puzur-Aššur from Il-wēdāku): (3) *ta-áš-pu-ra-am* (4) *um-ma a-ta-ma* (5) dumu *i-li-a i-na é* (6) *ší-ik-ri-im ma-lá* (7) *li-bi-šu-ma e-ta-wu-ú* (8) *a-šùr ù il₅-kà* (9) *li-ṭù-lá* ... (18) kb *lá-qá-am* (19) *lá i-mu-a x x* (20) *ku-wa-am šu-um-kà* (21) *i-za-kà-ar-ma* (22) *a-na-ku áš-ta-pu* (23) *áb-na-am a-na* (24) *pì-šu ma-ha-ṣa-am* (25) *lá a-le-i*, "You wrote to me: 'The son of Iliya vented his feelings in the bar.' By Aššur and your own god! ... He refused to take the silver. He was mentioning your name and I remained silent. I could not bring myself to hit his mouth with a stone."

[11] Kt m/k 14 (to Šumi-abīya and Nazi from Aššur-malik): (3) *a-na-kam lu-ùh-ra-ah-šu* (4) *i-na ší-ik-ri-šu a-na* (5) gal *sí-kà-tim iq-bi* (6) *um-ma šu-ut-ma* dam.gàr *ša* (7) *i-na ha-ra-nim e-pu-šu-ni* (8) *ta-ma-ar ki-ma* gal *sí-kà-tim* (9) *a-wa-tim a-ni-a-tim* (10) *iq-bi-a-ni um-ma a-na-ku-ma* (11) *šu-ma ke-na-ma iq-bi* (12) *a-ṣé-er ší-bu-tim* (13) *lá-áš-pu-ur-ma a-wa-tám* (14) *a-dí ša-ak-šu-dim* (15) *lu-ša-ak-ší-du um-ma* (16) gal *sí-kà-tim-ma* (17) *me-er-e : a-ta mì-ma* (18) *lá ta-ša-pá-ar ù* (19) *kà-sà-am ša* ᵈ*a-šùr* (20) ᵈutu *aⁱ-ga-ma-li-a* (21) *ú-šar a-dí : eš₁₅-ri-šu* (22) *iš-tí-a-am*. Translation: Hecker 2006, 89f.

[12] Larsen 1971.

[13] CCT 4, 3b (to Aššur-nādā and Ilī-ālum from Kuzazum): (22) ... *šu-ut i-ṣé-ri-a* (23) *a-wi-il₅-ma ma šu-wa-tí* (24) *ta-qí-ip-ma i-a-tí* (25) *ú-lá ta-aq-tí-pá-ni* (26) *mì-šu-um pu-ru-i* (27) *i-kà-ri-im* sig₅ (28) *ta-áš-ku-un*, "Is he better than I am, that you entrusted him (with goods), but did not entrust it to me? Why did you abuse me so in a good colony?"

when others witnessed his misfortune; in that context the expression "my day (of misfortune)" is used.[14]

Using the boss's money for one's own business amounted to fraudulent behaviour.[15]

A good insight into the world of OA merchants is provided by Kt n/k 1192, which contains a dramatic account of the bankruptcy that befell the business of Lā-qēp's father and had its impact on Lā-qēp himself. Part of the letter reads in translation:

> "Speak to Aššur-taklāku: What more should I write to you? You are my brother, my lord! I gave you a *naruqqu*-(investment) 30 years ago and you are doing business (with it). Since then neither your report nor a letter from you (ever reached me). I added a five-year term to you and I gave a certified tablet to your representatives, saying: Let his consignments to my father's house be regular so that my father's house be honoured and I myself be honoured in the city gate; and let him be honoured in the colony; let him build a house and raise a child. Let him pull the investment of the city.
>
> You are my brother, my lord! Save me on the day that I need it! Save my own father's house and the spirits of my father's house. My father's house went down because of the votive offerings of <Aššur>. Two-thirds of a mina of gold from your *naruqqum* are earmarked for our father's votive offerings of Aššur. Now then, send me 15 minas of silver, the fixed sum of 3 minas of gold at a rate of 5 shekels each.

---

[14] Examples of this usage can be found in CCT 2, 33, where Šu-Kūbum writes: (2) ... *la li-bi₄* (3) *i-li-ma a-bu-ni* (4) *me-et a-wa-sú la iq-bi₄* (5) *šu-ma dam-qá-ku-um tí-ib-a-ma* (6) *a-tal-kam é a-bi₄-ni šé-šé-er* (7) *ma-nu-um ša mì-num* (8) *i-qá-bi₄-a-ku-ni a-wi-lu iš-té-en₆* (9) *ù ší-na la-am-nu-tum a-na* (10) *é a-bi₄-ni da-la-hi-im* (11) *i-za-zu a-me-er ú-um é-et a-bi₄-ni* (12) *la i-ma-i-du*, "Against the will of god our father died. He did not make his will. If it is fine with you, prepare to leave and put the house of our father in order. Who would say anything to you? One or two evil men are ready to interfere with the house of our father. Those who see the day of our father's house must not become many." KTH 7 (to Aššur-mūtappil from his sister Ahaha): (28) *ta-ki-li : ša ma-ma-an* (29) *lá ta-ša-me a-na* (30) *ú-um <<tí>> ga-ma-lim* (31) *ú ú-um e-tá-ri-im* (32) *i-hi-id-ma kb 10 ma-na* (33) *ša-am-qí-tám-ma : ma-ma-an ú-mì* (34) *lá e-mar-šu*, "Do not listen to anybody's slander. For the day of granting a favour and saving! Take care to send me 10 minas of silver; no one must see my day!" KTK 18 (Aššur-taklāku to Tarīša and Ammārum): (5) *a-me-er u₄-mì-ni i-ma-i-du*, "Those who see our day are getting numerous."

[15] KTS 1, 15: (13) ... *ma-tí ki-ma ša a-da-gu₅-lu-ma* (14) *i-kb-áp a-ba-e-ˀšuˀ-nu* (15) 10 *ma-na.ta kb i-na-šu-ru-ni-ma* (16) *a-ší-a-ma-tim i-pá-ni a-ba-e-šu-nu* (17) *ú-šé-bu-lu-ni-ma ú a-ba-ú-šu-nu* (18) *i-ša-me-ú-ni-ma li-ba-áš-nu* (19) *i-lá-mì-nu ma-tí a-mì-a-tim* (20) *a-na-ku e-pu-uš*, "Ever – as I observe that people withdraw 10 minas of silver each from the silver of their fathers and send it ahead of their fathers to make purchases, and when their fathers hear it they get angry – would I ever do such things?"

(...) At the time I gave you the *naruqqum* you did not have a slave, a slave girl, a *naruqqum*, or a house."[16]

2. THE MERCHANTS

There was a social distinction in Assur as well as in the Assyrian communities abroad between 'big' (*rabium*) and 'small' (*ṣahhurum*) free citizens (*awīlum*). It was defined along family lines, as a remark by the daughter and sons of the deceased Pūšu-kēn makes clear when they write in BIN 6, 59: "And since (Kulumāya) left he has shown contempt towards our father's spirit and [even] us he has thereby [treated] as 'small' persons".[17] Attaining a good position could be the responsibility of an adoptive father.[18] Families and individuals from both layers of society were actively involved in trade, with the merchants belonging to the 'big' people, the citizens holding slaves. Others besides professional merchants bought and sold to make some extra money. In the first place there were the female relatives of the traders, who manufactured textiles at home and sold these via their men in Anatolia. The king of Assur also entrusted merchandise to a trusted merchant, but it is not known how often the kings did this. According to KTS 1, 30, Asqūdum (perhaps the same individual as the 'palace servant' by that name mentioned in KTS 1, 55b) had received two donkeys loaded with 125 minas of tin, 30 *kutānus*, over 5 minas of extra-fine lapis lazuli and a lump of *amutum*-iron weighing 11 shekels to convey to Anatolia. Aduda, son of king Šarru-kēn, was active in Kanesh.[19] A senior official in the administration of the city-state, the *lapputāum*

---

[16] Kt n/k 1192 (Sever and Çeçen 2000, 175f.): (4) *a-na a-šùr-ták-lá-ku : qí-bi-ma* (5) *mì-nam : ma-da-tim lu-lá-pí-tá-a-kum* (6) *a-hi a-ta be-l[í a-ta iš]-tù* mu.30.šè (7) *na-ru-qám : a-dí-na-kum-ma : ta-ma-kàr* (8) *war-ki-tám-ma ù-lá té-er-ta-kà ú-lá* (9) *na-áš-pé-er-ta-kà : u₄-me-e* mu.5.šè (10) *ú-ra-dí-a-kum ù ṭup-pá-am ha-ar-ma-am* (11) *a-na ša ki-ma : ku-a-tí : a-dí-in um-ma* (12) *a-na-ku-ma : ma-áš-kà-na-tù-šu : a-na* (13) *é a-bi-a lu kà-a-na-ma : é a-bi-a* (14) *lu kà-bi-it : ù a-na-ku : i-na ká a-bu-lim* (15) *lu kà-áb-tá-ku : ù i-na kà-ri-im šu-ut* (16) *lu kà-bi₄-it : ù é-tám le-pu-uš* (17) *lu šé-ra-am lu-ra-bi : a-na-ah-tám* (18) *ša a-lim^ki li-iš-du-ud : a-hi a-ta* (19) *be-lí a-ta : a-na : u₄-um ˹e˺-ṭá-ri-im* (20) *eṭ-ra-ni : é a-bi-a i-a-˹am˺ ù e-ṭá-me* (21) *é a-bi-a : e-ṭé-er : a-šu-mì ik-ri-bi ša <a-šur>* (22) *é a-bi-a ha-lá-aq i-na-ru-qí-kà* (23) *2/3 ma-na kù.gi a-na* (24) *ša a-šùr : ša a-bi-ni : i-lá-ak* (25) *ù 3 ma-na kù.gi 5 gín.ta* (26) *ší-im-tám : 15 ma-na kb* (27) *šé-bi-lam-ma : ...* (38) *... i-nu-mì na-ru-qám* (39) *a-dí-na-ku-ni : lá! ir am-tám na-ru-qám* (40) *ú é-tám ú-lá tí-šu.*

[17] Translation Larsen 1976, 288. See also Kt c/k 175: (17) *a-na ṣa-hu-ru-tim* (18) *ša ke-na-tim iš-ta-ak-nu-ni-a-tí,* "(They gave us nothing.) They really treated us as 'small' persons."

[18] AKT 4, 69: (7) *... a-ba-am* (8) *ù um-ma-am* (9) *lá tí-de₈-ma a-na-ku* (10) *ú-ra-bi-kà* (11) *a-na-ku e-né-en* (12) *ú-ša-ar-ší-ú-kà* (13) *ù ma-za-za-am* (14) *sig₅ : ša i-ṣé-ri-kà* (15) *sig₅ uš-ta-zi-<iz>-ma,* "You did not know (your) father and mother, and it was I who raised you! I surely gave you insight and provided you with a good position that is even better than you (deserve)." See for this text also Veenhof 2009, 202.

[19] Kt j/k 201 (Balkan 1965, 152): (1) *15 ma-na* (2) *an.na ku-nu-ki* (3) *ša puzur₂-a-šur* (4) *ru-ba-im ...* (apqid) *...* (12) *igi a-du-a-a* (13) *dumu ša-ru-ke-en₆* (14) *ru-ba-im,* "I entrusted 15 minas of tin, under the seals of king Puzur-Aššur (to PN) ... Witness: Aduya, son of Šarru-kēn, the king."

Hupitum, and a priest of Adad, engaged in trade by financing merchants.[20] The son of Aššur-šad-ilī, another *laputtāum*, worked as a harnesser (*kaṣṣārum*) for Kuliya (AKT 4, 29:13).

The general word for trader was *tamkārum*. A master or principal was called *ummiānum*. Among the masters some attained the status of bankers. They dwelled in Assur, where they engaged in money-lending and buying for the merchants they represented. One activity in which a master (*mēr ummiānim*, i.e. a member of the group of *ummiānu*) was involved in Anatolia is the shipment of large quantities of silver to Assur.[21] A trader could be working for another trader or a master as his agent (*šamallā'um*),[22] but it is unknown if this was a contract-based relationship. The harnesser, *kaṣṣārum*, and the *sāridum*, were involved in conveying the merchandise by donkey. Although both terms were used for junior personnel and sometimes overlap, *sāridum* is mostly used for temporary personnel that was hired in Assur or along the route (see also below). The tenure of a *kaṣṣārum* appears to have been longer term, and individuals could be identified as the harnesser of a specified individual.

The Assyrian firm was based on kinship ties, which promoted loyalty and reduced costs.[23] An Assyrian boy would first learn the craft by working as a *kaṣṣārum* for his father, for his uncle or for another person. Working for someone else could be occasioned in various circumstances. One of these, by invitation, is mentioned in the letter Kt c/k 45, in which the sender, Aššur-bēl-šadue, expresses his frustration at the behaviour of a certain Alahum: "Aššur knows it! I sought your brotherhood and gave you half a mina of silver as working-capital. And I sent you after merchandise of some 5 minas of silver. You said: 'I shall make a profit for you.' Instead of making me a profit, you robbed me in your house. You charged me with two-thirds of a mina of losses."[24]

---

[20]   VS 26, 32: (18) *um-ma hu-pí-tum* nu.bànda (19) *ù* ah.me *ša* ᵈ*im-ma* kb (20) *ù* kù.gi *ša ah-ša-lim* (21) dam.gàr-*ri-ni : ni-ṣa-ba-a*[t], "Hupitum, the *lapputāum*, and the priest of Adad, said: The silver and gold belong to our agent Ah-šalim; we will take it."

[21]   Kt c/k 259: (5) *iš-tí* dumu *um-mì-a-nim ke-nim* (6) *ša* kb 1 gú *iš-tí-šu i-lu-ku* (7) 30 *ma-na*.ta kb *iš-ri-ša-ma* (8) *a-na* é *be-tí-a šé-bi₄-lá-nim* (9) *ú šu-ma tá-da-ga-lá-ma* (10) *i-na wa-ar-ki-tim* (11) kb 5 gú *iš-tí* dumu *um-<mì>-a-nim* (12) *ke-nim i-lá-ak* 1 gú 20 *ma-na* (13) kb ... (16) *šé-bi₄-lá-nim*, "Send 30 minas each normally to my house by a reliable independent trader with whom 1 talent of silver is going (to Assur). But if you observe that later 5 talents of silver will go with a reliable independent trader, send me 1 talent 20 minas of silver!"

[22]   Larsen 1977, 126f.

[23]   The 'house' (*bētum*) of Alahum, part of whose archive is among the Kt c/k texts, is a typical family firm. It consisted of Alahum himself as the boss (called 'our father' by the others), his two sons, Aššur-malik and Aššur-bēl-šadue, and a servant called Tahašaili. These people closely cooperated with Aššur-ṭāb, the *šamallā'um* of Alahum. This group is assisted by other relatives of Alahum as well as by persons not related through kinship. Alahum and Aššur-ṭāb each manage a *naruqqum* and hence have their own masters and investors. They also have their own representatives in different towns.

[24]   Kt c/k 45 (unp. Ankara): (4) ... *a-šur lu i-de₈* (5) *a-na a-hu-tim áš-e-kà-ma* (6) 1/2 *ma-na* kb *be-ú-lá-tim* (7) *a-dí-na-kum-ma ù wa-ar-ki* (8) *lu-qú-tim ša* kb 5 *ma-na* (9) *aṭ-ru-ud-kà um-ma a-ta-ma* (10) *né-ma-lam ù-ša-ar-ša-kà* (11) *a-pu-ùh né-me-lim ša-ar-šu-im* (12) .... *a-ta-ma i-na* (13) *é-tí-kà ta-am-ta-áš-ha-ni* (14) 2/3 *ma-na* kb *bi₄-it-qá-tim* (15) *ta-áš-ku-nam-ma.*

A fully recognised merchant was someone who had obtained enough experience and credibility to become the manager of a joint-stock contract (*naruqqum*).[25] Such a long-term partnership was formed under the auspices of the city. It involved a dozen or so other persons (including women) who put an amount of gold or other assets at the disposal of the merchant for a contracted term in return for a share in the profits. Only two such contracts have been found in Kültepe. One of these concerns the *naruqqum* of Amur-Ištar, worth 30 minas of gold, and running for 12 years, starting in L64.[26] The other is the contract of Elamma, worth 27 minas 51 shekels of gold with a term of 10 years, starting in L77 (Kt 91/k 482). The case of a 30-year old investment in a *naruqqum*, mentioned in Kt n/k 1192 (see above), seems to be a case of a manager not repaying the investments after the end of the term.

After a successful life in Kanesh, a merchant would move to Assur and remain active in trade for his own firm and as a banker and representative for one or several other traders. He could become a member of the city council or of one of its committees. His wealth would be invested in shares in joint-stock investments, credit, and some houses in town.

3. THE PRACTICE OF BUSINESS

Against the background of the religious and social conventions, and within the political and legal framework set by the government of the city-state of Assur, the merchants conducted their trade. The general principles observable in other times and places largely apply here as well. It was important that the working capital remained active. Money should be used and not remain idle.[27] Therefore, it was of great importance to obtain credit as a vehicle for swift action, to enlarge one's business and to overcome occasional periods of financial hardship.[28] Granting credit was necessary when selling goods to agents and others. Silver, but also copper (and tin in Anatolia) could be borrowed at a 'merchant's house' (*bēt tamkārim* for Assyrian, 'the house of an Anatolian', *bēt nuāim*, for Anatolian moneylenders).[29] Goods should be sold as quickly as possible upon arriving at the specified location, and many letters advise sending on the transporter immediately and not giving him a night's sleep. Costs could not always be avoided but should be as low as possible. Due to the extensive network of trade settlements and the good communications between the various parts of Anatolia, Assyrian merchants were able to obtain accurate information about current events

---

[25] Larsen 1977; 1999.

[26] Kay 313, see Hecker 1999, 564. The L-numbers render eponym-years and refer to the list in Veenhof 2003a.

[27] Veenhof 1987.

[28] Veenhof 1999a.

[29] The redemption of indebted Assyrians from "the house of an Anatolian" occurs, e.g., in Kt a/k 447:6; Kt 91/k 433:12; KBo 9, 1:5.9.

that influenced the market situation and made decisions accordingly. A trader could be aggressive in buying and selling, in dealing with defaulting debtors and unreliable partners, but the overall wisdom was to act prudently. Legal cases against debtors and others were frequent. To prevent time- (and money-)consuming lawsuits,[30] conflicts were initially solved by means of arbitration and private summonses, a common phenomenon in mercantile circles.[31]

The main activity of all merchants was the export of tin and textiles to Anatolia, but this does not mean there was no diversification of trade. Differences could be geographical, when certain firms positioned their representatives in specific key regions. For example, imported goods could first be sent to the copper-producing region around Durhumit, and then the copper would be transported to the main towns to be sold for silver. Depending on the size of the firm and its network of partners, the organization of the sales might differ, with a firm having only a few staff but relying heavily on the services of agents. Some merchants had easier access to the rulers and elite than others and were able to acquire specific goods for them, such as lapis lazuli, carnelian, and iron, thus increasing their stock in trade. Assyrians occasionally dealt in goods with limited profit, such as salt.

4. MARKETS AND PRICES

4.1 Markets

Here the evidence for buying and selling and how and where this was done will first be discussed, and then the evidence for prices and the question of what determined them will be investigated. The terms "supply", "demand", and "market" are used in the conviction that market forces were at work also in this period. There are two strongly opposed camps in the discussion about whether the economy of ancient Mesopotamia can be considered a market economy. On the one side, there is the view taken by Polanyi and his followers, arguing that markets and trade were peripheral and that there were no self-regulating markets (Mayhew *et al.* 1985). At the other end of the spectrum stand M. Silver (1995) and D. Warburton (2003), who argue that the market in fact guided the Mesopotamian economy. As an example of that, Warburton assumes that tin production in Anatolia ceased when Assyrian merchants were able

---

[30] This was particularly the case when a merchant had to testify in Assur and had to abandon his activities in Anatolia for several months. Unless he was forced to go (*nasāhum* Š), often at the behest of an attorney, a merchant was granted what appears to have been reasonable time to go to the desired town. Dealing with a procedure in Anatolia, a colony ordered that someone should go to Kanesh within 6 months to testify on the basis of his written documents (ICK 1, 86 + 2, 141). A term of 1 year to go to Assur was common (AKT 3, 92:15; Kt c/k 561; Kt 92/k 491). A term of 2 years occurs in Kt 91/k 307:16.

[31] Veenhof 2003c.

to procure this metal more cheaply elsewhere. With the growing realization that self-regulating markets do not exist, and that other factors (state, culture etc.) always interfere with market forces and thus contribute to the outcome of economic processes, the OA economy can preferably be characterised as an embedded market economy.

The OA trade consisted of purchasing in Assur tin and textiles and occasionally small amounts of other luxury goods (lapis lazuli, carnelian, iron, shells), and selling these commodities for silver and gold in Anatolia. There was a demand for tin and quality textiles in Anatolia and for silver and gold in Mesopotamia. The textiles were woollen and some linen fabrics made in Babylonia, as well as small quantities of locally produced garments. Babylonian caravans transported the Babylonian textiles (denoted as Akkadian at the time) to Assur. The most common textile bought in Assur was the woollen *kutānum*. This is the type of textile to be understood where purchases include unspecified 'textiles' (*ṣubātum*). There were different sizes of a material. According to TC 3, 17, a textile should measure 9 by 8 cubits (approximately 4.5 × 4 m = 18 square metres).[32] The linen garments were long rolls.[33] A donkey-load of textiles comprised 25 to 30 *kutānus*. As textiles are discussed by Michel and Veenhof (2010), the reader is referred to that publication for details on the varieties and qualities.

Tin was also brought to Assur by foreign traders, and they are referred to as *harrānum ša māt šapiltim* "the caravan of the Lower Country" in AKT 3, 73 and 74.[34] The caravan may have started in Susa, but the regions where the tin was mined were much further away and must be sought in Central Asia. The tin arrived in the shape of rectangular ingots called *lē'um* "board". No other shapes of ingot, such as round or plano-convex, have yet been attested. The metal presumably was cast as ingots at or near the region where the metal was processed, and it is likely that standard ingots were used of approximately the same dimensions and weight at the different smelting centres. Ingots of the *lē'um*-type occur in OA texts as well as in documents from the Mari archive, and seem to have had an average weight of approximately 10 minas or 5 kg.[35]

The texts inform us that tin was bought with silver or copper at an unspecified location in Assur and then brought to the 'house' of a merchant, awaiting shipment to Anatolia. The tin destined for sale in Anatolia was wrapped in textiles and the package was put under sealings; hence its name *annukū kunukkū* "sealed tin". This tin will have been in the shape of ingots. The 'sealed tin' was distinguished from the 'hand-tin' (*annak qātim*), bought to pay expenses en route. This would have been smaller lumps of tin from broken-up ingots. A standard donkey-load of tin weighed 2 talents 10 minas (about 65 kg). The tin was carried in half-packs (*muttātum*) and a top-pack

---

[32] Veenhof 1972, 104f.

[33] Kt c/k 249:29ff.: 1 túg *ki-ta-am*, *ša* 40 *a-ma-tí* 2 *ší-ta* 15, *a-ma-tí*, "1 linen textile of 40 cubit (= 20 m) and 2 of 15 cubit (= 7.5 m)".

[34] Dercksen 2004, 25ff.

[35] A weight of 9 minas 7 shekels is attested in AKT 3, 49:23–24. According to the Mari document ARM 23, 555, dealing with a supply of tin from Susa, the total weight of 3 particular *lē'us* is 32 minas 15 shekels, and that of 2 such ingots is given as 18 minas. A quantity of tin weighing 8 minas 51 2/3 (!) shekels is mentioned in ARM 23, 557, and may well refer to the weight of a single ingot.

(*elītum*). The tin carried in half-packs was protected by a wrapping of textiles (*šurum/ kutānum ša liwītim*). With four textiles per donkey-load, each textile was wrapped around 30 minas of tin (three ingots); the tin in the top-pack was not wrapped in such a textile. It is unknown whether the tin was sold ready packed.

The supply of tin varied according to the season, and was occasionally disrupted because of other circumstances.

Apart from the merchandise itself, donkeys and their equipment (pack-saddles, bags, leather straps, ropes, fodder) were purchased in the city. Donkeys would usually be obtained at a *gigamlum* or paddock but occasionally supplies were insufficient (as in I 571:9). The merchandise and most of the surviving donkeys were sold for silver and gold in Anatolia, often having first been exchanged for copper, the metal most widely available as a means of payment. Practically all purchases in Assur were made with cash. Credit was sometimes granted by the City Hall.

The central markets in this segment of an international trading network were Assur and Kanesh. Assur represented the hub where silver and gold were exchanged for tin and textiles, connecting the Babylonian area and Iran with Anatolia. Kanesh was the major city-state in Central Anatolia and closest to Mesopotamia. It was also the place where all imports from Assur had to be cleared before they could be sent on to other areas, so for this reason the central Assyrian commercial settlement was located there. Kanesh was at the heart of the Anatolian network, linking copper-producing regions in the north (Durhumit) with the main urban centres, such as Wahšušana and Purušhattum, in the west. Purušhattum apparently formed the westernmost limit of Assyrian commercial activity. This town presumably had contacts with the Aegean world, which possessed some rich silver deposits. Anatolia was divided into three main areas: Kanesh, Hattum north of the Kızılırmak, and Purušhattum in the west. The main articles of trade (tin, textiles, silver, gold) had various places of origin and were shipped over long distances. This made trade highly vulnerable to any logistic disruption caused by political turmoil or otherwise. Purchases of lapis lazuli, carnelian and iron appear to have been marginal compared to turnover of the two main goods.

The word *mahīrum* denotes the actual market place and the price current there. The place or places where merchandise was bought in Assur are rarely indicated.[36] A heavy textile was bought "on the market" according to TC 2, 7:28. Frequently, however, the central economic institution of the town, the City Hall (*bēt ālim*) also known as the House of the Eponym (*bēt līmim*), is mentioned as the seller of goods. Representatives of a person called Asānum brought silver into the City Hall in order to purchase copper according to Kt a/k 913:11. Puzur-Aššur dashes any hopes Pūšu-kēn might have of obtaining iron and lapis lazuli by writing that "they do not sell (them) at the House of the Eponym" (TC 2, 9). A debt in silver arising from textiles bought at the House of the Eponym is mentioned in TPAK 1, 143:3–4. There are no references to tin being bought there but it seems probable that it could have been.

---

[36] See Dercksen 2004, 33–7.

A third place to buy goods was at a 'house' owned by a businessman (e.g., "our father") or by an individual for whom trade was a side-line, such as a priest of the moon god Suen (TC 3, 129:10′–11′). The word *bētum* in this context does not necessarily indicate a shop, but rather a house where merchandise was stored and sold. The owner of such a 'house' may have obtained the goods from the City Hall. The places where the products made by craftsmen (footwear, pack-saddles, bags, ropes, etc.) were purchased are never indicated.

A market building called *mahīrum* and supervised by a *rabi mahīrim* is known from various Anatolian towns.[37] It was the place where merchants would meet, and in some cases legal disputes began there.[38] If goods functioning as a means of payment, such as copper or silver, were absent from or insufficiently available at the market, trade was stalled. By contrast, enough money meant that goods could be sold and that debtors might dispose of silver.[39]

4.2 Prices

Details about the prices of the main articles of trade in Assur and in Kanesh were given by Garelli (1963), Larsen (1967), and Veenhof (1972; 1988). The merchants could live and work abroad under the protection of treaties which Assur had concluded with foreign rulers. These treaties deal with many aspects, but they do not contain fixed prices for merchandise. The correspondence between merchants makes it abundantly clear that they had a clear notion of what constituted a fair price, and what was expensive or cheap. Obviously, it was known that a shortage led to higher prices, and that abundant supply would lower a price. Examples for this will be given below. The purchase prices for tin and textiles in Assur show fluctuations over time, which are often difficult to assess in the absence of a datable event. But apparently different prices were not demanded for a given commodity at one particular time. The only difference noticeable is that occasionally a higher price was paid for hand-tin compared to the price of tin as merchandise (see below). It seems that the market at Assur was too small to allow for competing sellers requiring different prices. On a larger, regional scale, involving several towns, there could be markets where the prices differed from one another, as in Anatolia. There, for example, according to the letter Kt v/k 128, the price of good copper was 77 shekels of copper for 1 shekel of silver in the town of Ulama, but 73 in Šalatuar.[40]

---

[37] Dercksen 2004, 31–3.

[38] Kt c/k 108+ (unp. Ankara): (48) *ú a-dí ma-lá ú ší-ni-šu ri-ig-ma-am* (49) *i-ma-hi-ri-im i-dí-i um-ma šu-ut-ma* (50) *a-wi-lam ta-ma-ša-ha*, "He repeatedly raised a complaint at the marketplace, saying: 'You (pl.) are robbing the gentleman!'"

[39] TC 3, 111: (13) *i-nu-mì wa-áš-ba-ku-ni* (14) *iq-bi₄-ú-nim um-ma šu-nu-ma* (15) *ší-mu-um i-na ma-hi-ri-im lá-šu* (16) *ú-ma-am a-ša-me-ma* (17) *ší-mu-um i-na ma-hi-ri-im* (18) *ma-ad kb ša-áš-qí-lá-šu-nu-ma*, "When I stayed (there) they told me: 'There is no merchandise on the market'. Today I hear that there is plenty of merchandise on the market. Collect the silver from them".

[40] Dercksen 1996, 159.

Slightly different local prices over a period of some weeks or even months are mentioned in ATHE 38: "Why do you complain 'Who is selling tin for poor copper in Durhumit?' When Suea arrived, they were selling tin at 9 or 10 minas (of copper) per (mina of tin), but I sent it to you at 11."[41]

Knowledge about which goods were in demand and where there was a shortage of means of payment was obtained either from personal experience or through agents or colleagues. So, for example, "Since they are saturated with tin here, I had Uzubiškum carry 1 talent 20 minas of tin and 60 textiles to Purušhattum. I hear that *makūhu*-textiles are scarce in Purušhattum; buy for a value of 10 minas of silver and send (them) to me, so that 1 or 2 minas of silver will come up for you (as a profit)."[42] The local market prices for tin that are mentioned in the texts include those in Assur and in Hattum (see below).

As long as the trade in Anatolia functioned well, with returns being sent regularly to Assur, there was a steady demand for tin and textiles in that city. The main determining factor for price in Assur, therefore, was the level of supply of these articles.[43] Disruptions in the market in Assur were often caused by political problems. The supply of Akkadian textiles was interrupted because of disturbances in Babylonia, according to VS 26, 17: "As for the purchase of Akkadian textiles, about which you wrote, the Akkadians have not entered the city since you left. Their country is in revolt. If they arrive before winter, there will be the merchandise of your life and we shall make purchases for you. Moreover, we will pay from our own silver. Take care to send silver!"[44] At the time of writing of letter TC 2, 7, there was a disruption in the supply of tin, Akkadian textiles, and *kutānu*-textiles made of Šurbu-wool: "There is no tin (even) at 13 each or a decent package. 10 or 20 donkeys, the missing amount, have been bought at the paddock. (When) they (i.e., the caravan with tin) enter (Assur) we will buy tin and send it to you by the earliest express delivery. For the silver of my shipment, I did not buy any tin because tin is expensive. When tin comes in I will buy it and bring it to you together with your tin. And the merchandise of Akkadian textiles, if it has become normal, I will buy for a value of 1 mina of silver. As for the *kutānu*-

---

[41] ATHE 38 (to Puzur-Aššur from Ikāya): (2) … mì-š[u] (3) ša ta-na-zu-mu-ú (4) ma-nu-um i-na du-u[r-h]u-mì-it (5) ša an.na a-na urudu lá-mu-nim (6) i-ta-na-dí-nu i-nu-mì (7) sú-e-a i-li-kà-ni (8) an.na 9 ma-na.ta ú 10 ma-na.ta (9) i-ta-na-dí-nu (10) a-na-ku 11 ma-na.ta (11) ú-šé-bi-lá-kum. A rate of 20 minas of good copper per mina of tin is given in Kt h/k 40:7.

[42] Kt n/k 1689 (Sever 1995, 130; letter to Aššur-imittī in Kanesh from Hurāsānum): (18) ki-ma a-na-kam an.na (19) ša-bu-ni 1 gú 20 ma-na (20) an.na ù 60 túg.hi.a (21) a-na pu-ru-uš-ha-tim (22) ú-zu-bi₄-iš-kà-am (23) ú-šé-bi₄-il₅ a-ša-me-ma (24) ma-ku-hu i-na pu-ru-<uš>-ha-tim (25) wa-qar ša 10 ma-na (26) kb ša-a-ma (27) šé-bi-lá-ma (28) kb 1 ma-na ú 2 ma-na (29) ku-a-tí le-li-a-kum.

[43] Note that the price of tin in Mari dropped to 12–14 during the years of direct imports from Susa, as against 10–11 in the preceding period, and 8 in the year after the good relations ended; see Joannès 1991, 76.

[44] VS 26, 17: (4) a-šu-mì ší-im : túg ša a-ki-dí-e (5) ša ta-áš-pu-ra-ni (6) iš-tù : tù-uṣ-ú a-ki-dí-ú (7) a-na a-lim^ki ú-la e-ru-bu-nim (8) ma-sú-nu : sá-hi-a-at-ma (9) šu-ma a-ku-ṣí im-ta-aq-tù-nim-ma (10) ší-mu-um ša ba-la-ṭí-kà (11) i-ba-ší ni-ša-a-ma-ku-um (12) ú kb i-ra-mì-ni-ni (13) ni-ša-qal kb i-hi-id-ma (14) šé-bi₄-lam.

textiles you keep writing to me about, there is no Šurbu-wool. We will buy 1 heavy textile on the market and send it to you."[45] Another example of the fact that tin was preferred is contained in CCT 5, 5b,[46] from which it emerges that potential buyers were willing to wait for some time if necessary.[47]

Therefore, shortages in tin could lead to increased spending on textiles. It is reported in CCT 6, 47c: "As for the silver you sent here, since tin is delayed we have not bought tin. We will buy textiles for the silver and I will despatch it to you by the first caravan leaving. (Every) 10 minas of tin that comes up to you (in Kanesh), lie on top of your tin, later on I will have no tin."[48] At the same time, a shortage in Assur and the resulting higher price there influenced asking prices in Anatolia according to Pa. 22 (L29–579): "Thus says Imdilum, speak to Aššur-ṭāb: Adu is bringing 2 talents 2 minas of tin and 5 good quality *kutānus* to you under my seals. (...). 6 shekels each for my tin and 15 shekels each for my textiles, sell (the textiles) together with the tin for cash. If that cannot be done, let my tin remain packed (lit.: under its sealings). I repeatedly informed you that tin is delayed. Although I informed you (about this), you write to me in your letter: 'I have sold your tin at 7 shekels each.' Report to me if there is still unsold tin left. I must not get angry. But if you have already sold (it), send me the refined silver – the silver of the *qīptum* - under seal. And (sell) my textiles at 15 shekels each!"

We know of one particular case in which the city of Assur responded to a temporary shortage of tin, its main import. According to a decision by the city assembly, "one can (only) buy tin for one-third (of the money)".[49] The motivation for this decision to limit expenditure was clearly to distribute more evenly among the merchants later on the extra tin that would reach the market once the expected caravan from the Lower Country arrived.

---

[45] TC 2, 7: (9) an.na 13 gín.ta ú šu-uq-lúm (10) za-ku-tum lá-šu : anše 10 (11) *ù* 20 *bu-tù-uq-tum* (12) *i-na ki-kam-lim* : *ša-am-ú* (13) *e-ru-bu-nim-ma* : an.na (14) *ni-ša-am-ma i-ba-tí-qí-im* (15) *pá-nim-ma* : *nu-šé-ba-lá-kum* (16) *a-na* kb *ša šé-pì-a* (17) *ki-ma* an.na *ba-at-qú-ni* (18) *mì-ma* an.na *ú-lá áš-a-am* (19) an.na *e-ra-ba-ma a-ša-a-ma* (20) *iš-tí* an.na-*ki-kà* : *a-ba-kà-kum* (21) *ú ší-mu-um ša a-ki-dí-e* (22) *šu-ma* : *i-ta-áš-ra-am* (23) *ša* kb 1 *ma-na a-ša-a-am* (24) *a-na ku-ta-ni ša ta-áš-ta-na-pá-ra-ni* (25) *ša-áp-tum* (26) *šu-ur-bu-i-tum* : *lá-šu* (27) 1 túg *kà-ab-tám i-na* (28) *ma-hi-ri-im ni-ša-a-ma* (29) *nu-šé-ba-lá-kum.*

[46] CCT 5, 5b (to Pūšu-kēn from Ahuqar): (5) ... *ša* 33 *ma-na* (6) kb an.na *ša-ma-nim* (7) *eq-lúm li-iṣ-ba-sú* (8) *ba-at-qú-um ù wa-tù-ru-um* (9) an.na *ba-ab-šu lá-šu* (10) 17 *ma-na* kb (11) *ša dingir-ma-lik ub-lá-ni* (12) *i-na ku-nu-ki-šu i-ba-ší* (13) *i-na e-ra-ab* an.na (14) *a-ma-lá té-er-tí-kà* (15) *ni-ša-a-ma-ku-um* (16) ki *ba-tí-qí-im nu-šé-ba-lá-ku-um,* "(P. had written:) 'Buy for me tin for a value of 33 minas of silver.' Let the earth seize it! Expensive or cheap, there is no opportunity (for) tin. The 17 minas of silver which Ili-malik brought here is still lying under his sealings. When tin comes in we will buy for you tin according to your order and send it to you by express delivery."

[47] See also BIN 6, 59: (13´) ... *an-nu-ku* (14´) *a-na-kam wa-aq-ru* 14 gín.ta (15)´ [*ù*] *ša-ap-li-iš i-za-az* (16´) *a-dí* itu.1.kam *ù* itu.2.kam *a-wa-tum* (17´) *lá i-za-ku-wa,* "Tin is expensive here (i.e., in Assur). It stands at 14 each or even lower. The matter will not improve in 1 or 2 months."

[48] CCT 6, 47c (Šu-Hubur to Pūšu-kēn): (9) ... kb (10) *ša tù-šé-bi-lá-ni* (11) *ki-ma* an.na *ša-du-ú-ni* (12) an.na *ú-la ni-iš-ta-a-am* (13) *ša* kb-*pí* túg.hi-*tí* (14) *ni-ša-a-ma iš-tí* (15) *pá-ni-ú-tim-ma* (16) *a-ṭá-ra-da-kum* (17) an.na 10 *ma-na* (18) *ša e-li-a-ku-ni* (19) *i-šé-er* an.na-*ki-kà* (20) *ri-bi-iṣ* an.na (21) *wa-ar-kà-tám* (21) *ú-lá i-šu.*

[49] AKT 3, 73: (23) *i-na dí-in a-*[*lim*ki] (24) *ša-li-iš-tám* an.[na] (25) *i-ša-ú-mu.*

Occasionally there appear to have been temporary shortages of silver, but this did not affect buying. It is known that copper was widely used as a means of payment in Assur, but there is as yet little evidence for its use in the export trade. Five textiles were bought with copper in KTB 2:8. Only one instance is known where a caravan is largely paid for with copper. According to KTS 2, 36 + Bursa 3776, 100 *kutānus*, 20 bags, the harness of the donkeys and the payment for the *sa'adum* were all paid with copper (worth 10 minas 18 1/2 shekels of silver at 100:1), whereas the 4 donkeys, the 20 minas of hand-tin and the exit-tax were paid in silver (2 minas 47 2/3 shekels). The whole caravan was eventually paid with the silver that had been sent to Assur. Apparently, the representatives in Assur had preferred to use copper until the silver arrived from Kanesh.

In Anatolia, there will have been a continuous demand for tin and high quality textiles, partly due to the re-exporting of these commodities to more distant places, such as Purušhattum, and Assur was the sole intermediary delivering tin to Anatolia. With a more or less steady demand, there are two main factors that account for price fluctuations: the availability of money, usually in the form of silver and copper, and the level of supply of imported goods. Moreover, the longer the term for commission sales, the higher would be the expected returns.[50] If silver was in short supply, cash sales were impossible. One had to wait until better times and exploit possible alternatives. According to KTS 1, 18: "Do you not hear that silver is hard to obtain and that there is no payment for textiles? Silver is hard to obtain here. You say in your tablet: 'Sell my merchandise at any price and come here!' There is gold as payment, let us obtain gold for you. We will stay for one or two months and then obtain silver for you. Since you did not order it, we did not want to take gold."[51] Some shortages were known to last for a limited time only, such as those caused by harvesting or a festival.[52]

---

[50]   For an assessment of prices asked for commission sales, cf. a passage from 'C 42 Holzmeister' in a transliteration by B. Landsberger: (15) *a-na-kam : áš-ta-al-ma* (16) *um-ma a-hu-um : eb-ru-ma* (17) *1/2 ma-na.ta* 1 *ku-ta-ni* (18) 6 *gín.ta a-na an.*[*na*] (19) *e-eṣ*, "I asked around here and brothers and friends say: Half a mina (of silver) per *kutānum* and 6 shekels each for tin is few."

[51]   KTS 1, 18 (to Imdilum from Amur-Ištar and Uzua): (21) ... *lá ta-áš-ta-na-me-e* (22) *ki-ma* kb-*pu da-nu-ni* (23) *ù a-na túg ší-mu-um lá i-ba-ší-ú* (24) kb-*pu a-na-kam da-nu i-na* (25) *ṭup-pì-kà um-ma a-ta-ma ší-mì* (26) *ba-tí-iq ù wa-tur₄ dí-na-ma a-tal-kà-nim* (27) *a-na ší-mì-im* kg *i-za-az* (28) kg *lu né-pu-ša-kum itu.1.kam* (29) *iš-té-en₆ ù* 2 *itu-kam ni-sà-hu-ur-ma* (30) kb *né-pá-ša-kum ki-ma lá té-er-ta-kà* (31) kg *lá-qá-am lá ni-mu-a*.

[52]   Kt n/k 1689 (Sever 1995, 129): (4) *ší-mì ta-dí-in-ma* (5) urudu *i-ba-ší sí-kà-tum* (6) *ú-ṣa-ma i-na ma-hi-ri-im* (6) kb *ù* kg *lá-šu* ... (14) *sí-kà-tum a-na* (15) 10 *u₄-me-e i-tù-ra-nim-ma* (16) kg *a-ša-a-ma* (17) *ki a-li-ki ú-šé-ba-lá-kum*, "My goods have been sold and the copper is there. The *sikkātum* left (town) and there is no silver or gold on the market. ... The *sikkātum* will return here within 10 days and then I shall buy gold and send it to you with the travellers."

I 598 (to Puzur-Aššur from Il-wēdāku): (3) *ta-áš-pu-ra-am um-ma* (4) *a-ta-ma lu* kb *lu* kù.ki (5) *ša* 5 *ma-na* kb (6) *šé-bi-lam₅ : a-na-kam* (7) *sí-kà-tum-ma* (8) *ma-hi-ru-um : pá-ru-ud* (9) *a-dí* 2 *u₄-me sí-kà-tum* (10) *i-pá-ṭá-ra-nim* (11) *a-ma-lá té-er-tí-kà* (12) *lu* kb *lu* kù.ki (13) *ú-šé-ba-lá-kum-ma*, "You wrote to me as follows: 'Send me either silver or gold for a value of 5 minas of silver!' Here, it is the time of *sikkātum* and the market is disturbed. The *sikkātum* will disband within two days. (Then) I shall send you silver or gold in accordance with your instruction". The *sikkātum* refers to a periodical event, possibly of a religious character.

The exceptionally high price of 4 for tin is referred to in combination with the high, but by no means exceptional, price of half a mina of silver for a textile in a letter: "After the plague of Purušhattum they have been selling tin at 4 shekels each and textiles at 30 shekels each for cash."[53] One of the effects of this plague will have been that traders (Assyrian and non-Assyrian) avoided the city, which led to a shortage of imported goods. A shortage of silver seems unlikely (the cash sales were for silver), which makes it likely that the demand for tin exceeded the stocks available to the Assyrians in the area. Whereas customers in this case were prepared to buy tin at a rate of 4, there is no evidence that they would do the same at 3 1/2 or even higher rates. It is unknown whether such a price would introduce another supplier of tin on the Anatolian market. Unless the supply of tin through Assur (or from an alternative supplier) completely broke down, the customers would probably wait until more tin arrived in the not too distant future.

Was there a relationship between the price of tin and that of a *kutānu*-textile in Assur? Larsen (1967, 152) collected evidence of prices paid in Assur, which together with some other texts can be rendered thus:

tin (ht = hand-tin)	*kutānu* (k.)	
16 1/2 and 15 (ht)	3 1/3	CCT 3, 5a (4 *šuru* and 5 *k.* cost 1/2 m)
16	5 3/4	Pa. 15 (110 *k.*, 8 fine *k.*, 2 *kamsu* cost 11m 30 2/3 shekels)
15 2/3	8 1/4	VS 26, 151 (25 *k.* cost 3m 26 1/2 shekels)
15 and 14 (ht)	3.6	TC 3, 43 (230 *k.* cost 13m 46 2/3 shekels)
15 (ht)	4 2/3	Pa. 15 (26 *k.* cost 2m)
14	3 1/6	TC 2, 6 (10 *k.* cost 31 2/3 shekels)
14 (ht)	5 3/4	TC 2, 14 (63 *k.* cost 6m 1 1/3 shekels)
14 (ht)	3 1/2	TC 3, 36 (350 *k.* cost 20m 25 shekels)
14 (ht)	8.18	BIN 6, 65 (22 túg cost 3m)
14 and 13 (ht)	5 2/3	KTS 2, 10 (32 *k.* cost 3m)
14 (ht) ca.	6.1	KTS 2, 36+ (100 *k.* cost 16t 50 2/3 m of copper)
13 1/4 and 13 (k, ht)	4	CCT 3, 27a (114 *k.* cost 7m 32 1/4 shekels)
13 (ht)	5.8	KTS 1, 23 (175 *k.* cost 16m 53 shekels)
12 1/2 (ht)	5	CCT 3, 22a (149 *k.* cost 12m 30 1/2 shekels)

One could interpret the last data as evidence for a higher price for textiles when tin was expensive. The prices of *kutānu* are average prices and often rounded off. The real average price in many cases contains unusual amounts of grains (še). For example, the textiles in TC 2, 6, cost 3 shekels 48 grains each, those in TC 2, 14, 5 shekels 132.4

---

[53] Kt n/k 1339 (Çeçen 1995, 63): (10) *iš-tù : mu-ta-ni* (11) *ša pu-ru-uš-ha-tim* (12) 4 gín.ta an.na 1/2 *ma-na.ta* (13) túg.hi.a *i-ta-aṭ-lam* (14) *i-ta-dí-nu*.

grains. Such prices are evidently absurd and it is likely that the total amount of the expenses on textiles often included an extra payment or a discount.

The evidence for sale prices in Anatolia, on the other hand, shows that high tin prices usually corresponded to high prices for textiles.

The effect of supply can be illustrated with the help of two examples, which were written against the background of the imminent arrival of one or more caravans from Assur. CCT 4, 8b implies a causal relationship between an abundant supply and the fall of the price of tin. The sender of this letter wants to sell the tin available to him and even wishes for more tin to be borrowed for him from a merchant. The borrowing is presented as a commission sale: "I want to sell the tin before tin becomes too plentiful here; moreover, obtain for me tin for a value of 10 minas of silver at the office of a merchant for a long-term commission, as they are (currently) giving it."[54] A similar awareness is apparent in this passage from CCT 4, 11b: "You are my brother! Act according to your status of a gentleman and exchange the tin for silver before the tin of the caravan arrives. (...) The caravan will arrive in [x] days. Sell the tin and do not keep (any of) it!"[55]

The influence of market forces on supply (production) and demand (consumption) in the economies of Assur, Babylonia and Anatolia was not absolute. The only cases of increased production as a result of growing demand concern textiles in Babylonia and in Assur itself, and also the breeding of donkeys and the manufacture of their harnesses. An increase in the standard of living of successful merchant families in Assur may be seen from their purchase of houses.

5. STRATEGIES FOR BUYING AND SELLING

5.1 *The purchase of goods in Assur*

The price of tin determined how much of the money available was spent on textiles. The 'normal' price of tin fluctuated between 16 and 14 shekels of tin per shekel of silver. A rate of 15 (for some merchants this was 16) is the critical point determining whether the silver must be spent only on tin (15 or higher), or half on tin and half on

---

[54] CCT 4, 8b (to Imdilum from Al-ṭāb): (12) ... *la-ma* an.na (13) [*a-n*]*a-kam i-mì-du-ni* (14) an.na *la-dí-in-ma* (15) *ù ša* 10 *ma-na* kb (16) an.na *é* dam.gàr (17) *a-na* u_4-*me-e pá-tí-ú-tim* (18) *ki-ma i-du-nu-ni* (19) *le-qé-a-am*.

[55] CCT 4, 11b: (16′) ... *a-hi a-ta* (17′) *ki-ma a-wi-lu-tí-kà e-pu-uš-ma* (18′) *lá-ma* an.na *ša illat-tim* (19′) *e-ru-ba-ni* an.na *a-na* kb (20′) *ta-er* ... (31′) ... *illat-tum* (32′) [*a-x*] u_4-*me e-ra-ba-am* an.na *dí-in* (33′) *lá tù-kà-al-šu.* Cf. further I 571 (to Pūšu-kēn from Puzur-Aššur): (12) *a-bi a-ta be-lí a-ta* (13) *lu-qú-tám ša šé-ep* (14) *al-be-lí la-ma e-lá-tum* (15) *e-ru-ba-ni-ni a-li* (16) kb 1 gín *e-li-ú a-ṣé-er* (17) *ša ki ku-a-tí al-be-lí lu-bi₄-il₅-ma* (18) *a-na i-ta-aṭ-lim* (19) *li-dí-nu*, "You are my father, my lord! Concerning the merchandise transported (to you) by Al-bēlī, let Al-bēlī bring (it) to your representatives wherever a shekel of silver can appear, before the caravans arrive; let them sell (it) for cash."

textiles (below 15).[56] This has to do with the margin for profit and will be discussed below. A rate of 14 was considered expensive according to BIN 6, 59. At 13 and lower (12 1/2 or 12), tin was considered too expensive for commercial purposes and was only bought as hand-tin. Whereas in most cases the prices of tin and hand-tin are the same, occasionally hand-tin was more expensive: 9.1% (16 1/2 and 15, CCT 3, 5a), 7.1% (14 and 13, KTS 2, 10), 6 2/3% (15 and 14, TC 3, 43), 2.8% (15 75 še and 15, Kt 92/k 142), and 0.6% (14 1/3 and 14 1/4, Kt 91/k 419). Especially in view of the fact that usually there is no price difference, these cases are hard to explain. A different seller could have been involved, or an extra payment similar to the surcharge in silver, although that was around 1/2%:

> 0.53% (6 shekels) according to Pa. 15 // LB 1200 (*nikbus*; tin at 16);
> 0.55% (3 shekels) in I 480:9 (*nuraddi*; tin at 14 1/2);
> 0.55% (3 1/3 shekels) in TC 2, 6:10 (*tēṣubī nuṣib*; tin at 14).

In his analysis of purchases at Assur, Larsen (1967, 146–147) demonstrated that the transportation costs and taxes for a load of textiles are higher than those for a shipment of tin bought for the same amount of money, with the tin needing only half the transport capacity (see also below).

The tin price in Assur (*mahīr ālim (Aššur)*) at a specific moment could be used as a standard to calculate the price in silver in Anatolia.[57] Likewise, the price in Central Anatolia could be referred to as "the market price of Hattum" (*mahīr Hattim*, Kt c/k 228:31).

Whoever the sellers in Assur were, they rarely sold their goods on credit. Purchases

---

[56] This is clear from the following letters: Kt c/k 531 (Kura is bringing 30 minas of silver): (6) *ší-ma-am ša ba-lá-ṭí-a* (7) *ša-ma-nim šu-ma an.na* (8) 15 *gín.ta ù e-li-iš* (9) 4 *gú ù it-ra-sú* (10) *ša-a-ma-nim ù ší-tí kb* (11) *túg.hi.a šu-ma an.na* (12) *ša-pì-il* (13) *ša ta-dá-ga-lá-ni* (14) *ší-ma-am ša-a-ma-nim*, "Buy for me a purchase of my life. If tin is 15 shekels each or higher, buy for me 4 talents and its extra and (for) the rest of the silver (buy) textiles. If tin is lower, buy for me goods as you deem fit."

Kt 91/k 434 Elamma (concerning 30 minas of silver brought by Ah-šalim): (7) *šu-ma* 15 *gín.ta* (8) *i-ba-ší an.na ša-ma-ma* (9) *šé-bi-lá-nim* (10) *šu-ma i-na* 15 *gín.ta* (11) *ba-tí-iq mì-iš-lam* (12) *an.na mì-iš-lam* (13) *túg.hi.a ša-ma-ma*, "If a rate of 15 shekels each exists, buy tin and send it to me. If the rate is lower than 15 shekels each, buy half tin and half textiles." Courtesy K. R. Veenhof.

Kt 91/k 530 Elamma (Dān-Aššur is bringing 24 minas of silver): (8) *šu-ma : an.na* 15 *gín.ta* (9) *ù e-li-iš : 2 gú* (10) *an.na ša-ma-nim* (11) *šu-ma la ki-a-am* (12) *ku-ta-ni, ša-ma-ni-im*, "If tin is 15 shekels each or higher, buy for me 2 talents of tin. If that is not so, buy for me *kutānus*." (The reply is contained in Kt 91/k 532, from which it emerges that no tin was bought.) Courtesy K. R. Veenhof.

KTS 2, 26 Imdilum (Kutallānum is bringing 20 minas of silver): (4′) … *šu-ma* (5′) *an.na* 16 *gín.ta* (6′) *ù e-li-iš i-za-az* (7′) *ša* 10 *ma-na kb an.na sig₅* (8′) *šu-uq-lam ša-ma-nim* (9′) *ša* 8 *ma-na kb ku-ta-ni* (10′) *ša* 1 *ma-na kb ší-ma-am* (11′) *ša a-ki-dì-e i-a-ti* (12′) *ù ša* 1 *ma-na kb* (13′) *a-na tám-kà-ri-im* (14′) *mì-iš-lam [lu-b]u-šé* (15′) *pá-aṣ-ú-tim mì-iš-lam* (16′) *ku-sí-a-tim dam-qá-tim* (17′) *ša-ma-nim-ma* … (21′) *šu-ma i-na* 16 *gín.ta an.na* (22′) *ba-at-[qu]m i-za-az* (23′) [x x x x] x x [x x] *ku-ta-ni*, "If tin stands at 16 shekels each or higher, buy for me good tin (in package(s)) for 10 minas of silver, for 8 minas of silver *kutānus*; for 1 mina of silver (buy) Akkadian textiles for me and for 1 mina of silver for the merchant – half white garments, half good *kusītus*. If tin stands lower than 16 shekels each … *kutānus*."

[57] E.g. in I 521:7; Kt c/k 459: 19–22: due in Purušhattum at a rate of 17; Kt c/k 639b:28; TPAK 1, 94:12.

were paid in cash and with borrowed money if necessary. Making purchases took some time, which partly explains different prices mentioned in the same text. According to LB 1219 (to Pūšu-kēn from Aššur-malik): "For the gold of your votive gifts, which you sent here with Ahuqar and Ea-šar, they continue to buy *kutānu*s, but the money has not yet been spent on buying. They will completely spend it within 5 days and then I shall bring it to you personally."[58]

A legitimate question is whether there was a difference in price according to the quantity of goods purchased, as suggested by Veenhof (1988). Compare the following quantities of textiles and the average price per textile:

Quantities bought in Assur and average price per textile in shekels of silver (*k.* = *kutānum*; túg = 'textile'):

10 *k.* at 3 1/6, TC 2, 6
10 *k.* at 4.6, Kt 92/k 142
10 *k.* at 5, C 29
17 1/2 *k. ša qātim* at 6 1/2; and 5 *k.* at 6 1/2, BIN 6, 228:3
22 túg at 8.2, BIN 6, 65:18–19
25 *k.* at 8 1/4, VS 26, 151
25 *k.* at 8.5, LB 1230
26 *k.* at 4.6, Pa. 15
32 *k.* at 5.6, KTS 2, 10
36 *k.* at 5.8, Kt 91/k 484
36 túg at 3.9, Kt 91/k 419
63 *k.* at 5 3/4, TC 2, 14
64 *k.* at 6.8, ICK 1, 82
75 *k.* at 5.2, I 836:5
85 túg at 4.2, Kt 92/k 143
100 *k.* at 6.1, KTS 2, 36+Bursa 3776; (Imdilum), hand-tin at 14
100 *k.* at 5.6 and 10 *k.* at 5, CTMMA 1, 75 (to Imdilum), 8t 40m tin at 16
110 *k. ša qātim* + 8 fine textiles + 2 *kamsum*, on average 5.75, Pa. 15 (to Pūšu-kēn), gold 6 5/6, tin at 16
114 *k.* at 4, CCT 3, 27a// KTS 1, 38a (to Enlil-bāni), 2t 15m tin at 13 1/4, 48m tin at 13, hand-tin at 13
117 *k.* + 1 heavy *abarnium* at 3.3, I 435:10 (to Imdilum); gold 7 2/3, 2t 10m tin at 14
120 *k.* at 4.7, Yale 13092 (to Pūšu-kēn); 15m kb brought; hand-tin at 14
149 *k.* at 5, CCT 3, 22a (to Pūšu-kēn); gold 7 1/3 and 8 2/3 , hand-tin at 12 1/2
175 *k.* at 5.8, KTS 1, 23 (to Pūšu-kēn); 30 m hand-tin
177 *k.* at 5.1, I 704:7 (to Pūšu-kēn); hand-tin at 13 1/2
200 *k.* at 5.15, VS 26, 13 (to Imdilum)

---

[58] LB 1219: (3) *a-na kù.gi* (4) *ša ik-ri-be-kà* (5) *ša a-ṣé-er a-hu-qar* (6) *ù i-a-šar tù-šé-bi₄-lá-ni* (7) *ku-ta-ni* : (eras.) (8) *iš-ta-na-ú-mu-ni-ma* (9) *ší-mu-um* (10) *i-ša-a-mì-im* (11) *mì-ma* : *lá ga-me-er* (12) *a-dí* 5 *u₄-me* (13) *i-ša-a-mì-im* (14) *i-ga-mu-ru-ma* (15) *i-pá-ni-a* (16) *a-ba-kam.*

230 *k.* at 3.6, TC 3, 43 (to the merchant, from Šu-Kūbum and Iliya; transp. Ela)
350 *k.* at 3.5, TC 3, 36 (to Pūšu-kēn, from Kulumāya)

Quantities of 100 textiles or more often occur in combination with high tin prices and result from the fact that all or most of the money was invested in textiles:

a)   100 *k.* at 6.1, hand-tin at 14, KTS 2, 36+Bursa 3776 (Imdilum).
b)   114 *k.* at 4, 1 donkey-load of tin at 13 1/4, more tin at 13, hand-tin at 13, CCT 3, 27a// KTS 1, 38a (Enlil-bāni).
c)   117 *k.* + 1 heavy *abarnium* at 3.3, 1 donkey-load of tin at 14, [hand-tin at x], I 435:10 (Imdilum); gold 7 2/3.
d)   120 *k.* at 4.7, hand-tin at 14, Yale 13092 (Pūšu-kēn).
e)   149 *k.* at 5, hand-tin at 12 1/2, CCT 3, 22a (Pūšu-kēn); gold 7 1/3 and 8 2/3.
f)   175 *k.* at 5.8, hand-tin at 13, KTS 1, 23 (Pūšu-kēn).
g)   177 *k.* at 5.1, hand-tin at 13 1/2, I 704:7 (Pūšu-kēn).
h)   200 *k.* at 5.15, hand-tin at 14 1/2, VS 26, 13 (Imdilum).
i)   350 *k.* at 3.5, hand-tin at 14, TC 3, 36 (Pūšu-kēn); gold 7 1/3.

Note that at a tin price of 14 and 13 1/4 still one donkey-load of tin was purchased in c and b. At lower tin prices, large quantities of textiles were bought if there was sufficient money:

110 *k.*, 8t 40m tin at 16, CTMMA 1, 75 (Imdilum).
110 *k. ša qātim* + 8 fine textiles + 2 *kamsum*, on average 5.75, 2 donkey-loads of tin at 16, Pa. 15 (Pūšu-kēn); gold 6 5/6.
230 *k.* at 3.6, 1 donkey-load of tin at 15, hand-tin at 14; TC 3, 43; gold 8 1/4, 6 2/3.

The purchase prices for tin and textiles transported according to Kt c/k 866 are unknown. That letter from Alahum deals with a caravan of 21 donkeys carrying 10 talents of tin and a total of 401 textiles.

A small collection of the evidence on the average prices for the donkeys, their harness and their fodder shows that the quantity did not influence the price there either. The price of a donkey will have been influenced by the individual animal's characteristics. The prices for harnesses differ slightly, perhaps as a result of differences in required items.

Prices in shekels of silver of donkeys, harness, and fodder:

TC 2, 6:	1 donkey at 16; harness: 2; fodder: 3
LB 1230:	1 donkey at 16 1/2 ; harness: 2 1/3
Pa. 15:	1 donkey at 21 1/2; harness: 2 1/2 ; 6 donkeys at 20; harness: 2 1/6
I 836:	3 donkeys at 14 3/4; harness: 2 2/3
TC 2, 14:	4 donkeys at 18 1/2 ; harness: 3.16; fodder: 1 3/4

I 435:	5 donkeys at 16; harness: 3; fodder: 3 1/5
CCT 3, 22a:	5 donkeys at 19.2; harness: 3; fodder: 2
KTS 1, 23:	6 donkeys at 20; harness: 3 1/6
CTMMA 1, 75:	7 donkeys at 16.1; harness: 2.9; fodder: 2 1/2
I 704:	8 donkeys at 19 1/3; harness: 3; fodder: 1 1/4
TC 3, 43:	9 donkeys at 18.9; harness: 3 1/3

In conclusion, it does not appear to have been customary to pay less per item for larger quantities. It certainly did not occur with tin (see the appendix below), nor with donkeys (where differences in age and strength influenced the price), and the evidence for textiles is so unclear that the idea of a bulk discount can only be contemplated in cases where over 200 textiles were bought.

5.2 The sale of goods in Anatolia

The aim was to earn money by swiftly bringing the imported merchandise on to the market where it would be profitably sold, to obtain the proceeds of the sale within a reasonable period and to send them (via Kanesh) to Assur in order for new purchases to be made. Factors of importance were: information about the market situation; logistical support (people and means of transportation), and avoiding costs where possible, for example by the evasion of taxes through smuggling. Instructions often arrived by letter from Assur or from a town closer to where the goods were sold. Each day a person was forced to stay in a town not his own, he spent money on food and lodging.[59] Unless a trader urgently needed money, he would delay a sale that would yield less than hoped for by simply storing the merchandise until a better price was possible, by giving it on commission for a fixed term, or by sending it to another place. According to TC 2, 22, a merchant sent 2 1/2 minas of extra fine lapis lazuli and a cup of lapis. His instructions read: "If (you can get) 6 minas of silver or higher, sell the lapis, but if (you can get) half a mina of *pašallum* gold or higher, sell the cup. Should this opportunity not arise and you do not sell, then let the lapis and the cup wait until

---

[59] Kt c/k 591: (10) ... ᵈ*a-šur ù i-lu* (11) *e-ba-ru-tim li-ṭù-lá* (12) 40 u₄-*me-e a-šu-mì-šu i-na ha-qá* (13) *lu as-hu-ur* kb (14) 2 *gín ù* 3 *gín* (15) *lu ag-mu-ur*, "Aššur and the gods of the colleagues be witnesses! I truly remained because of him in Haqqa for 40 days. I truly spent 2 or 3 shekels of silver."

VS 26, 29 (to Aššur-nādā and Uṣur-ša-Aššur from Ilī-ālum): (15) *lá li-bi₄* dingir-*ma i-na ša-lá-tù-ar* (16) itu.8.kam (17) *uk-ta-ṣí-du-ni ù ša* (18) kb 20 *ma-na lu-qú-tum qá-dí-a-ma* (19) *kà-ṣú-ud*, "Unfortunately, they detained me in Šalatuar for 8 months; moreover, merchandise for a value of 20 minas of silver was detained with me."

Dalley, Edinburgh 10 (to Puzur-Aššur from Il-wēdāku): (3) *lá li-bi* dingir-*ma : ša-tám* (4) *iš-té-et : sú-ku-ur-tum* (5) *i-ší-ki-in-ma : qá-dí-ma* (6) dumu *a-šùr : šu-um-šu : ú né-nu* (7) *ni-tám-sà-ar*, "Unfortunately, a blockade was imposed for one year and we have been obstructed together with some other Assyrian."

Donbaz, Sadberk 10: (15) ... *a-šu-mì* (16) kb *a-ni-im iš-tù* 4 *ša-na-tim* (17) *kà!-ṣú-da-ku ú bu-lá-tí-a* (18) *i-na a-kà-li-im ag-ta-ma-ar*, "Because of this silver I have been detained for 4 years! And I spent my working-capital by eating."

I arrive." Storing tin when prices were too low is mentioned in Pa. 22 (see above). Another reference to this practice is contained in BIN 6, 127: "*Inquire about* the tin. If there is a rate of 6 1/2 or 5 to refined silver, now, sell it. Send Nunua here. If it is not like that, let it be stored until spring."[60]

Caravans from Assur had to be cleared by the palace of Kanesh before the goods could be sold. This clearance – stressing the great importance of the state of Kanesh in Central Anatolia – involved the levying of the *nishatum*-tax on textiles and tin and the possibility that the palace wanted to exercise its right of pre-emption (*ša šīmim*) on as much as 10% of the textiles. These levies, to which the city-state of Assur had committed itself by treaty, frequently were avoided by bringing the merchandise illicitly into Anatolia. It was not brought through Kanesh, but through a side track to the east leading to Durhumit. Use of this smuggling route, the *harrān sukinnim*, was punishable by imprisonment and fines. Many merchants tried their luck and sent part of the goods via the smuggling route to save some money. Pūšu-kēn did so as well and was once caught and sent to prison in Kanesh.[61] Smuggling is implied in Kt 91/k 416: "If the rate is 8 shekels each to silver, sell the tin and send me your report. If there is no rate of 8 shekels each to silver, (...) they must not bring the tin beyond Šalahšua (to Kanesh). To save my tin, they must bring the tin beyond Timelkia to Durhumit."[62] According to this text, paying taxes in Kanesh makes the sale of tin unprofitable if the rate is higher than 8, and the smuggling route to Durhumit is preferred instead.

The merchandise could be sold for cash (*ana itaṭlim*) or on credit to an agent (*tamkāram qiāpum, ina ṣēr tamkārim nadāʾum, ana tamkārim waššurum*). All these possibilities are mentioned in CCT 2, 34, a letter sent from Assur by Šu-Kūbum to Pūšu-kēn and Innāya: "You are my brothers! Each take half of the tin and textiles and deposit the equivalent in silver out of your own money when you can do me a favour, and let the silver come here with Innāya. I must not get angry. If you cannot take the tin and textiles and cannot do me a favour, then give it either for cash or for a long-term or for a short-term commission, and do what is best for me. Send me your report."[63] Cash sales often include the remark *batiq u wattur* "expensive or cheap", that

---

[60] BIN 6, 127 (Šu-Anum to Eddināya, Nūr-Ištar, and Nunua): (13) *wa-ar-kà-at* an.na (14) [x x] x *šu-ma* 6 1/2 gín.ta (15) [*ú*] 5 gín.ta (16) *a-*[kb] *ṣa-ru-pí-im* (17) *a-˹ni˺-ma i-ba-ší* (18) *dí-na-ma nu-nu-a* (19) *ṭur₄-da-˹nim˺ šu-˹ma˺* (20) *lá ki-a-am* (21) *a-dí d*[a]*-˹áš˺-e li-ni-dí.*

[61] According to ATHE 62 the candour with which merchants discussed smuggling in their correspondence is comparable to that of those involved in the Dutch trade during the mid-18th century AD in New York, for which see Truxes 2001, 88–92.

[62] Kt 91/k 416 (courtesy K. R. Veenhof): (9) *šu-ma* 8 gín.ta (10) *a-na* kb an.na (11) *dí-na ù té-er-ták-nu* (12) *li-li-kam* (13) *šu-ma* 8 gín.ta (14) *a-na* kb *lá-šu* ... (16) an.na *a-na e-ba-ar* (17) *ša-lá-ah-šu-wa* (18) *lá ú-šé-tù-qú* (19) *ki-ma ša-la-am* an.na-*ki* (20) *e-ba-ar tí-me-el-ki-a-ma* (21) an.na *a-na dur₄-hu-mì-it* (22) *lu-šé-tí-qú.*

[63] CCT 2, 34: (11) *a-hu-a a-tù-nu* an.na (12) *ù* túg.hi.a *mì-iš-lá le-qé-a-ma* (13) kb *me-eh-ra-tim i-ra-mì-ni-ku-nu* (14) *ki-ma ta-ga-mì-la-ni-ni* (15) *id-a-ma* kb (16) *i-šé-ep i-na-a li-li-kam* (17) *li-bi₄ lá i-la-mì-in* (18) *šu-ma* an.na *ù* túg.hi.a (19) *lá ta-lá-qé-a-ma lá ta-ga-mì-lá-ni* (20) *lu a-na i-ta-aṭ-lim* (21) *lu a-na u₄-me pá-tí-ú-tim* (22) *lu a-na u₄-me qúr-bu-tim* (23) *dí-na-ma a-li ba-lá-ṭí-a* (24) *ep-ša ù té-er-ta-ku-nu* (25) *li-li-kam.*

is, at any reasonable price. To exclude any risk, owners often add that first the silver must arrive and only then can the merchandise be handed over.[64] However, it was not unusual for customers (mainly Anatolian dignitaries) to pay only after some time.[65] Large quantities of textiles could be ordered for a special occasion. An order for 130 textiles for a wedding by an *alahinnum* was annulled according to BIN 4, 45:32ff.

The sale price for tin ranges from 10 to 4 shekels of tin per shekel of silver. 9 1/2 is a poor price according to I 430. The 'normal' price fluctuates between 9 and 6. A shortage of silver would exclude cash sales and instead a term of 4 weeks is granted for 7 1/2 according to TC 3, 49. Sales on a fixed term commission could be for short (*ana ūmē qurbūtim*) or long (*ana ūmē patiūtim*) terms; short-term appears to be 2 months or less. A detailed study of the terms is still lacking. Veenhof has provided a diagram showing the frequency of terms expressed in *hamuštum* "week", with most of the terms between 1 and 20 weeks.[66] Most of the agents seem to have been independent, and were not always available or willing to accept the terms. This appears from CCT 6, 35a: "I buttonholed a few agents for tin at 9 shekels each and *kutānus* at 15 shekels a piece for a fixed commission of 40 weeks, but there is none (willing/available). I will give on commission should an agent come my way".[67] Another example comes from Medelhavsmuseet 1977/12: "According to your instruction I am offering Ikuppiya and Ahu-waqar each 1 talent of tin and 10 *kutānus* (to sell on commission), but they refuse."[68]

The largest collection of data on prices involving a single merchant concerns Šalim-ahum. The tin prices he or his representatives in Anatolia charged range from 10 to 6:

10	BIN 4, 27 (25 weeks)
9 'or higher'	Pa. 19:7 (short-term)
8	BIN 4, 61 (interest bearing loan); I 426 (short-term)
7	AKT 3, 65:32ff.; BIN 4, 61:27 (50 and 45 weeks),35 (48 weeks); I 426:13 (long-term),39 (long-term); RA 59, 26:11

---

[64] KTS 1, 20: (12′) ... *a-na i-ta-aṭ-lim* (13′) *li-dí-nu lá ú-šu-ru lá i-qí-pu* (14′) *a-dí* kb *e-ru-bu* an.na (15′) *ù* túg.hi.a *lá ú-šu-ru* kb (16′) *le-ru-ub-ma* an.na *ù* túg.hi.a (17′) *lu-ṣú*, "Let them sell for cash. They must not release, nor entrust (merchandise) in commission. Until the silver arrives, they must not release the tin and textiles. Let the silver enter first, and then the tin and textiles may leave".

[65] CCT 2, 15 (to Puzur-Aššur from Il-wēdāku): "When the *alahinnum* ordered (goods) from me, they said: 'We will get 1 talent of silver for you within a month.'" ICK 1, 13 (Innaya no. 159) mentions a debt of 12 1/2 minas of silver and 100 *naruq* barley owed by Happuala, the shepherd of the queen, since 4 years interest accrues according to the rate of Kanesh.

[66] Veenhof 1997a, 21. In mid-18th century AD England and New York, a credit of one year to merchants and shopkeepers was customary for wholesale products. But for tea, for example, cash payment or a term of three months was used, see Truxes 2001, 81.

[67] CCT 6, 35a (to Šalim-ahum from Pūšu-kēn): (7′) ... dam.gàr *iš-tí-in* (8′) *ù ší-na* 9 gín.ta (9′) an.na 15 gín.ta *ku-ta-ni* (10′) *a-na* 40 *ha-am-ša-tim* (11′) *ag-ri-ma la-šu šu-ma* (12′) dam.gàr *i-ta-áš-ra-am* (13′) *a-qí-áp*.

[68] Veenhof 1984, Medelhavsmuseet 1977/12 (to Imdilum from Puzur-Ištar): (14) ... 1 gú.ta an.na (15) *ù* 10.ta *ku-ta-ni a-ma-lá* (16) *té-er-tí-kà a-na i-ku-pí-a* (17) *ù a-hu-wa-qar* (18) *ú-kà-al-ma : lá-qá-a-am* (19) *ú-lá i-mu-ú*.

6   AKT 3, 78:15 (claim on employee); TC 1, 26:29 (*lā tabattaqam*); TC 2, 3:12.18
             (*ulā ibattaq*)

The information from texts I 426 (a–c) and BIN 4, 61 (d–f) in context is as follows:

short-term (*ana ūmē qurbūtim*):
a) 50 *kutānu* at 20g, 5t 4m 40g tin at 8

long-term (*ana ūmē patiūtim*):
b) 20 *kutānu* at 30g, 4 *šuru* at 15g, 2t 2m 8g tin at 7
c) 26 *kutānu* at 30g, 2t 4m 39g tin at 7, 1 donkey at 30g
d) 20 *kutānu* at 30g, 10 *šuru* at 15g, 2t 59m tin at 7; 28m kb due within 50 weeks, the rest
in 45 weeks
e) 20 *kutānu* at 30g, 4 *šuru* at 15g, 2t 14m 10g tin at 7; due within 48 weeks

The remaining merchandise in BIN 4, 61 is given as a loan against 30% interest
(p.a.) to Ilī-ašranni, the transporter, at the same prices as a short-term commission:

(f) 17 *k.* at 20g, 1 *šurum* at 10g, 39m 50g tin at 8

It appears from this evidence that Šalim-ahum (or his partners in Anatolia) charged
a higher price for long-term commissions than for short-term ones. The discount
compared to prices for long-term commissions offered to Ilī-ašranni in (f) was profitable
for that person if he paid within one year. Otherwise the total amount of monthly
interest would have undone the advantage of the reduced prices.
     Although it is likely that long-term commissions always yielded more than short-
term ones, the evidence does not present a clear picture. The prices for tin can be
arranged by the duration of the term.

4 weeks:	7 1/2	TC 3, 49
15 weeks:	6	Kt 91/k 520
5 months:	8	AKT 3, 95
25 weeks:	10	BIN 4, 27
40 weeks:	9	CCT 6, 35a (refused)
45 & 50 weeks:	7	BIN 4, 61
48 weeks:	7	BIN 4, 61
15 months:	6	TC 2, 72

The sale prices for textiles (in shekels of silver) are:

4 weeks	30	20 *k.*, BIN 4, 4:6
short-term	20	50 *k.*, I 426
> 3 months	9	50 túg, Kt c/k 449:29

20 weeks	15	50 *k.*, CTMMA 1, 72:5
30 weeks	12	220 túg, Kt c/k 346:10
long-term	30	20 *k.* and 26 *k.*, I 426
50 & 45 weeks	30	20 *k.*, BIN 4, 61 (50 and 45 weeks; 48 weeks)

The possibility to sell the tin at a discount under the current market rate is mentioned in several letters. Twice a specific formula is used, *ina/*(accusative) price *etāqum-ma tadānum*, "to sell beyond the price." The king of Assur wants a quick sale and writes in AKT 2, 22: (14) an.na 1/2 gín *zi-šu* (15) *ki-ma i-za-zu* (16) *et-qá-ma dí-na*, "Go beyond the current price of tin by half a shekel ... and sell (it)". Such a discount is prohibited by Šalim-ahum according to MDOG 102, 86: (23) *i-na* an.na 1 gín.ta (24) *e e-tí-qú-ma e i-dí-nu*, "They must not sell the tin 1 shekel below the (market) rate." An alternative expression is the use of a form of the verb *batāqum* "to cut off" (Veenhof 1988, 253 n. 33).

Frequently the credit contract contained the stipulation that a defaulting agent had to add interest. For that reason, the month and year (often also the week-eponyms) during which the contract was drawn up are mentioned in the bond. When the reliability of the agent was doubtful, the creditor could demand a pledge and/or a guarantor. Bad experiences aroused a general concern about employing reliable agents. Some merchants employ the expression "do not attach too much value to 1 or 2 months" in this context. This expression and its cognate were last discussed extensively by Veenhof (1972, 407–409 *be'ālum* G/N; 443–445 *šēqurum*). His conclusion was that it refers to giving "a few months more credit, in order to guarantee a transaction free of risk" (Veenhof 1972, 445). It would mean that an agent would be commissioned for a term that was a few months longer than what one of his colleagues would agree to, probably at a higher price; or, that the representative had to wait a few months before beginning to charge default interest. This contrasts with comparative evidence for a strategy to limit the risk of bad debts by reducing the length of the term as much as possible.[69] That would be the case if the Assyrian expressions meant that the merchandise could be kept in store for one or two months until a trustworthy agent could be found. However, according to BIN 4, 25, Šalim-ahum expressly rules out such a possibility: "My tin and textiles should not be stored (*lā innaddi*). Give them on a fixed term to an agent who is like you. Your agent must be reliable! Do not attach too great value to one or two months. And let your report come here." This (later) wisdom was not shared by Šalim-ahum, Aššur-idī, and other Assyrians who employed these expressions in their letters.

Goods could be commissioned throughout the year, provided that seasonal weather did not make it impossible for donkeys to reach Kanesh and other markets or for agents to travel. Winter time was often problematic.

---

[69] "It is our Interest to sell for the shortest Credit possible, because the shorter the payments the less risque of bad debts," from a letter written in 1755 quoted in Truxes 2001, 81 n. 148.

6. PROFITABILITY AND LOSSES

Before turning to the actual costs and yields, it is important to note that as a general rule the OA merchants considered a net profit of 50% to be possible. This enabled debtors to repay their debt by trading with the money put at their disposal. A successful business trip (*harrānum*) comprised sending money to Assur, buying goods there, sending them to Kanesh and selling them in Anatolia. Two such trips were possible in a single year. Three examples can be given to illustrate a 50% proft.

AKT 3, 13:

"E. has 30 minas of refined silver on A. as a claim. From the week of Ilī-nādā he will pay within 22 weeks. If he does not pay, he will add 1 1/2 shekels per mina per month as interest. Month of *Kuzallū*, eponymy of Aššur-imittī, the sailor (L105/xi). For this silver, A. will make available 20 minas of silver, its import tax added, and he will go to the city (of Assur) and E. will buy merchandise in the city. The merchandise will go from the city to Kanesh and it belongs to E. The merchandise will cross the land in both directions in the name of A. His fixed term had elapsed and I added a term of equal length."[70]

KTHahn 24 (= EL 109):

"As for the 15 minas of refined silver, its import tax added and satisfied with his transport fee, which Š. had D. bring to the city, to P., E. and I., to make purchases, (the) silver from here and the merchandise from there will cross the land in the name of "the merchant". The merchandise will go from the city (to Kanesh), and if D. wants to, he will take the merchandise and pay 22 1/2 minas of silver."[71]

KUG 11 (= EL 216):

"Concerning the 30 minas of silver which E. son of A. had given to I., and for

---

[70] AKT 3, 13: (5) 30 *ma-na* kb *ṣa-ru-pá-am* (6) *i-ṣé-er a-šùr-i-dí en-um-a-šur* (7) *i-šu iš-tù ha-muš-tim ša* (8) *dingir-na-da a-na* 22 *ha-am-ša-tim* (9) *i-ša-qal šu-ma la iš-qúl* (10) 1 1/2 *gín.ta a-ma-na-im* (11) *i-itu.kam ší-ib-tám ú-ṣa-áb* (12) *itu.kam ku-zal-li : li-mu-um* (13) *a-šùr-i-mì-tí ma-lá-hu-um* (14) *a-na* kb *a-nim* 20 *ma-na* (15) kb *ni-is-ha-sú diri* (16) *a-šùr-i-dí i-ša-kán-ma* (17) *a-na a-lim*[ki] *i-lá-ak-ma* (18) [*ší-mu*]-*um i-na a-lim*[ki] (19) *en-um-a-šùr i-ša-a-am* (20) [*lu-q*]*ú-tum iš-tù a-lim*[ki] (21) [*a-kà*]-*ni-iš e-li-a-ma lu-qú-tum* (22) [*ša*] *en-um-a-šùr-ma* (23) [*lu-qú-t*]*um : gána-lam₅ a-na-num ù* (24) *a-lá-num a-šu-mì a-šùr-i-dí-ma* (25) *e-tí-iq u₄-mu-šu : im-lu-ú-ma ú* (26) *u₄-me-e ma-lá u₄-me-ma ú-ra-dí.*

[71] (1) 15 *ma-na* kb *ṣa-ru-pá-am* (2) *ni-is-ha-sú diri* (3) *ša-du-a-sú ša-bu* (4) *ša* ᵈ*utu-ba-ni a-na a-lim*[ki] (5) *a-na ṣé-er pí-lá-ha-a* (6) *en-na-nim ù dingir-ba-ni* (7) *da-da-a-a a-na ší-a-ma-tim* (8) *ú-šé-bi-lu* kb (9) *a-na-nu-um lu-qú-tum* (10) *a-lá-nu-um gána-lam₅* (11) *a-na šu-mì dam.gàr* (12) *e-tí-iq lu-qú-tum* (13) *iš-tù a-lim*[ki] (14) *e-li-a-ma šu-ma* (15) *li-bi-šu lu-qú-tám* (16) *i-lá-qé-ma* 22 1/2 *ma-na* (17) kb *da-da-a i-ša-qal.*

which he would travel twice to the city with the silver and pay 1 talent of silver..."[72]

According to I 438 even a 100% profit could be made in a single business trip as part of a special arrangement.

The merchandise was taxed by Assyrian and other authorities. Before leaving Assur an export-tax (*waṣītum*) of 1/120 was levied over the value of merchandise plus donkeys. Notwithstanding the fact that usually an amount is set aside for this tax, some merchants owed large debts of unpaid export-tax to the city's tax-office, the City Hall. Between Assur and Kanesh a *dātum* was levied over the tin, textiles and donkeys. It was levied as an amount per talent of "tin value", to which end the value of the merchandise was expressed in a single valuta, the *awītum* or declared value (Dercksen 2004, 151ff.). For the goods sent to Anatolia this valuta was tin and a textile had a value of 2 minas and a donkey was valued at 1 1/3 to 2 minas of tin. The *dātum* was paid in tin and for that purpose hand-tin was bought in Assur at approximately 5 minas per talent of "tin value". Since the actual expense was often higher, the amount of hand-tin was systematically insufficient.

(a) Amount of hand-tin as a percentage of the *awītum* (tin/textiles and donkeys; hand-tin excluded; italics indicate 1 donkey-load of tin)

5.81%	*TC 2, 6*
6.52%	BIN 6, 65
6.58%	*CCT 2, 2*
6.58%	*CTMMA 1, 75 (sec. car.)//Sadberk no. 13*
6.67%	Kt 92/k 142
6.67%	VS 26, 151
6.81%	CTMMA 1, 75 (first car.)
6.98%	*CCT 2, 2 (sec.)*
7.14%	CCT 4, 17b
7.14%	*RA 59 no. 27*
7.21%	Kt 91/k 484
7.28%	Kt 91/k 419
7.67%	CCT 4, 7a
7.73%	CCT 3, 22a
7.81%	Pa. 15
7.86%	Yale 13092
8%	*CCT 3, 5a*

---

[72] (1) 30 *ma-na* kb *ša* (2) *en-um-a-šur* dumu *a-ni-nim* (3) *a-na il₅-we-da-ku* (4) *i-dí-nu-ma* kb *a-na a-lim*[ki] (5) *ší-ni-šu : i-lu-ku-ma* (6) 1 gú kb *i-ša-qú-lu-ma*. After two business trips the expected profit was 100% of the capital sum. This particular arrangement did not work, and the rest of the document tells us that this case was closed by the payment of only 25 minas of silver.

8.09%	TC 3, 43
8.12%	Kt 92/k 143
8.15%	TC 2, 14
8.29%	KTS 1, 23
8.33%	TC 1, 47
8.82%	CCT 3, 2a
8.92%	CCT 3, 27a
8.93%	TC 3, 36
9.10%	BIN 6, 12
9.26%	I 704
9.52%	Kt c/k 227
9.62%	I 836
9.62%	VS 26, 13
10.71%	BIN 4, 30
13.83%	KTS 2, 10

The actual expenses per talent of *awītum* as established at the end of the journey vary:
4m 6 1/4 g per talent, Kt 91/k 483 (= 6.83%)
4m 20 1/4 g per talent, AKT 3, 75 (= 7.22%)
5m 5g per talent, AKT 3, 76 (= 8.5%)
5m 45g per talent, BIN 4, 29 (= 9.58%)
7m 33g per talent, LB 1250 (= 12.5%)

The clearance by the palace of Kanesh consisted of levying a *nishātum* of about 3% on the tin and of 5% on textiles, with the possibility of pre-empting up to 10% at a discount. Consignments sent between towns in Anatolia were taxed by the Assyrian authorities with the *šaddu'atum* of Karum Kanesh, unless the owner was a fee-paying registered merchant (*šāqil dātim*). In addition, local rulers levied tolls. For the return caravans, the valuta was silver and every shekel of gold was valued at 8 shekels of silver. In Kanesh, an import duty (*nishātum*) of one-twentyfourth and a transport tariff of one-sixtieth (*šaddu'atum*) of the declared value (making 7/120 or 5.83% altogether) were added to a consignment of money. On top of all these regular taxes, caravans had expenses for food and fodder, lodgings, repairs, replacement for animals or personnel, and special transportation costs across the mountains (*taššiātum*).

To calculate the profit on one donkey-load of tin we may start from the purchase of such a load made for Pūšu-kēn according to RA 59, no. 27.

> Bought in Assur: 2 talents 10 minas of tin and 10 minas of hand-tin, at 14g 15 še, in all 10 minas 39 1/3 shekels; 4 *kutānu*: 28 shekels; 1 donkey: 20 shekels; harness 1 1/2 shekels; export-tax: 5 shekels 135 grains. Total costs: 11 minas 34 shekels of silver. (The *dātum* is paid for with the hand-tin. The *nishātum* in

Kanesh is 6 minas of tin. The sale of the donkey in Kanesh covers other expenses.) Available for sale: 2 talents of tin. The *nishātum* and *šaddu'atum* (6%) are deducted from the yield. The letter Pa. 22, quoted above, had Imdilum insisting on a price of 6 because tin in Assur was scarce (here it is estimated at about 14).

Selling at 7: yield minus 6% = 16 minas 6 shekels; profit 4 minas 32 shekels = 39.1%.

Selling at 6 1/2: yield minus 6% = 17 minas 21 1/4 shekels; profit 5 minas 47 1/4 shekels = 47.8%.

Selling at 6: yield minus 6% = 18 minas 48 shekels; profit 7 minas 14 shekels = 63%.

In this case (with expensive tin in Assur) a profit of 50% can only be made if the tin is sold at less than 6 1/2. If the tin had been bought in Assur at a cheaper rate of 15 and sold in Kanesh at 7, the profit would be 57%. If it had been sold at 8, the profit would only be 38%. Not surprisingly then, a 50% profit depended on margin.[73] Moreover, it becomes understandable why a tin rate of 15 in Assur was used as a critical limit. The profit margin is related to the high transaction costs. In this calculation, only the direct costs have been taken into account as these are more or less known. To function as a firm in Anatolia also involved buying a house in Kanesh and perhaps elsewhere, costs of living, of traveling, of membership of the Karum organization (including the payment of an annual mandatory fee (*dātum*) of 12 minas of silver or more). Extra expenses related to reclaiming debts from defaulters and writing off losses from bad debts, theft, and the high interest rates (customary 30% p.a.). Good relations with bankers and others in Assur involved sending regular gifts of silver.

Impressive as the profit margins are, set-backs occurred. As one person wrote, "who does not experience losses?"[74] A merchant who for some reason had suffered financial losses had to beg for support from relatives and wealthy merchants, who would be concerned to prevent one of their group from going bankrupt.[75] Helpful support consisted of lending money with which to continue to conduct trade.[76]

---

[73] Larsen 1967, 43 and Veenhof 1988, 249 arrived at similar conclusions on the basis of purchase and sale prices.

[74] LB 1209a: (5) ... *ma-nu-um i-bi$_4$-[sà-e]* (6) *lá e-mar.*

[75] Several of the well-known merchants experienced financial difficulties, such as Pūšu-kēn (Dercksen 1999, 85f.) and Innāya. For the latter, cf. I 547 (Innāya to Uṣur-ša-Aššur, Ikuppiya and Tarām-Kūbi): (7′) *x-lá-tí-a ú i-bi$_4$-sà-e-a* (8′) *tí-de$_8$-a a-na ú-um ga-ma-lim* (9′) *ù e-ṭá-ri-im*, "You know of my ... and my losses – for the day of doing a favour and rescuing". TC 1, 54 (Innāya to Šu-Suen and Ikuppiya): (9) *i-bi-sá-e lá tí-de$_8$-a* (10) *ù u$_4$-ma-am : i-bi$_4$-sà-e* (11) *ma-du-tim a-ta-mar*, "Do you not know about my losses? Today I have suffered severe losses." Cf. also Ka 423 (Donbaz and Veenhof 1985, 152; to Enna-[...], Puzur-Aššur): (8) *a-ṣé-er i-bi-sà-e pá-ni-ú-ti[m]* (9) *ša ta-áš-k[u-n]i : u$_4$-ma-am 3-ší-š[u]* (10) *i-bi-sà-ú-a lu šu-té-ṣú-bu-ni* (11) *ù iš-tù : i-na é.gal-lim wa-áš-ba-ni-ni* (12) *kb : ma-dum : lu gám-ru-ú*, "In addition to the previous losses which she ..., today, my losses have tripled! Moreover, much silver has been spent since we were staying at the palace."

[76] I 517 (address broken off): (1′) [x x x x x k]b (2′) [*i-bi-sà-e a-t*]*a-mar* (3′) *ù kb ša i-ba-ší-ú* (4′) *a-na hu-ša-hi-a a-ga-mar-ma* (5′) *mì-ma lá i-ri-ha-am* (6′) *e-ri-ú-um a-na-ku* (7′) *ú-ša-áb ú-lá e-ri-um* (8′)

7. GOLD

Gold has a special position among the objects of trade.[77] It was a highly prized material and one letter contains the somewhat deprecatory remark "When they see gold, (their) hands and feet tremble" referring to unspecified "men" (*awīlū*).[78] It was made into jewellery and formed the valuta of the *naruqqum*-joint-stock investments in a way that is still imperfectly understood. But most importantly, gold was most fitting as an offering for the gods. The commonest reference to votive offerings (*ikribum*) concerns golden sun-symbols (*šamšum*).[79] The strong value attached to gold by the city of Assur is apparent in the law that prohibited the sale of gold to non-Assyrians which is alluded to in an official letter:

"Thus (said) the ruler, speak to the Kanesh colony: The tablet containing the verdict of the City concerning gold which we sent to you, that tablet has been cancelled. We did not draw up any (new) rule about gold. The rule concerning gold is the same as previously: one may sell it to another, (but) in accordance with the wording on the stele: no Assyrian whatever shall give gold to an Akkadian, an Amorite, or a Shubarean. Whoever does so shall not remain alive."[80]

This policy can be explained from the motive of trade: the city needed the gold to pay for the imported tin and as part of the financing of *naruqqus*. Hoarding could also have been a motive, and the obvious benefactors in the OA context would be the temples

---

a-na-ku : a-mì-ša-am ú-ṣí-a-am (9′) *be-lí a-ta šu-ma li-ba-kà* (10′) *lá a-ha-liq* kb lu 2 *ma-na* (11′) *lu* 3 *ma-na šé-bi₄-lá-ma* (12′) *ša-tám iš-té-et li-be-el-kà* (13′) [t]úg.hi.a *ù* an.na : *i-na* (14′) [*be*]-*tí-kà-ma lá-áš-a-ma* (15′) [*ša k*]*i-ma ku-a-tí qá-sú-nu* (16′) [*l*]*i-iš-ku-nu-ma lu-šé-bi₄-lá-ma* (17′) [kb] 1 *ma-na le-li-a-ma* (18′) [*x x x x x*] *iš-tí a-hi-im* (19′) [*ú eb-ri-im*] kb 1 *ma-na* (20′) [*ù* 2 *m*]*a-na er-ša-ma* (21′) [*x x x x e*]*ṭ-ra-ni*, "[...] I have suffered losses of [x] silver. And I am spending the silver that is still there for my daily needs, so that nothing will remain for me. I am living as a destitute man, but I do not want to go there as a destitute man. You are my lord! If you please, let me not perish. Send me silver, either 2 or 3 minas, and let it be used away from you for one year. Let me buy textiles and tin in your own house, let your representatives state your claim on it and then I will send (the goods) so that 1 mina of silver will come up for me. [...] Ask brother and friend for 1 or 2 minas of silver for me and save me!"

77   On this topic, see Dercksen 2004, 81–3; 2005, 25–7; Veenhof 2008a, 88–9.

78   BIN 4, 99 (to Hanunu and Saha from Puzur-Aššur): (13) kù.ki *e-mu-ru-ma* (14) *qá-ta-an : ú šé-pá-an* (15) *i-ra-hu-ba.*

79   The manufacture of a sun-disc at the *kārum* office (presumably in Kanesh) is mentioned in ICK 1, 139:6. A š. of 1 mina of gold occurs in Pa. 10:13.

80   Kt 79/k 101 (Sever 1990, 262): (1) *um-ma wa-ak-lúm-ma* (2) *a-na kà-ri-im* (3) *kà-ni-iš*ki (4) *qí-bi-ma ṭup-pá-am* (5) *ša dì-in a-lim*ki (6) *ša a-šu-mì* kù.gi (7) *ša ni-iš-pu-ra-ku-nu-tí-ni* (8) *ṭup-pu-um šu-ut : a-ku-uš* (9) *a-šu-mì* kù.gi *i-ṣú-ur-tám* (10) *ù-la né-ṣú-ur* (11) *a-wa-tum ša* kù.gi (12) *pá-ni-a-tum-ma* (13) *a-hu-um a-na a-hi-im* (14) *a-na ší-mì-im* (15) *i-da-an* (16) *ki-ma : a-wa-at* (17) *na-ru-a-im* (18) dumu *a-šùr šu-um-šu* (19) kù.gi *a-na a-ki-dí-im* (20) *a-mu-ri-im* (21) *ù šu-bi-ri-im* (22) *ma-ma-an* (23) *la i-da-an* (24) *ša i-du-nu* (25) *ú-lá i-ba-lá-aṭ.* See the analyses in Veenhof 1995, 1733–1735 and 2003b, 95.

in the city-state. This appears to be confirmed by the following lines from Kt c/k 446: "The colony (of Kanesh) has taken an oath (by the emblem of Aššur) because of the gold of Adad: the colony will inspect anybody who has gold in his possession or wants to bring it under seal to the city."[81] As a result of this measure, the writers of the letter have sold the gold they had at a good rate (9.4), and they have sent the proceeds in silver to Assur. Apparently the investigation by the colony would also affect their gold. The search by the Assyrian authorities in Kanesh is therefore a general one, aimed at all merchants, and does not appear to be directed at one particular person or family heavily indebted to Adad. Such a divine claim on one person is known from a small dossier of texts dealing with Sabasia's debt, which was most recently discussed by D. Schwemer.[82] The origin of the debt is not mentioned in the extant material. Like a reference to gold owed to Adad in Kt a/k 447,[83] a debt may be incurred in consequence of a pledge made to Adad.

Since the measure announced in Kt c/k 446 seems to have had consequences for all the gold in the hands of Assyrian merchants present in Kanesh at that time, and in the absence of any temple of Adad in Anatolia which might have been plundered, the search by the colony can at present best be explained as being motivated by an extraordinary, or perhaps even a regular, taxation of gold. If it is assumed that the gold was destined for the temple of Adad in Assur we have a parallel to the taxation of the colonies in Anatolia to co-finance the construction of new city walls with 10 minas of silver, as described in the letter from the *nībum* published as TC 1, 1.[84] Another possibility is that merchants were obliged to send a certain amount of gold to Assur, but this remains hypothetical.

Despite the obvious great symbolic value of gold, obtaining it was not the first objective of the traders. Gold only plays a modest role in the shipments sent back to Assur, and when it is included, it is first exchanged (presumably at the City Hall) for silver before being used as money to buy merchandise. The most desired quality of gold was *pašallum*, as in TC 1, 47, in which Aššur-idī writes: "Your gold was sold. You said: 'I shall send it to you as soon as possible.' No-one among you should send me any alluvial gold or any *kuburšinnu*-gold; if the *pašallu*-gold is of good quality, then send me some" (Larsen 2002, 58–9).

The archive of Alahum (Kt c/k) contains a number of documents in which gold is obtained. A quantity of 2 1/2 minas of *pašallum* gold was bought in Purušhattum for 53 talents 10 minas of copper at a rate of 58 minas of copper for 1 shekel of gold according to Kt c/k 759:4, thereby reducing the weight of goods to be shipped to

---

[81]   Kt c/k 446 (Itūr-il, Aššur-malik, Enna-Suen, Aššur-bēl-šadue to Šu-Ištar): (7) ... *a-šu-mì* (8) kù.gi *ša* ᵈim *kà-ru-um* (9) *ik-ri-ba-am iš-ku-un* (10) *ma-ma-an ša* kù.gi (11) *i-šu-ú lu a-na a-lim*ᵏⁱ (12) *kà-ni-ik ú-ba-lá-ma* (13) *kà-ru-um e-ma-ar.*

[82]   Schwemer 2001, 258–63.

[83]   Dercksen 1996, 105.

[84]   Dercksen 2004, 62–4.

Kanesh from 1595 kg (copper) to only 1 1/4 kg (the gold). Kt c/k 440 and 442 list claims by Aššur-ṭāb, and those mentioned in Kt c/k 442 total 1 mina 33 1/2 shekels of gold:

> 24 shekels due from E. and A., 12 shekels within 2 years, 12 shekels within 3 years from L96/x;
> 20 shekels due from P., to be paid within 2 years from L96/x;
> 12 shekels due from M., 6 shekels within 2 years, 6 shekels within 3 years from L96/x;
> 12 shekels due from E., 6 shekels within 2 years, 6 shekels within 3 years from L96/x;
> 12 shekels due from A., 6 shekels within 2 years, 6 shekels within 3 years from L96/x;
> 6 shekels due from E. and I., to be paid within 9 months from L94/ii.
> 5 shekels due from U., to be paid within 2 years from L96/x;
> 1 1/2 shekels (c/k 440 adds: to be paid within 1 year) from L96/x;
> 1 shekel due from I. and his brother, to be paid within 5 months, from L92/vi.

These claims must be regarded as payment for merchandise given in commission to agents. It is noteworthy that the larger sums are to be paid in two equal instalments and have a fixed term of 2 and 3 years.

The price of gold in silver in Anatolia ranged from 10 to 4 (from expensive to cheap), depending on its quality:

10	OrNS 50, 102 no. 3:11 (extra fine *pašallum*)
9.4	Kt c/k 446 (in Kanesh)
8 1/2 or 9	Kt c/k 48:37 (Kanesh, fine *ša dāmē*)
8 or 9	CCT 3, 47a (buy gold if 8 or 9, not if > 9)
8 1/4	Sadberk 12:40 (extra fine *pašallam* in Purushattum)
8 1/8	Kt n/k 1340 (Sever 1995, 136; silver in short supply)
8	AKT 2, 9:11; Kt c/k 54:11.20; Kt 91/k 550:20; Neṣr C1; WAG 48-1463 (*ša abnišu*)
8 and 6	RA 58 Goudchaux 1
7 2/3	TPAK 1, 8:17
7 1/2	TC 3, 40:6
7 1/4	I 649:14′
6 1/2	CCT 5, 37a:24; TPAK 1, 200:4; Kt c/k 462:7
6	CCT 2, 39; Kt c/k 172+:16; Kt c/k 257:22; TPAK 1, 21a:9; TPAK 1, 203:24; WAG 48-1463 (*ša tiamtim*)
5 1/2	AKT 2, 27 (*kuburšinnum* and *ša abnīšu*)
5 or 4	TC 2, 2:28–29

As mentioned above, consignments of gold that were sent from Kanesh to Assur were sold for silver after arriving in Assur. The exchange rates that were used in Assur are comparable to those in Anatolia. They are:

8 5/6	BIN 6, 65:7
8 2/3 (fine) and 7 1/3	CCT 3, 22a
8 1/2 and 7 5/6	BIN 4, 30:6–7
8 1/2 and 8 1/3	CCT 6, 30b:8.10
8 1/4 for 1 1/2 minas of gold; 1/2 mina of *kuburšinnum* at 6 2/3, TC 3, 43:6	
7 2/3	I 435:6; Kt 91/k 524:8
7 1/3	TC 3, 36:4
5 1/4	Kt 91/k 484:13

These prices suggest that there was no great difference between the price of gold in Anatolia and in Assur. This is corroborated by a unique piece of evidence of pleading with the specialists determining the value of gold in Assur. In OrNS 50 no. 3 the owner writes from Kanesh that in his opinion the extra fine *pašallum* gold he is sending to repay a debt to a former Eponym ought to fetch a rate of 10 in silver. He also informs the addressees that he bought (?) the gold at the same rate and that the excise over this gold had been added.[85] Gold therefore only served to a small extent as merchandise, and more often as currency, just like silver. It is not known whether merchants were obliged to send a certain amount of gold to Assur.

The ratios of gold to silver in the *naruqqum*-system, where usually no actual gold was invested or paid out, are 4 at the time of contributing a share, and 8 when the inlays become available at the end of the term. The inlay is therefore obtained at half the price of what appears to be customary in Assur, and the 100% increase is realized by the expected growth of the *naruqqum*-holder's assets. In contrast with the 50% increase during one successful business trip, discussed above, the number of such trips does not play any role in the *naruqqum*-system, since the shareholders already received their part in the profits.

Mathematical exercise tablets found in Assur contain a rate of 5 1/2 for *zakium* gold (Ass 13058e) and 3 1/2 for 'red' gold (Ass 13058f). Veenhof (2008a, 37 n. 95) commented on these rates, which are low for OA standards, and suggested they were similar to Old Babylonian evidence, "which may indicate that the tablets are 'Late(r) Old Assyrian'".

Two (perhaps related) texts from the archive of Pūšu-kēn contain an oddity in that gold is used there for the purchase of grain in Assur. TC 3, 35 contains a reference that he sent 10 shekels of gold to Assur to enable his relatives there to store grain (*ana uṭṭatim šapākim*). According to BIN 6, 118, Pūšu-kēn's daughter Ahaha took 1 mina of silver and 6 shekels of gold to buy barley.

---

[85] For this text see Dercksen 2004, 38.

8. DEBTS AND THE CHARGING OF INTEREST

The seemingly ambigious attitude of the merchants towards outstanding claims is striking. On the one hand, interest was charged from defaulting debtors and at times for the whole duration of the loan. In other cases, it often appeared extremely difficult for the creditor to collect the money and some loans lasted a staggering length of time, even when interest had to be added. The creditor's inability to collect a debt could have different reasons, such as loyalty or shame that prevented him from starting legal proceedings.

A good overview of how overdue debts could become is provided by the so-called *Sammelmemoranda*, referred to in Akkadian as a *ṭuppum* (or *tahsistum*) *ša ba'abātim* "tablet (or memorandum) of outstanding debts" or a *meher ṭuppē harrumūtim* "a copy of the bonds in envelope". The siglum L + number again refers to the eponymy-year according to Veenhof 2003a. These tablets were used as an authority to collect money when the original bonds were kept in a different place. For example, AKT 4, 25 contains the text of debts dated to L102/iv (due within 20 weeks), L114/iii, L117/ix, and L128/vi (mentioned first). AKT 4, 26 contains debts dated to L69/vii (due within 10 months), L96/x, L97/x (due in 1 year), L101/viii (due within 20 weeks), L105/ix (due within 20 weeks), L105/vii (due within 10 weeks), L105/vii, and L110/i (mentioned first). The oldest debt in AKT 4, 25 (of 1 mina of silver) is therefore at least 25 years overdue, the one in AKT 4, 26 (of [x] shekels of silver) is at least 40 years overdue.

An important source is the memorandum Kt c/k 839 (Donbaz 1985; Veenhof 1985), in which Alahum figures as the creditor. There, the most recent debt is from L97, while the oldest debts stem from year L80, 17 years earlier. The date of the bonds, the duration of the debt and the amount involved (m = mina, g = shekel, kb = silver) are as follows:

80 (10 weeks)	0m 36g kb
80/xii (15 weeks)	5m 10g kb
80/xii	14m kb
82/xi (1 year)	2m kb
83/ix (20 weeks)	2m kb
83/x (2 years)	3m 10g kb
83/xii (55 weeks)	14m kb
83/xii (5 weeks)	9m 5g kb
84/ii (1 year)	5m kb
85/iv (6 weeks)	0m 36g kb
85/v (20 weeks)	1m kb
85/viii	9m 14g kb
85/ix	11m kb
85/x (45 weeks)	14m kb
87 (20 weeks)	2m 8g kb

87/viii (20 weeks)	0m 50g kb
89/i	*11m 10g tin*
89/iii	6m 28g kb
89/v (5 months)	1m kb
89/vi (1 year)	6m 15g kb
89/vi (3 weeks)	6m 15g kb
90/v (40 weeks)	1m kb
90/v (1 year)	0m 30g kb
91/iv (1 year)	0m 40g kb
91/viii (20 weeks)	17m kb
97/viii (20 weeks)	1m kb

The extensive period of at least 40 years, documented in AKT 4, 26, appears to be the longest running debt attested in the OA evidence.[86] In correspondence and other genres of text the longest period a merchant quotes is 30 years. After his presumed departure from active life in Anatolia, thirty years previously, Aššur-idī continually paid his contribution to the Kanesh colony, according to CCT 5, 6a:5. The same period occurs in Kt n/k 1192, a long letter by Lā-qēp, describing to Aššur-taklāku how he gave him a *naruqqum*-investment thirty years ago.[87] A defaulting debtor who was unable to repay the full amount of capital and interest at once, might be offered a rescheduling of his debt with payments in instalments. This occurs in Kt c/k 791: "I settled the case of Ugawa and Šikmadu: I have received 2 1/2 minas of silver as an initial payment of the

---

[86] For the (Neo-)Assyrian view on life expectancy, J. C. Fincke kindly refers me to STT 400, where it is said that 40 years is a man's middle age, 50 years "short days", 60 years a normal age, 70 years "long days", 80 years old age, and 90 years advanced old age. The OA texts do not contain direct details about age; kings Erišum I and Šarru-kēn each reigned nearly 40 years.

[87] Other references to debts of 4 years or longer are:
4 years: CCT 2, 21a; CCT 3, 49b; Kt c/k 63/b; KTS 2, 36+ (a debt due within 3 months is now 4 years old).
5 years: Debts: ATHE 34; BIN 4, 19; Cole 4; KTS 2, 71; as period of work: AAA 1, 14; I 663; TPAK 1, 156.
6 years: BIN 6, 260; JCS 14, 11; TPAK 1, 57:33.
7 years: AKT 3,86 (1 m 22 1/2 shekels of silver).
8 years: Kt c/k 122:40 (instead of 2 and 3 years); Kt 91/k 165 (*tadmiqtum* of 5 shekels of silver); TC 3, 58:24.
10 years: Kt 91/k 157 (15 minas of refined copper; 6 shekels of silver); KTS 1, 13b (17 shekels of silver; cf. KTS 1, 13a); OIP 27, 62 (3 2/3 minas of silver and interest).
11 years: Kt c/k 63/b (instead of 1 year); KUG 35 (instead of 2 years).
13 years: CCT 4, 9b Amur-Ištar to Ennam-Aššur: "5 minas of silver has been running against you on interest for 13 years. When you came here to meet me, I did not ask you for an offering, nor did I show you any anger."
20 years: AKT 4, 51: see below, note 89.
Debts originating from an *ebuṭṭum*-loan running for 20 years are mentioned in KTS 1, 40 and its parallel text CCT 3, 30, and in Kt c/k 277 ("send the silver and its interest for 20 years").
25 years: Unapše owed 1m 15g for 25 years according to Kt k/k 4 (North-Syrian merchants).
30 years: for 30 years no report of silver had been sent to Assur according to TC 3, 1.

silver. They will pay 2 minas of silver within 2 months, they will pay 5 minas of silver within 10 weeks, they will pay 3 minas of silver within 20 weeks."[88] The word *niqi'um* 'offering' was used for earnest money or advance payment, and was more or less expected by the creditor.[89] If, after strong pleas and pressure a debtor still refused to pay, the creditor had to resort to legal procedures.

Financial obligations of a merchant to an institution could have severe consequences. The City Hall in Assur levied taxes and sold merchandise. If the debt was not remitted fully, the Eponym could resort to sealing the merchant's house and eventually to selling it.[90] Several OA kings proclaimed an *addurārum* "freedom" for their city to relieve the burden of debt, but it is not known how this affected the merchants. A specific instance of economic policy, which consisted of reversing forced house sales, is reported in TPAK 1, 46.[91]

The word *ṣibtum* "interest"[92] is usually a fixed sum to be added monthly to a round sum, such as ten shekels, a mina, or a talent, but at other times it is simply a sum to be added to the capital. Interest was charged for loans taken from "a merchant's house" (*bēt tamkārim*), for arrears due to the Eponym in Assur, and often for defaulting debtors.[93] Amounts of silver and other metals used as money or merchandise were often borrowed at interest in Assur and Anatolia to speed trade or to fulfil an obligation. A consignment of silver that was or soon would be in transit served to repay the loan.[94] Such credit was once interrupted in Assur according to I 502.[95] With

---

[88] Kt c/k 791 (unp. Ankara): (3) *ša ú-ga-wa ù ší-ik-ma-du* (4) *a-wa-tí-šu-nu ú-ga-me-er-ma* (5) 2 1/2 *ma-na* kb *a-na* (6) *ni-qí* kb *al-[qé]* (7) 2 *ma-na* kb *a-na* 2 itu.kam (8) *i-ša-qú-lu* 5 *ma-na* kb (9) *a-na* 10 *ha-am-ša-tim* (10) *i-ša-qú-lu* 3 *ma-na* kb (11) *a-na* 20 *ha-am-ša-tim i-[ša-qú-lu]*.

[89] As this meaning does not occur in the dictionaries some examples of its use will be given here. AKT 3, 81: (31) *šu-ma* kb *lá-šu* 10 *gín.ta* (32) *ni-qí-am eṭ-ra-nim* (33) *lá té-zi-ba*, "If there is no silver then take away for me 10 shekels each as an offering; do not give up."

AKT 4, 51: (11) ... *iš-tù* 20 *ša-na-tim* (12) *qá-qá-ra-am : da-nam* (13) *ta-aṣ-ba-at-ma ša-na-sú-ma* (14) *áš-ta-na-pá-ra-ku-ma* (15) *lá* kb : *ša* 1 *ṭup-pì-kà* (16) *tù-šé-ba-lam : ú-lá ma-tí-ma* (17) kb 10 *gín ni-qí-a-am* (18) *tù-šé-bi-lam : ù ki-ma* (19) *ni-qí-e-em šé-bu-li-im* (20) *a-ta tù-ni-e-ma* (21) *ta-wi-ni-tám : ta-áš-ta-na-pá-ra-am*, "You have been on 'strong ground' for 20 years, and although I write to you every year, you do not send the silver for a single one of your bonds. You have never sent me 10 shekels of silver as an offering. And instead of sending an offering you cheated me and you keep writing to me ....".

[90] Dercksen 2004, 72–3.

[91] Veenhof 1999b.

[92] On the question of interest in texts from Kültepe, see Veenhof 1997a, 68; Dercksen 2004, 109; for interest from Old Babylonian evidence, see Van De Mieroop 1995.

[93] Some debts were partly interest-bearing and partly for a fixed term. In Kt c/k 499 half of the debt was to be interest-bearing and the other half due within 20 weeks.

[94] Ka 295 (Donbaz 1991, 103): (1′) ... *a-na* (2′) *[ma-lá a-hu-um a-na] a-hi-im* (3′) *[a-ṣí]-ib-tim i-du-nu le-qé-a-ma* (4′) *a-na é kà-ri-im* (5′) *šu-uq-lá-ma*, "Take (silver) as one gives to another at interest and pay it to the office of the colony." Biggs 1988, 38 Burton-tablet: (46) *gi-im-lá-ni ù šu-ma lá ta-ga-mì-lá-ni ki-ma a-hu* (47) *a-na a-hi-im ṣí-ib-tám i-du-nu i-ṣé-ri-a le-qé-a*, "Do me a favour! If you cannot do me a favour, take (silver) at my expense like one gives (silver at) interest to another." But cf. lines 49–50: "Do not take interest at my expense lest you add more misery to what I already have!".

[95] I 502 (to Innāya from Aššur-malik): (18) *a-ta lá tí-de₈-e* : *ki-ma* (19) kb 1 *ma-na a-hu-um* (20) *a-na a-hi-im a-na ṣí-ib-tim* (21) *lá i-du-nu-ni*, 'Don't you know that one does not give 1 mina of silver at

the aim of avoiding paying unnecessary interest the correspondence often contains advice to send money in order to repay the debt "lest the interest become too much" and the merchant become annoyed. However, there are enough references to long overdue debts to show that not every trader cared about the payment of interest. Whereas some creditors were willing not to charge interest when the debt was only a few months overdue,[96] others were keen to get all that they were legally entitled to receive. A legal decision by the city assembly and recorded on the stele made it possible for the guarantor to charge extra interest (*ṣibat ṣibtim*) over the interest that had to be paid on money he had borrowed from a merchant's house in order to fulfil his obligation.[97]

Interest usually was paid in the same substance as that in which the debt had been incurred. However, creative solutions existed, such as the offer by Imdilum to pay the interest by selling textiles as a *tadmiqtum* for the women who had lent silver to him.[98]

The most common rate of interest during the Level II period was that of 1 1/2 shekels per mina per month, i.e. a rate of 30% per year.[99] It is attested in documents from L66 (Kt 91/k 428:8) until L135 (Enna-Suen son of Kurara, Kt j/k 300/viii). This rate was also known as "according to the decree of the colony" (*kīma awat kārim*), which expression first occurs in L79/ix (ATHE 3); the same expression existed during the Level Ib-period (18th c.), and may indicate the same rate.[100] Other rates of interest are:

---

interest to another?"

[96] BIN 6, 55 (Pūšu-kēn to Amur-Ištar): (10´) *šu-ma* 1 itu.kam *ù* 2 itu.kam (11´) *e-ta-at-qú ṣí-ib-tám* (12´) *ú-lá a-lá-qé*, "Should the term expire by only 1 or 2 months I will not take interest" (concerning a *qīptum* of 12 weeks).

[97] Veenhof 1995, 1724.

[98] ICK 1, 192: (10) ... kb *ša iš-[tí]* (11) *a-wi-la-tim a-ṣí-ib-tim* (12) *ta-al-qé-a-ni-ni* (13) kb *a-wi-lá-tim* (14) *šu-uq-la-ma* (...) (18) kb 1 gín *ṣí-ib-tám* (19) *mì-ma i-ṣé-ri-a lá i-lá-qé-a* (20) *ki-ma ṣí-ib-tí-ší-na* (21) túg.hi.a *lu-šé-bi₄-lu-nim-m[a]* (22) kb 1 gín *ra-mì-ni* (23) *lá-ak-bu-ús-ma lu-da-mì-iq-ší-na-tí* (24) *ù* túg. hi.a *ša ku-tal-lá-nu-um* (25) *na-áš-ú-ni* : *e-ra-ba-ma* (26) kb 1 gín *ra-mì-ni* (27) *a-kà-ba-as-ma* (28) [*k*]*i-ma ṣí-ib-tí-ší-na* (29) [*lu*]-*da-mì-iq-ší-na-tí* (30) [*ṣ*]*í-ib-tám i-ṣé-ri-a* (31) *lá i-lá-qé-a-ma* (32) *li-bi₄-i* : *la i-ma-ra-aṣ*, "As for the silver which you borrowed for me from the women, pay the silver to the women. (...) They must not take a shekel of silver at my expense as interest. Let them send me textiles instead of the interest due to them, and I shall exert myself for every shekel of silver and sell it as a *tadmiqtum* for them. Or when the textiles arrive that Kutallānum is transporting, I shall exert myself for every shekel of silver and sell it as a *tadmiqtum* for them. But they must not take interest at my expense lest I become angry."

[99] Old Babylonian interest rates are 20% for silver and 33 1/3% for barley according to the Laws of Ešnunna and those of Hammurabi.

[100] KBo 9, 35 (*kīma awat* [...]); KBo 9, 36 (*kīma awat kārim* [...]); OIP 27, 20 Ališar (*kīma* [*awat*] *kārim*). Common annual rates of interest attested in texts from Level Ib are 20% (KBo 9, 20; AKT 3, 1; AKT 3, 2), and 30% in UF 7 no. 1.

16 2/3% p.a.:	10 shekels per mina per year, AKT 3,38:5.10 L73.
20% p.a.:	1 shekel per mina per month, e.g. CCT 1, 2:6.17.35, or expressed as 12 shekels per mina per years, e.g., AKT 3, 20 L68; AKT 3,69 L69 en L68; TC 3, 219.
25% p.a.:	15 shekels per mina per year, ICK 1, 10; ICK 1, 143 L59.
40% p.a.:	2 shekels per mina per months, e.g. ICK 1, 148.
50% p.a.:	30 shekels per mina per years, rare, e.g. in Kt 92/k 210 L105.
60% p.a.:	3 shekels per mina per months, e.g., KTB 4.
90% p.a.:	4 1/2 shekels per mina per month, AKT 1, 59 (Anat. deb.).
100% p.a.:	5 shekels per mina per month, I 466:2-´3.
120% p.a.:	6 shekels per mina per month, ICK 1, 83; or expressed as 1 shekel per 10 shekels per month, CCT 1, 10a (EL 97) L47; CCT 1, 6b; VS 26,95; BIN 4, 57:15-18; or expressed as 1 mina per 10 minas per month, BIN 4, 207; ICK 1, 118.
160% p.a.:	8 shekels per mina, Kt c/k 114:18.

Anatolian debtors were usually charged a high rate and they had to provide additional goods in kind, such as bread, grain or fattened oxen.

The *hamuštum* "week" was the smallest period for calculating the start of a debt or the duration of interest. However, bonds often only mention the month and (eponymy) year as the starting point, and these are also the two units of time stipulated in letters.[101]

The interest appears to have been calculated per month or per year for a debt lasting 12 months or more. An annual payment is reported in KTS 1, 12: 13–15, "May he bring this year's interest into our house". Interest for half a year was also charged according to other texts.[102]

9. THE COST OF LIVING

The merchant families in Assur and in Anatolian towns in general did not grow grain or keep cattle. The food had to be bought. Some merchants in Anatolia, who had married a local wife, did keep some animals, and occasionally grain was accepted as means of payment. The majority, however, had to purchase grain, meat (butchered or whole animals), and other items.[103] We find much data on prices of food and other

---

[101] Kt c/k 602 (unp. Ankara): (25) ... itu.kam-am (26) ú li-ma-am ša iš-tù (27) u₄-mì-im ša kb ha-bu-lu-ni (28) šé-bi₄-lam, "Send me the month and the eponym from which they owe the silver"; cf. TC 3, 80:18.

[102] TC 3, 16 (3) a-šu-mì kb ša tár-ma-na (4) 1 ma-na-um 15 gín.ta (5) ša mì-šál ša-tim ṣí-ib-tám (6) i-dí-a-ma kb al-té-qé, "Concerning the silver of Tarmana, 15 shekels per mina, he deposited with me interest of half a year and I have taken the silver."

[103] Dercksen 2008a; 2008b.

necessities.[104] Costs of living included food, oil, firewood[105] and clothing. An allowance of 2 shekels of silver and 30 litres of wheat per month was given to a man (presumably in Kanesh) who had been hired as an attorney.[106] This amount of wheat is comparable to what is known from other periods in Mesopotamia. For example, a monthly ration of 30 litres of bread and 60 litres of wine is mentioned in an Old Babylonian text from Ur.[107] A woman in Assur complains that she is forced to eat the same quantity as a slave girl, just 20 litres per month.[108] A *karpatum* (a vessel of 30 litres) of wheat cost about 5 shekels of silver, so the attorney would have received an allowance for food and other small expenses of in all about 7 shekels of silver.

In general, women did not travel but stayed in the town. They were supported by their husbands or other male relatives. This dependency frequently led to hardship when the household in Assur was short of money, or even had none at all. Complaints and cries for help form a recurrent topic in some of the letters sent by female relatives to traders.[109] Some additional income could be obtained by domestic textile production,

---

[104] Details of buying food are also attested by Old Babylonian documents, for example in AbB 13, 68. A text listing various expenses on food etc. priced in silver, such as Kt 88/k 71, is paralleled by UET 5, 607 and 636, for which see Charpin 1986, 62–8.

[105] 1 wagonload of firewood cost between 1 and 1 1/2 shekels of silver; 1: TC 3, 197:18; 1 1/6: Kt a/k 537:4; 1 1/2: Kt a/k 537:2.

[106] For the legal case between Imdilum and his son Puzur-Ištar and their *rābiṣum* Laliya, see Veenhof in VS 26, p. 27 *ad* no. 118. VS 26, 118: (9´) 2 gín.ta kb *ù* 1 baneš.ta g[ig] *a-na* (10´) *ú-ku-ul-tí-kà i-na* itu.1.kam-*im a-ˀ ta-na-díˀ-na-[ku]m*, "I am giving you each month 2 shekels of silver and 1 *ṣimid* of wheat for your food." Compare Puzur-Ištar's discourse to Laliya in CCT 4, 38c: (2) *iš-tù ta-li-kà-ni* (3) *i-na é a-bi-a qá-dí a-ma-[tim]* (4) *ta-kà-al ú ta-ša-tí ú a-ma-[kam]* (5) 5 *ṣa-bu-um e-ba-ru-tí-ni* (6) *ša pá-du-ga-ni-kà i-na* (7) *é-tí-ni iš-ta-tí-ú-ni* (8) *i-na wa-ar-ki-tim* (9) *a-ša-tám ta-hu-úz-ma* 2 *gín* (10) [k]b *ù* 1 baneš.ta gig *ku-a-[tí]* (11) [*a-t*]*a-dí-na-kum* ..., "Since you came here, you are eating and drinking in my father's house together with the slave girls (?) And there five of our colleagues, belonging to your *padugannum*, have all been drinking at our house. Later on, you married a wife and I regularly gave you 2 shekels of silver and 1 *ṣimid* of wheat."

[107] UET 5, 636, see Charpin 1986, 62, lines 30–31.

[108] BIN 4, 22: (19) *iš-tí a-ma-tí-kà-ma* (20) *ú-uš-ta-am-hi-ru-ni* (21) géme 20 *qa e-kà-lá* (22) *ú a-na-ku* 20 *qa a-kál*, "They put me on the same level with your own slave girls; the slave girls eat 20 litres, and I eat 20 litres."

The quantity of barley or wheat stored in a house was reported to her relatives in Anatolia when a woman had died in Assur. For example, after the death of Pūšu-kēn's wife "1300 (*qa*) of barley was stored in the containers" (TC 1, 30: (7) [x] *li-im* 3 *me-at še-um i-na* (8) *ha-ri-a-tim ša-pí-ik*). A relative of Enlil-bāni did not leave behind any silver or copper, but unspecified quantities of bronze and 'beer-bread' as well as 1500 (*qa*) of barley, of which 500 (*qa*) was spent to feed "the house of your father" (TC 3, 66: (15) *ù li-im* 5 (16) *me-at še.am té-zi-ib* (17) *šà.ba* 5 *me-at še* (18) *a-na a-kà-al* (19) *é a-bi4-ku-nu ga-me-er* (20) *ší-tí še-im i-ba-ší*).

[109] Kt a/k 478/b (unp. Ankara): (9) *ma-tí-ma kb* 1 *gín ú-lá tù-šé-ba-lam* (10) *ú-lá ta-áš-ta-me-e ki-ma da-nu-tum* (11) *i-na a-lim*ki *ša-ak-na-at-ni* (12) *i-nu-mì i-na bu-bu-tim a-mu-tù* (13) *i-na kb ta-qá-bi-ra-ni*, "You never send me a shekel of silver! Don't you hear that there is an emergency situation in the town? When I die of hunger you will bury me with silver?"; BIN 6, 197: (7) ... *kb ša i-a-tí* (8) *i-lá-kà-ni* : *a-na é pì-lá-ah-išt*[ar] (9) *iš-ta-aq-lu-šu* : *ú qá-t*[*ám*] (10) *ša a-šùr-na-da* : *a-na* ˹é˺ (11) *a-lim*ki *a-na hu-bu-li-šu* (12) *iš-ta-aq-lu-šu a-na-kam* : *kb* (13) 1 *gín a-na ba-lá-ṭí-ni* : *lá-šu-m*[a] (14) *sú-úh-ru-um i-na bu-bu-*

which was sent to Anatolia to be sold there as a *tadmiqtum*. Such a dire situation is vividly described in some of the letters sent by Tāram-Kūbi to her husband Innāya. A letter from Assur sent to Alahum contains the following lines: "You wrote to me: 'Send me 2 *kutānus*!' I fell ill and spent the 10 shekels of silver that you had sent me. I had to stay in bed for 2 months, but (your) representatives did not ask how I was doing. Nor did they give me an offering for expenses. Ever since you left (Assur) they never gave me a single shekel of silver (...). If you are my father, let your message come here and just as the (men of) the town give a subsistence allowance to their daughters, so may they give me (one)."[110]

A moving letter is AKT 4, 63, possibly written by a *gubabtum*-priestess: "Do those who become angry with their sisters remain angry for ever? What have I done to you? Ever since you departed ten years ago, you do not mention my name. I am living in my own house and you are troubling yourself. You are my brother! Help me with a shekel of silver and I will pray on your behalf in front of my god Aššur."[111]

A rare example of a man writing about similar shortages from a town somewhere in Anatolia is contained in CCT 4, 45b: "My dear brother, send me there 15 or 20 minas of wool so that I can leave (that) behind with them (fem.) (to pay for) their (fem.) food. Then I will get ready and depart. Why have you locked me in the city like a woman for ten months? And here nobody gives me a loan. Here, winter just caught up with me. There is not even a single loaf of bread or firewood or textiles to clothe them (fem.)."[112]

Providing the necessities of life was the responsibility of the husband or father and those unwilling to comply could be forced to do so by court order. This appears from a verdict by the colony at Wahšušana (Kt 88/k 269, Bayram and Çeçen 1995, 11), according to which an Assyrian merchant, who had left his wife behind without any means of subsistence, had to provide her with a monthly allowance of 8 minas of

---

tim (15) *i-mu-a-at-ma lá ta-ša-ra-[ni* (x)], "The silver that comes here has been paid for the house of Pilah-Ištar. Even the share of Aššur-nādā has been paid to the City Hall for his debt. There is here not a single shekel of silver for us to live on. The children are dying from hunger and you do not take care of me."

[110] Kt c/k 43 (unp. Ankara): (7) ... *um-ma a-ta-ma* (8) 2 *ku-ta-né šé-bi-lim am-ra-aṣ-ma* (9) 10 gín kb *ša tù-šé-bi-lá-ni* (10) *ag-da-ma-ar itu.2.kam i-na* (11) *e-er-ší-im a-ni-dí-ma mu-zi-zu* (12) *da-tí-ma la iš-ú-lu ù a-na* (13) *ga-me-ri-ma ni-qí-am lá i-dí-nu* (14) *iš-tù tù-úṣ-ú-ni ma-tí-ma* (15) 1 gín kb ... (16) *lá i-dí-nu-nim* ... (31) *šu-ma a-bi a-ta té-er-ta-kà* (32) *li-li-kam-ma ki-ma a-lu-um* (33) *ip-re a-na me-er-ú-a-tí-šu-nu* (34) *i-du-nu li-dí-<nu>-nim.*

[111] AKT 4, 63 (to Adu from Šīmat-Aššur): (3) *ša iš-tí : a-hu-a-tí-šu-nu* (4) *i-za-ni-ú-ni a-dí* (5) *du-ri-ma : i-za-ni-ú* (6) *mì-nam e-pu-uš-kà-ma* (7) *iš-tù : tù-ṣú-ni* (8) *iš-tù 10 ša-na-tim* (9) *šu-mì-ma lá ta-za-kàr* (10) *i-na é bé-et* (11) *ra-mì-ni-a uš-ba-ku-ma* (12) *li-ba-kà : tù-lá-ma-nam* (13) *a-hi a-ta i-na kb* (14) 1 gín *áš-ra-ni-ma igi a-šùr* (15) *i-lí-a : lá-ak-ru-ba-kum.* See also Veenhof 2009, 201.

[112] CCT 4, 45b: (11) *a-hi a-ta a-ma-kam sík.hi.a* (12) 15 *ma-na ú-ul* 20 *ma-na* (13) *šé-bi-lá-ma ú-ku-ul-ta-ší-na* (14) *le-zi-ib-ší-na-tí-ma* (15) *lá-at-bi₄-a-ma lá-tal-kam* (16) *mì-šu-um ki-ma* (17) *sí-ni-iš-tim iš-tù* itu.10.kam (18) *i-qé-ra-áb a-lim^ki* (19) *ta-áp-ta-ah-a-ni-i* (20) *ú a-na-kam a-ha-ba-li-im* (21) *ma-ma-an lá i-da-nam* (22) *a-na-kam ku-ṣú-um ik-ta-áš-da-ni* (23) *lá ninda iš-té-en lá e-ṣú-ú* (24) *lá túg.hi.a a-lu-bu-uš-tí-ší-na* (25) *i-ba-ší.*

šikkum copper (about 3 shekels of silver) for her food, oil, and firewood. In addition to that he had to give her each year one textile (*ṣubātum*). Specific provisions for wives and unmarried daughters are often included in a merchant's last will. According to ICK 1, 12, the two sons, Iya and Ikuppiya, will give their sister Ahatum (a *gubabtum*-priestess) 6 minas of copper per year. In addition, they will give her a breast-piece from their offerings. Moreover, Ahatum will inherit three debt-notes from her father which represent claims of 1 talent 12 minas of tin, 1 1/2 talents of copper and 1 1/2 minas of silver (in all about 15 minas of silver).

The last will published as RA 60, 133 Thierry states that a sum of 5 minas of silver will be lent at interest and that the interest will serve to defray the costs of living of two women. The common rate of interest of 30% a year amounts to 1 1/2 minas of silver.

A text from Level Ib, Kt 01/k 325/b (Albayrak 2004), contains the provision that a sister (*gubabtum*) will receive 1 textile and 1 *šitrum*-textile for three years. After that period she will receive 20 shekels of silver per year. The 20 shekels per year amount to 1 2/3 shekels a month.

Calculating these monthly allowances gives 1 2/3 shekels of silver for a *gubabtum*-priestess, 8 minas of *šikkum* copper (about 3 shekels of silver) for a woman (+ 1 textile a year), 3 3/4 shekels of silver each for two women (RA 60, 133 Thierry), and 2 shekels of silver and 30 litres of wheat for a man. This agrees with the 2 or 3 shekels of silver which a trader had spent during a 40 days' stay according to Kt c/k 591 (footnote 59, above).

Of a different nature but interesting from a comparative perspective, are the costs of funerals. The diverse evidence was discussed recently by Michel (2008, 182f.) and it shows that the costs of burial (*ana qubūrim*) varied: 23 shekels of silver (TPAK 1, 212); 34 shekels of silver (Kt m/k 1, see Hecker, *TUAT NF* 1, 54); 22 1/6 shekels of gold, worth 2 minas 57 1/3 shekels of silver, to bury Aššur-ṭāb (Kt c/k 54:8ff.). An even more expensive burial is mentioned in Kt 94/k 1023, according to which 7 talents of copper were spent (reference in Veenhof 2008b, 114). According to Kt 91/k 423, the mortuary rites (including the bewailing) of a mother and sons cost 19 1/2 shekels of silver (Veenhof 2008b, 111).

10. THE HIRING OF PERSONNEL AND THE PAYMENT FOR SERVICES

10.1 The *sāridum*

Harnessing the donkeys was done by *kaṣṣārus* and *sāridus*. The former enjoyed a long-term relationship with a merchant. They received a sum of silver (rarely copper), as a *be'ūlātum*, which served as an interest-free loan with which to do business.[113] The latter were hired temporarily and usually only for part of the journey.

kaṣṣārum contracts contain a clause that the creditor can hire a *sāridum* at the expense of the *kaṣṣārum* if he should break his contract. A three-year term of employment is mentioned in Kt a/k 433: "When he returns the silver (i.e., 30 shekels), he may go where he likes. If he deserts me, I will hire a *sāridum* and Q. will pay the hire of the *sāridum* in full. Within three years Q. will not return the *be'ūlātum* of A. If he does, Q. will pay (twice the amount)."

A five-year term occurs in AAA 1, 14: "Puzur-Anna gave 20 shekels of refined silver as the *be'ūlātum* of Šu-Ištar. He is being held with the silver. Aguza, his father, received the silver. From the very moment that they begin packing, he will stay (*uššab*) with Puzur-Anna for five years. They will not break the contract and he will not leave. If they break the contract and he has left, he will pay 2 minas of silver."

Instead of a financial punishment, other contracts threaten an additional term of work as a fine. The penalty can be three years: Kt a/k 473b (unp. Ankara): the working capital is 26 shekels of silver, "He will not leave for three years. If he breaks the contract and leaves, he will work for me (*qātī iṣabbat*) for (another) three years. Then he will pay his *be'ūlātum* and leave." (ll. 8–14). A five-year penalty is noted in I 663: "If B-A. breaks the contract by returning his *be'ūlātum* to B., he will, after he returns his *be'ūlātum*, work for B. (*qāt B. iṣabbat*) for five years." A period of 12 (?) years as punishment is mentioned in I 729.

Since a *be'ūlātum* in principle was an interest-free loan, which the employee could use for trading, some employees preferred not to return it on completing the term, and some texts include as penalty monthly interest on the servant's *be'ūlātum*.[114]

Some idea of the pay a *sāridum* received when he hired himself out for a specific section of the journey can be gained from the following records:

    15 shekels of silver as hire from Assur as far as Hahhum, Kt c/k 456.
    11 shekels of silver as hire from Qaṭṭara as far as Hahhum, CCT 1, 31a.
    12 shekels of silver from Eluhut as far as Haqqa, TC 3, 164.
    7 shekels of silver as hire from Hahhum as far as Kanesh, TC 3, 24.

This evidence means that hiring a *sāridum* from Assur to Kanesh would cost round about 22 shekels of silver. The distance from Assur to Qaṭṭara is about 140 km, from Qaṭṭara to Hahhum about 400 km, and from Hahhum to Kanesh about 300 km. So the rate of pay from Assur to Hahhum is 1 shekel of silver for about 36 km. Using the same ratio for the 7 shekels paid from Hahhum to Kanesh, according to TC 3, 24, gives a distance of 252 km. The 8 shekels of silver paid in Assur for hiring a *sāridum*, according to Kt c/k 227:18, would be enough to reach Apum or the following station. Provisionally, it seems that the cost of hiring a harnesser would be about 1 shekel of silver for 36

---

113   Kienast 1989; Veenhof 1994.
114   Kt 91/k 473 (1 shekel per month); 1 1/2 shekels per mina per month is used in Kt a/k 393 and 1 1/2 minas per talent per month in Kt a/k 445 (*be'ūlātum* in copper).

km or less. In Mesopotamian terms, where 1 *bēru* equals about 10.8 km, this is slightly less than 3 1/2 *bēru*. The average distance covered per day can be estimated as 25 km.[115]

These approximate calculations put penalty clauses in *be'ūlātum*-contracts into perspective. According to such contracts from Level Ib and a reference in TPAK 1, 156a from Level II in a similar context, there was a customary rate of 1 shekel of silver per *bērum* which the *kaṣṣārum* had to pay to hire a substitute if he left his job prematurely. For instance in Kt n/k 30 (Level Ib): "I will hire a *sāridum* hireling in his stead at his expense and he will pay in full the hire of hirelings, (being) 1 shekel of silver per *bērum*."[116] Since it is unlikely that a substitute *sāridum* would cost three times as much as a regular one, it can be assumed that the triple payment, a *šušalšum*, is a punishment. This is mentioned in the *sāridum*-contract Ank. 14-2-80: "Seal of Aššur-idī. Seal of Ennum-Aššur. Aššuriš-tikal had no cylinder seal and therefore he did not seal. Aššuriš-takil of Zalpa is satisfied with 4 1/2 shekels of silver as his hire. If he disappears anywhere during his capacity as a *sāridum*, he will pay triple."[117]

Although there seems to have been no problem to find people in Assur or along the route willing to be hired as a *sāridum*, it was still an expense. A merchant trying to save some silver wrote in Kt c/k 395: "The man gave me H. for harnessing, but he fell ill in Apum and I had to leave him behind. I hired a *sāridum* instead of him from Apum until Hahhum. (…) Send one strong servant to me in Hahhum. I do not want to hire someone instead of him again."

Sometimes a worker could hardly refuse a contract, as when someone had been redeemed and consequently had to work for the redeemer to pay off his debt. A five-year period is used in TPAK 1, 156a (tablet): "Šuppianika, wife of Aššur-rēṣī, has redeemed Enna-Suen son of Ennam-Aššur for 26 1/3 shekels of silver from the native. He is being held with the silver. He will work for her for five years. If he breaks the contract and leaves before the end of his term, he will pay her 1 mina of silver. If he disappears somewhere, she will hire (a *sāridum*) at his expense at a cost of 1 shekel per *bērum*; Enna-Suen will pay in full the hire of the *sāridum*. (Three witnesses)."

10.2 Porters and Messengers

The hiring of individuals to carry goods from one place to another was a common feature. A well-known letter found in Mari refers to porters carrying snow over a distance of 10 or 20 *bērus*, or 108 or 216 km.[118] OA evidence for the use of porters (*ša*

---

[115]   Dercksen 2004, 255.

[116]   Donbaz 2008, 52f.: (17) *pu-ùh-šu ag-ra-am sá-ri-dam* (18) *a-ga-ar-šu-ma ig-re-e ag-re-e* (19) *be-ra-a* 1 *gín.ta* kb *ú-ma-lá.*

[117]   Ank. 14-2-80 (Günbattı 1987, 31): (sealing A) (1) *kišib a-šùr-i-dí* (2) *kišib en-um-a-šùr* (3) *a-šur-iš-tí-kál* (sealing B) (4) *ku-nu-kam lá i-šu-ma* (sealing A) (5) *ú-lá i-ik-nu-uk* (sealing B) (6) 4 1/2 *gín* kb *a-šur-iš-ta-ki-il₅* (7) *ša za-al-pá* (8) *ig-re-šu ša-bu* (9) *šu-ma i-na sà-ra-dim* (10) *a-e-ma* (11) *ú-dá-pè-er šu-ša-al-šu-um* (12) *i-ša-qal* (sealing A).

[118]   ARM 1, 21; cf. FM 1, 72; edited by Durand 1997, no. 418.

biltim, pl. *ša bilātim*) and their pay has been collected in Dercksen 1996, 62f. As an alternative to the use of donkeys or wagons, porters could be used to convey tin (to Ninaša, ATHE 66:4–6), copper, textiles and other objects. These hirelings were accompanied by a member of the firm or would go accompanied by other travellers (BIN 4, 63: *išti ālikim panîmma ṭurdaššu*). Porters were customarily provided with food. The letter CCT 2, 40 contains a reference to people from Kanesh who had carried three bags with 300 kg of copper, and the sender writes "give them 6 shekels of silver as their hire and instruct the boys to feed them with bread!"[119] The list with expenses in the Schoneveld collection includes "37 1/2 grains (of silver) for meat for those who carried the barley as proceeds of the slave here".

Means of transport could also be hired, as seen in Kt 92/k 313: "In accordance with your instruction about the 10 talents of good quality copper, we hired some people from Kanesh here and they are bringing (the copper) by wagon to you. Give them there 12 1/3 shekels of silver. Let Puzur-Aššur's representatives give him 6 1/3 shekels of silver. Let those of Šu-Hubur pay 2 1/3 shekels of silver to you. Pay a total of 21 shekels of silver to the caravan people from Kanesh. Three sacks with copper under your seals and 1 wagon are at your disposal. Puzur-Aššur here spent 5 minas of copper on food for them. We paid 5 2/3 minas of copper for the (rent of) the wagon."[120]

Whereas porters seem usually to have been recruited from among the local Anatolian population, messengers were usually Assyrians.[121] These were not the envoys of the city, who functioned as ambassadors for Assur, or merchants appointed by the Karum Kanesh or another Assyrian settlement for a specific task, but other Assyrians hired to deliver a message or tablet. Such a messenger could be called an *agrum* 'hireling' or a *šiprum*, the common OA word for envoy or messenger. When a merchant dispatched letters while travelling in a caravan or staying in another town, he needed someone for that task. This could be a person he knew,[122] or someone else. CCT 1, 29, for example, is a list of expenses incurred by members of a caravan that had not yet crossed the Euphrates. Apart from the usual payments to local chiefs, the costs for two messengers sent ahead are recorded: "15 shekels of tin for the messenger we sent to Kanesh (...) 7 shekels of tin for the messenger we sent to Tegarama."[123] The hiring of someone to

---

[119] CCT 2, 40: (4) 3 *i-la-tum* 5 gú (5) urudu *ma-sí-a-am šu-qúl-ta-ší-na* (6) *ku-nu-ki-a kà-ni-ší-ú* (7) *na-áš-ú-ni-ku-nu-tí* (8) 6 gín kb *ig-re-šu-nu* (9) *dí-na-šu-nu-tí ù ṣú-ha-re* (10) *ša-hi-za-ma ak-lam* (11) *lu-ša-ki-lu-šu-nu*.

[120] Kt 92/k 313 (Gökçek 2006, 188f.): (4) *a-ma-lá té-er-tí-kà* (5) 10 gú urudu sig₅ *a-na-kam* (6) *kà-ni-ší-e ni-gu₅-ur-ma* (7) *i-na e-ri-qí-im* (8) *ù-bu-lu-ni-ku-um a-ma-kam* (9) 12 1/3 gín kb *dí-in-šu-nu-tí* (10) *ša ki-ma puzur₄-a-šur* (11) 6 1/3 gín kb *li-dí-nu-šum?* (12) *ša ki-ma šu-hu-bu-ur* (13) 2 1/3 gín kb *li-iš-qú-lu-ni-kum* (?) (14) šunigin 1/3 ma-na 1 gín (15) kb *a-na kà-ni-ší-e* (16) *ša ha-ra-na-tim šu-qú-ul* (17) 3 *i-lá-tum* urudu *ku-nu-ku-kà* (18) *e-ri-qú-um ku-a-tí i-za-za-ku-um* (19) *a-na-kam puzur₄-a-šur* (20) 5 ma-na urudu *a-na ú-ku-ul-tí-šu-nu* (21) *ig-mu-ur* 5 2/3 ma-na urudu (22) *a-na e-ri-qí-im ni-iš-qú-ul*.

[121] On this topic, see Veenhof 2008c.

[122] Cf. Kt 91/k 163: (6) 6 gín kb *ig-re* (7) *ší-ip-ri-im* (8) *tap-pá-i-a*, "6 shekels of silver, hire of a messenger, my partner."

[123] CCT 1, 29: (1) 15 gín an.na *a-na* (2) *ší-ip-ri-im ša a-kà-ni-iš* (3) *ni-iš-pu-ru ...* (8) ... 7 gín (9) an.na

forward a letter is described in RA 59, 122 Sch. 19: "People brought us your message, but Šu-Enlil was not here; he has gone to Kuburnat. We hired (someone) and dispatched (the messenger) to him."[124]

The costs of repeatedly hiring messengers could easily reach 1 mina of silver.[125] Like other persons travelling to Assur, messengers sent to Assur received some money as an "offering" (*niqi'um*).[126] The hiring of a messenger to go from Kanesh to Assur is reported in Kt n/k 1192: "Hire (someone) for 10 shekels of silver so that people bring my tablets and the city and my lord (i.e., the ruler of Assur) may take care of me."[127]

10.3 The attorney (rābiṣum)

To solve complex legal cases, one could hire an attorney. According to the Erišum inscription found in Kültepe, the attorney was made available by the palace in Assur. Texts from everyday life show that the right to engage an attorney was granted by an official decision made by the city council. A suitable person could then be selected and instructed and an agreement reached about his wages (*igrū*) and how they would be paid together with his expenses (*gamrum, ukultum, dātum*). Usually the attorney received half of his wages in Assur and the rest after completing his task. Attorney's wages are known to range from 30 (Iddin-Aššur, Kt c/k 128), to 50 (Laliya, TC 1, 24), or even 55 shekels of silver (Aššur-ṭāb, TC 1, 24). The danger that a hireling would suddenly give up his mission also applied to attorneys. Their contract contained the stipulation that in such a case they would have to repay the money already received.[128]

The Kt c/k archive contains a file about a certain Iddin-Aššur, who had been hired

---

a-na ší-ip-ri-im ša (10) *a-té-ga-ra-ma ni-iš-pu-ru.*

[124] RA 58, 122 Sch. 19: (5) *a-ni-ša-am* (6) *na-áš-pé-er-ta-kà* (7) *ub-lu-ni-ma* (8) *šu-ᵈen.líl* (9) *lá-šu : a-na ku-bu-ur-na-at* (10) *i-ta-lá-ak* (11) *ni-gu₅-ur-ma* (12) *a-ṣé-ri-šu* (13) *ni-iš-ta-pá-ar.*

[125] Kt c/k 63/b: (15) 2 1/2 *ma-na kù.gi en-nam-/a-šur* (16) *ša ší-ma-lá iš-tù* (17) [L93] *ha-bu-lam* (18) *a-na mu.1.šè ša-qá-lam qá-bi* (19) *u₄-ma-am* 11 *ša-na-tum im-ta-/al-a* (20) *ù a-ší-ip-ri-ma* (21) kb 1 *ma-na ag-ta-mar*, "Ennum-Aššur from Šimala owes me 2 1/2 minas of gold since L93. He had to pay within one year. Today, 11 years have elapsed! Moreover, I have spent 1 mina of silver on messengers."

RA 59, 169 no. 30: (15) *ag-ra-am : a-na* 1 *ma-na.ta* (16) kb : *a-šu-mì a-wa-tim* (17) *a-ni-a-tim a-gu₅-ra-ni-ma* (18) *áš-pu-ra-ni*, "(That) I hired because of this affair a hireling for 1 mina of silver each time and dispatched (him)."

[126] The passage in I 429:56–59 may be best interpreted in that way.

[127] Kt n/k 1192 (Sever and Çeçen 2000, 176): (60) ... *a-na* kb 10 gín *a-gur₁₆-ma ṭup-pí-a lu-ub-lu-nim-ma* (61) *a-lu-um ù be-li : li-šu-ru-ni.*

[128] TC 1, 24: (4) 5/6 *ma-na* kb *ig-ru-šu ša lá-li-a* (5) *ša ra-bi₄-ṣú-tí-šu šà.ba* 1/3 *ma-na* 5 gín (6) kb *il₅-qé : ší-tí* kb 1/3 *ma-na* 5 gín (7) kb : *a-wa-at-ni i-kà-ša-ad-ma* (8) *i-tù-wa-ri-šu* kb *i-lá-qé šu-ma* (9) *té-er-tí e-té-zi-ib-ma : a-šar ša-ni-um* (10) *i-ta-lá-ak* kb *il₅-qé-ú : ú-ta-ar* (11) *i-na ṭup-pí-šu ša ku-nu-ki-šu : a-ni-a-tum* (12) *lá-áp-ta* : 5/6 *ma-na* 5 gín kb (13) *i[g-ru-šu] ša a-šùr-dùg ša ra-bi₄-ṣú-tí-šu* (14) [kb] *ig-ri-šu ša-bu*, "50 shekels of silver is the hire of Laliya for his work as attorney. Of this he has received 25 shekels of silver. The rest of the silver, 25 shekels, he will receive on his way back when he wins our case. If he disregards my instruction and goes somewhere else, he will return the silver that he received. These (words) are written in his document, sealed with his sealings. 55 shekels of silver is the hire of Aššur-ṭāb for his work as attorney. He is satisfied with the silver of his hire."

as an attorney after the death of Aššur-ṭāb. His wages amounted to 30 shekels of silver,[129] and another text informs us that this attorney received a total of 26 shekels of silver for his food (Kt c/k 394).

10.4 Assyrian scribes

It is a basic assumption in OA studies that many merchants and some of their wives and daughters were able to read and write. Poorly written texts are considered as proof of this. Still, many letters and legal documents will have been written by professional scribes. The fee they charged for their activity is almost never mentioned. A rare example is contained in Kt c/k 394: (18) *ú 1/2 ma-na* 5 *gín* (19) kb *a-na ṭup-pé-e* (20) *ša ší-bi ha-ru-mì-im* (21) *ša é a-šur-dùg* (erasure) (22) *ta-ag-mu-ur* (erasure), "You spent 35 shekels of silver to certify the witnessed documents of the house of Aššur-ṭāb". Another case may occur in KTS 2, 9: (33) *a-na ṭup-pé-e ša ší-bi ša a-šu-mì* (34) *i-ku-nim* dumu *sà-ma-a al-ta-qé-ú* (35) kb 1 *ma-na ù e-li-iš ag-mu-ur-ma*, "I spent over a mina of silver on the witnessed documents that I have taken because of Ikūnum son of Samāya."[130] These amounts may have included a payment to the witnesses as well.

11. SLAVERY

The use of slave labour (*wardum*, "slave"; *amtum*, "slave-girl"; collectively *ṣubrum*) was widespread. Slaves and slave-girls were counted among the standard possessions of a household and as such were part of the assets of a merchant. Most slaves apparently did domestic work, and some slave-girls were bought as millers (*ṭē'ittum*) to grind flour. A slave could have a profession that brought his owner money, such as a barber.[131] The price of slaves and slave-girls varies from 15 to a little over 30 shekels of silver. Through the purchase contract or inheritance document, the owner excercised full

---

[129] Kt c/k 128: (20′) ... *i-dí-a-šùr ra-bi-iṣ-ni* (21′) *a-na 1/2 ma-na* kb *ni-gu₅-ur-šu* (22′) 15 *gín* kb *a-na-kam ni-dí-šu-um* (23′) *a-ma-kam* 15 gíb kb *dí-na-šu-um*, "We hired Iddin-Aššur, our attorney, for half a mina of silver. We gave him 15 shekels of silver here. Give him 15 shekels there."

[130] The "half a shekel each" in CCT 3, 37a may refer to the calculation of interest (half a shekel per mina per month): (16) ... *ú a-dí* (17) *ṭup-pì-im e-pá-ší-im* (18) *ša ta-áš-pu-ra-ni* (19) 1/2 *gín.ta iš-tù* (20) *u₄-mì-im-ma li-né-pì-iš* (21) *a-dí* : *ší-be-e* : *ṭup-pá-am* (22) *a-na-kam lá né-pu-uš*, "As for making a tablet, about which you wrote me, let it be made from today for half a shekel (of silver) each. We did not draw up a tablet here because of the witnesses."

[131] KTK 19: (18) *šu-ma ṣú-ha-ru-um* (19) *iš-tù za-al-pá* (20) *e-ru-ba-am iš-tí* (21) *pì-lá-ah-ištar ṭù-ur-da-ni-šu* (22) *ṣú-ha-ra-am* (23) *kà-lá-ri-a-am a-na* (24) *ga-lá-bu-tim i-dá-šu*, "If the boy arrives here from Zalpa, send him here with Pilah-Ištar. He will give the Kilarite boy to become a barber."

UF 7, no. 2 (from the Level Ib-period): (5) *ṣú-ha-ra-am za-áb-ra-am* (6) *ga-lá-ba-am a-na 1/2 ma-na* kb (7) *a-na ší-im ga-me-er* (8) *ta-dí-nam* 17 *gín* kb (9) *a-dí-na-ku-um*, "You sold me the slave boy, a barber, for half a mina of silver, as the full price; I gave you 17 shekels of silver."

legal authority over his slaves, and could sell them at his discretion.[132] A number of individuals often bearing an Assyrian name and identified as the slave of another Assyrian, were active in trade, for example as transporters of merchandise across Anatolia.[133] Their status clearly was higher than that of (mainly Anatolian and Syrian) slaves, and such Assyrians must be regarded as employees of a firm, but not belonging to the family. Some servants of Assyrian institutions appear as transporters or debtors: Nūr-ki-ili, slave of the colony (BIN 4, 160:14); Asqūdum, slave of the palace of Assur (KTS 1, 55b:3); and a servant of the City Hall (Kt 93/k 76:32, Veenhof 2008a, 110).

The number of slaves varied for each household.[134] Šīmat-Ištar complains to Alahum that she has only a single female miller, while Alahum has ten slave-girls in his house in Kanesh.[135] In an attempt to raise money, Aššur-idī orders his sons living in Kanesh to sell the house, the two slave girls and the two female millers, send him the silver and find a house to rent.[136] Other details arise from the division of property in last-wills, as in Kt c/k 843b, where the wife gets three slaves and the son one.

The background of the slaves is diverse. Children could be bought from their mother or other relatives (AKT 3, 41; Kt 88/k 1003; TPAK 1, 161), including from Assyrians (the daughter of Šalim-Aššur is sold for 14 shekels of silver in ICK 2, 76), and some men were forced to sell themselves (TPAK 1, 160). A slave-girl of north Syrian origin was bought in Uršu and brought to Kanesh, according to Kt 87/k 179 (Hecker 1997, 164f.). The town of Kilar (location unknown) was a popular source of slaves. Slave-girls from Kilar are mentioned in CCT 3, 14 and Kt p/k 5:3 (Level Ib), and the slave to be trained as a barber was from the same place (KTK 19). Two 'fullers' from Kilar (2 *áš-lu-ku ki-lá-ri-yu*) are listed in Kt 73/k 14:28 (Level Ib).

The purchase of a captive (*asīrum*) as a slave is attested in a limited number of texts. The current view that this word in OA refers to a container or a piece of equipment (Michel 2001, 115, 485) does not fit all contexts. A price of 40 minas of copper for an *asīrum* is given in Kt c/k 685, which is equivalent to about 13–40 shekels of silver, and

---

[132] E.g. ICK 1,69, where Lā-qēp advises Hutala, his Anatolian wife, to sell the slave-girl if she is not satisfied with her.

[133] For example, Abī-ilī w. of Puzur-Aššur son of Itūr-il, TC 3,129:2′; Aššur-bāštī w. of Kulumāya, CCT 1,38a:15; Šamaš-taklāku w. of Pūšu-kēn, ATHE 31:12; Duna w. of Ahuqar, KTK 67:19; Ennum-[...] w. Sasia: Kt 91/k 181:6; Ištar-pilah w. of Amur-Ištar, AKT 1, 33; Kakki w. of Imdilum, CCT 3,1:11; Šalim-bēlī w. of Suen-nawer, ICK 1,136:1; [...]bani w. of Kuna, AAA 1,16:8′; w. of Hananum, CCT 1,18b:12; w. Kura, CCT 3,12a:13; w. of Uṣur-ša-Aššur, Kt m/k 18:16. Other indebted persons are simply referred to as 'slave', e.g. Išar-bēlī, CCT 1, 32a:10; Mannum-ki-Aššur, I 677:3.8.27.

[134] For Old Babylonian evidence, cf. Stol 2004, 910.

[135] Kt c/k 266 (unp. Ankara): (25) *ki-ša-ma géme ša ke-na-tim* (26) *i-na ma-ah-ri-a té-zi-ib* (27) *géme iš-tí-a tù-uš-té-ṣa i-nu-mì* (28) *a-qá-bi-ú-ší-ni um-ma a-na-ku-ma* (29) 5 *qa té-ni lá ta-mu-a* (30) *ù* 2 *qa e-ṣa-am té-a-na-am lá ta-mu-a* (31) *a-tù-nu a-ma-kam* 10 *a-ma-tum* (32) *ma-ah-ri-ku-nu uš-ba a-na-ku a-na-kam* (33) *a-na té-i-tim a-na a-lim*[ki] (34) *ki-li-šu ú-sà-la*, "Forgive me, but you left a real slave-girl behind to work for me. The slave-girl quarrels with me. When I tell her 'Grind 5 litres', she refuses. Even as little as 2 litres she refuses to grind. Over there, you have 10 slave-girls at your disposal. Here, I appeal to the whole city for a (single) female grinder."

[136] TC 3, 88 edited by Larsen 2002, no. 40.

can only refer to a donkey or a slave. The purchase of a "strong *asīrum*" in TC 3, 98, in order to carry a mill-stone, is another argument for interpreting the word as a captive, who could function as a slave, in at least these two texts.

APPENDIX: THE PRICE OF TIN[137]

Purchase prices, in shekels of tin per shekel of silver, in ascending order of cost. The number of asterisks indicates the number of transactions.

17:	****
16 1/2:	**
16:	***** *****
15 2/3:	*
15 1/2 g 15 še:	*
15g 75 še:	*
15:	***** ***** ***
14 3/4:	*
14 1/2:	****
14 1/3:	*
14 1/4:	**
14g 15 še:	*
14:	***** ***** *
13.9:	*
13 2/3:	**
13 1/2:	*
13 1/4:	*
13:	****
12 1/2:	**
12:	*

References

17	AKT 3, 39:37 (as equivalent of hire); Kt 91/k 484:19 Elamma (4t 20 m 8g tin, 30m hand-tin); TC 1, 47:11 (Aššur-idī, 2m hand-tin); TC 3, 157:20.29 (price of tin spent en route).
16 1/2	BIN 6, 12:12 (2t 10m tin + 12m hand-tin bought from Imdilum); CCT 3, 5a (Aššur-idī, 2t 10m sealed tin, but 12m 5g hand-tin at 15).
16	AAA 1, 4:3′; C 29 // CTMMA 1, 75 (2t 10m tin, but 10m hand-tin at 15); I 571:4.7; KTS 2, 26:5′, 21′; KUG 7:17; KUG 27:17; Pa. 15 (L29-569) 4t 20m 3 1/3 g tin + 40m hand-tin; RA 59, 31:8; TC 1, 29:33; TC 3, 26:3 (10t tin).

---

[137] References from unpublished Kt 91/k and 92/k texts courtesy of K. R. Veenhof.

15 2/3	VS 26, 151:4 (10t 50m tin + 50 m hand-tin; *kutānu* 8 1/4 g, *šuru* 4 1/2 g).
15 1/2 gín 15 še	CCT 4, 7a:9 (35m 10g tin and 5m hand-tin).
15 gín 75 še	Kt 92/k 142 (4t 20m tin, but 20m hand-tin at 15).
15	BIN 4, 47:16-17.39 (7 1/2 t tin); C 29 // CTMMA 1, 75 (10m hand-tin, but 2t 10m tin at 16); CCT 3, 2a:20-21 (15m hand-tin); CCT 3, 5a:24 (12m 5g hand-tin); CCT 4, 17b:6 (30m tin, of which 2m hand-tin); I 762:4′; Kt c/k 42:47; Kt c/k 531:8; Kt 91/k 434:7; Kt 91/k 530:8; Kt 92/k 142 (20m hand-tin; but 4t 20m tin at 15g 75 še); TC 3, 43:15 (2t 20m tin, 50m hand-tin at 14); VS 26, 47:19.
14 3/4	Kt 91/k 417:4 (Elamma, 2t 56 2/3 m incl. hand-tin).
14 1/2	BIN 4, 30:16 (3t 37 1/2 m); I 480:5 (2t *kunukkū*; 11 2/3 m hand-tin); KTB 17:4 (5t30m tin + [x] t hand-tin); VS 26, 13 (40m hand-tin = 2m 45 1/2 g at 14 1/2).
14 1/3	Kt 91/k 419:8 Elamma (2t 10m tin).
14 1/4	Kt 91/k 419:11 Elamma (15m hand-tin); Kt 92/k 143 (2t 10m tin + 25m hand-tin).
14 gín 15 še	RA 59, 27 Pūšu-kēn (2t 10m tin + 10 m hand-tin).
14	BIN 6, 65:18 Aššur-mūtappil (2m 55g hand-tin); I 435:9 Imdilum (2t 10m tin); I 836:9 Pūšu-kēn (15m hand-tin voor 1m 4g); KTS 2, 10: 2t tin (but 26m hand-tin à 13); KTS 2, 36+: Imdilum, 17 (20m hand-tin); TC 2, 6 Šalim-ahum and Šu-Hubur (2t 10m and 9m hand-tin); TC 2, 14:12 Šu-Hubur (15m hand-tin); TC 3, 36 Pūšu-kēn (1t 5m hand-tin); TC 3, 43:35 (50m hand-tin); Yale 13092:19 Pūšu-kēn (22m 10g hand-tin).
14 or lower:	BIN 6, 59: 14′ (expensive).
13.9	Sadberk 13 Pūšu-kēn (2t 10m + 10m hand-tin) // CCT 2, 2: 17–31, furthermore 2t 7m tin + 9 m hand-tin at 14 5/6, and 13 2/3 for 6m 33g.
13 2/3	Kt 91/k 418 Elamma (2 1/2 m tin); TC 3, 134:4′ (6t 58 2/3 m).
13 1/2	I 704:19 Pūšu-kēn (40 1/2 m hand-tin).
13 1/4	KTS 1, 38a:13 Enlil-bāni (2t 15m) // CCT 3, 27a:12.
13	KTS 1, 23:9 30m hand-tin; KTS 1, 38a:16 [13] ([40m] en [8m], 23 (37 1/2 m hand-tin) // CCT 3, 27a:23; KTS 2, 10: 26m hand-tin (2t tin at 14); TC 2, 7:9 Pūšu-kēn.
12 1/2	CCT 3, 22a Pūšu-kēn (almost 24m hand-tin); Kt 91/k 418:20 Elamma (hand-tin and 2 1/2 m at 13 2/3).
12	Kt c/k 227:11 (4m hand-tin).

The sale of tin

Prices for tin in silver in Anatolia in ascending order of cost.

10	*****
9 1/2	*
9 1/4	*

9	***** ***
8 5/6	*
8 1/8	*
8	***** ***** ****
7 1/2	****
7	***** ***** *
6 3/4	**
6 1/2	**
6	***** ***** ***** *
5 1/2	*
5 1/4	*
5	***
4	*

References

10   BIN 4, 27 Šalim-ahum (L86/v) (*kutānu* 15g); CCT 6, 16a:27 (*šitapku*; *šuru* 8g, *kutānu* 15g); Kt c/k 189:2; Kt 91/k 301:20; TC 2, 24:16 (Ikunum < Pūšu-kēn, *kutānu* 13g, *šuru* 8g).

9 1/2   CCT 2, 49a:8 (in Hahhum).

9 1/4   I 430:6 poor price, Imdilum angry; textile 8 3/4 g.

9   BIN 4, 29:23 (1t 2m 15g of Aššur-imittī); CCT 4, 50b Pūšu-kēn ([x x] 1? an.na biltim š[a...], [sà-a]h-ru-da-na-i-e an.na 10 [.. gín]./ta, [i-z]i-iz 9 gín.ta an.na-kà, [x-x]-dí-šu-ma); CCT 6, 35:8′ (Pušuken; *ana* 40 weeks, *kutanu* 15g); I 686:15; I 789:3′; Kt c/k 208:8; Kt 91/k 455:16; Pa. 19 (Šalim-ahum).

8 5/6   TC 3, 2:11 (6t 55 1/2 m tin, fine *kutānu* 26 1/4 g).

8 1/8   CCT 4, 23a:11 (Pūšu-kēn, 4t 5m 8g).

8   AKT 3,95 (5 months; 109 *kutānu* at 10g); AnOr 6, 15:19–20 (*ešartum* of Nihria < Pūšu-kēn); AnOr 6, 17:7; TMH 27, 436:4; BIN 4, 23:30 (tin given to Lulu for 8:1); BIN 4, 61:54 (39m 50g) Šalim-ahum, L81/xi; BIN 6, 72:5 Innaya (16 5/6 m tin); CCT 4, 25c:18′ (Wahšušana, *kutānu* 15g); CCT 5, 17b:15f. (2t 40m tin for 20m silver); I 426:51 (short-term); Kt 91/k 298:10 (*ana* 20 weeks); Kt 91/k 416:9; Sadberk no. 12:14 (sale for Imdilum, 3t tin; *kutānu* 10g); TC 3, 24:33 (Šalim-ahum < Pūšu-kēn, rate of Kanesh).

7 1/2   CCT 2, 24:9 (1t 42g) sold by Enna-Suen; Kt c/k 256:4 Tahašali > Aššur-malik (1t); Kt 91/k 447:4 Elamma (*niplātum* of Hinaya); TC 3, 49:8 (for Imdilum, no cash, silver hard to obtain: 50m tin at 7 1/2 + *kutānu* 13 1/2 g to U. for 4 weeks, 50m tin at 7 1/2 + *kutānu* 13 1/2 g to I. for 4 weeks).

7   AKT 1, 82 Imdilum (not 7, but 9 because silver is scarce; *kutānu* 20g, *šuru* 12g); AKT 3, 65:32–36 Šalim-ahum (*kutānu* 30g, *šuru* 15g); BIN 4, 61:27 Šalim-ahum L81/iii (2t 59m for 45-50 weeks) and .35 (2t 14m 10g for 48 weeks); I 426:13 Šalim-ahum (2t 2m 8g) .39 (2t 4m 39g); CCT 4, 9a:12; I 678:7 (textile 20g); Kt g/k

	199:32; KTS 1, 57e (textile 30g, within 50 weeks from L83); RA 51 HG 74:7 (1t sold in Ulama); RA 59, 26:11 (35m of Šalim-ahum); TC 3, 46:9 and Pa. 22:22 (Imdilum).
6 3/4	CTMMA 1, 74:21 (Imdilum); ICK 1, 154.
6 1/2	BIN 6, 127:14–18 (sell tin for silver if 6 1/2 or 5, otherwise store the tin); ICK 1, 81; Kt c/k 449:3′ (in Purušhattum).
6	AKT 3,78 Šalim-ahum (textile 30g); BIN 4, 19:15 (4t Hinaya); C 17 and TC 1, 8 Alāhum; C 42; I 761:6; Kt 91/k 520:12; KTH 11:6; KTS 2, 34:10; Pa. 22 Imdilum (but sold for 7; fine *kutānu* 15g); TC 1, 26:29 (Šalim-ahum); TC 2, 3:12.18 (Šalim-ahum); TC 2, 72; TC 3, 136:7′; TC 3, 203:5ff.; TC 3, 72 (6 and 5 1/2).
5 1/2	CCT 5, 2a:35.
5 1/4	Kt c/k 172+:10.
5	KBo 9,6 (*tapšu* tin not sold for 5; Level Ib); Kt c/k 353:18; KTS 2, 53:6.
4	Kt n/k 1339 // Kt 91/k 175 (cash payment 'since the plague of Purušhattum').

REFERENCES

Albayrak, I. (2004) 'She will live, eat and be anointed together with them' *ušbat aklat u paššat ištišunu*. In J. G. Dercksen (ed.) *Assyria and Beyond. Studies Presented to Mogens Trolle Larsen*, 9–20. Leiden: Nederlands Instituut voor het Nabije Oosten.

Balkan, K. (1965) Review of L. Matouš, Inscriptions cunéiformes du Kültepe, Prague 1962 (= ICK II). *Orientalistische Literatur-Zeitung* 60, 146–162.

Bayram, S. and Çeçen, S. (1995) 6 Neue Urkunden über Heirat und Scheidung aus Kaniš, *Archivum Anatolicum* 1, 1–12.

Biggs, R. D. (1988) An Old Assyrian letter. In E. Leichty, P. Gerardi and M. deJ. Ellis (eds) *A Scientific Humanist. Studies in Memory of Abraham Sachs*, 33–38 (Occasional Publications of the Samuel Noah Kramer Fund 9). Philadelphia: The University Museum.

Charpin, D. (1986) *Le clergé d'Ur au siècle d'Hammurabi*. Geneva/Paris: Droz.

Çeçen, S. (1995) *mūtānū* in den Kültepe-Texten, *Archivum Anatolicum* 1, 43–72.

Dercksen, J. G. (1996) *The Old Assyrian Copper Trade in Anatolia*. Istanbul: Nederlands Historisch-Archaeologisch Instituut in het Nabije Oosten.

Dercksen, J. G. (1999) On the financing of Old Assyrian merchants. In: J. G. Dercksen (ed.) *Trade and Finance in Ancient Mesopotamia*, 85–99 (PIHANS 84). Istanbul: Nederlands Historisch-Archaeologisch Instituut.

Dercksen, J. G. (2004) *Old Assyrian Institutions* (PIHANS 98). Leiden: Nederlands Instituut voor het Nabije Oosten.

Dercksen, J. G. (2005) Metals according to documents from Kültepe-Kanish dating to the Old Assyrian Colony Period. In Ü. Yalçın (ed.), *Anatolian Metal III*, 17–34. Bochum: Deutsches Bergbau-Museum.

Dercksen, J. G. (2008a) Subsistence, surplus and the market for grain and meat at ancient Kanesh. *Altorientalische Forschungen* 35, 86–102.

Dercksen, J. G. (2008b) Observations on land use and agriculture in Kaneš. In C. Michel (ed.) *Old Assyrian Studies in Memory of Paul Garelli*, 139–157. Leiden: Nederlands Instituut voor het Nabije Ooste.

Donbaz, V. (1985) New evidence on the reading of the Old Assyrian month-name *kanwarta* with an edition of the memorandum kt c/k 839. *Jaarbericht Ex Oriente Lux* 28, 3–9.

Donbaz, V. (1991) A small archive of Innāya – an Assyrian merchant. *Revue d'Assyriologie* 85, 101–108.

Donbaz, V. (2008) The archives of Eddin-Aššur son of Ahiaya. In C. Michel (ed.) *Old Assyrian Studies in Memory of Paul Garelli*, 47–62. Leiden: Nederlands Instituut voor het Nabije Ooste.

Donbaz, V. and Veenhof, K. R. (1985) New Evidence for some Old Assyrian Terms. *Anatolica* 12, 131–155.

Durand, J.-M. (1997) *Les Documents épistolaires du palais de Mari, Vol. I* (Littératures anciennes du Proche-Orient 16). Paris: les Éditions du Cerf.

Garelli, P. (1963) *Les Assyriens en Cappadoce*. Paris: Maisonneuve.

Gökçek, L. Gürkan (2006) The use of wagons (*eriqqum*) in ancient Anatolia according to texts from Kültepe. *Zeitschrift für Assyriologie* 96, 185–199.

Günbattı C. (1987) Ankara Anadolu Medeniyetleri Müzesi'nde bulunan üç tablet. *Ankara Üniversitesi Dil ve Tarih-Cografya Fakültesi Dergisi* 1987, 189–199.

Hecker, K. (1997) Über den Euphrat... Ortsbezogene Restriktionen in aA Kaufurkunden. *Archivum Anatolicum* 4, 157–172.

Hecker, K. (1999) In nova...,. *Archív Orientální* 67, 557–565.

Hecker, K. (2006) Altassyrische Briefe. In M. Lichtenstein (ed.), *Texte aus der Umwelt des alten Testaments*, NF 3: *Briefe*, 77–100. Gütersloh: Gütersloher Verlagshaus.

Joannès, F. (1991) L'étain, de l'Élam à Mari. In L. De Meyer and H. Gasche (eds) *Mésopotamie et Elam. Actes de la XXXVIème RAI Gand, 10-14 juillet 1989*, 67–76 (Mesopotamian History and Environment, Occasional Publications I). Ghent: University of Ghent.

Johnston, S. I. (ed.) (2004) *Religions of the Ancient World. A Guide*. Cambridge, MA/London: Belknap Press of Harvard University Press.

Kienast, B. (1989) The Old Assyrian *be'ūlātum*. *Journal of Cuneiform Studies* 41, 87–95.

Larsen, M.T. (1967) *Old Assyrian Caravan Procedures*. Istanbul: Nederlands Historisch-Archaeologisch Instituut in het Nabije Oosten.

Larsen, M.T. (1971) Slander. *Orientalia* 40, 317–324.

Larsen, M.T. (1976) *The Old Assyrian City-State and its Colonies* (Mesopotamia 4). Copenhagen: Akademisk Forlag.

Larsen, M.T. (1977) Partnerships in the Old Assyrian trade. *Iraq* 39, 119–145.

Larsen, M.T. (1999) Naruqqu-Verträge (*naruqqu*-contracts). *Reallexikon der Assyriologie* 9, 181–184.

Larsen, M.T. (2002) *The Aššur-nādā Archive* (Old Assyrian Archives 1). Leiden: Nederlands Instituut voor het Nabije Oosten.

Mayhew, A., Neale, W. C. and Tandy, D. W. (1985) Markets in the Ancient Near East: a challenge to Silver's argument and use of evidence. *Journal of Economic History* 45, 127–134.

Michel, C. (2001) *Correspondance des marchands de Kaniš au début du IIᵉ millénaire avant J.-C.* Littératures anciennes du proche-Orient 19. Paris: Éditions du Cerf.

Michel, C. (2008) Les Assyriens et les esprits de leurs morts. In C. Michel (ed.) *Old Assyrian Studies in Memory of Paul Garelli*, 181–197. Leiden: Nederlands Instituut voor het Nabije Ooste.

Michel, C. and Veenhof, K. R. (2010) The *textiles* traded by the Assyrians in Anatolia (19th–18th Centuries BC). In C. Michel and M.-L. Nosch (eds), *Textile Terminologies in the Ancient Near East and Mediterranean from the Third to the First Millennia BC*, 210–271 (Ancient Textiles Series 8). Oxford: Oxbow Books.

Nakata, I. (1971) Mesopotamian merchants and their ethos. *Journal of the Ancient Near Eastern Society* 3/2, 90–101.

Schwemer, D. (2001) *Die Wettergottgestalten Mesopotamiens und Nordsyriens im Zeitalter der Keilschriftkulturen.* Wiesbaden: Harrassowitz.

Sever, H. (1990) Yeni Kültepe Tabletlerinde Geçen (Kīma awāt naruā'im) Tabiri ve Değerlendirilmesi. *Dil ve Tarih-Coğrafya Fakültesi Dergisi* 34, 251–265.

Sever, H. (1995) Anadolu'da borsa ve enflasyonun ilk şekilleri. *Archivum Anatolicum* 1, 123–136.

Sever, H. and S. Çeçen (2000) Naruqqum – ortaklığı hakkında yeni bir belge. *Archivum Anatolicum* 4, 167–176.

Silver, M. (1995) *Economic Structures of Antiquity.* Westport, CT/London: Greenwood Press.

Stol, M. (2004) Wirtschaft und Gesellschaft in altbabylonischer Zeit. In D. Charpin, D. O. Edzard and M. Stol, *Mesopotamien. Die altbabylonische Zeit*, 643–975 (Orbis Biblicus et Orientalis 160/4). Fribourg/Göttingen: Academic Press/Vandenhoeck & Ruprecht.

Truxes, T. M. (2001) *Letterbook of Greg & Cunnigham 1756-1757. Merchants of New York and Belfast.* Oxford: Oxford University Press for the British Academy.

Van der Toorn. K. (2004) Sin, pollution, and purity. Mesopotamia. In Johnston (ed.), 499–501.

Van De Mieroop, M. (1995) Old Babylonian interest rates: were they annual? In K. Van Lerberghe and A. Schoors (eds) *Immigration and Emigration Within the Ancient Near East*, 357–364. Leuven: Peeters.

Veenhof, K. R. (1972) *Aspects of Old Assyrian Trade and its Terminology.* Leiden: Brill.

Veenhof, K. R. (1984) An Old Assyrian business letter in the Medelhavsmuseet. *Medelhavsmuseet Bulletin* 19, 3–9.

Veenhof, K. R. (1985) Observations on Old Assyrian memorandums. *Jaarbericht Ex Oriente Lux* 28, 10–23.

Veenhof, K. R. (1987) 'Dying tablets' and 'hungry silver'. Elements of figurative language in Akkadian commercial terminology. In M. Mindlin, M. J. Geller and J. E. Wansbrough (eds) *Figurative Language in the Ancient Near East*, 41–75. London: School of Oriental and African Studies.

Veenhof, K. R. (1988) Prices and trade. The Old Assyrian evidence. *Altorientalistische Forschungen* 15, 243–263.

Veenhof, K. R. (1994) Miete. C. Altassyrisch. *Reallexikon der Assyriologie* 8, 181–184.

Veenhof, K. R. (1995) 'In accordance with the words of the stele': Evidence for Old Assyrian legislation. *Chicago-Kent Law Review* 70, 1717–1744.

Veenhof, K. R. (1997a) The Old Assyrian *hamuštum* period: a seven-day week. *Jaarbericht Ex Oriente Lux* 34, 5–26.

Veenhof, K. R. (1999a) Silver and credit in Old Assyrian trade. In J. G. Dercksen (ed.) *Trade and Finance in Ancient Mesopotamia (MOS Studies 1). Proceedings of the First MOS Symposium (Leiden 1997)*, 55–83 (PIHANS 84). Istanbul: Nederlands Historisch-Archaeologisch Instituut.

Veenhof, K. R. (1999b) Redemption of houses in Assur and Sippar. In B. Böck, E. Cancik-Kirschbaum and T. Richter (eds) *Munuscula Mesopotamica. Festschrift für Johannes Renger*, 599–616. Münster: Ugarit-Verlag.

Veenhof, K. R. (2003a) *The Old Assyrian List of Year Eponyms from Karum Kanish and its Chronological Implications.* Ankara: Türk Tarih Kurumu.

Veenhof, K. R. (2003b) Trade and politics in ancient Assur. Balancing of public, colonial and entrepreneurial interests. In C. Zaccagnini (ed.) *Mercanti e politica nel mondo antico*, 69–118. Rome: "L'Erma" di Bretschneider.

Veenhof, K. R. (2003c) Old Assyrian period. In R. Westbrook (ed.) *A History of Ancient Near Eastern Law* I, 431–483 (Handbuch der Orientalistik 72/1). Leiden/Boston: Brill.

Veenhof, K. R. (2008a) The Old Assyrian Period. In K. R. Veenhof and J. Eidem, *Mesopotamia. The*

Old Assyrian Period, 13–264 (Orbis Biblicus et Orientalis 160/5). Fribourg/Göttingen: Academic Press/Vandenhoeck & Ruprecht.

Veenhof, K. R. (2008b) The death and burial of Ishtar-lamassi in karum Kanish. In R. J. van der Spek (ed.) *Studies in Ancient Near Eastern World View and Society Presented to Marten Stol*, 97–119. Bethesda, MD: CDL Press.

Veenhof, K. R. (2008c) Communication in the Old Assyrian trading society by caravans, travelers and messengers. In C. Michel (ed.) *Old Assyrian Studies in Memory of Paul Garelli*, 199–246. Leiden: Nederlands Instituut voor het Nabije Oosten.

Veenhof, K. R. (2009) A new volume of Old Assyrian texts from Karum Kanesh. *Jaarbericht Ex Oriente Lux* 41, 179–202.

Warburton, D. (2003) *Macroeconomics from the Beginning. The General Theory, Ancient Markets, and the Rate of Interest*. Neuchâtel: Recherches et publications.

Economic Development in Babylonia from the Late 7th to the Late 4th Century BC: Economic Growth and Economic Crises in Imperial Contexts

Michael Jursa[1]

This paper summarizes some of the findings of the START Project and places them into a wider context.[2] The principal focus is on the defining characteristics of the Babylonian economy in the 'long sixth century' between the fall of the Assyrian empire (612 BC) and the Babylonian revolts against Xerxes in 484 BC. For the subsequent period, i.e., the late Achaemenid period and the Hellenistic age, the documentation for which is much less variegated and overall less abundant, some incisive changes in the socio-economic framework can be identified that, notwithstanding all structural continuity in the ecological and technological background, altered the basic characteristics of the economy. A preliminary model for the as yet incompletely understood developments in the later Persian period is presented here to allow this paper to be linked up with van der Spek's contribution on the economic history of Hellenistic Babylonia in the present volume.

[1] This paper is based on research conducted under the auspices of the START project until 2009 and thereafter under the auspices of a project entitled "Imperium and Officium," both funded by the Fonds zur Förderung der Wissenschaftlichen Forschung (Vienna).
   [2] Much of the following can also be found in the monograph Jursa 2010, on which this paper draws heavily.

INTRODUCTION

The body of written sources on which we can draw for writing an economic history of Babylonia is one of the largest text corpora that survives from antiquity: well over 24,000 cuneiform tablets dating to the late seventh, the sixth, and the early fifth century are currently available for study, and many more remain unpublished. Perhaps four thousand archival tablets from the later centuries are known (many of them still unpublished). The earlier material from the beginning of the first millennium until the late seventh century consists of under 900 archival texts (not counting over 1,000 letters written in Babylonian that were found in the Assyrian royal archives of Nineveh).[3] Archaeological data have been under-exploited for the purposes of economic history, which is mostly owed to the lack of pertinent specialized research.[4] The most notable exceptions are the archaeological surveys that have furnished fundamental information on the development of settlement patterns (Adams 1981).

Methodologically, positivistic philological approaches have long dominated research on the Mesopotamian economies: the field in general was (and remains) quite sceptical of 'grand narratives' and theory-based interpretations. The most frequently employed model is that of a two-sector economy, consisting of a 'subordinate' 'domestic sector' (which is largely village-based) and the 'hegemonial' institutional sector dominated by the large urban institutional *oikoi* of the temples and palaces. In both sectors, especially in the 'domestic sector', subsistence production is the dominant mode of the economy; the institutional households are dependent on their own domains and on (quasi-)servile labour and on the surplus production and the surplus labour of the domestic sector. Economic exchange beyond subsistence production and resource extraction on the part of the institutional *oikoi*, especially (long-distance) trade, draws largely from the surpluses of the institutional sector and is needed for procuring prestige goods, but on the level of everyday consumption its importance is very limited.[5] This model is employed famously by Moses Finley in his *Ancient Economy* where he emphasises the fact that in Egypt and the Ancient Near East temples and palaces, with their redistributive bureaucracies, performed essential social and economic functions.[6] For this reason, Ancient Near Eastern sources, economic structures and generally history were to be kept separate from the Graeco-Roman equivalents where these institutions normally did not play such an important role. This argument is still widely accepted,[7] and indeed, from a Mesopotamian perspective,

---

[3] Jursa 2005; Nielsen 2011, 5–6 with note 17; Hackl 2013.

[4] But note, e.g., Baker in this volume for an approach that integrates philological and archaeological data.

[5] References for this model and its proponents can be found in Jursa 2010, 13–26.

[6] They owned, he claims, most of the arable land, monopolised trade, and organised all aspects of social life (economic, religious, political and military) through their bureaucracy.

[7] For Finley see the pertinent quotes in Manning and Morris 2005, 12–13 (the book largely concerns this very question). Finley's argument was recently repeated by the editors of the *Cambridge Economic History of the Greco-Roman World* in their justification of their choice of thematic coverage (Morris *et al.* 2007, 8).

the value of the two-sector economy – if not its universal applicability – especially for the early periods of Mesopotamian history is beyond doubt. There is, however, rich evidence that cannot be accommodated by the model, such as the Old Assyrian case (Dercksen, this volume) with the central role of trade and its underlying market-oriented structure for the economy of the city state of Assur. Crucially for the concerns of the present paper, the two-sector model does not explain sufficiently the structure (and performance) of the Babylonian economy of the Iron Age, especially during its best-documented phase, the long sixth century. For this period, most specialist scholars have adopted more or less 'modernist' readings. In this vein, Jursa (2010) suggested casting the economic phenomena that distinguish the period into the mould of an explanatory model that sees a conjuncture of several independent demographic, social, economic and political factors leading to a period of 'Smithian' growth. The methodology employed draws on tenets of Douglass North's New Economic History, emphasizing economic performance as well as economic structure, and investigating the impact of institutional change on economic development.

Babylonian society in the first millennium BC was predominantly agrarian. Local irrigation agriculture depended on two leading crops: the extensive cultivation of barley made comparatively lavish use of land and sparing use of the scarce resources of seed, water and labour. Date gardening, the second distinctive agrarian regime abundantly attested in this period, implied a far more intensive use of land (and water).[8] Labour requirements and returns were higher than in the case of arable farming. Sheep breeding was the third principal agrarian activity. Flocks belonging to central and southern Babylonian owners were often pastured in the north and northeast of the country, east of the Tigris.

In our period, several interdependent ecological, economic, social and political factors combined to change the nature of the economy within this general framework. By the eighth century BC, the climatic anomaly that had contributed to the crisis of the Near Eastern world around the turn of the millennium was over: the climate grew wetter, the conditions for arable agriculture in the alluvial flood-plain of southern Mesopotamia improved markedly, population density started to increase again, and a phase of increasing urbanisation began (Adams 1981). The ascent of the Neo-Babylonian empire at the end of the seventh century brought to an end a period of political unrest and war caused by the Assyrian domination over Babylonia. As the centre of an empire whose sphere of influence stretched from the Levant in the West to the foothills of the Iranian plateau in the east, Babylonia could reap the benefits both of peace, and of imperial domination.

This combination of ecological, demographic and political factors gave an important impetus to economic development. The close to one and a half centuries following the fall of Assyria saw an increase of agrarian productivity and a change in the focus of agricultural production, which was increasingly market-oriented. A large part of

---

[8] Fernea 1970 presents ethnographical data on the Iraqi dual-crop regime and the way it shapes (shaped) traditional nutrition in the country.

the urban population worked in non-agrarian and distinctly specialized occupations. For the first time in Mesopotamian history, a large part, probably at times the larger part, of the urban and rural work-force consisted of free hirelings who were paid money wages, not of compelled labourers. The economy was certainly monetised to a greater degree than ever before – silver served ubiquitously, both for high-value purchases and as low-range money. This is exemplified also by the rich data on prices and wages than can be fully contextualised. Few Babylonian city dwellers can have remained entirely untouched by the monetary economy. The available indications for consumption patterns point to a higher level of prosperity in comparison to earlier periods of Babylonian history.

The initial Persian conquest of Babylonia in 539 BC did not bring immediate and fundamental socio-economic change, but the consequences of the Babylonian rebellions against Xerxes in 484 BC constituted an important step, indeed, probably the crucial step, towards an elite change in what was then the Achaemenid province of Babylonia. The Babylonian upper classes who had been the main beneficiaries of the economic expansion of the long sixth century suffered politically, socially and economically. Their economic interests were certainly not served anymore by state politics as they had been under the Neo-Babylonian empire and, mostly by institutional inertia, in the first decades of Persian rule. Property rights were upset on a large scale. The expansion of the latifundia owned by Persian nobles and Babylonian supporters of Persian rule introduced into the Babylonian socio-economic system a class of agents who depended for their prosperity and status on their use of political power rather than on commerce and agricultural business founded on a stable legal system and market-based contractual exchange (Jursa 2014a). We discuss below the probable consequences of these changes for the economic system.

A model for economic development during the long sixth century

The overall development of the Babylonian economy in the 'long sixth century' can be explained by reference to a 'commercialisation model' of Smithian inspiration.[9] As is frequently suggested also for other periods (e.g. Dyer 2005), population growth can act as a stimulus for commercial development and technological progress; rising demand generates a positive feedback in the economy which offsets (for a while) the Malthusian threat accompanying demographic growth. Urbanisation allows an increase in the division of labour and economic specialisation, and thus leads to higher productivity. As administrative, religious and economic centres, cities are foci of high consumption and depend on an increasing pool of non-agricultural labour. They

---

[9]   Employing concepts that go back in part to Adam Smith, this is decidedly a 'modernist' model. See, e.g., Hatcher and Bailey 2001, 121–73 (for the medieval period), Hopkins 1978, and Millett 2001 (for the classical period). For the application of the model to the present period, see Jursa 2010, 783–800. This is not the place to review the modernist-primitivist (or the formalist-substantivist) debate.

stimulate the production of a growing agricultural surplus by offering market opportunities. There is thus a causal link between agricultural development and economic phenomena, especially commerce, which the city-oriented documentation allows us to observe in an urban setting only. The interplay of intensification and market-orientation of agricultural production, urbanisation, increasing division of labour and technological improvements can be expected to lead to an increased productivity per capita and thus to intensive economic growth, i.e., to an increase in real incomes and hence in economic 'well-being' throughout society. We will briefly review here some of the data on which this model is based (Jursa 2010, 785). Special emphasis will be placed on the role of the state as an important catalyst sustaining the process of agrarian change, monetisation and commercialisation of economic life by directing (some of) the 'benefits of empire' into the economy: it is here that important changes occured in the fifth century.

Demography

According to Adams 1981, the results of wide-ranging archaeological surveys in northern and north-eastern Babylonia suggest "a growth in the population of the region by more than five times during a span of five to seven hundred years" beginning in the late eighth century (Adams 1981, 178). "We are dealing with fairly abrupt, probably state-directed, policies of settlement formation in the case of the urban communities" (ibid.). Other scholars point out that the surveys did not cover the area with the greatest concentration of Babylonian cities in the alluvium along the new, western course of the Euphrates, where the demographic expansion was most likely less rapid (Brinkman 1984). Nevertheless it is certain that in our period not only did more people live in Babylonia than in the preceding centuries, but also more of them lived in larger settlements. According to Adams's figures half the settled surface area was taken up by settlements of a surface area of more than ten hectares, settlements he designates as cities. Notwithstanding uncertainties about settlement density, it is probable that such settlements had more than 1,000 inhabitants each (taking 1,000 as a minimum figure for the inhabitants of a site of ten hectares); they also had fairly differentiated internal structures and institutions that generated textual documentation.[10] This means that according to these findings, in the large area covered by the survey, around half of the population lived in socio-economic contexts that can be considered to have been urbanized, and that are well documented by texts.

---

[10] The textual documentation is heavily concentrated on urban contexts, but the countryside is by no means outside its general focus owing to the multiple links through rents and taxation between the city and the countryside. Some village archives are known (Jursa 2005 for a survey of the documentation).

Michael Jursa

Table 5.1 Comparative data for barley seed rates and yields in Iraq (references: Jursa 2010, 49)

	Seed rate		Average yield	
	litre/ha	kg/ha	litre/ha	kg/ha
2040–1700 BC	46.3	28.7	1,389	861
Sixth century BC Sippar	71.1	44.8	1,728	1,071
Iraq, 1940s	80.6–206.5	50–128	1,355	840

Agriculture

The evidence for agrarian change, intensification of production and local and regional specialisation, including cash-crop production, is rich and variegated. For most regions of Babylonia an expansion of the cultivated surface at least from the late seventh century onwards can be documented either on the basis of archaeological surveying (Adams 1981) or on the basis of the documentary record, or both (van Driel 1988, a seminal article; Jursa 2010, 316–468, on which much of the following is based).

The agricultural landscape of Babylonia exhibited a degree of regional agricultural specialisation. The south, and especially the Sealand in the far south of Babylonia, was (at least occasionally) a major supplier of grain to more northern parts of Babylonia, where date gardening dominated.[11] Animal husbandry dominated in the trans-Tigridian area, allowing also distant institutions such as the Eanna temple to specialize in the production of wool as a cash-crop.

By the sixth century, traditional arable farming had changed towards a more intensive form of cultivation. The basic principles of cultivation had of course remained unaltered: as in earlier periods the seeder plough and the comparatively low seeding rates produced high returns on seed while land was used extensively, rather than intensively – the system was still intended to economise on the scarce resources of seed, labour and irrigation water, but not land. In such a system, a slight shift of the quantitative parameters can produce significant change. Neo-Babylonian seeding rates and yields were higher and furrow spaces narrower than, for instance, in the second millennium BC. This additional investment of labour and resources produced higher returns than in earlier periods. The evidence is as follows.

Neo-Babylonian farmers used as much as 53 percent more seed than their Bronze Age predecessors (but far less than traditional Iraqi farmers in the mid-20th century who did not use the seeder-plough, but broadcast the seed). A plough team of the Ur III period (c. 2040 BC) was expected to deal with 39–52 ha of land, a huge workload for a ploughing season which was feasible only because of the wide spacing of the furrows: another indication of the low intensity of farming in this period (Halstead

---

[11] Cities in southern Mesopotamia had a belt of garden land around them in which citizens held individual plots, much as is the case for Iraqi cities today. The evidence from Sippar, for instance, shows that in our period widespread horticulture was a phenomenon on a different scale in northern Babylonia; it determined the character of the agrarian landscape not just in the vicinity of the cities.

1990, 189). In our period, the maximum workload prescribed for a plough team was 37.5 ha, but in practice teams often tilled as little as half this figure. This means a narrower spacing of the furrows than in the second and third millennium BC. In short, Neo-Babylonian arable farming was more intensive than third and early second millennium practice. This higher investment of resources (seed, land and labour) achieved an increase of average yields by about a quarter. For a traditional pre-modern agrarian system, this is a significant difference (note in comparison the relatively poor performance of traditional 20th-century agriculture in the area). It reflects the innovative character of Neo-Babylonian agriculture, and must be read as evidence for widespread and structural economic change.

The period experienced a continuous expansion of the cultivated area. Both textual data and the archaeological surveys tell us about large-scale 'interregional' systems of irrigation canals. These, according to Adams' reading of the survey data, appeared in this form for the first time in Mesopotamian history and fundamentally changed the agricultural landscape in the later first millennium BC. The textual documentation gives us the crucial additional insight into the agricultural focus of these newly-created estates: they illustrate the large-scale shift to date-growing and the concomitant increase in productivity. In comparison to barley growing, date gardening is a more intensive form of agriculture; the yield per surface area is much higher. Date gardening is obviously more labour-intensive than arable farming in absolute terms, but it is also more productive in terms of output per capita: the labour productivity of date gardening exceeded that of arable farming by a margin of at least ten and potentially more than one hundred percent (Jursa 2010, 50–1): one agricultural labourer, by moving from arable farming to working in a productive date garden, could as much as double the output of his work in terms of calories of food produced. Such a shift had always been theoretically possible in Babylonia, but in our period, the necessary preconditions, i.e., a growing population that could meet the high labour requirements, stable political conditions, and a willingness of the state to invest in the agrarian infrastructure, were present in an ideal form. The strong preponderance of horticulture on privately owned land, and sometimes also on institutional land, is therefore a key factor for understanding the economic structure of our period: Babylonia being a largely agrarian society, the shift to horticulture on a large scale caused a society-wide increase in the available agricultural surplus.[12]

Money and monetisation

Exchange in sixth-century Babylonia was monetised to a significant degree (Jursa 2010,

---

[12] The fact that this preference for horticulture was indeed an extremely common phenomenon follows also from the observation that Babylonians in our period drank beer made of dates, not of barley, as had been common in earlier periods. This would not have been possible if the basic parameters of agricultural production had not changed.

469–753; see also Graslin-Thomé 2009, 238–52).[13] The most common money medium was weighed silver. It came in certain forms and in specified degrees of purity. Other metals were used to a much lesser degree in this period.[14]

In comparison with eighth-century data, the archives of the sixth century, especially the temple archives, demonstrate that the range of economic situations in which silver money was used had expanded substantially. In the institutional sphere, silver was the near-exclusive means of payment for all transactions reaching beyond the confines of the temple households. Furthermore, and contrary to the postulate of the traditional redistributive household model, also a large part of the internal payments within the temple household were in fact made in the form of silver money. Those temples for which there are sufficient data can be shown to have depended on cash-crop agriculture and to have used to a considerable degree free hired workers who were paid silver wages rather than forced servile labour. The temples could not have functioned without monetised exchange with the outside economy.

The importance of silver-based transactions for the non-institutional sector of the economy emerges from the private archives of city dwellers (Jursa 2010, 624–60). Silver was a common means of hoarding wealth (for those who had any wealth to hoard). It appears frequently in dowry lists and estate divisions, but staples do not. This is exactly the opposite of the situation in the Old Babylonian period, around 1650 BC, when, according to structurally identical dowry texts etc., silver was rare and grain was used as a means of hoarding wealth. In our period valuable items – land as well as movable goods such as animals or slaves – were as a rule bought and sold for silver only. 'Cheap' monies (barley, wool, base metals) and barter could be used to acquire items of everyday consumption, but also silver had a role to play in this respect. A comparison of prices of dates and barley in the second millennium BC with Neo-Babylonian prices shows that the purchasing power of silver in our period had fallen by 50 to 65 percent (see Jursa 2010, 630 note 3337). As a result, silver retained its utility also for low-value transactions: the smallest quantity of silver we can prove changed hands, 1/40 of a shekel, 0.2 grams, bought around 3 litres of grain at the time.

Hired mass labour, far more than compelled labour, provided the backbone of the labour force levied by temples for the numerous royal building projects to which they were required to contribute. In this way large amounts of money were brought into circulation also among the less affluent strata of the free population, both urban and rural. The agency of the crown played a major role in this respect: much of the wealth that financed the ambitious building programmes of the period in the final count was provided by the king. The vast amounts of surplus silver that the Neo-Babylonian

---

[13]   Note: 1 Babylonian shekel = 8.3 g; 1 Babylonian mina = 60 shekels = 0.5 kg; 1 *kurru* = 180 l = 144 kg (dates), 111.6 kg (barley), 99 kg (sesame).

[14]   See also Graslin 2009, 357. Copper and tin were used very rarely indeed according to the extant sources (Jursa 2010, 474), but at least temples used gold as a means of purchase more often than just occasionally (PTS 2267, YOS 17, 360, etc.: this aspect of the Neo-Babylonian economy remains to be investigated in depth).

monarchy spent in this way must have originated from the benefits it reaped from its domination over its imperial periphery: the spoils of Assyria, the tribute from Syria and the Levant. The use of silver money predominated also in the realm of taxation and payments for substitute labour service (Jursa 2010, 645–60). Both under the Chaldean monarchy and under Persian rule, the state was not so much interested in taxes paid by individual Babylonian households as in forced labour and military service. Nevertheless, the tax system had an effect on the use of money and the monetisation of the economy. In order to discharge their obligations, heads of households who were subject to royal demands for labour service hired substitute labourers or soldiers (who had to be paid in cash) if they could afford to do so. Private households therefore had to have access to ready silver: landowners at least were to some extent forced into the market for staples. Agricultural producers without additional sources of income had to sell some of their crops for cash; otherwise they would have lacked the means required for dealing with the demands made by the state. Thus, the monetisation of the economy in the sixth century could not have been as far-reaching as it was had it not been for the particular political background conditions of the period and for the state's role in promoting (indirectly and unwittingly, no doubt) the use of silver money.

Labour and labour specialization

The ubiquitous use of silver money determined labour relations. Silver was paid also for the services of professionals as diverse as mercenaries and wet-nurses. Free hirelings who were demonstrably employed full-time, e.g., as harvesters or builders in the city and the countryside, were practically always paid silver wages as the major part of their recompense. In many cases, silver was in fact the only form of recompense paid for hired labour, free or otherwise. Apprenticeship contracts by which (young) men, sometimes also trained craftsmen, were apprenticed to master craftsmen who were supposed to teach them their craft and specialist skills show that a highly differentiated labour force existed also, and perhaps especially, outside the institutional sector of the economy (Hackl in Jursa 2010, 700–25): some apprentices were not simply trained as "weavers," but as manufacturers of specific types of luxury garments using specific materials ("multi-coloured tunics", "garments made of byssos"); some bakers were apprenticed to 'ethnic' masters to learn the manufacture of special types of 'ethnic' bread ("common bread, *long* bread ('baguettes') and Egyptian bread"). This clearly reflects an environment of 'refined' consumption well beyond basic subsistence needs and well beyond the reach of unspecialised household production. But labour specialisation did not only occur on such 'elevated' levels of the economy: there were independent laundry businesses, which, given the moderate cost, could be patronized not only by the rich (Waerzeggers 2006). The delegation of a mundane household task like washing laundry to specialised wage-earning outsiders is a good example of the degree of labour specialization that had arisen in the long sixth century: it is only congruent with an economic environment strongly characterised by monetisation and a far-reaching division of labour.

State agency in the long sixth century and the economy

As can be seen from the foregoing summary, state institutions and political agency had a demonstrable impact on economic development in Babylonia, both under the Neo-Babylonian monarchy as well as under Persian rule.[15] Of all the specific contributions of the state to the economy that could be mentioned, the most decisive may be the fact that the Neo-Babylonian monarchy, and later the Persians, at least until the reign of Darius, managed to bring political stability and internal peace to Babylonia, the necessary precondition for the economic development of the long sixth century after the nadir the country had reached during the war against the Assyrians in the mid-seventh century.

Agricultural change was promoted by the large-scale state-sponsored building projects that aimed at land reclamation and amelioration and transformed parts of the rural landscape of Babylonia. Royal land allotment schemes of the seventh and early sixth century gave the important initial impetus for the reclamation of the barren or at least under-used land around the cities after decades of war and unrest. The crown also promoted administrative change and measures towards an increase in efficiency in institutional agriculture. Overall the role of the crown in shaping the institutional, administrative and technical foundations of Neo-Babylonian agriculture was essential: the principal productive sector of the Babylonian economy grew both in aggregate and in terms of productivity per capita, by a far-reaching shift to horticulture at the expense of arable farming as a result of the favourable institutional background conditions created by the Neo-Babylonian kings and their administration. These interventions of the crown in the economy also maintained their efficacy after the fall of the empire: with their large-scale canal building schemes the Neo-Babylonian kings had started a trend that would eventually transform the Babylonian landscape.

At least indirectly, if not necessarily through a consciously adopted policy, the crown promoted commercial development by furthering entrepreneurial activities at the interface between the institutional and the private economy (e.g., Wunsch 2010). In general, the legal institutions that sustained the increasing monetization of the economy and generally the commercial expansion of the period are a product of Mesopotamian tradition, but some innovations can be identified that occurred under the influence of the changing economic system. Contractual law was mostly traditional, but some new contract types emerged. The most important of these is represented by partnership contracts which expanded the potential offered by the old *commenda*-type business partnership contracts that had existed already in the first half of the

---

[15]   For the political history of the period and state institutions see, e.g., Da Riva 2008, Kleber 2008 and Jursa 2014b for the Neo-Babylonian period; for the Persian empire, Briant 1996 and 2002 and Tolini 2011.

second millennium BC. Neo-Babylonian law reached a considerable degree of refinement in these contracts by distinguishing company property from the private property of the investors, thereby implicitly allowing the company to become a legal persona in its own right. Cheques and by the fourth century BC also deposit banking had been developed, although little can be said about the scale of this phenomenon (Jursa 2006). There were attempts by the state to set fixed interest rates[16] and establish rules for regulating money-based exchange – rules that also aimed at creating a firmer base for taxing exchange. Perhaps the most significant innovations in this field concerned quality control for silver as effected by the state. By 545 BC, even before the Persian conquest, silver could bear an official mark guaranteeing its fineness. By the end of the sixth century silver was in circulation that was said to be of such-and-such a fineness, to be useable for commercial exchange, and to bear a mark of guarantee, all of which facts were warranted by the (royal) treasury.[17] These interventions in the economy had a long-term effect; later Achaemenid practice demonstrably built on Neo-Babylonian precedents.

Another contribution of the Neo-Babylonian kings to the economic expansion during their reign consisted in their ambitious building activities (e.g., Beaulieu 2005; Da Riva 2009, 109–13; Joannès 2011). They brought large amounts of silver into circulation for the purpose of the construction of huge new temples, palaces, city walls and cross-country defensive structures and by offering employment for much of the year. This allowed many urban unskilled labourers to subsist largely on money wages (Jursa 2010, 661–81). As these activities must have been financed to a significant degree with tribute and booty from Assyria, Syria and the Levant, this was the most unstable and transient of the immediate effects of royal policies on the economy: once royal spending was reduced, building activities slowed down or ceased, as did the flow of silver into Babylon that was caused by imperial domination over the west. In this respect then, the Persian conquest did mark a major caesura.

The manner in which the state drew on the economic resources of its population had direct and indirect consequences for the economic development of Babylonia (van Driel 2002; Jursa 2010, 645–60). Both under the Neo-Babylonian kings and under Persian rule royal demands for (cash) taxes and for labour and military service contributed to the increasing monetisation of economic exchange: willingly or unwillingly, taxpayers were forced into the monetary economy. In the Neo-Babylonian period, money spent on corvée labour was used locally. The principal recipients were large numbers of hirelings of urban and rural origin; this assured a wide circulation of silver

---

[16] Interest rates were initially regulated by custom but sometimes by institutional interference. Throughout most of the sixth century, they remained fixed at 20% p.a. At the beginning of the sixth century they were more flexible and tended to be lower, in later centuries they were often much higher, as much as 40% p.a. The reason for this development is unknown (see most recently Hackl and Pirngruber 2013).

[17] However, it is unclear how this warranty was conveyed: possibly this silver circulated in leather bags bearing a seal of the treasury where it had been assayed, but this description may also be a very cumbersome way of saying "coin" (Jursa 2010, 474–90).

also among the poorer strata of society. The Persian conquest at first brought little structural change in the system. However, the cumulative load of labour and service obligations increased and probably peaked under Darius I.

The reign of Darius I brought also two important novelties. First, the forced service of Babylonian corvée workers and soldiers outside the country, particularly in Elam, caused a flow of cash out of Babylonia. A substantial part of the silver that was spent on this endeavour eventually ended up in local circulation again, since it was paid to Babylonian substitute workers and hired soldiers, but nevertheless a certain withdrawal of funds from Babylonia must have occurred.

Second, the Persians imposed on Babylonia the obligation to contribute to the maintenance of the Achaemenid royal court. The Babylonian tablets document food deliveries to Iran that were paid for and managed by Babylonian taxpayers as part of their obligations towards the state (*upiyātu*; Tolini 2011, 314f.). The private archives that mention them refer to the duty imposed on priests (and their mother temples) to finance the hauling of these foodstuffs to Susa – using no doubt a waterway that was constructed with Babylonian labour and funds in Susiana.[18] The origin of the staples themselves is not stated in the texts – while a part may have come from the priests and their communities, the fact that the sources emphasize the duty of hauling rather than that of providing the foodstuffs makes it seem more likely that the principal source of the staples was different: royal estates, the estates of Persian aristocrats and their Babylonian clients, and the taxes in kind paid by temples to the royal administration. In any case it must have been an important flow of goods, since the transport costs were a special burden on Babylonian urban communities. In fact, if, as is suggested by Greek sources, Babylonia indeed had to contribute a substantial part of what was consumed by the Persian royal establishment, and if the figures for the consumption of goods in Persepolis are indicative also of what was consumed by the court at Susa, this would have resulted in an important withdrawal of foodstuffs from intra-Babylonian circulation (Henkelman 2010, 687 for relevant figures).

The foregoing remarks summarise the role of the state, especially of the Neo-Babylonian monarchy, as a catalyst determining economic development in sixth century Babylonia, in particular with regard to agrarian change and the monetisation and commercialisation of economic life. To a large extent the state achieved this result by investing the spoils that had been brought from the imperial periphery to the imperial centre. The impact of these policies, of the institutions they shaped and of the economic development they supported, can be seen in the data that reflect economic 'well-being': prices and proxy data reflecting prosperity levels. These also show, as a mirror-image of the effects of Neo-Babylonian policies, the probable consequences of the claims Persian imperial rule made on Babylonian resources.

---

[18]   As Tolini has shown, the Persians constructed a waterway connecting Susa to the Tigris following an old bed of the Karun and thereby created an important conduit for the flow of perhaps predominantly Mesopotamian goods to the imperial city (Tolini 2011, 288f., 293f.).

THE PERFORMANCE OF THE BABYLONIAN ECONOMY IN
THE LONG SIXTH CENTURY

In Ancient Near Studies, economic performance is traditionally discussed on the basis of data bearing on production. An alternative approach, taking its cue from D. North and his school, must focus on consumption and the standard of living. Such an approach has rarely been followed in the present field, since the nature of the textual record from Babylonia imposes a primary focus on production (while archaeological data, on the other hand, lend themselves more easily to an investigation of consumption). Recently, however, several studies on first millennium Babylonia have drawn on the rich price data offered by the textual record for the purpose of addressing the issue of prosperity and economic well-being (e.g., van der Spek 2006, van der Spek *et al.* [forthcoming]; van Leeuwen, van Leeuwen-Li and Pirngruber [forthcoming]; much of the following is based on Jursa 2010, 804–16).

Prices and price development

For Iron Age Babylonia the existence of commodity markets can be considered a given, at least from the late seventh century onwards (e.g., Pirngruber 2012 and van der Spek in this volume for the Late Achaemenid and Seleucid periods; Jursa 2010 *passim* for the long sixth century). It has been established beyond doubt that the prices reported in the Babylonian astronomical diaries are market prices that are subject to seasonal fluctuations and to the laws of supply and demand. The statistical proof is conclusive: prices moved unpredictably and could not be foreseen by consumers, and they were strongly interrelated through substitution and complementarity (e.g., Temin 2002, Pirngruber 2012, van Leeuven and Pirngruber 2011, van der Spek *et al.* [forthcoming]). Quantitative approaches to the performance of these markets has been discussed especially for the Late Achaemenid and Seleucid data found in the Astronomical diaries (in addition to the studies cited above, see van der Spek 2014), while their context is somewhat better understood in the Neo-Babylonian and early Achaemenid periods (Jursa 2014a and 2013a). We will not belabour this point and simply present, first the development of barley prices (fig. 5.1) and of date prices (fig. 5.2) in grams of silver per tonne, allowing a comparison with the corresponding graphs in van der Spek's paper in this volume, and then a synoptic view of the price data for the sixth century BC (see Jursa 2010, 734–53).

The following graph (fig. 5.3) shows the price development of the main commodities in comparison. The prices of -560 have been set at index=100. We use moving ten-year averages.

At the beginning of the century, prices fell. This trend was reversed around the middle of the century, when barley, sheep, date and slave prices started to increase: it should be noted that the general increase in prices began before the fall of the Babylonian empire to the Persians in 539 BC. Only in the case of dates was there a

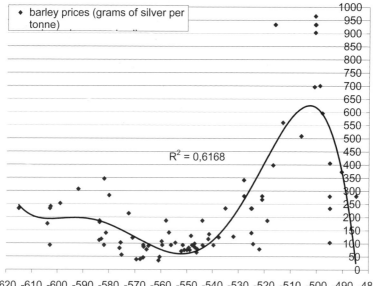

Fig. 5.1 Barley prices (grams of silver per tonne) (data: Jursa 2010, 443–448)

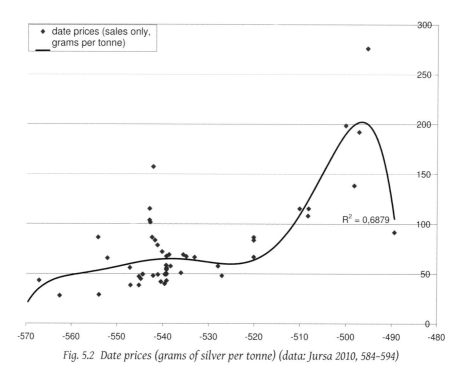

Fig. 5.2 Date prices (grams of silver per tonne) (data: Jursa 2010, 584–594)

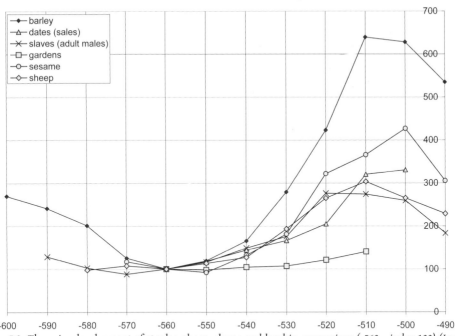

Fig. 5.3 The price development of staples, sheep, slaves and land in comparison (-560 = index 100) (Jursa 2010, 746)

slight interim reprieve from roughly -540 to -520, i.e., until the beginning of the reign of Darius. The increase was dramatic in the case of barley and less pronounced, but still quite strong, for the other commodities. The otherwise very stable garden prices exhibit a moderate (at least nominal) increase. The increase culminated around -510 or slightly later; the very end of the sixth century and the beginning of the fifth experienced still high, but slightly falling prices.

The data concern diverse commodities that depend on quite different supply and demand structures and come from sources of different geographical and socio-economic origin. Nevertheless, they follow roughly the same long-term trend: they reflect a single economic system, and clearly, in this sector of the economy, prices were determined primarily by the interplay of supply and demand (of goods and money) – no other mechanism could have yielded a similarly consistent result.

The decreasing prices in the first half of the sixth century reflect the general economic recovery and expansion of the time: supply of most commodities increased substantially. The rising prices thereafter are more difficult to explain. There can be no doubt that the level of prices during the later reign of Darius is that of an exceptional crisis – in the following centuries, prices climb to comparable levels only during the wars of the successors (see Pirngruber 2012). The origins of this development are manifold (Jursa 2010, 745–53). One root of the price inflation is monetary; it is a result of the huge influx of silver into the Babylonian economy that began with Nebuchadnezzar and continued until the fall of Babylon to the Persians, if not, to some degree, beyond this point (as some public building projects, which were the main conduit for this influx of silver, were continued under Persian rule). To some extent, there was a supply crisis. We know that the climate was turning towards a drier phase in the second half of the sixth century, and there is explicit evidence for failed barley harvests during the reign of Cambyses (Kleber 2012) – there may have been more such episodes later in the century, which drove up barley prices well above the general trend. Was there also a demand crisis? Demographic growth as such could have driven up commodity prices, but then it would also have driven down wages, which was not the case: wages increased more or less in step with the general price trend (Jursa 2010, 673–81). The price of labour is also represented by the price of slaves, which more than doubles between the years -560 and -510 (Jursa 2010, 741–45). The pattern is thus not consistent with a 'price revolution' triggered by growing internal demand (see, e.g., Fischer 1991, 76–7). If a demand-driven component is assumed to have contributed to the price increase, it would have had to be external demand, both for commodities and for labour. The only plausible explanation is the assumption that the Persians withdrew substantial resources of manpower and staples from the province, especially under Darius. The labour-component of this hypothesis is sufficiently documented to be unproblematic (Jursa and Waerzeggers 2009). As was discussed above, the withdrawal of significant quantities of staples from intra-Babylonian consumption on the other hand can only be documented on the basis of the data for the *upiyātu* deliveries and the construction of the *nār kabarri* (see note 18), which implies the need for a labour-saving waterway from Babylonia to Susa. The huge quantities of staples that were consumed at the court at Persepolis (Henkelman 2010) allow us to assume that the court in Susa was equally expensive and would have needed as many contributions from outside of Susiana as possible. It therefore seems likely that the price inflation at the end of the sixth century was not only driven by monetary reasons and a supply shock that was owed to failed harvests, but was also, and perhaps to a significant extent, driven by a demand shock that resulted from the Persians' extraction of resources from the province of Babylon.[19] The falling prices at the end of the century may reflect a more stable supply, less pressing demands on the part of the Persians (the intense phase of building at Susa was over), and certainly a degree of deflation:[20] Babylonia was no longer a net importer of silver as the centre of an empire, tribute went into the cashbox of the Great King at Susa, and no king in Babylon kept spending fortunes on reconstructing palaces and temples.

---

[19] Jursa and Schmidl (forthcoming) argue that, notwithstanding the general inflation of commodity prices, land prices remained stable or even decreased in real terms owing to the overall difficult economic situation and because land ownership was increasingly less profitable owing to the heavy tax burden imposed on privately owned land by the Persian rulers.

[20] However, it can be excluded that the Persians withdrew very significant quantities of silver from circulation within Babylonia at this stage.

Prosperity in the sixth century

Living standards are most commonly measured in terms of real income or real wages, but for the purposes of economic history various indices can substitute for, or supplement, quantitative data of this kind. Many of these indices are archaeologically observable. The categories of proxy data for living standards include: stature, nutrition, mortality and life expectancy, disease patterns, material culture and housing.[21] Morris' study of such parameters for economic prosperity in Iron Age Greece can be taken as an illustration of a study along these general lines and as a guide for identifying the phenomena one might look for in the more or less contemporaneous record from southern Mesopotamia. Morris concludes from his data that the standards of living in Iron Age Greece increased significantly between 800 and 300 BC.[22] An analogous investigation for Babylonia, while desirable, remains a task for the future; the comparative lack of archaeological data is a severe impediment. Textual data can substitute for archaeological information at least to some extent: a comparison of Old Babylonian (c. 2000–1600 BC) and Neo-Babylonian dowry and inheritance documents for instance shows that the material culture in the later period was significantly richer than in the Middle Bronze age (Jursa 2010, 806–11).

Drawing on the rich price and wage data discussed above, it is possible to calculate Babylonian wheat wages, i.e., the quantity of wheat (or, in other words, calories of food) the average daily wage of an unskilled free worker could buy – an important index that allows cross-cultural comparison of economic wellbeing (for the concept: Scheidel 2010; Jursa 2010, 811–16). While in most Ancient and many Medieval societies, wheat wages of 3.5–6.5 litres predominate, Babylonians of our period earned wheat wages of 9.6–14.4 litres, significantly more than their predecessors of the late third and early second millennium BC (4.8–8 litres). This is a strong indication of unusually high prosperity levels during the first two thirds of the long sixth century. A recent study (van Leeuwen, van Leeuwen-Li and Pirngruber [forthcoming]) employs a structurally similar methodology for a comparison of welfare levels in Han China, Imperial Rome and Babylonia from the sixth to the second centuries BC. The authors base themselves on the cost of standardized 'baskets' of vital commodities (distinguishing a 'bare bones basket' and a 'respectability basket') and the average wages of unskilled workers. The aim is to calculate a 'welfare ratio,' i.e., the relationship between the income of one worker and the living cost of a household (defined here as four adult equivalents: three adults and two children). For Han China (100 BC) then, the welfare ratio (for the 'bare bones' basket) is 0.87[23], for Roman Egypt (1st century AD) and Imperial Rome of Diocletian's edict it is 0.55 and 0.65–0.78 respectively, and for Babylonia of the pre-crisis sixth century, 0.71–1.04, depending on the set of parameters

---

[21] See Morris 2005, 106f. He points out that "age-specific stature and the real wage moved together in early modern Europe."

[22] Morris 2004 and 2005.

[23] In other words, the average wages of an unskilled worker cover 87 percent of the living costs of an average family. For Beijing around 1750, the figure is 0.94.

used. The data for prosperity levels, such as they are at the moment, thus lend weight to the production-oriented analysis summarized in the foregoing pages: a coherent image of a comparatively prosperous period benefitting from incoming wealth (owing to Babylonia's imperial domination over much of the Near East) and a higher productivity per capita (owing to agricultural change) emerges.

BABYLONIA IN THE FIFTH AND FOURTH CENTURY

The narrative that results from the reading of the economic data from Babylonia in the long sixth century that is proposed here amounts to a limited Smithian success story, as they occasionally occur also in other pre-modern economies. The importance of this case lies in its particularities, in the combination of longue-durée factors of demography and climate with certain much more transient political and socio-economic factors. In particular, it is imperial domination that allowed agrarian change and expansion and monetization and, overall, a modicum of economic growth and increasing prosperity.

The economic development in Babylonia in the fifth and fourth century, up to the Macedonian conquest, cannot be reconstructed in similar detail: the textual documentation is far less abundant and leaves large gaps in our knowledge of the history of the period. It is clear that the revolts against Xerxes in the second year of his reign (484 BC) were a major watershed in the history of Babylonia under Persian domination: as a consequence, many of the most important clans of northern Babylonia practically disappear from view. Their members were removed from their positions of power in provincial, city and temple administration: changes which are visible in the record and which demonstrably affected the core institutions of Babylonian society. These families were substituted by Persians or by Babylonian supporters of Persian rule of generally less prominent origin (Waerzeggers 2003/4; Kessler 2004; Baker 2008; Waerzeggers 2010, 9; Jursa 2013). Many questions remain regarding both the political, social and economic implications of the replacement of the indigenous elite by (ethnic or social) outsiders and the subsequent development of the province (see, e.g., Henkelman *et al.* 2011). It is not intended here to survey and discuss the available data in detail. Rather, we present, on the basis of previous studies,[24] some general thoughts on the process of socio-economic change in the province in this period that draw on the understanding of the sixth-century economy that has been outlined above and try to gauge the effects of the transformation of Babylonian institutions that occurred, or began, in 484 BC.[25]

---

[24] The textual data bearing on Babylonia as a Persian province have recently been synthesized by Tolini 2011, 441–604, who could build on the work, of, i.a., van Driel, Joannès, van der Spek and Stolper. See now also Hackl 2013 for rich new information on Late Achaemenid Babylon.

[25] Much of the following is argued more extensively in Jursa 2014a, where detailed references can be found.

Quantitative data from the Late Achaemenid period are scarce and offer little help for our problem. The relative prosperity of the sixth century had resulted in part from the process of monetization and commercialization of economic exchange, which functioned in a comparatively free and efficient institutional framework. In comparison, the evidence for commercial exchange in the fifth and fourth centuries is in part contradictory and does not yield itself easily to generalization. We do find 'proto-banking' in the early fourth century at the latest, indicating a demand for more complex and objectified 'financial services' (Jursa 2006), but on the other hand interest rates were significantly higher in the late period than in the long sixth century: frequently they go up to forty per cent per annum, that is, to double the level common in the later part of the long sixth century (Hackl and Pirngruber 2013; Jursa 2010, 490–9): the cost of borrowing money had increased. If this change in interest rates was based primarily on economic factors and not on (Persian?) custom, it would be an argument in favour of assuming a contraction of the monetary base in Babylonia in the later Achaemenid period. In fact, a certain degree of deflation, *ceteris paribus*, has to be postulated *a priori* in any case as a long-term effect of the shift of the imperial centre away from Babylon to Iran, and the resulting withdrawal of specie from circulation within Babylonia.[26] Unfortunately the development of commodity prices can only be sketched in outline. The barley prices that are known from the late fifth century are comparable to the high prices of the late sixth and early fifth century, but price levels in the fourth century were lower, while price volatility remained high. This is also true for other commodities as well (Hackl and Pirngruber 2013). Wage data are largely absent for the fifth and fourth centuries (Jursa 2010, 676), but this fact can be compensated for by a comparison with the salaries in kind paid to institutional dependants. In the long sixth century, these salaries paid in kind ('rations') were demonstrably linked to wage levels and the costs of living (Jursa 2010, 296–301), a nexus which must have existed also in the later period. It is therefore significant that institutional salaries in Babylon in the late fifth and the fourth centuries tended to by paid out according to the 90 litre and the 65 litre standards for monthly payments (Hackl and Pirngruber 2013). This corresponds to the standard used in Southern Babylonia in the mid-sixth century, but is significantly lower than the standard 180-litre salary paid in northern Babylonia towards the end of the sixth century and at the beginning of the fifth. This must mean that wages too had decreased in the intervening period. Overall therefore, the available data are at least congruent with the assumption of a continuing gradual contraction of the monetary base of the economy that follows from the interpretation of the data of the long sixth century, in particular with regard to the partly inflation-driven price and wage increase of the late sixth and early fifth centuries.

The most important socio-economic changes of the period occurred in the countryside which, by the end of the fifth century, had undergone at least a partial

---

[26] Owing at least as much to a reduction of royal spending (in comparison to the sixth century) as to a direct withdrawal of funds by taxation.

transformation: ownership patterns had changed. The estates held by the Great King himself and by members of his family and other Iranian nobles had been greatly extended, and much land was also in the hands of Babylonian families who owed their career and their fortunes not to their traditional position in Babylonian society, but to their cooperation with the Iranian conquerors.[27] Many of these estates were held as royal land grants. Land in the hand of Persian nobles and members of the royal family is likewise well attested, as is land held by royal officials of Babylonian origin. This new group of landowners may have in part held newly-reclaimed estates, especially in the Nippur region (Jursa 2010, 405–18), but in general their rise implies a decline in the fortunes of other social groups.

The Babylonian urban elites suffered severely at the beginning of the fifth century, in the aftermath of the rebellions against Xerxes. The case of Uruk can serve as a model (Kessler 2004): in the aftermath of the rebellion against Xerxes reprisals targeted those leading families of the city whose roots lay in Babylon. These northerners, who had dominated socio-economic life in Uruk, were removed from their offices, the importance of the northern Babylonian gods Marduk and Nabû in the local cult was drastically reduced, and the local god Anu was promoted to chief deity in Uruk. The Urukean priesthood transferred their offices from Eanna to the Anu temple, which experienced a steep ascendency at the time while the old Eanna temple was allowed to fall into ruin (Kessler 2004, 250–1; Kose 1998, 9–16). That much is evident from the available textual (and archaeological) record. The change in the countryside that the demise of the fortunes of the northern Babylonians entailed is less visible, but it must nevertheless necessarily be inferred from the record: since the northerners lost their properties in the city, their houses and temple offices, they must also have lost their fields, and it is clear that the beneficiaries were the crown, Persian nobles, and Babylonian supporters of Persian rule, in the case of Uruk mostly the local priestly families who very well may have resented the domination of the northerners over their local temple. Changes of this kind, in analogy to the well-documented case of Uruk, can be expected in all cities where the old clans disappeared – effectively, they must have occurred, *mutatis mutandis*, all over northern Babylonia, foremost in the capital itself.[28] Thus, 484 BC entailed an overturning of property rights and a shift of socio-economic power in the countryside. These changes favoured a type of landownership that was less strongly based on traditional and legally sanctioned property rights; rather, it had its roots in the political and military power of a new rent-seeking elite.[29] Landownership for these classes was a corollary, or consequence,

---

[27]   This aspect of landownership in Late Achaemenid Babylonia has mostly been studied with respect to the Murašû archive (locus classicus: Stolper 1985, 52–69; van Driel 1989 and 2002, 194–203, 230–2); for additional references see Jursa 2014a.

[28]   Note also, e.g., the evidence for the appropriation of temple lands (of Bēl) by Persian nobles (e.g., BE 9, 59; Stolper 1985, 42–4) and for the integration of land farmed by temple personnel into the Persian system of military conscription and taxation (PBS 2/1, 94).

[29]   John Ma, quite appropriately, entitled a forthcoming interpretative essay on the business dealings of an Achaemenid noble "Aršama the Vampire."

of holding political power; it was not primarily acquired commercially. The relationship between landowners and tenants/labourers was largely dependent on patterns of socio-economic domination rather than contract-based.[30] Tenancy patterns also changed. Multiple layers of leases could allow numerous parties rights to the same piece of land and to the water on which it depended (e.g., Stolper 2005). Typically, Iranian overlords and their bailiffs stand in the background of complex constructions of leases and sub-leases which involved Babylonians of different social status (landowners and managers/businessmen alike) as well as cultivators of different ethnic backgrounds: mostly Babylonians and West Semites. While agricultural entrepreneurs of the sixth century had most often relied on free agents who shared their social background and sometimes were family members (e.g., Hackl *et al.* 2011, 181–2, Jursa 2005, 69–71), in the fifth century it was more often slave agents with far-reaching powers who acted for elite landowners, Iranians and rich Babylonians alike.[31] Overall returns of farming were not higher than in the sixth century (Jursa 2010, 407), so pressure on the cultivators necessarily increased owing to the practice of multiple sub-leasing, even though this is difficult to prove in detail. Certainly, coercion and the use of force play a more important role in the documentation on agriculture than in the sixth century,[32] the importance of compelled labour in agriculture and elsewhere increased at the expense of contractual labour. One finds an ever-increasing manifestation of the effects of political power at all levels of agrarian production.

A similar argument can be made for commerce and agricultural management. In the sixth century, agricultural business and the management of estates had depended on the agency of upper-class Babylonians who were involved in the local and interregional commodity trade, often drawing on capital raised from their peers through loans or through the creation of business companies. However, the importance of private capital investment in business ventures was eclipsed by that of institutional property that was made available to commercial purposes. Land, but also access to manpower and movable capital as well as rights to dispose of various funds and taxes, could be contracted out to businessmen, both within the institutional sphere and without it (e.g., van Driel 1999; Jursa 2010, 193–206, 252–6). Individual entrepreneurs and entrepreneurial families specialized in institutional property management in the sphere of agriculture and livestock breeding as well as in tax farming: the temples and the royal household made use of the service of such men to facilitate the administration of their holdings. Patronage and connections to the royal household were important for entrepreneurial success, especially on the uppermost levels of this kind of business, but there is also some evidence for entrepreneurs offering bids for certain franchises with the intention of outdoing their competitors. On the lower rungs of the scale of the entrepreneurial engagement with institutional business,

---

[30] For the evidence see van Driel 2002, 203–18; Jursa 2014a.

[31] This is well in evidence in the Tattannu and the Bābāya (or Kasr) archives: Stolper 1995; 2005; 2007; Jursa 2010, 375–82.

[32] See, e.g., Stolper 1985, nos. 91, 102, 103, 104, BE 9, 57, PBS 2/1, 21.

businessmen certainly competed with each other, and access to institutional funds seems to have been granted normally on the basis of considerations that were foremost of an economic nature (but this does not exclude the importance of patronage and social ties also in these cases).

In the fifth and fourth century, access to institutional capital (land, manpower, rents, taxes, liquid capital) for commercial purposes continued to be conceded to businessmen. The Murašû family, for instance (Stolper 1985 etc.), a family of Babylonian businessmen, specialized in institutional property management and tax farming, mainly by offering credit for tax purposes to holders of royal land grants. Overall, the family acquired a vast accumulation of immobile capital in the form of land granted to them as leases or taken as pledges, and of mobile capital in the form of dependent or indebted (quasi-indentured) agricultural labour. The produce of the land under the Murašû's control was sold to consumers in the city of Nippur (or elsewhere) or to the royal authorities. Thereby the Murašû acted as middlemen between the agricultural producers and taxpayers on one hand and the Persian overlords on the other with regard to production and resource extraction, but also with regard to consumption. No Babylonian entrepreneur or entrepreneurial family of the sixth century worked on a comparable scale and had a similar degree of control over the several means of agricultural production: land, water, credit and, at least indirectly, also labour. Yet the Murašû's was but one of several such businesses acting at the intersection between the ruling elite (the state) and the socio-economic substructure that supported it: similar concentrations of the means of production in the hands of members of the political elite and the entrepreneurs who worked with their backing can be documented also in the area of Babylon and Borsippa.[33] This reflects the overall tighter hold of the ruling elite, at least over the rural economy, that distinguished the fifth from the sixth century, as was argued above – the effects of political power being in this case channelled through the agency of the entrepreneurial family of the Murašû. In fact, political domination served also as a constraint on the entrepreneurial activities that were conducted in its service: the Murašû's business was taken over and either terminated or entrusted to other agents by the Achaemenid price Aršam.[34] Again what we see is consistent with the assumption of a restriction of freely negotiated commercial, market-based activity and a more important role of forms of economic interaction that were shaped by the political reality of Persian (i.e., foreign) imperial rule and its oppressive character.

---

[33] See, e.g., for the Tattannu archive, BM 120024, edited in Jursa and Stolper 2007, and van Driel 1989, 204.

[34] Stolper 1985, 23–4; but see also van Driel 1989, 204.

CONCLUSION

The long sixth century, especially the period of Neo-Babylonian empire, emerges from the analysis of the rich source material as an unusually prosperous phase of Babylonian history: the country benefitted from incoming wealth (owing to Babylonia's imperial domination over much of the Near East) and a higher productivity per capita (owing to agricultural change). Far-reaching monetization, unparalleled in Ancient Near Eastern history, and an increasing market-orientation of economic exchange were further factors that led to this 'golden interval' of economic growth accompanying demographic expansion: the several elements that led to and sustained this process can be cast into a 'commercialization model' for economic growth of Smithian inspiration.

As happens frequently, this prosperity was harnessed by a new ruling class in a way that eventually undermined its foundations: the affluence of Babylonia in the long sixth century was not of very long duration. In the later fifth century and thereafter, after the decline of the fortunes of the traditional Babylonian urban elites owing to the events of 484 BC and thereafter, the economic centre of gravity shifted to other social agents and to some extent away from the cities to the large rural estates of the Achaemenid empire's ruling class. These new rent-seeking elites took control of the economic structures and institutions of Babylonia with the intent of extracting a maximum of resources from the province. Thereby they most likely caused an at least partial reversal of the economic innovations of the long sixth century that had contributed to the creation of the Babylonia's exceptional prosperity in the first place. Nevertheless, the agrarian expansion continued also under Xerxes and his successors, and the economy remained comparatively strongly monetized, if less so than in the preceding century. The structural factors described distinguish this Iron Age economy in fundamental ways from its Bronze Age precursors and establish a strong link of continuity with Hellenistic Eastern Mediterranean economies. It is certainly not justifiable anymore to exclude Iron Age Babylonia from the general discussion on the Ancient Economy advanced by Moses Finley decades ago (note 7).

REFERENCES

Adams, R. McC. (1981) *Heartland of Cities, Surveys of Ancient Settlement and Land Use on the Central Floodplain on the Euphrates*. Chicago: University of Chicago Press.

Baker, H. D. (2008) Babylon in 484 BC: the excavated archival tablets as a source for urban History. *Zeitschrift für Assyriologie* 98, 100–116.

Baker, H. D. and Jursa, M. (eds) (2005) *Approaching the Babylonian Economy. Proceedings of the START Project Symposium Held in Vienna, 1-3 July 2004* (Alter Orient und Altes Testament 330). Münster: Ugarit-Verlag.

Beaulieu, P.-A. (2005) Eanna's contribution to the construction of the North Palace at Babylon. In Baker and Jursa (eds) 2005, 45–73.

Brinkman, J. A. (1984) Settlement Surveys and Documentary Evidence: Regional Variation and Secular Trend in Mesopotamian Demography. *Journal of Near Eastern Studies* 43, 169–180.

Da Riva, R. (2008) *The Neo-Babylonian Royal Inscriptions* (Guides to the Mesopotamian Textual Record 4). Münster: Ugarit-Verlag.

van Driel, G. (1988) Neo-Babylonian Agriculture. *Bulletin on Sumerian Agriculture* 4, 121–159.

van Driel, G. (1989) The Murašûs in Context. *Journal of the Economic and Social History of the Orient* 32, 203–229.

van Driel, G. (2002) *Elusive Silver. In Search of a Role for a Market in an Agrarian Environment. Aspects of Mesopotamia's Society.* Leiden: NINO.

Dyer, C. (2005) *An Age of Transition? Economy and Society in the Later Middle Ages.* Oxford: Oxford University Press.

Fernea, R. A. (1970) *Shaykh and Effendi. Changing Patterns of Authority Among the El Shabana of Southern Iraq.* Cambridge, MA: Harvard University Press.

Fischer, D. H. (1996) *The Great Wave. Price Revolutions and the Rhythm of History.* New York: Oxford University Press.

Graslin-Thomé, L. (2009) *Les échanges à longue distance en Mésopotamie au Ier millénaire. Une approche économique.* Paris: de Boccard.

Hackl, J. (2013) *Materialien zur Urkundenlehre und Archivkunde der spätzeitlichen Texte aus Nordbabylonien.* PhD Dissertation, Vienna University.

Hackl, J., Janković, B. and Jursa, M. (2011) Das Brief-Dossier des Šumu-ukīn. *KASKAL* 8, 177–221.

Hackl, J. and Pirngruber, R. (2013) Prices and related data from Northern Babylonia in the Late Achaemenid and Early Hellenistic periods, ca. 480–300 BC. In R. J. van der Spek, B. van Leeuwen and J. L. van Zanden (eds.), *A History of Market Performance from Ancient Babylonia to the Modern World.* London: Routledge.

Halstead, P. (1990) Quantifying Sumerian Agriculture Some Seeds of Doubt and Hope. *Bulletin on Sumerian Agriculture* 5, 187–195.

Hatcher, J. and Bailey, M. (2001) *Modelling the Middle Ages. The History & Theory of England's Economic Development.* Oxford: Oxford University Press.

Henkelman, W. F. M. (2010) Consumed before the King. The table of Darius, that of Irdabama and Irtaštuna, and that of his Starap, Karkiš. In B. Jacobs and R. Rollinger (eds), *Der Achämenidenhof / The Achaemenid Court,* 667–775 (Classica et Orientalia 2). Wiesbaden: Harrassowitz.

Henkelman, W. G., Kuhrt, A., Rollinger, R. and Wiesehöfer, J. (2011) Herodotus and Babylon reconsidered. In R. Rollinger *et al.* (eds), *Herodot und das Persische Weltreich - Herodotus and the Persian Empire,* 449–470 (Classica et Orientalia 3). Wiesbaden: Harrassowitz.

Hopkins, K. (1978) Economic growth and towns in classical antiquity. In P. Abrams and E. A. Wrigley (eds), *Towns in Societies. Essays in Economic History and Historical Sociology,* 35–77. Cambridge: Cambridge University Press.

Joannès, F. (2011) L'écriture publique du pouvoir à Babylone sous Nabuchodonosor II. In E. Cancik-Kirschbaum, M. van Ess and J. Marzahn (eds), *Babylon. Wissenskultur in Orient und Okzident* 113–120 (Topoi. Berlin Studies of the Ancient World 1). Berlin: de Gruyter.

Jursa, M. (2005) *Neo-Babylonian Legal and Administrative Documents. Typology, Contents and Archives* (Guides to the Mesopotamian Textual Record 1). Münster: Ugarit-Verlag.

Jursa, M. (2006) Agricultural Management, Tax Farming and Banking: Aspects of Entrepreneurial Activity in Babylonia in the Late Achaemenid and Hellenistic Periods. In P. Briant and F. Joannès (eds), *La transition entre l'Empire achéménide et les royaumes hellénistiques,* 137–222. Paris: de Boccard.

Jursa, M. (2008) The Remuneration of Institutional Labourers in an Urban Context in Babylonia in the First Millennium BC. In P. Briant *et al.* (eds), *L'archive des Fortifications de Persépolis. État des questions et perspectives de recherches*, 387–427. Paris: de Boccard.

Jursa, M. (2010) *Aspects of the Economic History of Babylonia in the First Millennium BC: Economic Geography, Economic Mentalities, Agriculture, the Use of Money and the Problem of Economic Growth.* With contributions by J. Hackl, B. Janković, K. Kleber, E. E. Payne, C. Waerzeggers and M. Weszeli. Münster: Ugarit-Verlag.

Jursa, M. (2013) Epistolographic evidence for trips to Susa by Borsippean priests and for the crisis in Ezida at the beginning of Xerxes' reign. *Arta 2013.*

Jursa, M. (2013a) Market efficiency and market integration in Babylonia in the 'Long Sixth Century' BC. In R. J. van der Spek, B. van Leeuwen and J. L. van Zanden (eds), *A history of Market Performance from Ancient Babylonia to the Modern World.* London: Routledge.

Jursa, M. (2014a) Factor markets in Babylonia from the late seventh to fourth century BC. *Journal of the Economic and Social History of the Orient* 57, 173–202.

Jursa, M. (2014b) The Neo-Babylonian Empire. In M. Gehler and R. Rollinger (eds), *Imperien und Reiche in der Weltgeschichte. Epochenübergreifende und globalhistorische Vergleiche*, 121–148. Wiesbaden: Harrassowitz.

Jursa, M. and Schmidl, M. (forthcoming) Babylonia as a Source of Imperial Revenue from Cyrus to Xerxes. In B. Jacobs and W. Henkelman (eds), *Proceedings of the symposium "Die Verwaltung im Achämenidenreich - Imperiale Muster und Strukturen. Festkolloquium zur 80-Jahr-Feier der Entdeckung des Festungsarchivs von Persepolis", Basel, 14.-17.5. 2013.*

Jursa, M. and Stolper, M. W. (2007) From the Tattannu Archive Fragment. *Wiener Zeitschift für die Kunde des Morgenlandes* 97, 243–281.

Jursa, M. with contributions by C. Waerzeggers (2009) On aspects of taxation in Achaemenid Babylonia: new evidence from Borsippa. In P. Briant and M. Chaeuveau (eds), *Organisation des pouvoirs et contacts culturels dans les pays de l'empire achéménide*, 237–269. Paris: de Boccard.

Kessler, K. (2004) Urukäische Familien versus babylonische Familien. Die Namengebung in Uruk, die Degradierung der Kulte von Eanna und der Aufstieg des Gottes Anu. *Altorientalische Forschungen* 31, 237–262.

Kleber, K. (2008) *Tempel und Palast. Die Beziehungen zwischen dem König und dem Eanna-Tempel im spätbabylonischen Uruk* (Alter Orient und Altes Testament 358). Münster: Ugarit-Verlag.

Kleber, K. (2012) Famine in Babylonia. A microhistorical approach to an agricultural crisis in 528–526 BC. *Zeitschrift für Assyriologie* 102, 219–244.

Kose, A. (1998) *Uruk. Architektur IV. Von der Seleukiden- bis zur Sasanidenzeit.* Mainz: Zabern.

van Leeuwen, B. and Pirngruber, R. (2011) Markets in pre-industrial societies: storage in Hellenistic Babylonia in the medieval English mirror. *Journal of Global History* 6, 169–193.

van Leeuwen, B., van Leeuwen-Li, J. and Pirngruber, R. (forthcoming) The standard of living in ancient societies: a comparison between the Han Empire, the Roman Empire, and Babylonia. *European Review of Economic History.*

Manning, J. G. and Morris, I. (eds) (2005) *The Ancient Economy. Evidence and Models.* Stanford: Stanford University Press.

Millett, P. (2001) Productive to some purpose? The problem of ancient economic growth. In D. J. Mattingly and J. Salmon (eds), *Economies beyond agriculture in the classical world*, 17–48. London: Routledge.

Morris, I. (2004) Economic growth in Ancient Greece. *Journal of Institutional and Theoretical Economics* 160, 709–742.

Morris, I. (2005) Archaeology, Standards of Living, and Greek Economic History. In Manning and Morris (eds), 91–126.

Morris, I., Saller, R. P. and Scheidel, W. (2007) Introduction. In W. Scheidel, I. Morris and R. Saller (eds), *The Cambridge Economic History of the Greco-Roman World*, 1–12. Cambridge: Cambridge University Press.

Nielsen, J. C. (2011) *Sons and Descendants. A Social History of Kin Groups and Family Names in the Early Neo-Babylonian Period, 747-626 BC*. Leiden: Brill.

Pirngruber, R. (2012) *The Impact of Empire on Market Prices in Babylon in the Late Achaemenid and Seleucid periods, ca. 400-140 B.C.* PhD Dissertation, VU Amsterdam.

Scheidel, W. (2010) Real Wages in Early Economies: Evidence for Living Standards from 1800 BCE to 1300 CE. *Journal of the Economic and Social History of the Orient* 53, 425–562.

van der Spek, B. (2006) How to measure prosperity? The case of Hellenistic Babylonia. In R. Descat (ed.), *Approches de l'économie hellénistique*, 287–310. Saint-Bertrand-de-Comminges: Musée archéologique de Saint-Bertrand-de-Comminges.

van der Spek, B. (2014) Factor and commodity markets in Hellenistic and Parthian Babylonia (331–61 BC). *Journal of the Economic and Social History of the Orient*.

van der Spek, R. J., van Leeuwen, B. and van Zanden, J. L. (eds) (2013) *A History of Market Performance from Ancient Babylonia to the Modern World* (Routledge Explorations in Economic History). London: Routledge.

Stolper, M. W. (1985) *Entrepreneurs and Empire. The Murašû Archive, the Murašû Firm, and Persian Rule in Babylonia*. Leiden: NINO.

Stolper, M. W. (1995) The Babylonian Enterprise of Belesys. In P. Briant (ed), *Dans les pas des Dix-Mille: Peuples et pays du Proche-Orient vus par un Grec*, 217–238. Toulouse: Presses universitaires du Mirail.

Stolper, M. W. (2004) The Kasr Texts, the Rich Collection, the Bellino Copies and the Grotefend Nachlass. In J.-G. Dercksen (ed), *Assyria and Beyond: Studies Presented to Mogens Trolle Larsen*, 511–549. Leiden: NINO.

Stolper, M. W. (2005) Farming with the Murašûs and Others: Costs and Returns of Cereal Agriculture in Fifth-Century Babylonian Texts. In Baker and Jursa (eds), 323–342.

Stolper, M. W. (2007) Kasr Texts: Excavated but not in Babylon. In M. T. Roth (ed), *Studies Presented to Robert D. Biggs, June 4, 2004*, 243–283. Chicago: Oriental Institute.

Temin, P. (2002) Price Behaviour in Ancient Babylon. *Explorations in Economic History* 39, 49–60.

Tolini, G. (2011) *La Babylonie et l'Iran. Les relations d'une province avec le Coeur de l'empire achéménide (539-331 avant notre ère)*. Dissertation, Université de Paris I, Paris.

Tolini, G. (forthcoming) Les ressources de la Babylonie et l'approvisionnement de la Table de Darius le Grand.

Waerzeggers, C. (2003/2004) The Babylonian Revolts Against Xerxes and the 'End of Archives'. *Archiv für Orientforschung* 50, 150–173.

Waerzeggers, C. (2006) Neo-Babylonian Laundry. *Revue d'Assyriologie* 100, 83–96.

Waerzeggers, C. (2010) *The Ezida Temple of Borsippa, Priesthood, Cult, Archives* (Achaemenid History 15). Leiden: NINO.

Wunsch, C. (2010) Neo-Babylonian Entrepreneurs. In D. S. Landes, J. Mokyr, and W. J. Baumol, (eds), *The Invention of Enterprise: Entrepreneurship from Ancient Mesopotamia to Modern Times*, 40–61. Princeton: Princeton University Press.

6

Legal Institutions and Agrarian Change in the Roman Empire

Dennis Kehoe

In this paper, I hope to contribute to the Vienna START project's efforts to model agrarian change in the ancient Near East by investigating how property rights maintained by the state affected the organization of agriculture in an ancient society. I will focus on the Roman Empire, but I believe that my methodology can be usefully applied to other ancient societies. It is notoriously difficult to determine whether, or to what extent, ancient societies experienced economic growth. Real economic growth, the kind that can promote greater specialization of labour and urbanization, requires agrarian change (Johnson 2000; Scheidel 2007). The possibilities for agrarian change in an ancient economy were subject to severe constraints, the most important of which were technological and demographic, as discussed in many chapters in the *Cambridge Economic History of the Greco-Roman World* (Scheidel *et al.* 2007). Certainly the Roman Empire experienced a significant economic expansion that fostered a remarkable urban culture. Much of the impetus for economic growth in Roman cities came from elite landowners' spending there the incomes they achieved from their agricultural holdings (Erdkamp 2001; Jongman 1988). Urban expansion depended on a transfer of wealth from the agrarian economy, which was itself made possible both by population growth and by the development and dissemination of new technologies, such as the increasing use of the lever-press, as well as new types of irrigation and the increasing use of water mills (Wilson 1999; Wilson 2002; Horden and Purcell 2000, 231–97). These developments would have made it possible to farm more intensively. However, within the constraints imposed by population and technology, legal institutions, including property rights and contractual arrangements, and the courts that enforced them, affected the conditions under which wealth was extracted from the rural world to support the urban economy. Legal institutions, then, would have played a significant role in shaping the relations between city and country, and, more broadly, would have affected the welfare of many people.

We can learn a great deal about the role of law in the rural economy by considering various forms of farm tenancy. Farm tenancy was an institution basic to the Roman economy. It represented a widespread method of exploiting estates both in Italy and the provinces. Farm tenants provided labour, and sometimes they also helped absentee landowners in managing their holdings. In addition, some farm tenants contributed substantial resources of their own, including livestock and even slaves, and so reduced the level of investment that landowners had to make in cultivating their land.[1] Farm tenancy existed side by side with other forms of cultivation. For example, the villa economy of early imperial Italy involved the cultivation of compact estates with slave labour under the management of a slave bailiff, or *vilicus*. But in regions where this type of agriculture was practiced, such as on the west coast of Italy, other farms were worked by owner-cultivators or tenants (Kehoe 2007b, 553–9). In the interior of Italy and other regions of the empire, farm tenancy was a common way for landowners to exploit estates. In Egypt, farm tenancy played an important role in the village economy, alongside small-scale owner cultivation. Some larger estates in Egypt were exploited with wage labour, including permanent salaried labourers residing within the estate and other workers hired on a daily basis (Rathbone 1991; Banaji 2001). Although most of our evidence for wage labour on large estates comes from Egypt, it is also likely that there were estates in other parts of the empire cultivated primarily through wage labour (Rathbone 2005). In addition, throughout the period of the Principate and late antiquity, independent small-scale farmers continued to occupy a great deal of land, often cultivating it at a near-subsistence level. Even so, farm tenancy in some form was in all likelihood a ubiquitous institution, and it was one moreover in which the Roman government took a continuing interest, whether establishing rules for land tenure on state-owned land or responding to legal disputes involving private tenancy.

Analysing the likely economic effects of Roman policies is difficult, but we can learn from the rich theoretical perspectives engendered by the on-going debate about the relationship between legal institutions and the economy in the fields of Law and Economics and the New Institutional Economics (NIE).[2] The term New Institutional Economics refers to an interdisciplinary field involving scholars primarily in economics and law, but in other fields as well, who are concerned with the role of institutions in economics. These institutions include both laws and legally defined property rights, court systems, and the like, as well as informal institutions, such as social norms and customs, that shape how individuals engage in economic activity. This approach is to be contrasted with neoclassical economics because it takes into account basic constraints that affect economic activity, including the costs associated with creating

---

[1] My discussion of tenancy is based on a more extensive treatment in Kehoe 2007a, chapter 3, as well as Kehoe 1997, chs. 3–4. For the recent debate on Roman farm tenancy, see the essays in Lo Cascio ed. 1997, as well as Launaro 2011.

[2] For an introduction to NIE, see Mercuro and Medema 1997, 130–56; Klein 2000; for further discussion on the application of NIE methodologies to the ancient world, see Frier and Kehoe 2007, Kehoe 2007a, ch. 1, Kehoe 2012, 193–7, and Bang 2009.

and maintaining property rights, as well as the costs of obtaining information crucial to making informed decisions. Moreover, people's decision-making in economic matters is influenced substantially by broadly shared values and ideologies (Greif 2006). Changing the institutions that surround the economy can be very difficult; it involves not only the costs of moving to a potentially more efficient arrangement (North 1990, 92–104), but also overcoming or changing the perceptions and values that help to create existing arrangements (Greif 2006, 188).

The methodologies of law and economics and NIE have limitations. They do not necessarily explain the origins of institutions, which can be a product of complex legal and social factors (Rutherford 1994). Nor can they be used to generate any predictions about the scale of an ancient economy or its rate of growth over time. But these methodologies are helpful in that they allow us to predict the likely incentives created by institutional arrangements. At the very least, an analysis of the legal institutions surrounding the economy makes it possible to come to a more complete understanding about the factors that affected agrarian change in the ancient world.

The Roman government's policies on land tenure had their most immediate impact on state-owned lands, or imperial estates, where it fostered the security of tenure of small-scale tenants as a means to secure stable revenues. Imperial estates formed part of a vast system of property throughout the empire that the imperial government acquired over the years by various means, including bequest and confiscation. Under the administration of the imperial treasury, or Fiscus, they furnished considerable revenues, supporting, among other things, the state-sponsored programs of food distribution at Rome.[3] The Roman administration's policies regarding imperial estates were central to its efforts to secure revenues, but they also affected the broader agrarian economy, since the imperial government was by far the largest landowner in the Roman world. The policies that the Roman administration developed for managing its own estates thus established how a considerable portion of the empire's land was exploited, and it is likely that these policies also affected the terms of tenure on private land. As I will argue, the Roman administration consistently followed a policy of promoting the tenure rights of small-scale cultivators on imperial land as a means of securing stable long-term revenues, and this policy had ramifications for private land tenure as well.

The Roman government's intervention in the private economy, which largely came in the form of interpreting lease law as it responded to petitions from landowners and tenants (see below), was clearly more limited in scope. Still, in responding to petitions it was guided by similar considerations that informed its administration of state-owned land. With private tenancy, the task that the Roman legal authorities faced was not to favour landowners or tenants, but to define property rights as clearly as possible to encourage productive private bargaining between these two groups. In the process of responding to petitions, the Roman legal authorities tended to interpret

---

[3] For the revenues from imperial estates, see Duncan-Jones 1994, 47–63; Lo Cascio 2007.

legal issues in terms of Roman private law, even when the disputes standing behind the petitions originated from local and customary arrangements. The policies that the state followed in administering state land and in developing rules for private tenancy helped to create institutions that shaped land tenure, and these institutions severely constrained the Roman government as it sought, in the late third and early fourth centuries, to stabilize its sources of revenue.

We can appreciate the advantages and costs of the Roman government's policy of promoting and protecting small-scale cultivation by considering its administration of imperial estates in North Africa, as revealed by its responses to petitions involving land tenure rights.[4] The Fiscus sought stable, long-term revenues from its estates despite its ability to maintain only a minimal administrative structure to oversee the cultivation of the estates. At the same time, it had limited information about how best to achieve this. As a result, it seems likely that the regulations it developed for its estates in North Africa modified in some form land-tenure arrangements that already existed when the state acquired its properties (cf. De Ligt 1998–99).

To accomplish an overriding goal of realizing predictable and steady revenues, the Fiscus relied on several groups with varying property rights to the land. Production largely depended on sharecroppers, *coloni*, who occupied their land under perpetual leaseholds based on a first-century regulation called the *lex Manciana*, apparently an originally private lease regulation that the imperial administration adapted for imperial estates. Under the emperor Hadrian, the Fiscus developed a more general regulation, called the *lex Hadriana de rudibus agris* ("the law of Hadrian concerning unused lands"), to define the conditions under which *coloni* could occupy unused lands on imperial estates. The administration implemented this law through a communication from imperial procurators (the *sermo procuratorum*) that spelled out the precise rules under which unused lands could be occupied. The regulations in the *sermo* encouraged *coloni* to invest their labour and resources in cultivating vines, olives, and other tree crops. *Coloni* gained perpetual rights to their land as long as they kept it under cultivation, and they could bequeath their rights and also use them as security in loans.

The *coloni* were independent farmers who supplied the labour, livestock, and other resources to cultivate the land. But the rights established by the *lex Manciana* and the *lex Hadriana* did not give this group anything like full rights of ownership. Instead, they had to pay a share of their crops, generally one-third, as rent to middlemen, or *conductores*, who leased from the Fiscus on a short-term basis the right to collect the share rents and to cultivate certain lands not occupied by *coloni*. Besides paying their share rent, the *coloni* were responsible to provide a certain number of days of labour each year as well as the use of their draft animals to enable the *conductores* to cultivate these lands.

If offering the security of tenure through perpetual leaseholds represented a policy to promote the long-term investment in imperial land by small farmers, this method

---

[4] This discussion summarizes a longer treatment in Kehoe 2007a, ch. 2; see also Kehoe 2013.

came with substantial costs. For one, the Fiscus had few means to monitor the performance of *coloni*, or to adjust rents in accordance with the quality of the land. At best, the Fiscus set up incentives for *coloni* to cultivate land and invest in it for the long term, and then to achieve a modicum of monitoring it assigned to the middlemen *conductores* the task of enforcing the obligation of the *coloni* to pay rent. But the *conductores* for their part had little capacity to enforce how the *coloni* cultivated their land – whether they used appropriate methods and preserved the land for the future. The only sanction facing the *coloni* was that they faced the loss of their rights to land that they did not cultivate for two consecutive years.

Another disadvantage was that this property rights regime left little room for cooperative bargaining between the *coloni* and the *conductores*, say over sharing the costs of installing new plantations or maintaining or upgrading pressing installations. Instead, the administration effectively pitted two groups against one another, with the *coloni* having the incentives and responsibility to cultivate the land, and the *conductores* set over them to exact a portion of their production to provide revenues for the Fiscus. The role of the imperial administration was mainly to settle the disputes between these two groups that would inevitably arise. Such arbitration would never involve altering the terms of occupation in any fundamental way, but instead it would determine, within the set of rights established long in the past, what the obligations of the various groups with economic interests in the imperial estates were. The *coloni* were invested with firm property rights to their land, which they could only lose if they failed to cultivate it.

The logical consequences of pitting middlemen *conductores* against the *coloni* can be seen in the imperial government's response to a series of petitions in the 180s, in which *coloni* complained about abuses that they were suffering at the hands of *conductores* and corrupt procurators administering the estates. In the most complete of these, *coloni* on an estate called the *saltus Burunitanus* successfully petitioned the emperor Commodus for relief against the efforts of a middleman who, with the cooperation of the imperial procurator administering the estate, sought to raise their share rent and increase the number of days of labour that the *coloni* were required to provide. These *coloni* defined their rights to the land on the basis of the *lex Hadriana*, presumably the *lex Hadriana de rudibus agris*, and a document that they called the *perpetua forma* (perpetual rule or procedure). The response of the emperor to the complaints by the *coloni* about the abuses they were suffering – a corrupt procurator sent soldiers onto the estate and arrested and beat *coloni*, some of whom were Roman citizens – was to reassert the validity of these tenure arrangements. This certainly represented a victory for the *coloni*, but it also suggests the narrow range of options that the imperial administration had in formulating a policy toward imperial estates. The overriding concern of the state was to maintain the viability of the small-scale farmers cultivating the land, and to preserve this the state consistently sided with them in disputes with *conductores*. Indeed, some time after the petitions to the emperor Commodus, the administration offered the same terms of cultivation to would-be *coloni* that were originally established under Hadrian, as the republication under Septimius Severus (193–211) of the Hadrianic *sermo procuratorum* citing the *lex Hadriana de rudibus agris* indicates (De Vos 2000).

In Egypt, the Roman administration sought to achieve the same basic goals as with its estates in North Africa. It maintained control over the lands that had been under the direct administration of the Ptolemaic monarchy (Manning 2007; Rathbone 2007). The land inherited from the Ptolemies included royal land, *ge basilike*, and it was augmented by public land, or *ge demosie*, which included land confiscated from temples or other supporters of M. Antonius and Cleopatra. A third category of state land, created under the Principate, ousiac land, or *ge ousiake*, was granted to members of the Julio-Claudian family or close associates of the court (Parássoglou 1978); later the *ousiai* came under direct state control and were administered like other categories of state land. The conditions under which this land was cultivated certainly varied from region to region, but broad principles guided the state's policy in administering it. It was generally leased out in small parcels to cultivators who enjoyed substantial security of tenure (Rowlandson 1996, 76–101). Sometimes, the line between a private landowner and a cultivator of state land was blurred, with the same people performing both roles. Leasing state land was generally an attractive proposition, and it provided an additional source of income to economically independent farmers. One result of the state's maintaining control over large amounts of land and leasing it out under favourable conditions was to promote a more equitable distribution of land in Egyptian villages than was the case in other parts of the empire. This policy must have slowed the development of large private estates, which began to emerge in the second century and became a very important feature of the Egyptian agrarian economy from the third century until late antiquity.[5] Even in the third century and later, when much state-owned land had reverted to private hands, Egyptian villages continued to have a viable class of small farmers, such as Aurelius Isidorus from the village of Karanis in the early fourth century, who were both landowners and tenants at the same time and were financially capable of performing liturgies (Kehoe 1992, ch. 4).

In Egypt, then, the Roman government pursued a goal-oriented strategy to maintain its access to important revenues, in particular rents in kind of wheat, and its policy had distributional consequences for the economy of Roman Egypt. To return to the North African imperial estates, the Roman administration's policy of providing security of tenure for *coloni* precluded other approaches, such as returning or selling the estates back to private landowners, who could potentially make the estates more profitable by changing how they were cultivated. This would entail violating the property rights of the *coloni*, a step that the imperial government was not willing to take either in Africa or in Asia Minor, where a series of inscriptions preserves petitions from tenants on imperial properties (Hauken 1998). In Asia Minor, the major bone of contention

---

[5] For the development of estates in Egypt, see Rathbone 2007, 701–2, and now Monson 2012. Cf. Bagnall 1992, for a study of landholding patterns in Egyptian villages in the fourth century, and Sharp 1999, for a focused discussion of landowning in an individual village during the principate.

concerned the efforts of imperial tax officials and representatives of towns to impose tax and liturgy obligations (compulsory public services) on tenants from imperial estates. The imperial tenants, for their part, viewed such impositions as violations of their terms of tenure, and the Roman administration consistently took their side. In North Africa and Asia Minor, as well as in Egypt, the state sought, to the extent possible, to monopolize the resources of imperial tenants for its own purposes. Whether or not this made the most efficient use of resources to foster economic growth is unknowable, and it was certainly not something the imperial administration could measure. But it does seem to have represented a reasonable solution to a long-term goal of achieving stable revenues, even if it had some clear drawbacks.

This privileging of small-scale cultivation informed the Roman legal authorities' treatment of legal issues involving farm tenancy on private estates. The Roman legal authorities were especially concerned to respond to the private bargaining engaged in by landowners and tenants to overcome impediments to investment in agriculture, particularly those involving the tenant's security of tenure and the risk posed by weather. The interventions by the Roman government in issues involving land tenure (and, for that matter, in other areas of private law) characteristically came in the form of responding to petitions to the emperor. These responses, or rescripts, became an important way for the emperors, or their legal advisors, to modify the law.[6] In responding to petitions involving land tenure, the government tended to make preserving the legal relationship part of the solution to the legal problem and so supported the efforts of landowners and tenants to maintain mutually beneficial long-term tenure arrangements. The importance of long-term tenancy relationships in the Roman empire created legal complications for the imperial government, however, as it sought to sort out competing rights and claims of landowners and tenants land arising from local, customary tenure arrangements. This policy, then, involved a willingness to adapt the terms of the classical Roman farm lease to the realities of the Roman agrarian economy.

In the classical farm lease, the tenant leased the farm for a short period of time, generally five years, in exchange for a cash rent (Kehoe 1997, ch. 3; Frier 1979). In this type of lease, the main duty was to provide the tenant with a farm that he could cultivate, and this duty imposed on the landowner the responsibility to provide the fixed capital, including buildings, presses, and storage facilities – anything attached to the soil. For his part, the tenant was expected to provide movable capital, such as tools, livestock, and even slaves. The property that the tenant brought onto the farm remained pledged as security for the rent. If the policy of the state in administering

---

[6] During the Principate, it was a common practice for people in the empire to seek to resolve legal disputes by petitioning the emperor. In response to this, the government developed an office, headed by an equestrian official, the *a libellis*, to respond to petitions (Peachin 1996; Corcoran 1996; Connolly 2010). The emperor was not in a position to respond to the facts alleged in the petition but would instead establish what legal principles would apply. The successful litigant would then take the emperor's rescript back to a local court, where the judge would be bound to follow it.

imperial estates was to encourage long-term investment by the tenant, the conventional Roman farm lease provided a potentially serious impediment to this, since the tenant lacked the right of possession (Kehoe 1997, 183–209). The right of the tenant in Roman private law to remain on the land was insecure; for example, if the tenant's land were sold or bequeathed to a new owner, that person would not be obliged to honour the tenant's lease, since Roman law did not allow contracts to impose obligations on third parties. The tenant's only recourse would be against the original landlord, and his compensation for losing his lease would be monetary. The law did not impose an enforceable duty of specific performance (that is, making someone fulfil his or her obligations in a contract rather than paying monetary damages) on either landowner or tenant.

The position of private farm tenants, then, was much weaker than that of their counterparts on imperial estates, who enjoyed the security of tenure represented by perpetual leaseholds. The lack of any provision for specific performance can be seen as economically efficient, in that it allows for contracts to be breached when the benefits of doing so outweigh the costs and the party breaching the contract can compensate the other, to their mutual benefit (Shavell 2004, 379). But we can easily imagine that in the rural Roman world, monetary compensation would be cold comfort to a farmer who had lost his land, since he would have invested his labour and resources in cultivating it, and his losses could not easily be covered by money.[7]

But the petition process confronted the Roman legal authorities with tenure systems that accorded the tenant much stronger protection, and they recognized such arrangements as legally binding in terms of Roman law. For example, the emperor Alexander Severus (*CJ* 4.65.9, 234 CE) was willing to enforce a tacit or customary understanding that the tenant could remain on his farm even when it was sold or otherwise alienated; the tenant envisioned in this rescript seems to have had a de-facto right of possession (Kehoe 2007a, 124–5). The Romans had a useful legal principle to describe open-ended tenure arrangements in terms of Roman legal conventions, namely, the tacit renewal of the lease, or *relocatio tacita*. According to this principle, if the tenant remained in his tenancy without any objection on the part of the landowner, he was considered to have renewed the lease for another year under the same terms as had existed previously.

The policy of the Roman legal authorities to promote the tenant's continued cultivation of the land can be seen in its treatment of the thorny issue of risk in agriculture.[8] In the Mediterranean world, frequent droughts, even, or especially, quite localized ones, could threaten the ability of a tenant to pay rent (Horden and Purcell

---

[7] This is the so-called 'endowment effect,' which refers to the difference between the price that someone places on a good and the value that the market places on it. In Roman law, a tenant's compensation would be based on the market value of his lease. For discussion of the endowment effect, see Curran 2000.

[8] This section is based on Kehoe 2007a, 109–19 and Kehoe 2012, 197–205. For discussion of remission of rent in a broad historical perspective, see Capogrossi Colognesi 2005.

2000, 175–230). In classical Roman law, the tenant bore the risk for the size of the harvest and for the market price of the crops, and was entitled to an abatement or remission of rent only in the event of an unforeseeable disaster, such as an earthquake, unforeseeable weather conditions, or an invasion (Frier 1989–90; Du Plessis 2003). The tenant was responsible for all other risks, including those posed by normal variations in rainfall (Servius apud Ulp. *D.* 19.2.15.2; cf. Gaius *D.* 19.2.25.6). This distribution of risk can be seen as economically efficient, since it encouraged the tenant to take steps to reduce risk by diversifying crops, cultivating more drought resistant crops, and building up reserves. The landowner, from this perspective, could better bear the risk for unforeseen disasters; the landowner could diversity holdings geographically and was generally wealthier than the tenant and so better able to ride out a storm (cf. Posner and Rosenfield 1977). But losses resulting from crop failure, or *sterilitas*, posed a real problem, since they could be viewed as foreseeable risks, but would leave the tenant as unable to pay the rent as a catastrophic disaster for which the landowner bore the risk. The legal authorities addressed this situation, not by taking the side of landowners or tenants, but rather by facilitating negotiations or 'private ordering' between the two parties. It did this by defining their rights and obligations more precisely when the landowner did grant the tenant a remission of rent because of a poor crop. Such a policy stands behind a famous response of the earlier third-century jurist Papinian (Papin. apud Ulp. *D.* 19.2.15.4). Papinian did not envision termination of the lease contract as a remedy when a disaster prevented the tenant from paying the rent, as it would be in later civilian systems (such as the Napoleonic Code and the Louisiana Civil Code), but the jurist operated on the assumption that lease would endure beyond the individual growing season. Papinian's reasoning became part of governmental policy, as is indicated by a somewhat later rescript of the emperor Alexander Severus on the same problem (*CJ* 4.65.8, 231).

The continuing concern of the Roman legal authorities with the question of risk in agriculture raises the question to what extent the law and formal institutions of the state made a real difference in land tenure. At the very least, responding to petitions tended to enhance the authority of Roman legal institutions for settling disputes. Even if the vast majority of disputes involving land tenure were decided without recourse to any court, the authority of Roman legal institutions helped to establish what some scholars term an endowment of rights that informed private bargaining; private tenure systems developed in the "shadow of the law."[9] The Roman Empire's legal institutions were strong enough and responsive enough that turning to the law provided a viable, if costly, means of resolving disputes.

From another perspective, the rescript process offers us a glimpse at how the Roman legal authorities dealt with social practice. As Avner Greif has shown in his analysis of institutions surrounding commerce in the Mediaeval world, institutions are not simply the product of the efforts of well-placed people to protect their economic

---

[9] For the use of this concept to refer to divorce settlements in US courts, see Mnookin and Kornhauser 1979. For theoretical discussion of this concept, see Dixit 2004, 25–58.

interests, but they also embody values and even ideologies that individuals internalize (Greif 2006). So to a great extent the values underlying institutions create both constraints on the behaviour of individuals as well as impediments to more comprehensive institutional change. In the tenancy issues that the Roman legal authorities addressed, there must have been norms of behaviour that limited what each party would consider acceptable in his or her dealings with the other, although we can only infer some of these. A landowner could presumably not simply kick a tenant off the estate, and a tenant could not simply burn his crops or take other violent actions. For example, Libanius, the wealthy landowner and orator from fourth-century Antioch, complains about the failure of his and other tenants to observe due deference to their landlords, because of outside interference (*Or.* 47). Libanius' perspective on the breakdown of rural patronage should be taken seriously: landowners and tenants might have reasonable expectations about the nature of their relationship, whatever the formal law might indicate. To consider the legal issue of *remissio mercedis*, it is possible that rent abatements for *sterilitas* were to some extent normative. In developing their doctrine on this issue, then, the legal authorities were not simply allocating the costs of such remissions by defining property rights. Rather, they were doing something more, trying to make the law keep pace with social practice, in the sense of having the law rule over social norms by defining what a remission actually involved.

This meant that the law had to be flexible. We have seen this flexibility in the willingness of the Roman government to recognize as legally binding tenure systems that accorded the tenant a degree of protection not possible in classical Roman lease law (see above). One consequence of its flexibility was that the Roman government would be called upon to serve as a kind of referee to prevent landowners and tenants, but especially the former, from exploiting long-term tenure arrangements. This concern stands behind a constitution of Valerian and Gallienus (*CJ* 4.65.16, 260 CE), who ruled that, in a tacitly renewed lease, landowners were not to raise the rent. Later, the emperor Constantine recognized as legally binding customary rents, and he provided a remedy for tenants against landowners who raised these (*CJ* 11.50.1). This policy of protecting tenants was consistent with an overall concern to make sure that farmers remained on their land, since only by cultivating their land could they provide tax revenues to the imperial treasury. For example, in the early fourth century, creditors were prohibited from seizing property from farmers that they needed to cultivate their land (*CTh* 2.30.1; *CJ* 8.16.7, 315).

The Roman government's policy to protect the tenure of at least some small-scale cultivators affected the interests of landowners, small farmers, and the state. In the private sphere, according tenants secure tenure rights and offering them incentives to invest their own resources in the farm might serve the interests of risk-averse landowners. They, like the Fiscus in relation to imperial estates, would gain their revenues by skimming a portion of the surplus that their tenants produced. They would have little inclination to invest their own resources in their estates to increase productivity or to alter their crop choices in response to changing market conditions.

To be sure, there were landowners who took a very different approach to managing their estates, such as Aurelius Appianus in third-century Egypt, the running of whose estate is documented in the Heroninos archive (Rathbone 1991). This estate consisted of divisions organized around villages, and each division, or *phrontis*, was under the direction of a *phrontistes*, whose job was to oversee the cultivation of numerous individual parcels of land, many of them vineyards. A modest number of permanent wage labourers, supplemented by many more hired on a daily basis, performed most of the labour on the estate. The primary difference between an estate owner like Appianus and the ones who leased land out to multiple tenants is that Appianus was able to gain a greater profit as a result of controlling costs through economies of scale. Both types of landowners depended on the same market for agricultural production, and both were subject to the basic constraints imposed by an agrarian economy with few options for investing wealth.

These general constraints on the Roman agrarian economy limited the options available to the government in developing any sort of policy for the agrarian economy, and this situation was especially felt during times of crisis. Implementing a policy involving substantial changes in tenure systems would have involved considerable costs with little assurance of any long-term benefit, either to the imperial treasury or to society as a whole. We can trace the immense difficulty that the Roman government faced in altering time-honoured tenure arrangements by considering the economic implications of late antique fiscal legislation, which involved, beginning in the fourth century CE, taking the security of tenure implicit in many customary arrangements to its logical conclusion by binding of certain categories of farmers to the land they cultivated.[10] This policy, which was gradually and not uniformly implemented, adapted long-standing institutional arrangements, but it also had unforeseen consequences for incentives to invest. It tended to diminish the possibilities for the type of private bargaining that the state's legal policies under the Principate encouraged.

The key to the fiscal system of the later Roman Empire was tying individual farmers to their village of origin, their *origo* or *idia*. From the time of the Principate, individual cultivators were registered for tax purposes in their villages, and they were expected to remain there and contribute their share to the tax assessments that were imposed on villages corporately. In the later Roman Empire, the efforts to tie farmers to their villages of origin became more urgent, as the government imposed the responsibility to collect taxes to an increasing extent on landowners, and in some circumstances estates could be counted as the *origo* of farmers who were not otherwise registered in the census rolls as independent landowners. The binding of *coloni* who were registered as tenants did not create a new class of farmers dependent on increasingly wealthy

---

[10] For discussion of the development of the bound colonate in late antiquity, see the essays in Lo Cascio 1997, especially Carrié 1997, and Vera 1997 and now Grey 2007. For a broad treatment of the late Roman rural economy, see Whittaker and Garnsey 1998. I discuss the incentives created by late Roman fiscal policy in Kehoe 2007a, ch. 5.

landowners; rather, it provided a convenient way to organize the collection of taxes and the performance of liturgies at the local level (Grey 2007). By restricting the movements of *coloni* registered as tenants, the government could, in theory at least, help landowners meet their increasing responsibility, and liability, for the collection and payment of taxes by assuring them of having a labour force on hand to cultivate their land.

To maintain the viability of its fiscal system, the government had to mediate between landowners and tenants registered on their estates. On the one hand, it was concerned especially to restrict the movement of *coloni* who, with substantial resources of their own, would be especially attractive to landowners. To counter their mobility, the government, beginning in the reign of Constantine, imposed increasingly severe penalties both on *coloni* who fled their estates of origin and on landowners who took them in. On the other hand, the government provided a great deal of protection to *coloni* bound to their land. Landowners could not dismiss them, or even raise their rents. Thus, as we have seen, Constantine ruled that landowners could not raise customary rents, and in the same constitution this emperor established a process for tenants to seek redress against landowners who had raised their rent in contravention of existing arrangements (*CJ* 11.50.1). All of this imposed costs on the economy. But the persistence of laws restricting their mobility suggests that *coloni* and landowners had an incentive to flout them. However, any new contractual arrangements that they struck would have been outside of the control of the law, which would have created distortions in the market for the services of *coloni*. At the same time, landowners had little capacity to reorganize estates and thus little incentive to invest in improvements that might make them more productive. The more likely situation is that investment would be largely in the hands of *coloni*, and the role of landowners would be much more like that of a tax collector than any kind of business partner reaching cooperative arrangements with tenants.

An analysis of the likely economic consequences of Roman legal and administrative policy as it affected land tenure helps us to understand better the process of agrarian change in the Roman Empire. The government's policy of privileging small-scale cultivation, within the restricted sphere that it was able to affect, certainly had consequences for the Roman economy. These are impossible to measure empirically, but they can be predicted. Protecting the tenure rights of small farmers affected the relationships between city and the countryside, since it would have checked the capacity of large landowners to monopolize the surplus produced by peasant farmers, both because it gave greater economic security to imperial tenants themselves and also required private landowners to offer competitive terms of tenure. This is not to say that elite landowners did not have a great deal of power in the countryside; indeed they might exercise patronage over rural communities that would give them a great deal of leverage in dealing with their own tenants or other modest landowners (Grey 2011, especially 122–137). But the state provided some check on the power of such landowners. At the same time, the state's legal policies combined with social practices to foster a set of institutions that helped to drive the process of change in the Roman agrarian economy. This complex relationship between Roman law and the empire's agrarian economy suggests some of the ways in which legal institutions and property rights affected the agrarian economy of the ancient Near East.

BIBLIOGRAPHICAL ABBREVIATIONS

CJ   *Corpus Iuris Civilis*. Vol. II, *Codex Justinianus*. Ed. and rev. P. Krueger. Berlin, 1954. Reprint, Hildesheim, 1989.

CTh   *Codex Theodosianus*.

D.   *Corpus Iuris Civilis*. Vol. I, *Digesta*. Ed. T. Mommsen. Rev. P. Krueger. Berlin, 1963. Reprint, Hildesheim, 1988.

REFERENCES

Bagnall, R. S. (1992) Landholding in Late Roman Egypt: The Distribution of Wealth. *Journal of Roman Studies* 82, 128–149.

Banaji, J. (2001) *Agrarian Change in Late Antiquity: Gold, Labour and Aristocratic Dominance*. Oxford: Oxford University Press (repr. 2005).

Bang, P. (2009) The Ancient Economy and New Institutional Economics. *Journal of Roman Studies* 99, 194–206.

Bouckaert, B. and De Geest, G. (eds) (2000) *Encyclopedia of Law and Economics*, 5 vols. Cheltenham, UK, and Northampton, MA, Edward Elgar. [On-line edition (1999): http://users.ugent. be/~gdegeest/]

Capogrossi Colognesi, L. (2005) *Remissio Mercedis: una storia tra logiche di sistema e autorità della norma*. Naples: Jovene.

Carrié, J.-M. (1997) 'Colonato del Basso Impero': la resistenza del mito. In Lo Cascio (ed.), 75–150.

Connolly, S. (2010) *Lives Behind the Laws: The world of the Codex Hermoginianus*. Bloomington: Indiana University Press.

Corcoran, S. (1996) *The Empire of the Tetrarchs: Imperial Pronouncements and Government A.D. 284–324*. Oxford: Oxford University Press.

Curran, C. (2000) The Endowment Effect. In Bouckaert and De Geest (eds), vol. 1, 819–835.

De Ligt, L. (1998–99) Studies in Legal and Agrarian History I: The Inscription from Henchir-Mettich and the *Lex Manciana*. *Ancient Society* 29, 219–239.

De Vos, M. (ed.) (2000) *Rus Africum: Terra acqua olio nell'Africa settentrionale. Scavo e recognizione nei dintorini di Dougga (Alto Tell tunisino)* (Labirinti 50). Trento: Università degli studi di Trento/ Institut national du patrimoine de Tunis.

Dixit, A. (2004) *Lawlessness and Economics: Alternative Modes of Governance*. Princeton: Princeton University Press.

Duncan-Jones, R. (1994) *Money and Government in the Roman Empire*. Cambridge: Cambridge University Press.

Du Plessis, P. J. (2003) *A History of Remissio Mercedis and Related Legal Institutions.* Diss. Erasmus University, Rotterdam.

Erdkamp, P. (2001) Beyond the Limits of the 'Consumer City': A Model of the Urban and Rural Economy in the Roman World. *Historia* 50 (3), 332–356.

Frier, B. W. (1979) Law, Technology, and Social Change: The Equipping of Italian Farm Tenancies. *Zeitschrift der Savigny-Stiftung für Rechtsgeschichte (Romanistiche Abteilung)* 96, 204–228.

Frier, B. W. (1989–90) Law, Economics, and Disasters down on the Farm: 'Remissio Mercedis' Revisited. *Bulletino dell'Istituto di Diritto romano,* 3rd ser., 31–32, 237–270.

Frier, B. W. and Kehoe, D. P. (2007) Law and Economic Institutions. In Scheidel *et al.* (eds), 113–143.

Greif, A. (2006) *Institutions and the Path to the Modern Economy: Lessons from Medieval Trade, Political Economy of Institutions and Decisions.* Cambridge: Cambridge University Press.

Grey, C. (2007) Contextualizing *Colonatus:* The *Origo* of the Late Roman Empire. *Journal of Roman Studies* 97, 155–175.

Grey, C. (2011) *Constructing Communities in the Late Roman Countryside.* Cambridge: Cambridge University Press.

Hauken, T. (1998) *Petition and Response: An Epigraphic Study of Petitions to Roman Emperors 181-249* (Monographs from the Norwegian Institute at Athens 2). Bergen: Norwegian Institute at Athens.

Horden, P., and Purcell, N. (2000) *The Corrupting Sea: A Study of Mediterranean History.* Oxford: Blackwell.

Johnson, D. G. (2000) Population, Food, and Knowledge. *The American Economic Review* 90 (1), 1–14.

Jongman, W. (1988) *The Economy and Society of Pompeii* (Dutch Monographs on Ancient History and Archaeology 4). Amsterdam: Gieben.

Kehoe, D. P. (1992) *Management and Investment on Estates in Roman Egypt during the Early Empire* (Papyrologische Texte und Abhandlungen 40). Bonn: Habelt.

Kehoe, D. P. (1997) *Investment, Profit, and Tenancy: The Jurists and the Roman Agrarian Economy.* Ann Arbor: University of Michigan Press.

Kehoe, D. P. (2007a) *Law and the Rural Economy in the Roman Empire.* Ann Arbor: University of Michigan Press.

Kehoe, D. P. (2007b) The Early Roman Empire: Production. In Scheidel *et al.* (eds), 543–569.

Kehoe, D. P. (2012) Roman Economic Policy and the Law of Contracts. In T. A. J. McGinn (ed.) *Obligations in Roman Law: Past, Present, and Future.* Ann Arbor: University of Michigan Press, 189–214.

Kehoe, D. P. (2013) The State and Production in the Roman Economy. In A. Bowman and A. Wilson (eds), *The Agricultural Economy: Production and Consumption,* 33–53. Oxford: Oxford University Press.

Klein, P. G. (2000) New Institutional Economics. In Bouckaert and De Geest (eds), vol. 1, 456–489.

Launaro, A. (2011) *Peasants and Slaves. The Rural Population of Roman Italy (200 BC to AD 100).* Cambridge: Cambridge University Press.

Lo Cascio, E. (ed.) (1997) *Terre, proprietari e contadini dell'impero romano: Dall'affitto agrario al colonato tardoantico.* Rome: NIS.

Lo Cascio, E. (2007) The Early Roman Empire: The State and the Economy. In Scheidel *et al.* (eds), 619–647.

Manning, J. G. (2007) Hellenistic Egypt. In Scheidel *et al.* (eds), 434–459.

Mercuro, N., and Medema, S. G. (1997) *Economics and the Law: From Posner to Post-Modernism.* Princeton: Princeton University Press.

Mnookin, R. H., and Kornhauser, L. (1979). Bargaining in the Shadow of the Law: The Case of Divorce. *Yale Law Journal* 85, 950–997.

Monson, A. (2012) *From the Ptolemies to the Romans: Political and Economic Change in Egypt.* Cambridge: Cambridge University Press.

North, D. C. (1990) *Institutions, Institutional Change and Economic Performance.* Cambridge: Cambridge University Press (repr. 2002).

Parássoglou, G. M. (1978) *Imperial Estates in Roman Egypt* (American Studies in Papyrology 18). Amsterdam: Hakkert.

Peachin, M. (1996) *Iudex vice Caesaris: Deputy Emperors and the Administration of Justice during the Principate* (Heidelberger Althistorische und Epigraphische Beiträge 21). Stuttgart: Steiner.

Posner, R. A. and Rosenfield, A. M. (1977) Impossibility and Related Doctrines in Contract Law: An Economic Analysis. *Journal of Legal Studies* 6, 813–818. [Excerpted in A. W. Katz (ed.) (1998) *Foundations of the Economic Approach to Law*, 227–236. New York: Foundation Press]

Rathbone, D. W. (1991) *Economic Rationalism and Rural Society in Third-Century A.D. Egypt: The Heroninos Archive and the Appianus Estate.* Cambridge: Cambridge University Press.

Rathbone, D. W. (2005) Economic Rationalism and the Heroninos Archive. *Topoi orient-occident* 12–13, 261–269.

Rathbone, D. W. (2007) Roman Egypt. In Scheidel *et al.* (eds), 698–719.

Rowlandson, J. (1996) *Landowners and Tenants in Roman Egypt: The Social Relations of Agriculture in the Oxyrhynchite Nome* (Oxford Classical Monographs). Oxford: Oxford University Press.

Rutherford, M. (1994) *Institutions in Economics: The Old and the New Institutionalism* (Historical Perspectives on Modern Economics). Cambridge: Cambridge University Press.

Scheidel, W. (2007) Demography. In Scheidel *et al.* (eds), 38–86.

Scheidel, W., Morris, I. and Saller R. (eds) (2007) *The Cambridge Economic History of the Greco-Roman World.* Cambridge: Cambridge University Press.

Sharp, M. (1999) The Village of Theadelphia in the Fayyum: Land and Population in the Second Century. In A. K. Bowman and E. Rogan (eds) *Agriculture in Egypt from Pharaonic to Modern Times*, 159–192 (Proceedings of the British Academy 96). Oxford: Oxford University Press on behalf of the British Academy.

Shavell, S. (2004) *Foundations of Economic Analysis of Law.* Cambridge, MA: Belknap Press of Harvard University Press.

Vera, D. (1997) Padroni, contadini, contratti: *realia* del colonato tardoantico. In Lo Cascio (ed.), 185–224.

Whittaker, C. R., and Garnsey, P. (1998) Rural Life in the Later Roman Empire. In A. Cameron and P. Garnsey (eds) *The Late Empire, A.D. 337–425*, 277–311. Vol. 13 of *The Cambridge Ancient History*, 2nd ed. Cambridge: Cambridge University Press.

Wilson, A. (1999) Deliveries *Extra Urbem*: Aqueducts and the Countryside. *Journal of Roman Archaeology* 12, 314–331.

Wilson, A. (2002) Machines, Power and the Ancient Economy. *Journal of Roman Studies* 92, 1–32.

The Papyrological Evidence for
Water-Lifting Technology

Myrto Malouta

Technological innovation, especially in the area of agriculture, is highly relevant in a debate regarding the ancient economy, which was a mostly agricultural economy. Improvement in the technology of irrigation might be expected to have one of the most significant impacts on agricultural productivity, and that in turn on economic growth. The construction, as well as operation of complex machinery would also be an interesting element of discussion relating to the division of labour and labour specialisation. Successful comparison and quantification of data relating to the development of agricultural technology also makes a very useful contribution to estimating the degree of economic rationalism in the ancient world, as well as in the discord between that and the Finleyan model that supports the idea that wealth was meant to be acquisitive and not productive, that is, was not intended to create capital.[1] Furthermore, quantifiable data on technological innovation alongside population estimates contribute to the debate on whether this innovation led to *sustained* growth, or whether the economy did not manage to avoid the so-called "low equilibrium trap".[2]

In this paper I set out and try to analyse the papyrological data on water-lifting devices from the 3rd century BC to the 8th century AD. For further clarification I also juxtapose them with the relevant archaeological data, with an overview of which I shall start.

The archaeological evidence for water-lifting devices, mainly for the early Roman period, indicates their widespread use throughout the Empire. The following graph (fig. 7.1), kindly provided by Andrew Wilson, sets out the archaeological and literary evidence for water-lifting technology, with a view to indicating trends of uptake of

---

[1] Finley 1985[2], 144.
[2] Scheidel 2007, 55.

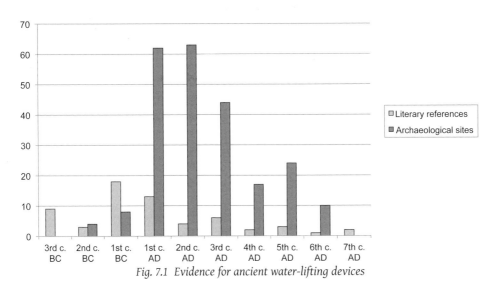

Fig. 7.1 Evidence for ancient water-lifting devices

water-lifting technology in the Empire in general. A word of caution is needed here: both archaeological and literary evidence include all kinds of water-lifting devices, including bilge-pumps from ships and tread-wheels from mines. Indeed, because of the nature of the evidence, only a fraction comprises irrigation machinery, whereas in the papyri, as we shall see, irrigation machinery constitutes the overwhelming bulk of attestations of water-lifting devices. However, if we agree with the opinion that treats different areas of technological development in antiquity as forming a mutually dependent technological system,[3] a comparative study of archaeological and papyrological data can be very enlightening, although at first glance we might appear to be comparing dissimilar finds. Furthermore, the archaeological data are drawn from finds in the Roman Empire as a whole, whereas the papyri by necessity are almost exclusively from Egypt. This does not negate the potential for using the two bodies of evidence together, but, especially since the emphasis here is on the papyrological side, it means that any comparison must be manifestly aimed at a microeconomic study of the particular province, rather than at attempting to reach conclusions about the whole of the Empire by generalising. While the view that Egypt is in some way idiosyncratic and therefore not representative of the physiognomy of the rest of the Empire is no longer fashionable, there are obvious particularities in its irrigation system which should not be overlooked and which do not allow us easily to extrapolate the finds to other provinces.

The main forms of water lifting devices known from archaeology are all attested in the Egyptian papyri of the third century BC to the eighth century AD. They are:

- the *shaduf*, in Greek mostly called *kêlôneion*, which consists of a horizontal lever

---

[3] Schneider 2007, 148.

balancing on a vertical beam. In the front hangs a container which is pulled down and dipped into the canal or reservoir below, and is then lifted by a counter-weight attached to the back of the horizontal beam.

- *Kochlias*, the water-screw or Archimedes screw, is a kind of displacement pump[4] in which a helix fitted within a solid cylindrical body, arranged diagonally with one end inside the source of water, lifts and pushes up quantities of water which it picks up as it turns.

- The water-wheel, which in Greek is called *trochos* and possibly *tympanon* (I shall return to the matter of terminology shortly), can be of various types, but the main principle is that it can lift water in a continuous movement to a maximum height equal to a little less than its diameter, by turning around an axle. It can store the water either in its main body (compartmented wheel), or in its rim (wheel with compartmented rim), or in containers attached to it around its rim.

- A similar principle, but allowing the lifting of water to a greater height, is that of the pot-garland or bucket-chain, in Greek probably *kullê kuklas*, where the wheel is not used directly to lift water, but rather to set in motion a long rope or chain from which hang a series of containers (wooden, bronze, or ceramic) which reach the water level below.

The compartmented rim wheel can be water powered (*noria*), where paddles attached to the outside of the cylinder ensure the perpetual motion of the wheel as it is driven by the flow of the water. This type of drive does not seem to have been very popular in Egypt, where water-lifting devices were mainly used to lift water out of slow-moving or stagnant water that was collected in canals and reservoirs. In that case, the simplest way of setting a water wheel in motion is by direct man-power by treading, but a more efficient, if more complicated and expensive way of operating water-wheels and pot garlands is with a mechanism that boosts direct man- or (usually) animal-power through a system of cog-wheels arranged at right angles. This allows for more efficient operation of larger wheels, which can lift larger amounts of water and through a greater height. This mechanism, and by extension the whole system of cog-wheels and water-wheel(s), is known in Arabic as a *saqiya*; in Greek it seems to be commonly referred to simply as *mêchanê*.

Because of the aforementioned potential value of the quantifiable data regarding water-lifting technology, I have set up a database in order to collect and analyse references to these devices in the papyri. I have accumulated all direct references to water-lifting devices, as well as references to water-lifting and artificial irrigation, even when the actual device used for that purpose is not specified. As it stands, the database contains 298 texts with 658 references to a minimum of 506 machines. The machines may in fact be many more, but I have chosen to count unspecified plurals

---

[4]   Oleson 1984, 296.

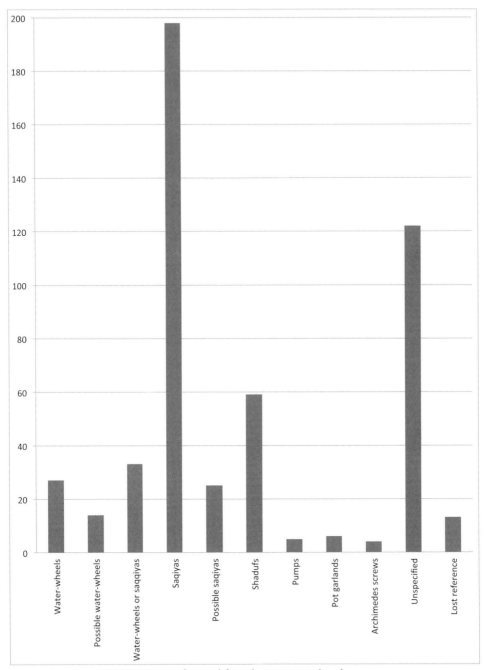

Fig. 7.2 *Types of water-lifting devices attested in the papyri*

as 2, although specified plurals are occasionally a lot more numerous.[5] The database is constructed in MySQL and is available at the Oxford Roman Economy Project website.[6]

In 122 cases there is little doubt that we are in fact dealing with a water-lifting device, and in many of these cases we can tell whether that device was used for irrigation, or for furnishing water for baths, etc. The exact type of the device, however, is not known in these cases. In 13 cases, usually because of damage to the papyrus, a reference to a part of the device is preserved, but again without allowing us to draw a secure conclusion as to which device we are dealing with. Of the rest, 27 can be interpreted as water-wheels; 14 as possible water-wheels; 33 as water-wheel or *saqiyas*; 198 as *saqiyas*; 25 as possible *saqiyas*; 59 as *shadufs*. We also find 5 pumps, 6 pot garlands, and 9 Archimedes screws (fig. 7.2).

The main complication when trying to establish the nature of each device is that the terminology of the device itself and many of the parts it comprises is still a subject of debate.[7] What is clear is that one must allow for regional or chronological variations in that terminology. The most obvious example is that of the *shaduf, kêlôneion* in Greek. If one were to take the papyrological evidence at face value, one would conclude that the *shaduf*, which features prominently throughout the Ptolemaic and early Roman times (it is of course a much earlier invention), ceases to exist at some point in the second century AD. This cannot be true. The *shaduf* is still in use today in Egypt, and, as it is one of the simplest and cheapest water-lifting devices, it would be hard to imagine that it gave way to its more costly and labour-intensive counterparts. What is more, Oleson, in his thorough study of *Greek and Roman Mechanical Water-Lifting Devices*, refutes the suggestion that the disappearance from the documents of certain kinds of devices depends on whether or not they were taxed.[8] He rightly points out that water-lifting devices feature in the papyri regardless of their status as taxable goods.[9] We hear of them when they are sold or hired, damaged and repaired, when labourers must be remunerated for operating them, or when accidents happen in them. The predominance of "unspecified" types of water-lifting devices after the 2nd century AD may in fact be due to such a switch in terminology that has not yet been accurately delineated. On that basis, the vague term *organon* which appears in the 2nd century AD may be used to denote the *shaduf*, or a number of devices including the *shaduf*. Similarly, the term *mêchanê*, which, when its meaning can be ascertained, means

---

[5]   A reference to 100 devices (*organa*) in P.Petr. III 43 is, however, possibly an erroneous reading.
[6]   http://www.romaneconomy.ox.ac.uk/.
[7]   Bonneau 1993; Oleson 1984; Rathbone 2007.
[8]   Bonneau 1971.
[9]   Oleson 1984, 131.

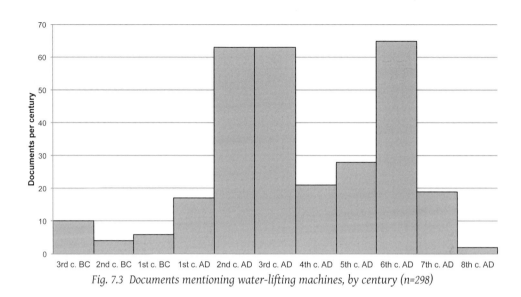

Fig. 7.3 Documents mentioning water-lifting machines, by century (n=298)

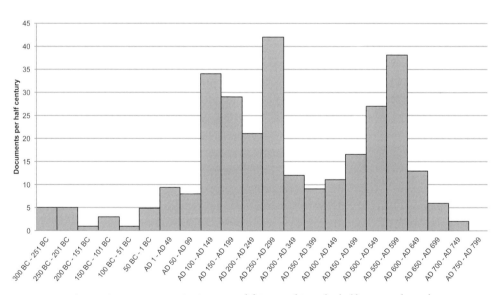

Fig. 7.4 Documents mentioning water-lifting machines, by half-century (n=298)

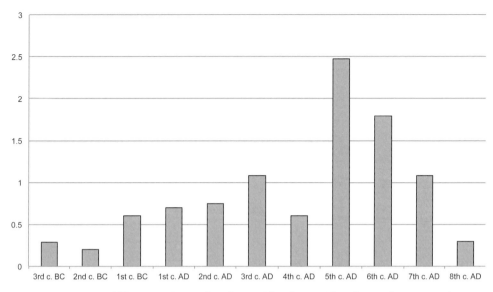

Fig. 7.5 Water-lifting papyri as % of total papyri (total papyri data from Haberman 1998)

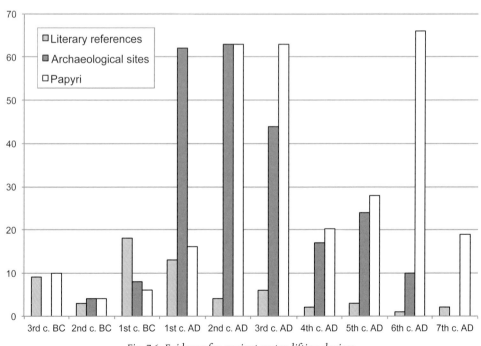

Fig. 7.6 Evidence for ancient water-lifting devices

the *saqiya*, should possibly be interpreted more flexibly, especially in view of the high number of *saqiyas* found in the surviving published papyri. One might of course choose to argue that an eventual increase in prosperity may have led to the greater affordability of more complex machines. While not impossible, this argument would assume sustained economic growth, the indication for which lies in evidence such as the kind under scrutiny here, and would therefore beg the question.

The vast majority of the attested devices come from the Oxyrhynchite Nome, namely 225 of them. Ninety-four come from the Arsinoite Nome, 71 from the Hermopolite, and of the rest, 60 of which are of unknown origin, notable are 6 from Alexandria and 1 from Nessana in Palestine – which represents our only attestation from outside Egypt. The picture is similar if we look for the origin of the papyri that carry the attestations, rather than the attestations themselves: 103 from the Oxyrhynchite Nome, 52 from the Arsinoite, 54 from the Hermopolite, 45 unknown, 2 from Alexandria, and the one from Nessana.

The distribution of papyri that mention water-lifting devices per century and half-century can be seen in figs. 7.3 and 7.4. In comparing these with the graph of the chronological distribution of all papyri, as compiled by Wolfgang Habermann,[10] what becomes immediately apparent is the massive peak that our data exhibit in the 5th and 6th centuries (fig. 7.5). Given the content of the data in question, however, this is not difficult to explain: the vast majority of 6th century texts included in this database belong to the Archive of the Apiones, a wealthy landed family, a lot of which consists of estate accounts. So it is to be expected that it would include many references to water-lifting devices, mainly relating to their maintenance. Besides, the archive comes from Oxyrhynchus, which also goes some way to explaining the preponderance of Oxyrhynchite sources.

The next step is to compare the data and their analysis with the archaeological finds. Fig. 7.6 is a preliminary attempt to integrate the available evidence.

I have already mentioned the limitations in the attempt to set the two datasets side-by-side for comparison. A lot more work is needed therefore to develop control datasets (perhaps isolate archaeological finds of water-lifting devices from Egypt? Or retain the geographical spread, but eliminate water-lifting devices that come from the context of shipping or mining?). A structured, comparative approach to evidence for water-lifting devices is the subject of a paper that Andrew Wilson and I have published in the Oxford Roman Economy Project volume on the agricultural economy of the Roman Empire.[11]

I hope that I have offered an adequate summary of the papyrological evidence for water-lifting devices. It seems from the data presented here that there was widespread use of the *saqiya* already in the 2nd and 3rd centuries AD, not only in late antiquity as is often suggested. Also the 5th and 6th century papyri seem to contain

---

[10] Habermann 1998, 147.
[11] Malouta and Wilson 2013.

proportionately more references to water-lifting than before. The reasons behind this might have to do to some extent with the type of document containing the evidence, the changing visibility threshold of different devices over time, or the aforementioned obscurity of some of the terminology used. What is, however, evident from all sources is that artificial irrigation was a significant component of agriculture in Roman and Byzantine Egypt.

REFERENCES

Bonneau, D. (1971) *Le Fisc et le Nil. Incidences des irrégularités de la crue du Nil sur la fiscalité foncière dans l'Egypte grecque et romaine.* Paris: Cuja.

Bonneau, D. (1993) *Le régime administratif de l'eau du Nil dans l'Egypte grecque, romaine et byzantine.* Leiden: Brill Academic Publishers.

Finley, M. I. (1985²) *The Ancient Economy.* London: Hogarth Press.

Habermann, W. (1998) Zur chronologischen Verteilung der papyrologischen Zeugnisse. *Zeitschrift für Papyrologie und Epigraphik* 122, 144–160.

Malouta, M. and Wilson, A. (2013) Mechanical Irrigation: Water-Lifting Devices in the Archaeological Evidence and the Egyptian Papyri. In A. K. Bowman and A. I. Wilson (eds) *The Agricultural Economy*, 275–307 (Oxford Studies in Roman Economy). Oxford: Oxford University Press.

Oleson, J. P. (1984) *Greek and Roman Mechanical Water-Lifting Devices: the History of a Technology.* Toronto: University of Toronto Press.

Rathbone, D. W. (2007) Mechanai (Waterwheels) in the Roman Fayyum. In M. Capasso and P. Davoli (eds) *New Archaeological and Papyrological Researches on the Fayyum*, 251–262. Galatina, Lecce: Congedo.

Scheidel, W. (2007) Demography. In Scheidel *et al.* (eds), 38–86.

Scheidel, W., Morris, I. and Saller, R. (eds) (2007) *The Cambridge Economic History of the Greco-Roman World.* Cambridge: Cambridge University Press.

Schneider, H. (2007) Technology. In Scheidel *et al.* (eds), 144–171.

8

Plagues and Prices: Locusts

Reinhard Pirngruber

1. INTRODUCTION

Locusts are long since known to have been a much-feared plague in the ancient Near East. Most prominently, they feature as one of the ten biblical plagues in the Book of Exodus (Ex. 10, 3–15) inflicted upon Egypt for the Pharaoh's refusal to release the Israelites from slavery and to let them leave the country. Similarly, cuneiform documents from Mesopotamia tell us about invasions of locust swarms and the damage caused by them: in SAA 10 364 (= ABL 1214), a letter from a diviner to an Assyrian king, we read (r. 11–13): 'If at the appearance of the moon (the star sign of) Scorpius stands by its right horn: [in th]at [year] locusts will rise and consume the harvest', [*ina* mu b]i buru$_5$$^{hi.a}$ zi-*ma* še.buru$_{14}$ gu$_7$. Further examples providing similar scenes of locusts having a detrimental impact on the land and, especially, on crops could be given.[1] They range in time from the Old Babylonian period to the reign of the Seleucids, and from Mari (Tell Hariri) in present-day Syria to the Mesopotamian heartland around Assur in the north and Babylon in the south. They also comprise various literary genres: besides omina and letters, royal inscriptions of Assyrian kings feature prominently, comparing the damage caused by the Assyrian army to the impact of locusts. In TCL 3, an account of the 8th campaign of Sargon II (721–705) against the king of Urarṭu and his allies in 714, the Assyrian king boasts (line 187): *ki-ma e-ri-bi di-ku-ti bu-ul* karaš-*ia i-na ú-šal-li-šú ad-di-ma* ú$^{hi.a}$ *tuk-la-ti-šú is-su-hu-ma ú-šah-ri-bu* a.gàr-šú, 'Like a swarm of locusts, I drove the cattle of my camp in his pastures, the herbs, his mainstay, they tore out and his fields they destroyed.'

In an article on this subject Karen Radner recently revealed the impact of such

---

[1]   See the references in CAD E 257 s.v. *erbu* c.; also Hunger 1972–75.

swarms in Northern Mesopotamia as documented by letters from provincial officials to their superiors or even the king:[2] the first two instances originate from the Habur region, the first from the time of Zimri-lim of Mari (1773–1759 BC, according to the Middle Chronology), the other from the reign of Tukulti-Ninurta I of Assyria (1243–1207 BC), and concern invasions of the Moroccan locust (*Dociostaurus maroccanus*). Interestingly, the first two invasions exhibit a similar pattern: both are, according to Radner, a direct consequence of a recently-fought war owing to which the inhabitants of the region were unable to take any counter-measures to contain the locust population, i.e., to prevent the eggs from hatching by means of burying them or similar. In the third instance the species causing the damage is the Desert locust (*Schistocerca gregaria*), and typically for this species, the geographical range was much wider and the invasion happened suddenly and unpredictably, not in connection to bellicose events.[3] The sources show that the administration took great pains to extinguish the plague by assigning troops to kill the locusts immediately. Unfortunately, the documentation for the aftermath of these locust invasions is too poor to signal any direct economic impact of these events.

In light of what has been discussed so far we would expect such invasions to have had heavy repercussions in the prices of agricultural crops. In the above mentioned article, numerous references are given of farmers abandoning their land and of crops being consumed by the locusts. A promising corpus for analysing such an impact on prices comprises the so-called Astronomical Diaries which contain not only monthly observations of planetary constellations but also narrate historical events;[4] among them we find more than 20 references to locust invasions. Furthermore, this corpus produces meticulous observations of the river level of the Euphrates and also records the prices of six basic commodities, among them barley, date and sesame, in a very exhaustive manner:[5] there are often prices for the beginning, the middle and the end of the month in question, and sometimes even daily movements are recorded.

In this paper, we shall investigate whether the numerous locust invasions that are reported in these Astronomical Diaries (Table 8.1) had an impact on the prices noted in the same corpus, and how this issue may best be addressed. We will first present an overview of earlier literature on the prices given in the Astronomical Diaries, then present the available data on our topic and finally discuss what can be concluded by its analysis. Also methodological aspects will be considered.

The price quotations of the Astronomical Diaries have already been the subject of

---

[2]   Radner 2004. The earlier dossier is also discussed by Ziegler 1999/2000.

[3]   The two species are not distinguished in the texts but were identified by Radner on the grounds of their biological characteristics; especially the geographical pattern of the invasions proved to be revealing. See Radner 2004, 7–11 with relevant literature.

[4]   Published in three volumes ADART I (1988), II (1989) and III (1996); see also the edition of Del Monte 1997 providing a historical commentary.

[5]   It is actually more correct to speak of exchange value rather than price, as for each product the amount (in litres, only in the case of wool in minas) which can be acquired for one shekel of silver is recorded.

various investigations, most notably Slotsky (1997) and Vargyas (2001). The approach of the former was to conduct a regression analysis on the data. Her method has been subjected to heavy criticism,[6] which pointed out the dangers of employing only statistical methods without considering the historical background. Due to Slotsky's superficial treatment of the data, her work yielded also some quite surprising results, most prominently the absence of any seasonal fluctuation in ancient Babylonia. Contrary to her results, seasonal fluctuation can actually be detected in the data and has been demonstrated in various ways.[7] Vargyas (1997; 2001) and van der Spek and Mandemakers (2003), for example, discussed all suitable references, that is, the years for which there are pre- as well as post-harvest prices available. Peter Temin (2002) demonstrated the existence of seasonal fluctuation (at least for barley and dates) by means of a more sophisticated statistical investigation, namely regression analysis employing seasonal dummies. Another weak point was the fact that Slotsky did not make use of all extant price data, but only the end-of-month quotations.

On the other hand, nothing has been published so far regarding the impact of the locust invasions on the prices as given in the Astronomical Diaries. The only reference is found in van der Spek (2006, 296) who stated that these invasions strangely enough had no effect on the prices. Indeed, there are a number of examples which confirm this view, such as the first diary to be discussed in the following section, AD -381, with prices remaining essentially the same before and after the invasion. But then again, there are also a few examples that are in clear contradiction to this phenomenon, most notably AD -346, indicating a sharp rise in the barley price (expressed as a decrease in the amount received for one shekel of silver) at the time of the locust invasion. Due to the relatively few attestations of locust invasions and in the light of what we have said so far about the dangers of overly superficial analysis, we consider it best to first discuss all instances of locust invasions separately, before turning to the question whether and on what basis generalisations can be made.

2. THE DATA: LOCUSTS AND BARLEY PRICES

We shall now look at each Diary containing a report of an invasion of locusts. We will focus on the barley price, for several reasons. Not only is it unquestioned that this cereal was the most important staple food, but we also have more records of its price than of other commodities and we know its exact harvest time, normally month II, *ayyaru* (between the end of April and the end of May),[8] whereas the harvest time for,

---

[6] E.g., in van der Spek and Mandemakers 2003.

[7] On the phenomenon of seasonal fluctuation more generally see, e.g., Abel 1974, 34–7

[8] Already Meissner 1932. See also, e.g., the numerous references in the Murašû archive from Nippur from the last quarter of the 5th century BC in which loans taken on in barley (or wheat) were almost always due in month II, ayyaru.

e.g., *kasû* is uncertain.[9] The question of the harvest time is important because once the crops had been harvested and stored it is unlikely that a locust invasion would have any repercussions on the price of the commodity.[10] Furthermore, barley is also a product for which the seasonal price fluctuation is established with absolute certainty.[11] All these factors, and of course also the general political circumstances,[12] have to be taken into account in this analysis.

As to the species of locusts concerned, it is important to note that the Moroccan locust is not native to Southern Mesopotamia,[13] so it is to be expected that we are dealing with invasions of Desert locusts. The concentration of the locust invasions between months XII and III (see Table 8.1), thus in spring and early summer, is hardly surprising and fits the reproduction cycle and the migration pattern of the Desert locust.[14]

We will of course not be able to tell anything about the impact of locusts if, for example, on a given tablet only the prices for months II and III are extant but the invasion took place in month VI. Thus, if possible, we also must consider the prices of the years preceding and following the diary in question in order to get a clearer idea about possible fluctuations.

Another very important point to be considered is the literary context of these reports of locust invasions. The Astronomical Diaries are generally interpreted as 'a kind of source-book and a scientific foundation of divination' (van der Spek 1993, 94). We hence must also account for the possibility that these invasions were recorded because of their relevance for divinatory purposes rather than because of their value as historical information. However, for various reasons the historicity as well as the potentially serious economic impact of the locust invasions recorded in our corpus seems very plausible. To begin with, the categories given above (ominous or historical interest) are of course not mutually exclusive. It has to be said that the diaries are in general a very reliable source based on personal observation, not only in their astronomical and meteorological sections but also with regards to their historical information.[15] Also, the degree of seriousness of the invasions will have varied from

---

[9] See the discussion in Vargyas 2001, 199. The plant has been identified as cuscuta by Stol 1994.

[10] It is surely not coincidence that all references in letters and royal inscription allude explicitly or implicitly to locusts invasions causing harm to crops (or grasses) standing on the field. I do not know of any example of a harmful impact of locusts on grain in storehouses or similar in the cuneiform documentation.

[11] Temin 2002, 57 concluded that on the basis of the extant prices seasonal fluctuation can not be established with absolute certainty for commodities other than barley and dates.

[12] On the possible impacts of political history – in the form of wars – on prices see van der Spek 2000.

[13] Radner 2004, 1118. Also Lion and Michel 1997, 710 attribute the invasions reported in the cuneiform documents from Mari to the Desert locust.

[14] For a convenient summary of the biological characteristics of these animals we refer again to Radner 2004, 7–11 (with relevant literature). For the migration pattern cf. her Abb. 2.

[15] See already the introduction by the original editors in ADART I, especially pp. 11–13 and 36; also van der Spek 1993 and 2000, 295–7 on the historicity of the price data.

case to case, resulting in the emergence of a picture that looks incoherent at first glance, which is exactly the case in the diaries. Most interesting and illuminating, though, are the occasional specifications given by the scribes of the tablets. In the diary AD -201D, u.e. 1 we read exceptionally ITU BI 23 bur[u₅ʰⁱ.]ᵃ *zi-a mim-ma* nu *ti-qé*, 'That month, day 23: locusts attacked but took nothing'. On the 8th of May 201 BC, and thus at the beginning of the harvest time, the scribe could not help but wonder that a locust swarm spared the crop growing in the fields. Another example one might adduce is AD -132D, r. 30, which states in the section of month XII (roughly March 132 BC): buru₅ʰⁱ.ᵃ sig₇ *i-ṣa zi-a*; 'a few green locusts attacked'. *Arqu* (sig₇) can actually mean both yellow and green,[16] which is interestingly enough exactly the colour combination of the Desert locust during its solitary phase (green body with yellow dots).[17] The additional designation *īṣu* (few) thus suits perfectly the context of this passage and the diary reports not so much an invasion ravaging the crops than an occurrence of a limited (but still notable) number of locusts in Babylonia. Another case in point might be the locust invasion of July 124 BC (reported in AD -123). As we know from Livy, there was also a locust invasion in Africa in the year 125/4 BC,[18] and it might well be that the same invasion is referenced in these very different sources: as can be seen in Radner 2004, Abb. 2, a migration pattern Africa-Mesopotamia is at any rate absolutely possible.[19]

Having made the case for the historicity of the locust invasions recorded in the Astronomical Diaries and having clarified the terminology, we shall proceed to describe the single attestations. In the following tables an overview of the price notations of the same diaries that also report locust invasions will be given. As the material is arbitrarily distributed in time and differs markedly as to the number and the precision of the extant notations, for clarity's sake we assign to each diary a different table combining all information from the different fragments. The respective locust invasions are inserted in bold letters in column one.

As to the terminology of the diaries, the standard unit in which barley is measured is the *qû* which roughly equals one modern litre. Most often, a month is divided into a tripartite scheme of sag (beginning)- murub₄ (middle)- and til (end) of the month. Occasionally, but especially in later times, a binary scheme en murub₄ (until the middle)- en til (until the end) occurs, and sometimes the price is given also for single days or shorter periods of days (e.g., from the 5th to the 7th). For brevity's sake, we will stick to the Akkadian terminology in the tables.[20]

---

[16] CAD A/II 300f. s.v. *arqu*.

[17] As can be seen on the frontispiece of Uvarov 1966. In its gregarious state the locust oscillates between brown, yellow and red.

[18] Livy, Per. 60; Obseq. 30. I owe this reference to Professor D. Rathbone (London).

[19] Radner 2004, 7–9.

[20] We assume that when there are indications for a certain month (without specification of a period) and then specifically for the end (til) of the same month, then the former period covers the entire remainder of this month (i.e., sag and murub₄; see typically the barley entry for month IX of AD -346).

AD -381

For the preceding year, -382, there is a diary extant. Unfortunately it does not give any price information on barley. The best, i.e., temporally closest information we get is from AD -384: in month IX (01.12–31.12.385 BC) the equivalent was 27 litres of barley (increasing to 30 litres at the end of the month). It thus confirms the low barley equivalents of these years (cf. van der Spek 2000, 294, Table 1).

The locust invasion is noted in the section concerning month III. For the same month the equivalent was given as 44 litres of barley per shekel of silver. Three months later, barley was slightly more expensive, the equivalent having dropped to 42 litres per shekel. Considering that the harvest in Mesopotamia takes place at the beginning of the year, this development is hardly surprising and is possibly owed to seasonal fluctuation. It is anyhow unlikely that this invasion had any impact on the barley price: it happened after the harvest, the crop was probably already safe in the storehouses.

Table 8.1 AD -381

Diary	Month		Julian date	Price (in qû)
AD -381B	I		08.04.–27.04. 382 BC	32
	-til		28.04.–06.05. 382 BC	36
Locust invasion	III		05.06.–04.07. 382 BC	44
	VI		01.09.–01.10. 382 BC	42
AD -380	X[1]		18.12. 381–05.01. 380 BC	96
AD -379	XI	(-murub₄)	14.02.–23.02. 379 BC	72
	XI	(-til)	24.02.–05.03. 379 BC	78

[1] As this date indication is still followed by *ina* til we assume, in accordance with what we have said above, that it is valid for the first two-thirds of the month in question.

AD -346

Unfortunately, this highly interesting diary is preceded by a gap of 20 years for which we have no diary. The next barley quotation is found only after 13 years (AD -332), giving slightly higher equivalents than AD -346 (oscillating around 144 litres per shekel).

The fact that the equivalents rose already during winter and thus before harvest time may seem a little bit odd at first glance, but this price movement has been explained by P. Vargyas with a shift in demand from barley to dates – the second most important foodstuff – in the period following the date harvest and the low price for dates connected to it.[21] In the last days of month XII, the equivalent drops dramatically by almost 50% from 120 to only 69 litres of barley per shekel of silver. In the very same period, a locust invasion is reported. It is likely in this instance that the crop was

---

[21]   Vargyas 1997, 339f.

severely damaged by the locusts, causing this price explosion. Although in general the prices fluctuated widely, fluctuations of this magnitude within so short a period of time hardly ever occur in the Diaries.

Additionally, we do not know of any major internal strife in Babylonia at this time that could have caused such a breakdown in the price: the revolt of the Sidonians under their king Tennes, which ultimately was ended in 345 by treason (and which afterwards entailed the deportation of a group of Sidonians to Babylon) went on already for quite some time, possibly at least since 347.[22] More generally, it is hardly conceivable that a local revolt in a faraway region had such a profound repercussion on the prices in Babylon.[23]

There are two additional interesting notes in line r. 33 in the same diary: itu bi [il] lu tar-is, 'This month (month XII), the flood did not occur.' This notice records a delay in the annual spring flood, but it is unlikely that this event caused the radical price increase. Firstly, as emerges from Brown (2002, 42, graph 1) showing the mean river level between the years -293 and -73, the height of the flood is expected only towards the end of April/beginning of May and thus about four weeks after the period referred to in this entry. Secondly, it is important to note that the crop in the last two to four weeks before the harvest does not need to be irrigated.[24] The delay or even absence of the spring flood has no immediate impact on the prices. Rather we would expect such an effect on prices to be caused by an exuberant spring flood which could damage the harvest by inundating the fields.[25]

The second notice reads: mu bi [bur]u$_{14}$ še-im sa-ma-nu tag, 'This year the barley harvest was affected by the samānu-disease.' This disease, an 'ergot-like blight, causing spots on the grain and having a poisonous effect on those who eat the grain' according to the CAD S 112, had certainly a detrimental impact on the harvest in terms of quality and quantity and might very well have influenced the prices. But the formulation (mu bi) of this passage is rather ambiguous and should very likely be interpreted differently, namely as referring to the harvest reaped in this (i.e., the preceding) year, possibly in month II of year -346. As there are no prices extant for the first half and more of this year, nor from prior and successive years, we have no possibility to explore the matter in depth. A parallel from another diary (AD -122), to be discussed below, can help to put the impact of this disease into perspective: in this instance the reference to samānu is made (again with the formulation mu bi, 'this year') in the astronomical section of month I and thus (as in our instance) slightly before the beginning of harvest time. The prices, as can be seen in the table under AD -123, did in fact drop in the same

---

[22] For this episode and its uncertain chronology see Briant 1996, 701–4 and the chronicle ABC 9 for the deportation.

[23] Van der Spek 2000, 307f. has argued that warfare abroad can even lead to falling prices.

[24] A dry period at this time is even considered advantageous for the ripening process; cf. Charles 1988, especially pp. 3–4 and 13.

[25] Only in the long run a low peak flood could have a detrimental impact on the economy as it was likely to cause a lasting low river level – a phenomenon which often brought with it higher prices according to Brown 2002, 46.

month, though not to the extent that they arrived at the very low equivalents of the preceding year, and certainly not by almost 50% within a few days. As is also clear from a broken price indication in month II referring to new barley, the reason for this increase in prices can also be attributed to seasonal fluctuation: in fact, the prices decreased again in month III.

In sum, this diary puts forward a very likely case for an exogenous price shock in the form of a locust invasion: it took place while the crop was still standing, the barley equivalent almost halves abruptly and there are no other convincing explanations. It cannot be excluded that the crop was affected by a parasite which aggravated this

Table 8.2 AD -346

Diary	Month		Julian date	Price (in qû)
AD -346	IX		03.12.- 22.12. 347 BC	102
	-til		23.12.- 01.01. 346 BC	108+
	X		02.01.- 21.01. 346 BC	114
	-til		22.01.- 30.01. 346 BC	120
	XI	-til	20.02.- 01.03. 346 BC	117
	XII	-sag	02.03.- 11.03. 346 BC	120
	-til		22.03.- 30.03. 346 BC	69
Locust invasion	-days 27-29		28.- 30.03 346 BC	

Table 8.3 AD -308

Diary	Month		Julian date	Price (in qû)
AD -308	I	(-sag)	10.04.- 19.04 309 BC	7.5
(-gibil)	-til		30.04.- 09.05. 309 BC	13.5
	V	(-til?)	26.08.- 03.09. 309 BC	9
Locust invasion: 19.09.	VI	(-murub₄?)	14.09.- 23.09. 309 BC	9
	(-til)		24.09.- 03.10. 309 BC	14
AD -307A	V	(1.-18.)	26.07.- 12.08. 308 BC	14.5
	19.-28.		13.- 22.08. 308 BC	13(+)

situation. It is striking that the invasion lasted for three days only but nevertheless caused such an economic breakdown.

AD -308

Note that for the year preceding (310/9) as well as for the year in question (309/8) in this diary the so-called 'Chronicle of the Diadochoi' (ABC 10 = BCHP 3, lines r. 29 and r. 33) gives an equivalent of 6 litres per shekel, which fits nicely with the very low equivalents in AD -308.

The very low equivalents of this period were caused by the constant wars fought by the Successors in the region. The period under discussion corresponds to the last phase in the battle for Babylon (fought in Babylon and its surroundings) between the ultimately victorious Seleucus and Antigonus the One-eyed.[26] The aforementioned locust invasion, owing to its post-harvest date, left no traces in the documentation of the prices. The month of September is also too early for sowing, so there were no fields of barley to be damaged.

AD -284

This diary's locust invasion (month XII) occurred after the period for which there are barley prices extant (only for month XI). For the following year, there is a diary extant (AD -283), but also without any information on the barley price. As the invasion took place with the barley crop still growing in the fields this loss of information is all the more regrettable.

AD -256

The price equivalents in the years 257 and 256 BC are quite low. AD -253 has been included to show that two years later the equivalent was again much higher,[27] as was the case in the preceding diary AD -259, which gives 90 litres in month X (30.12.260– 28.01.259 BC). AD -261 even gives 168 litres in month VII (25.09–23.10.262 BC).

This is a highly interesting case: the invasion took place shortly before or at the beginning of the harvest and according to the fragmentary diary lasted for one day only. The equivalent one month later, thus in the immediate post-harvest season with low prices to be expected, was at only 36 litres of barley for one shekel of silver. The prices were almost as high as during the period of the Successors which saw constant warfare in Babylonia.[28] There was also a war waged in the period in question, but one with quite different characteristics: the 2nd Syrian War (260–253 BC) was fought almost exclusively in the coastal regions of Asia Minor. Also, this war was a successful one for the Seleucids, resulting in a (temporary) re-conquest of larger portions of Asia Minor (including, among others, the city of Ephesos).[29] It is more than doubtful whether this war was capable of driving up the prices in Babylonia to such a great extent. Also, neither at the beginning (AD -259) nor towards the end of the war (AD -253) were prices approximately as high as in the period in question (257/6 BC).

The fact that the prices remained high for two years is hardly surprising given that

---

[26]   On the impact of these wars on prices see van der Spek 2000, 299–305. For the political history of Babylon in the period of the Successors cf. Boiy 2004, 117–37 (with a revised chronology in Boiy 2007).

[27]   In AD -251 month VII (04.10–02.11.252 BC) the equivalent rose to even 240 litres of barley per shekel of silver.

[28]   Grainger 1999, 323 in his graph on barley gives 23.5 *qû* as average for the period from 325 to 301 BC; van der Spek 2000, 294, table 1 gives a range between 6 and 51 *qû* for the period between 329 and 300 BC. For the political circumstance of that period, cf. the literature in footnote 26.

[29]   Will 1979[2], 234–43. For the parameters involved concerning wars abroad see van der Spek 2000.

Table 8.4 AD -256

Diary	Month		Julian date	Price (in qû)
AD -259	X		30.12. 260- 28.01. 259 BC	90
Locust invasion	02. II		05.05. 257 BC	
AD -256	III		03.06.- 02.07. 257 BC	36
	XI		25.01.- 23.02. 256 BC	24
AD -255	I		26.03.- 23.04. 256 BC	24
	II	(-til)	14.- 23.05. 256 BC	42
	VI		20.08.- 17.09. 256 BC	42
	VI$_2$		18.09.- 17.10. 256 BC	42
AD -253	VII		27.09.- 25.10. 254 BC	120
	IX		22.03.- 19.04 254 BC	108

Table 8.5 AD -237

Diary	Month	Julian date	Price (in qû)
AD -237	III	04.06.- 23.06. 238 BC	120
Locust invasion			
	(-til)	24.06.- 03.07. 238 BC	135

a failure of crops caused not only a scarcity of foodstuffs but also a shortage of seed-corn for the following season: this price sequence can perhaps be explained by the phenomenon that is commonly known as autocorrelation.[30]

AD -237

The only indication of barley in this diary dates from the same month in which the locust invasion took place; nevertheless, the price equivalent rose. Anyway, we assume that in month III (June, in this instance) the harvest had already taken place, consequently there was no crop damage. There is a gap of three years between both the preceding (AD -240) and the following diary (AD -234), impeding further analysis.[31]

AD -226A and AD -225

This is the only extant case of locusts invading in two subsequent years. Thus, the price indications for barley are presented in one single table here.

The next indication of barley is about 4 years later, in AD -222 month X (11.01–

---

[30] In the words of Karl G. Persson 1999, 55: 'when a harvest failed stocks were depleted, which would keep prices up next year because of smaller supply and greater demand if granaries were restocked.' His context is early modern Europe, but according to him (p. 61) 'high autocorrelation is a property of almost all types of price series'.

[31] It is interesting to note that this diary is the only one containing low prices in the period between 241 and 233 BC. For a discussion of the political circumstances in Babylonia of this period see van der Spek 2006.

Table 8.6 AD -226A and AD -225

Diary	Month		Julian date	Price (in qû)
AD -226A	II		03.05.- 22.05. 227 BC	102
	(-til)		23.05.- 01.06. 227 BC	108
Locust invasion	03. III		03.07. 227 BC	
AD -225	III	(-sag)	21.06.- 10.07. 226 BC	120
Locust invasion	09.-26. III		29.06.-16.07. 226 BC	
	-til		11.07.- 19.07. 226 BC	132
	IV		20.07.- 18.08. 226 BC	135

Table 8.7 AD -178

Diary	Month		Julian date	Price (in qû)
AD -179	IV		21.06.- 20.07. 180 BC	108
	V	(-til)	10.- 18.08. 180 BC	102
	XI		13.02.- 14.03. 179 BC	96
AD -178C	XII	(-sag)	04.03.- 13.03. 178 BC	81
	(-en til)		24.03.-02.04. 178 BC	78
Locust invasion	30.? XII		02.?04. 178 BC	
AD -177	X	(-sag)	24.12. 178- 02.01. 177 BC	64

09.02.222 BC), with somewhat lower equivalents (72 and, at the end of the month, 84 litres per shekel).

As was the case in the previously discussed diary, the invasions took place in both years after the harvest, during July only. Consequently, we do not expect any impact on the price of barley, an impression which is confirmed by looking at the prices.

AD -178

As this locust invasion took place at the beginning of April, and thus before harvest time, we might expect to find repercussions. Unfortunately, we hardly have any prices following this event in our documentation. It should be noted that in the following year we do have higher prices: at the end of December 178 BC the equivalent stood at 64 litres of barley per shekel of silver, whereas in March of the same year (therefore closer to the harvest, when a lower equivalent is expected) it was between 81 and 78 litres. The difference in the equivalent between the two years thus amounts to almost 20%. The development in these years might have been similar to the one described in the discussion of AD -256.

AD -164

The price pattern of this diary is dazzling: although there was a locust invasion during harvest time in 165 BC, the prices in the following months are among the lowest found throughout the period covered by the Astronomical Diaries: in October 165 BC, 378.5 litres of barley were received for one shekel of silver.[32] Shortly before the next harvest, by the end of March 164, barley was then suddenly no longer available. Interestingly enough, the year afterwards, 164/3 BC, sees then fairly high prices for the Seleucid period. For this period, van der Spek (2000, 294 table 1) gives an average range of between 90 to 225 litres of barley per shekel.[33]

A possible explanation of these notations can be found when considering the political circumstances: AD -163 (C$_2$ r17) reports the arrival of the corpse of the king. It is now known that Antiochus IV, after he had been forced to retreat from Egypt by the Roman delegates under C. Popillius Laenas (at the famous day of Eleusis 168 BC), turned his interest to the Upper satrapies in the East and tried to launch an *anabasis* into these regions similar to his father and predecessor Antiochus III. Inaugurated by the grand *pompē* of Daphne in 166, the campaign was never to happen as Antiochus IV died on the way (in Persis) of illness.[34]

The prices in the diaries now show an interesting analogy with what can be said about the price data from the time of the war of Antiochus III against Rome: the high equivalents (in 165/4) might be interpreted as reflecting a lack of silver, which was needed and requisitioned to cover the expenses of the war and the preparations for it. It is very likely that the influential factor causing the sudden disappearance of barley from the market in March 164 BC was the army on its way eastwards passing through Babylon at that time, depleting completely the already thinning granaries – we are shortly before a new harvest. Normally (e.g., AD -324B, 12–3) barley is only cut off (from the market) during years with an already low equivalent.[35] It is also conceivable that in 164/3 the army was still supplied with Babylonian grain, resulting in the low equivalents owed to the high demand.

One might also think of alternative explanations for this sharp price increase in 164/3. Of course, one could simply say that a bad harvest had taken place in 164. Any impact resulting from the locust invasion is very improbable in this instance. The unusually high equivalents for barley following the invasion, even if mainly explicable by lack of silver, also presuppose a certain availability of barley. It is thus unclear if, and to what extent, this price pattern is explained by, or even reconcilable with the locust invasion. If the invasion happened at the end of the month, it is possible that the harvest was already brought in and safe in the granaries, and the invasion had little or no repercussion at all on the prices. Thus, in the present case, emphasis in the attempt to explain the price pattern must be given to the political circumstances during these years.

---

[32]   The all-time low in the Astronomical Diaries dates from October 188 BC, which records 390 litres of barley per shekel of silver.

[33]   Similarly, Grainger 1999 gives an average of 138.9 litres for the period between 200 and 176 BC and for the years 175–151 BC 137.6 litres.

[34]   Will 1982², 344–8; Mittag 2006, 282–327.

[35]   See already van der Spek and Mandemakers 2003, 529.

Table 8.8 AD -164

Diary	Month			Julian date	Price (in qû)
AD -165	V			16.08.–13.09. 166 BC	372
AD -164 Locus invasion	II			07.05.–05.06. 165 BC	
	VII	(-sag)		02.10.–11.10. 165 BC	180+[1]
	(-til)			22.10.–31.10. 165 BC	378.5
	XII	(25, 26)		22.+23. 03. 164 BC	TAR-*as*
AD -163	II	(-sag)		26.04.–05.05. 164 BC	96
	VIII	(-murub₄)		31.10–09.11. 164 BC	69
	(-til)			10.–19.11 164 BC	72
	XII	(-murub₄)		26.02.–07.03. 163 BC	78
	(-til)			08.–16.03 163 BC	93

[1] Maximum possible: 359 litres of barley per shekel.

Table 8.9 AD -140

Diary	Month		Julian date	Price (in qû)
AD -142A	VIII		28.10- 26.11. 143 BC	114
AD -141	II	(-en murub₄)	24.04.- 08.05. 142 BC	150
	(-en til)		09.05.- 23.05. 142 BC	180
Locust invasion	III (between 04 and 06. III)		between 27. and 29.05. 142 BC	
AD -140	I	(-sag)	13.- 22.04. 141 BC	150
	(-murub₄)		23.04.- 02.05. 141 BC	156
	(-til)		03.- 11.05. 141 BC	132
	IV	(-sag)	10.- 19.07. 141 BC	168
	VII	(-sag)	06.- 15.10. 141 BC	102
	(-en murub₄)		16.- 20?.10 141 BC	108
	IX	(-en murub₄)	04.- 18.12. 141 BC	117
	(-en til)		19.12. 141- 02.01. 140 BC	120

AD -141

AD -140 also provides indications of barley for months X and XI; they do not differ much from the indications of month IX (the equivalent is higher by some litres). As they are not useful for the purpose of this investigation, they are not reproduced here.

Unfortunately, in this instance there is quite a gap in the documentation: the prices for the period after the locust invasion date from one year (and more) later. As the invasion took place at the end of May, thus only at the end of the main harvest period, repercussions are at any rate unlikely and in fact, as far as we can judge from the defective sources, non-existent.

AD -136

The preceding diary AD -137 yields a most extensive price section. It is not necessary

Table 8.10 AD -136

Diary	Month		Julian date	Price (in qû)
AD -136	X	(til)	09.01.- 18.01. 136 BC	57
	XI	(-en murub₄)	19.01.- 01.02. 136 BC	54
		(-en til)	02.02.- 16.02. 136 BC	52.5
Locust invasion	XII_B	(day 11)	29.03. 136 BC	
AD -134	VI	(-en murub₄)?	01.- 15.09. 135 BC	99
		(-en til)	16.- 30.09 135 BC	90+
	VII		1.- 20?.10. 135 BC	96
		(-til)	21.- 30.10 135 BC	99

Table 8.11 AD -132

Diary	Month		Julian date	Price (in qû)
AD -133	XI	(x-26)	x-11.02. 133 BC	120
	27		12.02. 133 BC	117
	28		13.02. 133 BC	114
	29		14.02. 133 BC	108
	XI	(1,2)	15.+16. 02. 133 BC	102
	-(3,4)		17.+18. 02. 133 BC	99
	-(5-7)		19.-21. 02. 133 BC	108
AD -132	VI	(-sag)	08.09.- 17.09. 133 BC	132
		(-en til)	18.09.-07.10. 133 BC	129
	VII		08.10.- 27.10. 133 BC	123
		(-en til)	28.10.- 06.11. 133 BC	108+
	VIII	(-sag)	07.11.- 16.11. 133 BC	126
		(-en 20)	16.11.- 26.11. 133 BC	120
		(20? en til)	27.11.- 05.12. 133 BC	105
Locust invasion	XII		05.03.- 14.03. 132 BC	105
		(-murub₄)	15.03.- 24.03 132 BC	114
		(-til)	25.03.- 03.04. 132 BC	114+
AD -130	XII	(-sag)	13.-22.03 130 BC	96

for our purpose to reproduce it fully here. Generally, the equivalents in the second half of this year (roughly November 138 to March 137) correspond to those of AD -136: between 50 and 60 litres of barley are given for one shekel of silver, with a tendency of decreasing equivalents towards the new harvest. The first half of the same year (May to August 138) has somewhat higher equivalents of about 75–85 litres per shekel and thus makes a good case for seasonal fluctuation. Again, we only have very fragmentary data. The locust invasion, though in March with possibly damaging impact, left no traces in the following diary, which is, however, from only about one and a half years later. There is another complicating factor though: the prices of AD -136 are fairly high for this period. Between 144 and 129 BC, the equivalent was usually above 100 litres of barley per shekel, with a depression between 138 and 136, which are known to have been very troublesome years. It was the period of the abortive

Table 8.12 AD -129

Diary	Month		Julian date	Price (in qû)
AD -130	XII	(-sag)	13.-22.03. 130 BC	96
AD -129	I	(-sag)	11.04.- 20.04. 130 BC	108+
(28.-30.)	II		11.05.- 09.06. 130 BC	114
Locust invasion	II	(28.- 30. II)	07.-09.06 130 BC	
(not good barley!)			11.05.- 09.06. 130 BC	120
	IV	(-sag)	10.07.- 19.07. 130 BC	132+
	VI		07.09.- 05.10. 130 BC	120

attempt of Demetrius II to re-conquer Babylonia for the Seleucids (reported in AD -137A, cf. Del Monte 1997, 111–12), of Elamite raids and the emergence of the kingdom of Mesene under Hyspaosines. These events obviously outweighed any possible impact of the locust invasion. This increase in the equivalents from -134 onwards can thus be tentatively explained by a calming of the political situation. In ADs -133 and -132, the barley equivalent moves between 100 and 130 litres per shekel of silver.

AD -132

Also in this instance the data are not very enlightening; the prices do not seem to be influenced by the locust invasion in March. Maybe it was a year with an early harvest, which is possibly reflected in the rising equivalents already in month XII, thus escaping from crop damage due to the locust invasion. It would be all too daring to attribute the slightly lower equivalent of two years later to this locust invasion.

AD -129

As the invasion took place at the end of the harvest only, the beginning of June 130 BC, we do not expect any repercussions. The price pattern confirms this assumption. The next extant barley indication dates from AD -125 (29.03.126 BC–15.04.125 BC). The equivalent is much lower, ranging between only 20 and 30 litres of barley per shekel throughout the whole year (indications for months I, VI and XII). The cause is probably to be seen once again in the political circumstances. The diary reports of continuous raids of Arabs and other internal problems in Babylonia. The satrap of Babylonia was ensnared in skirmishes in the south of the country and was later arrested at the command of the king.[36]

AD -123

AD -122 speaks of the samānu-disease having affected the barley harvest of this year, although the equivalents in the same year are higher than in the preceding year (see

---

[36] See Del Monte 1997, 136–43 for the pertinent texts.

Table 8.13 AD -123

Diary	Month		Julian date	Price (in qû)
AD -123	II	(-sag)	05.05.- 14.05. 124 BC	9
	(-5-10)		09.05.- 14.05. 124 BC	9.5
	III	(-en murub$_4$?)	03.06.- 22.06. 124 BC	30
	(-en til)		23.06.- 01.07. 124 BC	27.5
Locust invasion	a day between 20. and 23. IV		a day between 21. and 23.07. 124 BC	
	V	(-1-5)	01.08.- 05.08. 124 BC	31.5
Locust invasion	17. or 18. V		18. or 19.08. 124 BC	
AD -122	I	(-13-19)	07.-13.04 123 BC	72
	(-20, 21)		14.+15. 04 123 BC	63
	II	(-sag)	24.04- 03.05. 123 BC	57
	(-en til)		04.-23.05. 123 BC	51
	III	(-til)?	13.-21.06. 123 BC	90
	VI$_2$	(-til)?	08.-16.10. 123 BC	45

the discussion of AD -346 above). Both invasions mentioned are insignificant for our purpose as they happened in July and August respectively, when there was no barley growing in the fields. Thus they are unlikely to have influenced the barley price, as is also clear from the falling prices in the following year.

AD -108

Here is a possible case for the detrimental economic impact of a locust invasion, which according to the diary lasted throughout the whole of month II. It could at least explain the curious fact that barley was more expensive in month II than it was in month I. Even if we consider the possibility that the harvest had already started in this month (which is quite conceivable in this case as it corresponded to the month of April), we do not expect prices to rise immediately after harvest time.[37] It is important to note that also the following year 108/7 BC had lower equivalents – and substantially so. This rise in prices can again be interpreted as being caused by autocorrelation.

Little is known of the political history of these years, let alone its exact chronology. The reign of Mithradates II is generally assessed as quite a prosperous one in modern historiography (as it was already in antiquity, hence the epithet "the Great") after a period of weak Parthian kings, resulting in a re-conquest of formerly lost parts of the empire. His sovereignty over, and recognition as king of, Babylonia at least since 120 BC is undisputed.[38] This relative stability may also be reflected in the high equivalents of the years 112 to 109 BC, ranging roughly between 100 and 200 litres of barley per

---

[37] See also Vargyas 2001, 108f., giving quite an exact seasonal pattern: in normal years, the equivalent is highest in June, when all the harvest is put into market circulation and remains more or less stable during the period of summer before dropping again.

[38] Assar 2006, 134–49 and especially 136f.; Will 1979–82 Vol. II, 452–5.

Table 8.14 AD -108

Diary	Month		Julian date	Price (in qû)
AD -109	VIII		25.10.- 22.11 110 BC	80
AD -108	I	(1, 2)	18.+ 19.04. 109 BC	120
Locust invasion	II	(-sag)	18.05.- 27.05. 109 BC	72+[1]
	IV	(-en til)	05[?].08.- 14.08. 109 BC	102
	VI		13.09.- 12.10. 109 BC	72+
AD -107	IV	(-1-11)	05.-15.07. 108 BC	72
	(-12-14)		16.-18.07 108 BC	54+
	VII	(-x-16)	x-17.10. 108 BC	54
	(-en 17)		-18.10. 108 BC	51
	IX	(-29, 30)	28.+29. 12. 108 BC	27
	XI	(-x-12)	x-09.02. 107 BC	30
-not good barley	(-x-12)		x-09.02. 107 BC	31.5
	(-13, 14)		10.+11.02. 107 BC	33
	(15, 16)		12.+13.02. 107 BC	36
	(17-til)		14.-26.02 107 BC	40
	XII	(-en 18)	27.02.-16.03. 107 BC	40

[1] Maximum: 107 litres.

shekel of silver.[39] AD -107D, r. 39 mentions a son of Demetrius, interpreted by Del Monte (1997, 157) as a reference to Antiochus VIII Grypos. This Seleucid king had to cope during most of his reign with a dynastic struggle against his cousin Antiochus IX Cyzicenus.[40] Even if it is Antiochus VIII who is actually referred to in the Diary, it is most unlikely that he ever came even close to Babylonia, and there is nothing in the sources that suggests an eastern campaign. We thus assume that in this case the diary reports an event of this struggle between the cousins in Syria. The price pattern of the years 109 and 108 BC could thus reasonably well be explained by the aforementioned locust invasion.

AD -121 and AD -62: No barley prices extant.

3. SUMMARY AND IMPLICATIONS

The condition of the sources has proven to be somewhat disappointing for our analysis. As a matter of fact, the overwhelming majority of cases are inconclusive owing to various factors: often (e.g., ADs -381, -226, -225 -141, -123) the invasion took place after the harvest and consequently there was no crop on the field to suffer damage. The

[39] Grainger 1999 gives 68.4 litres per shekel as average price for the years 125–101 BC. Unfortunately there is a gap in the price documentation for barley from 119 BC until 112 BC.
[40] Cf. Wilcken 1894.

prices in these references show at any rate no increase in prices in the period after the invasion that could not be explained by other factors such as seasonal fluctuation. In two instances (AD -121 and AD -62) we have indications of a locust invasion but no prices are extant in these diaries. In AD -132, there are no price notations extant for the months after the invasion. AD -136 shows that the hypothetical impact of locusts could be largely outweighed by situations of political crisis such as enduring warfare, and the same holds true for AD -164, which is particularly difficult to interpret. Cases that can be interpreted as showing a positive correlation between locust invasions and price increases are few. The most convincing source is certainly AD -346 which shows the barley equivalent halving within a few days. Also for ADs -256, -178 and -108 the price movements, though less impressive, can reasonably well be explained by the impact of a locust invasion before or during harvest time. It is interesting to see, though, that these are exactly the cases that fulfil our postulated main criterion of a locust invasion during harvest time. The only two diaries that do not show the expected price pattern have been shown as pertaining to periods of internal war (AD -136) or campaigns involving at least an army passing through Babylonia (AD -164) and thus present additional difficulties of interpretation.

For the commodities other than barley, the situation of the data is even worse. Table 8.15 gives the equivalent for sesame in the years of locust invasions. Sesame was in Mesopotamia a summer crop and thus was planted after the barley harvest in late spring/summer and harvested after a ripening period of three months in September or October.[41] There is not a single case of a price fluctuation that might be attributed to the impact of locusts, largely owing to the paucity of references. For these commodities we would also have to account for the difficult nature of their price data: for products other than barley, not even seasonal fluctuation can be established with absolute (statistical) certainty.[42] Also, as barley is the most important of all the crops for which we have price notations, it is not surprising that it is prone to heavier fluctuations than the other commodities[43] – and is thus more likely to respond, at least for us in a more comprehensible way, to exogenous shocks.

With so few attestations, a generalisation of the impact of locust invasions by statistical analysis is hardly manageable. As can be seen by the very critical reactions to Slotsky (1997),[44] whose all too superficial analyses even smoothed away seasonal fluctuation, it is important to establish clear parameters before assigning oneself to such a task. We have seen in the discussion of the attestations that the case for locust invasions damaging a crop and thereby raising prices can neither be argued in a fully satisfactory manner nor can it be completely discarded. By taking into account the

---

[41] See Slotsky 1997, 36–9, with previous literature on the subject. Locust swarms attacking specifically sesame fields are not directly attested in Mesopotamian sources, but do occur in nature, cf. http://www.fao.org/docrep/007/j3968e/j3968e00.htm (accessed August 2010). I would like to thank Dr. Dorothea Bedigian for this and other references.

[42] Temin 2002, 57.

[43] As has been contemplated already by Grainger 1999, 313.

[44] Van der Spek and Mandemakers 2003; see also the various references in Vargyas 2001.

dates of the invasions, such a pattern seems at least possible. On the other hand, this procedure of taking into account only quotations of (roughly) the same months reduces even further our already scanty data:[45] even by pooling the data for months II and III in order to establish a post-harvest price for barley, we have only 16 years with prices attested in the whole second century BC,[46] and with substantial gaps: for the period between 180 and 140 BC, there are only two years with data on the barley price in the weeks following the harvest. The frequent economic disturbances caused by periods of war and internal strife, especially from the middle of the 1st century BC onwards (but there are also quite some examples from the Seleucid period), and the resulting fluctuations further exacerbate our situation.

As a preliminary conclusion one is tempted to say that we actually have available too few data, and that we are impeded by too many lacunae to apply reliable statistical methods, e.g., a simple moving average of monthly prices, to this subject. Before proceeding with such methods, one has to assess what can actually be deduced from our data, and how can it best be obtained. Desirable as a statistical analysis may be, it is of utmost importance to take into consideration all factors that might have left an imprint on the prices – and there are many, and a wide variety: damage caused by warfare and silver requisitions to pay an army,[47] the impact of autocorrelation, climate changes,[48] devaluation of the money[49] – as well as locust invasions. Otherwise we will inevitably run the risk of barking up the wrong tree.

Table 8.15 Locust invasions in the Astronomical Diaries

AD -381:

Diary	Month	Julian date	Price (in qû)
AD -382	II	17.05.- 15.06. 383 BC	7.5
Locust invasion	III	05.06.-04.07. 382 BC	
AD -381	V	03.08.- 01.09. 382 BC	15

This table provides an overview of all attestations of locust invasions in the Astronomical Diaries with their respective dates. The dates of the invasions have been changed from the Mesopotamian to the Julian calendar on the basis of Parker/Dubberstein[2] 1946, with minor corrections found in the ADART-volumes and on the website http://www.tyndale.cam.ac.uk/Egypt/ptolemies/chron/babylonian/chron_bab_intro.htm.

---

[45] Also Vargyas 1997, 342.

[46] But if extant, then the prices are recorded meticulously and mostly 3 times (beginning, middle and end) per month.

[47] Van der Spek 2000.

[48] Brown 2002. See also Abel 1974, especially pp. 267–272.

[49] Heichelheim 1930, 9–37 on the Ptolemaic empire.

AD -284:

Diary	Month		Julian date	Price (in qû)
AD -284	VII	(-sag)	09.10.-18.10. 285 BC	24
Locust invasion	06. XII		11.03. 284 BC	
AD -283	VII		28.09.-27.10. 284 BC	24

AD -237:

Diary	Month	Julian date	Price (in qû)
AD -237	III	04.06.- 03.07. 238 BC	8
Locust invasion	IV	04.06.-03.07. 238 BC	
	V	02.08.- 30.08. 238 BC	9

AD -226 and -225:

Diary	Month		Julian date	Price (in qû)
AD -226	III	(-sag)	02.06.- 11.06. 227 BC	30
Locust invasion	3. III		03.07. 227 BC	
	(-til)		22.06.- 30.06. 227 BC	24
AD -225	III		21.06.- 19.07. 226 BC	24
Locust invasion	09.-26. III		29.06.-16.07. 226 BC	
	IV		20.07.- 18.08. 226 BC	24

AD -178:

Diary	Month		Julian date	Price (in qû)
AD -178	XII		04.03.- 02.04. 178 BC	18
Locust invasion	30.? XII		02.? 04. 178 BC	
AD -177	X	(-sag)	24.12. 178- 02.01. 177 BC	30

AD -164:

Diary	Month		Julian date	Price (in qû)
Locust invasion	II		07.05.- 05.06. 165 BC	
AD -164	VII		02.10.- 21.10. 165 BC	39
	(-til)		22.10.- 31.10. 165 BC	42
	XII		26.02.- 27.03. 164 BC	42
AD -163	II	(-sag)	26.04.- 05.05. 164 BC	39
	(-en til)		06.-25.05. 164 BC	30+
	XI	(-en murub$_4$)	17.-31.01. 165 BC	42+

AD -136:

Diary	Month		Julian date	Price (in qû)
AD -137	III		08.06.- 07.07. 138 BC	12.5
	IV	(-sag)	08.-17.07. 138 BC	12
	(-murub$_4$)		18.-27.07. 138 BC	10
	IX		03.-22.12. 138 BC	9
	(-til)		23.-31.12. 138 BC	8
	X		01.-29.01. 137 BC	9
AD -136	VIII		23.10.- 20.11. 137 BC	15
	XII$_2$		18.03.- 16.04. 136 BC	10
Locust invasion	XII$_B$	(day 11)	29. 03. 136 BC	
AD -134	VII		01.-30.10. 135 BC	15
	XII		26.02.- 26.03. 134 BC	16

AD -123:

Diary	Month		Julian date	Price (in qû)
AD -133	XI	(-murub₄)	27.01.- 05.02. 133 BC	24
	(-en til)		06.-14.02 133 BC	22.5
AD -132	VI		08.09.- 07.10. 133 BC	21.5
	VII		08.10- 06.11. 133 BC	8?
	VIII	(-murub₄)	17.11.- 26.11. 133 BC	20
	(-en til)		27.11.- 05.12. 133 BC	21
	XI		03.02.- 04.03. 132 BC	20
Locust invasion	XII		05.03.- 03.04. 132 BC	21

AD -129:

Diary	Month		Julian date	Price (in qû)
AD -129	I	(-murub₄)	21.04.-30.04. 130 BC	24
	(- en til)		01.05.- 10.05. 130 BC	25
	II		11.05.- 09.06. 130 BC	24
Locust invasion	28.-30. II		07.- 09.06. 130 BC	
	IV	(x-26)?	x.07/08.- 04.08. 130 BC	21
	(-27-29)		05.08.- 07.08. 130 BC	18
	V	(-sag)	08.08.- 17.08. 130 BC	18
	(-murub₄)		18.08.- 27.08. 130 BC	16.25

AD -123:

Diary	Month		Julian date	Price (in qû)
AD -124	V	(-en murub₄)	11.-25.08. 125 BC	5
	IX	(-sag)	08.-17.12. 125 BC	9.5
	(-en til)		18.12. 125- 05.01. 124 BC	10
	X	(-en murub₄)	06.-20?.01. 124 BC	9
	(-en til)		x-04.04. 124 BC	8
AD -123	III		03.06.- 22.06. 124 BC	10
	(-til)		23.06.- 01.07. 124 BC	10.5
	IV (-en murub₄)		02.07.- 21.07. 124 BC	10.5
Locust invasion	a day between 20. and 23. IV		a day between 21. and 23.07. 124 BC	
	(-en til)		22.07.- 31.07. 124 BC	11.25
	V	(-en murub₄)	01.08.- 15?.08. 124 BC	11.25
Locust invasion	17. or 18. V		18. or 19.08. 124 BC	
AD -122	I	(-en til)	10.?-23.04. 123 BC	10.75
	VI₂ (-murub₄)		28.09.- 07.10. 123 BC	6
	(-en til)		08.- 16.10. 123 BC	9

AD -108:

Diary	Month		Julian date	Price (in qû)
AD -109	VIII		25.10.- 22.11. 110 BC	18
AD -108 Locust invasion	II		18.05.- 15.06. 109 BC	25?
	VII	(-sag)	13.10.- 22.10. 109 BC	22.5
AD -107	IV		05.07.- 03.08. 108 BC	21.25
	VII	(-x en 26)	x-27.10. 108 BC	16.5

The extant examples demonstrate that great care was taken to record the exact date of such events. More often than not the exact day is given, and in two instances (AD -284 and AD -123) even the time of the day is indicated. AD -225 shows that an invasion of longer duration was ideally recorded with the phrase ta ... en ... ('from ... to ...'). We assume that when the formulation simply says itu bi ('that month'), the invasion recorded occured during this whole month.

Table 8.16 Locusts and sesame

Source	Date of the invasion	Julian Date	Text
AD -381B Col. II	III	05.06.-04.07. 382 BC	itu bi zi-*ut* buru$_5$ tur z[i-a]
AD -346, r30	27.- 29. XII	28.03.-30.03. 346 BC	27, 28, 29 buru$_5^{hi.a}$ z[i-a]
AD -308, r11	16. VI	19.09. 309 BC	16 buru$_5$ tur zi-a
AD -284, r36	06. XII	11.03. 284 BC	*ina* kin.sig buru$_5$ mah zi-a
AD -284, r39	12. XII	17.03. 284 BC	*ina* kin.sig buru$_5$ zi-a
AD -256, 3	02. II	05.05. 257 BC	2 buru$_5^{hi.a}$ [zi-a]
AD -237, 14	III	04.06.-03.07. 238 BC	buru$_5^{hi.a}$ *sa-dir*
AD -226A, 23-24[1]	30. II	01.06. 227 BC	itu bi u$_4$ 30-*kam* buru$_5^{hi.a}$ zi-a
AD -226A, r1	03. III	03.07. 227 BC	3 buru$_5^{hi.a}$ zi-a
AD -225, 15[2]	09.-26. III	29.06.-16.07. 226 BC	itu bi ta 9 en 26 buru$_5^{hi.a}$
AD -201D, U.E. 1	23. I	08.05. 201 BC	itu bi 23 bur[u$_5^{hi.}$]^a zi-a *mim-ma* nu ti-*qé*
AD -178C, r14	30.$^?$ XII	02.$^?$04. 178 BC	buru$_5^{hi.a}$ sig$_7$ zi-a.
AD -164A, r4	II	07.05.- 05.06. 165 BC	[bur]u$_5$ tur.tur zi-[a]
AD -164A, r5	II	07.05.- 05.06. 165 BC	[bu]ru$_5$ mah zi-a
AD -141C, 16	a day between 04. and 06. III	a day between 27. and 29. 05. 142 BC	buru$_5^{hi.a}$ [... ...]
AD -136B, r4	11. XII$_B$	29.03. 136 BC	buru$_5^{hi.a}$ *i-ṣa* zi-a
AD -132D$_1$ r30	XII	05.03.- 03.04 132 BC	buru$_5^{hi.a}$ sig$_7$ *i-ṣa* zi-a
AD -129A$_2$, 13-14	28.-30. II	07.- 09.06. 130 BC	buru$_5^{hi.a}$ [... ...] *i-ṣa* zi-a
AD -123A, 28	a day between 20. and 23. IV	a day between 21. and 23.07. 124 BC	*ina* še-*rì* buru$_5^{hi.a}$ gal.gal *šá* ma-*diš* mah zi-a
AD -123A , r16	17. or 18. V	18. or 19.08. 124 BC	buru$_5^{hi.a}$ zi-a
AD -121, 5	1.-10. III	11.- 20.06. 122 BC	ta 1 en 10 zi-*ut* buru$_5$ t[ur]
AD -108A, 27	II	18.05.- 15.06. 109 BC	buru$_5^{hi.a}$ tur *sa-dir*
AD -62, 3	a day before 8. I	a day between 21. and 27.04. 63 BC	buru$_5$ gal.gal zi-a

[1] The actual text goes: (23) itu bi u$_4$ 30-*kam* {bu[ru$_5^{hi.}$]^a} /(24) buru$_5^{hi.a}$ zi-a. We assume a redundant writing.

[2] In addition to this summary, the same locust invasions are also mentioned in the astronomical day-to-day observations.

BIBLIOGRAPHICAL ABBREVIATIONS

ABC   see Grayson 1975
ADART   see Sachs and Hunger 1988–1996.
SAA 10   see Parpola 1993

REFERENCES

Abel, W. (1974) *Massenarmut und Hungerkrisen im vorindustriellen Europa. Versuch einer Synopsis.* Hamburg and Berlin: Parey.

Andreau, J. *et al.* (eds) (1997) *Économie antique. Prix et formation des prix dans les économies antiques* (Entretiens d'archéologie et d'histoire 3). Saint-Bertrand-de-Comminges: Musée archéologique départemental de Saint-Bertrand-de-Comminges.

Andreau, J. *et al.* (eds) (2000) *Économie antique. La guerre dans les économies antiques* (Entretiens d'archéologie et d'histoire 5). Saint-Bertrand-de-Comminges: Musée archéologique départemental de Saint-Bertrand-de-Comminges.

Assar, G. (2006) A revised Parthian chonology of the period 165–91 BC. *Elektrum* 11, 87–158.

Birot, M. (1993) *Correspondance des gouverneurs de Qaṭṭunân* (Archives Royales de Mari 27). Paris: Éditions Recherche sur les Civilisations.

Boiy, T. (2004) *Late Achaemenid and Hellenistic Babylon* (Orientalia Lovaniensia Analecta 136). Leuven: Peeters.

Boiy, T. (2007) *Between high and low. A chronology of the early Hellenistic period.* Frankfurt/Main: Verlag Antike.

Briant, P. (1996) *Histoire de l'empire perse de Cyrus à Alexandre.* Paris: Librairie Arthème Fayard.

Brown, D. (2002) The level of the Euphrates. In C. Wunsch (ed.), *Mining the archives. Festschrift für Christopher Walker on the Occasion of His 60th Birthday*, 37–56. Dresden: ISLET.

Charles, M. P. (1988) Irrigation in Lowland Mesopotamia. In J. N. Postgate and M. A. Powell (eds) *Irrigation and cultivation in Mesopotamia. Part I*, 1–39 (Bulletin on Sumerian Agriculture 4). Cambridge: Sumerian Agriculture Group.

Del Monte, G. (1997) *Testi dalla Babilonia Ellenistica. Vol. 1: Testi cronografici.* Pisa and Rome: Istituti Editoriali e Poligrafici Internazionali.

Grainger, J. D. (1999) Prices in Hellenistic Babylonia. *Journal of the Economic and Social History of the Orient* 42, 303–325.

Grayson, A. K. (1975) *Assyrian and Babylonian Chronicles* (Texts from Cuneiform Sources 5). Locust Valley, NY: J. J. Augustin.

Heichelheim, F. (1930) *Wirtschaftliche Schwankungen der Zeit von Alexander bis Augustus.* Jena: Fischer Verlag.

Hunger, H. (1972–75) Heuschrecken. *Reallexikon der Assyriologie* 4, 389–390.

Lion, B. and Michel, C. (1997) Criquets et autres insectes à Mari. *MARI* 8, 707–724.

Meissner, B. (1932) Ackerbau und Ackerwirtschaft in altbabylonischer und assyrischer Zeit. *Reallexikon der Assyriologie* 1, 19–21.

Mittag, P. F. (2006) *Antiochos IV Epiphanes. Eine politische Biographie* (Klio Beihefte, N.F. 11). Berlin: Akademie Verlag.

Parker, R. and Dubberstein, W. (1946^2) *Babylonian chronology 626 B.C. - A.D. 45.* Chicago: University of Chicago Press.

Parpola, S. (1993) *Letters from Assyrian and Babylonian Scholars* (State Archives of Assyria 10). Helsinki: Helsinki University Press.

Persson, K. G. (1999) *Grain markets in Europe 1500-1900. Integration and Deregulation* (Cambridge Studies in Modern Economic History 7). Cambridge: Cambridge University Press.

Radner, K. (2004) Fressen und gefressen werden. Heuschrecken als Katastrophe und Delikatesse im Alten Vorderen Orient. *Welt des Orients* 34, 7–22.

Sachs, A. and Hunger, H. (1988) *Astronomical Diaries and Related Texts from Babylonia*. I: *652-262 BC*. Vienna: Verlag der Österreichischen Akademie der Wissenschaften.

Sachs, A. and Hunger, H. (1989) *Astronomical Diaries and Related Texts from Babylonia*. II: *261-165 BC*. Vienna: Verlag der Österreichischen Akademie der Wissenschaften.

Sachs, A. and Hunger, H. (1996) *Astronomical Diaries and Related Texts from Babylonia*. III: *164-61 BC*. Vienna: Verlag der Österreichischen Akademie der Wissenschaften.

Slotsky, A. L. (1997) *The bourse of Babylon. Market quotations in the Astronomical Diaries of Babylonia*. Bethesda, MD: CDL Press.

Stol, M. (1994) Beer in Neo-Babylonian times. In L. Milano (ed.) *Drinking in Ancient Societies: History and Culture of Drinks in the Ancient Near East*, 156–183. Padua: Sargon.

Temin, P. (2002) Price behaviour in Ancient Babylon. *Explorations in Economic History* 39, 46–60.

Uvarov, B. (1966) *Grasshoppers and locusts. A handbook of general acridology*. Vol. 1. Cambridge: Cambridge University Press.

van der Spek, R. J. (1993) The Astronomical Diaries as source for Achaemenid and Seleucid history. *Bibliotheca Orientalis* 50, 91–101.

van der Spek, R. J. (2000) The effect of war on the prices of barley and agricultural land in Hellenistic Babylonia. In J. Andreau *et al.* (eds) (2000), 293–313.

van der Spek, R. J. (2006) How to measure prosperity? The case of Hellenistic Babylonia. In R. Descat *et al.* (eds), *Approches de l'économie hellénistique*, 287–310 (Entretiens d'archéologie et d'histoire 7). Saint-Bertrand-de-Comminges: Musée archéologique départemental de Saint-Bertrand-de-Comminges.

van der Spek, R. J. and Mandemakers, C. (2003) Sense and nonsense in the statistical approach of Babylonian prices. *Bibliotheca Orientalis* 60, 521–537.

Vargyas, P. (1997) Les prix des denrées alimentaires de première nécessité en Babylonie à l'époque achémenide et hellénistique. In J. Andreau *et al.* (eds) (1997), 335–354.

Vargyas, P. (2001) *A History of Babylonian prices in the First millennium BC, 1. Prices of basic commodities* (HSAO 10). Heidelberg: Heidelberger Orientverlag.

Wilcken, U. (1894) Antiochus VIII. *RE* 1 (Stuttgart), 2480–2483.

Will, É. (1979-82²) *Histoire politique du monde hellénistique*, 2 vols. Nancy: Presses Universitaires de Nancy.

Ziegler, N. (1999/2000) Review of Birot 1993. *Archiv für Orientforschung* 46/47, 324–336..

9

On Payment Transactions and Monetisation in the Rural Region of Late Antique Egypt: the Case Study of Small-Format Documents[1]

Sven Tost

(Ancient) historical research has long understood Late Antiquity as a period of continuous and general decline in politics, economics and culture, accompanied by numerous catastrophes.[1] This downward trend has been explained, on the one hand, by a number of internal and external political crises caused by usurpations and the invasions of Germanic tribes and, on the other hand, by the demographic effects of the Antonine and Cyprianic plagues. Political instability, population decrease, ruralisation, the isolation of settlement and marketing areas together with an increase in the barter economy have been considered to be long-term effects.[2] Official regulatory procedures and a failure of the reforms initiated by Emperor Diocletian and continued by Emperor Constantine may also have functioned as a kind of catalyst. It is assumed

[1] The present article was written within the context of the research project number 12341 "Neuedition und Auswertung griechischer Papyrusdokumente aus Ägypten. Forschungen zur Wirtschafts- und Geldgeschichte der Spätantike (A New Edition and Analysis of Greek Papyrological Evidence from Egypt. Research on the Economic and Monetary History of Late Antiquity)," which was funded by the Jubilee Fund of the Austrian National Bank. I give my sincere thanks to Jairus Banaji, Bernhard Palme, Fritz Mitthof, Bernhard Woytek and Constantin Zuckerman for our fruitful discussions.

Edward Gibbon, whose *History of the Decline and Fall of the Roman Empire* was published between 1776 and 1788, may be seen as the founder of this tradition of modern historiography. Demandt 1984 has discussed the reception history of the "Fall of Rome" in detail.

[2] The representatives of a primitivistic approach (see Bücher 1893, Weber 1891 and 1909, Jones 1964, Finley 1973) and the adherents to a modernistic approach (see, for example, Meyer 1895, Rostovtzeff 1926) are remarkably in accordance in understanding Late Antiquity as an epoch mainly characterised by barter.

that both rulers tried to check the inflationary economic development, which got out of control in the course of the third century, by introducing a new monetary system based on gold and copper coins instead of the former common silver and copper currency, and by applying accompanying measures. However, this attempt is alleged to have been doomed to failure from the beginning. The continuing economic misery together with military defeats, a constantly growing tax burden and the increasing erosion of imperial authority eventually paved the way to mediaeval feudalism and led to the end of Antiquity.

The socio-economic implications of this transformation process are the subject of a distinct academic discourse that has mainly taken place in the second half of the twentieth century and has often been ideologically charged. It has been termed "the first transition debate" and has been of interest to ancient historians, mediaevalists, archaeologists, cultural historians, philosophers, sociologists, political scientists and economists alike.[3] A crucial aspect of this debate is the question of whether the transition from Antiquity to the Middle Ages was a continuous process of transformation or rather a period of decline with a clear caesura.

The pessimistic approach of the end of the eighteenth and the entire nineteenth century when assessing the conditions of Late Antiquity has been largely nourished by the biased reports of contemporary authors such as Libanius and John Chrysostom. Only in the course of the twentieth century has this approach been more precisely defined and corrected, thanks to the analysis and consideration of the papyrological evidence from Egypt. In addition, the continuity theory of the Viennese mediaevalist Alfons Dopsch has provoked a reassessment of Late Antiquity.[4] No later than the 1970s, Peter Brown's contributions with their decidedly historico-cultural approach have resulted in a predominantly positive characterisation of this Late Antique–Early Mediaeval transition period.[5] Only recently have voices once again been heard which seem to favour a return to the traditional catastrophe-theory model. They have found a prominent and forceful supporter in Bryan Ward-Perkins and his programmatic work of 2005 entitled *The Fall of Rome and the End of Civilization*, arguing mainly from the economic development.[6] No matter whether this approach prevails in the medium

---

[3]   The fact that it has been hardly debated in Byzantine Studies is also due to the specific standpoint of that field which undermines the otherwise common periodisation with its division into Antiquity and the Middle Ages. For an earlier resumé and state of research see, for example, Anderson 1974. The so-called "second transition debate" deals with the transition from feudalism to capitalism.

[4]   See mainly Dopsch 1918–1920. Since 1997 there has even existed a series entitled *Transformation of the Roman World* which was devoted to the subject of this transformation and which currently comprises 21 individual publications. Since 2008 this series has been continued under a new title, namely *Brill's Series on the Early Middle Ages*; volume 22 is expected to be published by October 2013.

[5]   See, for example, Brown 1971 and 1978.

[6]   Ward-Perkins 2005 primarily discusses the situation in the West of the Roman Empire, yet he assumes a similar and clear downward trend for the Eastern Mediterranean in the sixth and seventh centuries. Only the Levant and Egypt must explicitly be excluded from this negative assessment.

term or results in changing the minds of some representatives of History, Classical and Ancient Studies, it may give a decided impulse for continuing and intensifying the transition debate in a much larger context.[7] In addition to the questions of imperial unity, immigration, culture and religion, the economic aspect is crucial for this re-ignited debate.

In a number of much discussed works, most of all in his controversial monograph *Agrarian Change in Late Antiquity: Gold, Labour, and Aristocratic Dominance*, Jairus Banaji has recently pleaded for a view that contradicts any kind of catastrophe theory.[8] According to Banaji it was precisely Constantine's adaptation of the gold currency system which brought about the nascent and thereafter continuing economic recovery and the higher degree of monetisation. In this reformed currency system the *solidus* was no longer struck at a rate of 60 to a Roman pound, but at a rate of 72. Banaji assumes that, owing to an almost complete monetisation of the taxation system at the end of the fifth century, gold coins were even circulating in rural catchments and used in private, low-value trade. It is certain that under the Eastern Roman Emperor Anastasius (ruled 491–518) the *solidus*'s fractions in divisional copper coins were based on a new and permanently stable mint price system, which must have strongly influenced daily exchange in the sixth and seventh centuries.[9] There is evidence that in the East of the Empire the copper currency of the *follis* gained massively in spending power in comparison to the gold currency of the *solidus* in the first half of the sixth century. However, in the course of the 560s there occurred a radical change, because the large property holders and the state became closer, leading to a seigniorial reaction.[10] Banaji's view is in any case representative of one of the two opposing positions in the currently re-ignited transition debate.

The following study takes the current state of this theoretical discussion into consideration and combines it with the question of monetary exchange in the rural catchments, using the case study of Late Antique Egypt. The research will mainly focus on the question of the extent to which the rural region was embedded in the monetised

---

The end of the Mediterranean home market may thus already be set in the first half of the fifth century.

[7] With regard to this revitalised transition debate one may, in addition to Ward-Perkins 2005, also mention Wickham 2005.

[8] See Banaji 1998, 2000 and 2007; especially 2007, 23–38 and the references supplied. Banaji follows there, among others, Mickwitz 1932, who in turn follows Stein 1928.

[9] See Zuckerman 2004, 65–6.

[10] See Sarris 2006, 222–7 with reference to Noeske 2002, table 25 (the development of the mint price of the *follis* in the Eastern mints, except for Alexandria, in the 6th and 7th centuries and the equivalents between AE and the solidus) and table 25A (the development of the mint price of the *follis* in Alexandria in the 6th and 7th centuries and the equivalents between AE and the *solidus*). For the question of spending power see, for example, the summary of price for staple food documented in papyri in Johnson and West 1949, 175–98. For the upward and downward revaluation of the *follis* in the 6th century see Zuckerman 2004, 81–5. For the ratio between gold and copper currency see West and Johnson 1944, 157–70, especially pp. 159–61 with a list of some dated papyri from the 6th century; see also Zuckerman 2004, 59–64.

economic cycles, and which sectors of the public administration and private business took part in these cycles. The study is based on the rich documentary evidence of papyri from Byzantine and early Arabic Egypt (fifth to eighth centuries), which are the only ones among the contemporary written evidence containing precise details of daily payments. Thus reliable information on the nature and the extent of the local money circulation can be gained from them.

CHARACTERISATION OF THE SOURCES USED

Based on the papyrological evidence, two categories of monetised exchange can be discerned: First, monetary transactions which deal with loans, donations, inheritance, dowries and purchases of goods or property, i.e. payments which require a singular payment of a large sum. These belong to the category of high-value transactions. Second, payments of insignificant sums, for example, payments of taxes, wages, rent, loans or daily purchases of staple food and clothes may be termed low-value transactions. As for the research question of the present study, mainly documents of the latter category are of importance as they cover exactly the sphere of daily exchange which gives the best indication for the degree of monetisation of a certain region or social class.

The sources which have been used for the present case study are small-format papyri which are mainly taken from the first, recently revised section of the edited corpus of the *Studien zur Paläographie und Papyruskunde III & VIII* (*Studies in Palaeography and Papyrology III and VIII*).[11] The entire corpus comprises no less than almost 1,400 documents that their previous editor, Carl Wessely, ordered not according to contents and chronology, but rather according to external criteria such as size, format and document formulation. The data that have been used in what follows consist of 70 single documents which are particularly telling with regard to the present research question because they deal with various cases of monetary payments.[12] Other documents, such as the recently re-edited receipts for wheat,[13] are by their nature much less suitable for the purpose of the present case study, as they increase the number of records for one and the same payment but do not corroborate their significance. The time of origin of the documents used also allows for a diachronic approach, covering the period between the fifth and the eighth century, i.e. late Roman-Byzantine, Sasanian and early Arabic Egypt.[14]

---

[11]   Wessely 1904 = SPP III. A new edition of the first part of this corpus can be found in Tost 2007 = SPP III² 1–118.

[12]   SPP III² 2; 5–15; 19; 21 A; 22–23; 24 B; 29; 33–38; 40–42 A; 43–44; 46–47; 56–59; 62; 64; 69–72; 73; 78–79; 82–83; 86–88; 90–92; 94–96; 98–100; 104–105; 109–110; 112 A–118.

[13]   Kreuzsaler 2007 = SPP III² 449–582.

[14]   For the question of dating see Tost 2007, XXXII–XXXIV. Only six of the 70 documents can be

The main advantage of this group of texts is doubtless the fact that, in addition to the diversity of contents, they cover a cross-section of the population due to their broad distribution over the social spectrum. This allows for an inclusion of the poorer rural classes who are of crucial importance for the question of the degree of monetisation. A further advantage is the unusually high degree of homogeneity of this group of texts in comparison with other, often rather disparate papyrological evidence.[15] This circumstance, as well as the remarkable quantity of data, lends itself to quantificatory analysis. The results must, however, be modified owing to the rather narrow geographical distribution of the documents in question – the majority demonstrably originates from one of three Middle Egyptian nomes, namely the Arsinoite, the Heracleopolite and the Hermopolite nomes.[16] About a quarter of the documents (17 pieces) can be attributed to one single archive which is clearly based on the documentation of the official correspondence of a certain Andreas, who in his function as a *grammateus* (among others?) was responsible for the affairs of the public employment sector in the village Tamauis in the Arsinoite nome.[17] These latter two facts already seem to indicate a symptomatic problem of the papyrological evidence: their doubtful significance for the evaluation and assessment of supra-regional conditions and developmental trends.

STATE OF RESEARCH AND METHODOLOGY

For a long time research in Ancient History has assigned to Egypt an exceptional role

---

more precisely dated thanks to their contents: SPP III² 95 (494/5?), 86 (593), 9 (603/4 or 618/9), 14 (between 605/6 and 612/3), 96 (640 or 655), 116 (640/1 or 655/6). Mainly based on palaeographical criteria, the following documents can be roughly dated: six documents to the 6th century (SPP III² 23, 62, 69, 109, 110 and 113), three to the middle of the 6th century (SPP III² 15, 19 and 87), 15 to the 6th/7th century (SPP III² 10, 29, 33, 37, 40, 56, 64, 73, 79, 100, 105, 112 A, 112 B, 114 and 117), one document to the end of the 6th or the beginning of the 7th cenury (SPP III² 44), 17 pieces to the beginning of the 7th century (SPP III² 2, 5, 6, 8, 12, 22, 36, 42 A, 70, 71, 72, 82, 82 *bis*, 90, 91, 92 and 118), two to the first half of the 7th century (SPP III² 43 and 78), 16 to the 7th century (SPP III² 7, 11, 21 A, 24 B, 34, 38, 41, 47, 57, 58, 59, 83, 94, 98, 99 and 104), one papyrus to the second half of the 7th century (SPP III² 88), two documents to the 7th/8th century (SPP III² 35 und 115) as well as one last document to the first half of the 8th century (SPP III² 46). Thus there emerges a clear focus on the 7th century (in total 40 texts) whereas the other periods are less well documented: 6th/7th century with 16 texts, 6th century with ten texts, 7th/8th century with two texts and the 5th and the 8th century with one text each.

[15]   This not only follows from the similarities with regard to the circumstances of their finding, origin and date of composition, but also from the common genre, character, format, type of document and form.

[16]   For the question of origin see Tost 2007, XXXIV–XXXV.

[17]   The following documents seem to have belonged to Andreas's Archive: SPP III² 2; 5–6; 8–9; 12–14; 22; 36; 70–72; 82–82 *bis*; 90–92.

among the provinces of the Roman Empire due to its particular geo-strategic position as well as to its function as Rome's breadbasket since the time of Augustus. This also seems to be manifested by the unique existence of the papyrological findings, although their survival is down to climate alone.[18] The often-postulated exceptional role of Egypt, as well as the privileged position of Italy, had, however, expired, at least in the course of the comprehensive changes within the state under Diocletian and Constantine between 284 and 337. It is very surprising that this fact is still hardly acknowledged in Ancient History, especially with regard to the assessment of Late Antique conditions.

For the papyrological perspective this change in Egypt's role was of comparatively small significance, since the origin of the material necessarily implies a focus on the Egyptian region. Yet it followed that due to this limiting focus research questions dealing with a broader historical context were often neglected, as studies concentrated on the conditions in Egypt.

The following approach attempts to combine the analysis of papyrological data with the question to what extent exchange was monetised, and to relate the resulting findings to the theoretical discourse of the transition debate. It will become apparent whether there existed a variation in degree of monetisation between the urban and the rural settlement areas, namely the *civitates,* the villages and hamlets, and whether various levels of monetisation can be found for the public administration sector, the private business sector, and individual classes of the population. These and other considerations are all summed up in the crucial question as to whether the positioning of Late Antique monetary exchange is limited to certain social classes and professions, and if so, what conclusions can be drawn from this. Needless to say, it is necessary to consider that the positioning of public or private business, and the aspect of social attribution depend on the contents of the documents and on the purpose of each documented transaction. Therefore the analysis must take this into consideration as a separate parameter. Also, the nomenclature of the documented currency and calculation units, i.e. the face value, as well as the amount of the sums paid, must be considered. We will not discuss in detail the occurrence of various mint prices, nor calculate the ratio between real and nominal value.[19] Due to the nature of this case study it is evident that the results presented can only be regarded as preliminary. Future research will broaden the present approach by comparing archaeological and numismatic evidence.[20]

---

[18]   For Egypt's in no way extraordinary legal status within the Roman Empire, the sole particularity of which was a provincial administration characterised by patrimonialism, see now Eich 2007, 378–99.

[19]   See also the section *Currency-related and Terminological Aspects as well as Amounts of Sums* below.

[20]   See von Reden 2007, 58–83, who uses a similar methodology when dealing with the question of the monetisation of the rural regions in Ptolemaic Egypt.

The local-geographical positioning (see Appendix, fig. 9.1)

As several of the documented locations indicate, more than half of the material discussed (namely 38 documents) may come from the Arsinoite nome and thus from the spacious and densely populated Fayum oasis. It is situated to the west of the middle Egyptian bank of the Nile and was one of Egypt's core economic regions since Ptolemaic times. Thanks to toponyms and other geographical references, five papyri can be attributed to the Heracleopolite nome[21] which borders the Arsinoite nome in the south-east, and six to the Hermopolite nome in the far south-west of Middle Egypt.[22] As for about a third of the 70 documents, namely 21, the question of origin and location cannot be answered.[23]

Urban or Rural Context (see Appendix, figs. 9.2a–d)

The majority of Arsinoite documents (34) may have been issued in the *civitas* Arsinoe/ Arsinoiton Polis,[24] even if no fewer than 21 of these texts have, at least formally, a clear relation to rural matters.[25] The contents of only three Arsinoite documents seem to indicate a rural place of issue.[26] As to one further certificate, its origin from the Arsinoite nome is beyond doubt, yet the place of exchange or issue is not stated.[27] At least six of the eleven documents of non-Arsinoite origin were issued in the respective *civitates* (Heracleopolis or Hermupolis).[28] As for the remaining documents, their attribution must remain unknown due to the fragmentary state of the texts or the absence of detailed statements.

Summarising the findings with regard to the place of issue within the individual districts, a significant preponderance of urban places of issue emerges (see fig. 9.2d). At the same time this resulting distribution must be modified in relation to the specific context of discovery, since all documents were discovered at excavation sites next to the cities of Medinet el-Fayum (Crocodilopolis/Arsinoiton Polis), Ehnas (Heracleopolis) and el-Aschmunein (Hermupolis).[29] Although these find spots are located in urban catchments, the existence of some clear connections to villages comes as no surprise

---

[21] SPP III² 24 B; 46; 59; 64; 86.

[22] SPP III² 42 A; 43; 78–79; 95; 118.

[23] SPP III² 10; 11; 29; 34; 37; 41; 44; 47; 62; 69; 94; 98–100; 105; 109–110; 112 A–113; 117.

[24] SPP III² 2; 5–9; 12–14; 21 A; 22; 33; 36; 38; 40; 56–58; 70–72; 73; 82–83; 87–88; 90–92; 96; 104; 114–116.

[25] SPP III² 2 (Tamauis), 5 (Tamauis), 6 (Tamauis), 7 (Tanis), 8 (Tamauis), 9 (Tamauis), 12 (Tamauis), 14 (Tamauis), 22 (Tamauis), 36 (Tamauis), 38 (Letus), 40 (Syron), 70 (Tamauis), 71 (Tamauis), 72 (Tamauis), 82 (Tamauis), 82 *bis* (Tamauis), 88 (Theaxenis), 90 (Tamauis), 91 (Tamauis), 92 (Tamauis).

[26] SPP III² 15 (Metrodoron), 23 (Kaminoi), 35 (Hermupolis).

[27] SPP III² 19.

[28] SPP III² 46 (Heracleopolis), 59 (Heracleopolis), 64 (Heracleopolis), 86 (Heracleopolis), 95 (Hermupolis), 118 (Hermupolis).

[29] See Tost 2007, XXXV, note 78. This is in accordance with the observations made on the basis of the entire papyrological evidence from Byzantine times, on which see Habermann 1998, 144–60.

thanks to the close interaction between the city (*civitas*) and its surroundings (*territorium*). This must be understood as an obvious indication of the monetisation of the rural region in these areas.

Public-administrative or private business context (see Appendix, fig. 9.3)

Half of the documentary evidence, i.e. 35 out of 70 cases, consists of documents which originated in the context of local administrative correspondence and which can therefore be attributed to the public sphere.[30] Twenty-eight documents stem most probably from a private business context.[31] Yet it must be stressed that in Late Antiquity a clear separation between private and public spheres is not always possible. A systematic distinction is difficult, not least because, owing to the distribution of public tasks and competences and the intersection of various spheres of interest, many state services or offices were undertaken by local owners of large estates.[32] In seven cases the context and background of documented payments must remain unresolved thanks to the deficient textual evidence.[33] One cannot therefore assume that monetary exchange was restricted to only one of the two spheres.

Social positioning (see Appendix, fig. 9.4)

For analysing the social embeddedness of monetary exchange, the aspect of social identities must be defined as comprehensively as possible. Since it is not possible to make reliable statements solely based on individual characteristics such as personal legal status, ethnicity, social origin and standing, material status, profession and function, the multi-layered but also ambiguous term 'milieu' is used as it seems to encompass all of these attributes.

With regard to the people involved, more than half of all documents, i.e. 41, belong to the lower level of the local administration[34] – they are either official internal

---

[30] SPP III² 2; 5–10; 12–15; 22–23; 24 B; 29; 34; 36–38; 40; 42 A; 43; 58; 70–72; 78; 82–82 *bis*; 88; 90–92; 95; 100; 118.

[31] SPP III² 33; 35; 44; 46–47; 56–57; 59; 64; 73; 79; 83; 86–87; 96; 98–99; 104–105; 109–110; 112 A–117.

[32] For this see Gascou 1985.

[33] SPP III² 11; 19; 21 A; 41; 62; 69; 94.

[34] SPP III² 2 (*archihyperetes*; *grammateus*), 5 (*grammateus*), 6 (*grammateus*), 7 (*symmachos*; *grammateus*), 8 (*symmachos*; *grammateus*), 9 (*archihyperetes*; *grammateus*), 10 (*hypo? -katastates*; *grammateus*), 12 (*grammateus*), 14 (*symmachos*; *grammateus*), 15 (official of the *komokatoikoi*; soldier), 19 (soldier), 22 (gate keeper; *grammateus*), 23 (?), 24 B (?), 29 (*grammateus*), 34 (*grammateus*), 35 (fireman and *pronoetes*; *symmachos*), 36 (*symmachos*; *grammateus*), 37 (*grammateus*), 38 (?), 40 (store keeper; *grammateus*), 42 A (?), 43 (official of the *komokatoikoi*?), 59 (*boethos*, son of a lamp lighter), 62 (*nyktostrategoi*), 69 (*boethos*), 70 (*grammateus*), 71 (*symmachos*; *grammateus*), 72 (*mandatarii*; *grammateus*), 78 (*boethos* of the *komokatoikoi*; *diastoleus*), 82 (*telonarches*; *grammateus*), 82 bis (*symmachos*; *grammateus*), 88 (?), 90 (*symmachos*; *grammateus*), 91 (*symmachos*; *grammateus*), 92 (*symmachos*; *grammateus*), 100 (officials of a village; *grammateus* of a domain), 109 (*grammateus*), 112 B (*grammateus*), 117 (*grammateus*),

correspondence between different levels,[35] or they deal with private business matters of office-holders or subordinate officials. Seven documents relate to people who worked in the agricultural service sector.[36] Their employers must have been members of the local landlords' class, similar to those who appear, for example, in three texts.[37] Craftspeople are mentioned in seven,[38] traders in three documents.[39] Representatives of the urban curial class are attested in two documents.[40] Two further cases even attest to members of the local imperial administration, mentioning pagarchs, state officials who were assigned to tax collection.[41] There are only five documents which cannot be positioned socially owing to the absence of any exact indications or the poor state of preservation of the writing material.[42] All of the evidence thus allows not only for the assumption of an intersection of individual milieux, but also for the suggestion of a high degree of monetisation of the local milieu, considering the documented involvement of several social classes, professions and public institutions.

Contents of the documents, i.e. purpose of the monetary payment (see Appendix, fig. 9.5)

Among 70 documents there are mainly tax and wage payments as well as loans attested. Twenty-eight documents deal with wage payments. Of these 22 alone relate to the public administrative sector,[43] whereas the remaining six deal with private

118 (*epikeimenos*; *boethos* and *diastoleus*).

[35] For this see the above section *Public-administrative or Private Business Context* and the documents which are attributed to the public sector there.

[36] SPP III² 21 A (sheep farmer), 44 (steward; tenant), 47 (steward; *symmachos*), 57 (?; abbot), 79 (steward), 96 (equerry; *chartularios*), 116 (shepherd; *chartularios*).

[37] SPP III² 33 (landlord; steward), 56 (donkey driver; landlord), 64 (landlord; episcopal general secretary).

[38] SPP III² 46 (?), 73 (two upholsterers), 87 (linen weaver, *enoikiologos*), 98 (*notarios*; goldsmith), 104 (potter), 105 (?), 113 (dyer).

[39] SPP III² 83 (female textile merchant; *geometres*), 114 (merchant?), 115 (grocer, papyrus merchant).

[40] SPP III² 86 (farmer; *riparius*), 95 (*komarchoi*; councilman)

[41] SPP III² 58; 94.

[42] SPP III² 11; 41; 99; 110; 112 A.

[43] SPP III² 2 (receipt for an annual wage of an *archihyperetes*; Andreas's Archive), 5 (receipt for an annual wage?; Andreas's Archive), 6 (receipt for an annual wage; Andreas's Archive), 7 (receipt for an annual wage? of a *symmachos*), 8 (receipt for an annual wage?; Andreas's Archive), 9 (receipt for an annual wage? of an *archihyperetes*; Andreas's Archive), 10 (receipt for the wage of a *hypo?-katastates*), 12 (receipt for an annual wage; Andreas's Archive), 14 (receipt for an annual wage? of a *symmachos*; Andreas's Archive), 22 (receipt of an annual wage? of a gate keeper; Andreas's Archive), 23 (receipt for a wage?), 29 (receipt for a wage), 36 (receipt for an annual wage? of a *symmachos*; Andreas's Archive), 37 (receipt for a monetary payment), 40 (receipt for the wage of a store keeper), 70 (receipt for an annual wage? for a woman; Andreas's Archive), 71 (receipt for an annual wage? of a *symmachos*; Andreas's Archive), 72 (receipt for an annual wage of two *mandatarii*; Andreas's Archive), 82 *bis* (receipt for an annual wage? for a *symmachos*; Andreas's Archive), 90 (receipt for an annual wage of a *symmachos*; Andreas's Archive), 91 (receipt for an annual wage of a *symmachos*;

employment.[44] The contents of ten documents consist of payments, bookings and accounts of taxes and fees,[45] while two others acknowledge the receipt of fees.[46] Payments relating to leases are mentioned in three cases.[47] Nine documents deal with loans, four of which seem to attest to the payment or the allocation of the loan sum,[48] four others confirm the repayment.[49] One last document states the receipt of a payment of interest.[50] In four cases the monetary refund of a purchase or a delivery of goods is attested.[51] Further individual documents relate to the paying-out of an inheritance,[52] of a compensation,[53] and of a reimbursement of provisions.[54] As to 11 documents, the purpose of their attested payments remains in doubt.[55] In sum, one gets the impression of an active low-value monetary exchange which covers a broad spectrum of daily transactions and gives a clear indication of the monetisation of a multitude of exchange. Even in cases where a payment in kind might be expected, e.g. contracts of lease, cash was used.

Andreas's Archive), 92 (receipt for an annual wage of a *symmachos*; Andreas's Archive).

[44] SPP III² 56 (receipt for the wage of a donkey driver), 57 (receipt for a wage), 86 (receipt for the wage of a farmer for irrigation), 87 (receipt for the daily allowance of a linen weaver = subsistence allowance), 96 (receipt for the wage of an equerry), 105 (receipt for a wage).

[45] SPP III² 15 (collective receipt for land tax), 24 B (account of *probata*-tax), 38 (receipt for land taxes), 42 A (double receipt for taxes, Magistor's dossier), 43 (receipt for monetary payment for *embole*), 78 (receipt for a payment in the context of a wheat tax), 82 (receipt for the fee for a monopoly for the dyestuff *krimnos*; Andreas's Archive), 88 (receipt for a monetary payment for *probata*-tax), 95 (receipt for tax), 100 (receipt for the freightage of wheat for taxes).

[46] SPP III² 34 (receipt for *synetheia*), 118 (receipt for an official fee; Magistor's dossier).

[47] SPP III² 44 (collective receipt for lease), 47 (receipt for long lease), 98 (receipt for lease).

[48] SPP III² 35 (receipt for land tax = "hidden" loan?), 59 (loan of a sum of money), 99 (receipt for tax = "hidden" loan?), 115 (loan of a sum of money).

[49] SPP III² 64 (receipt for a partial repayment of a loan of a sum of money), 109 (receipt for debt redemption), 112 A (receipt for debt redemption), 112 B (receipt for repayment of a loan?).

[50] SPP III² 113 (receipt for the interest of a loan).

[51] SPP III² 46 (receipt for the payment for delivered goods), 79 (receipt for the payment for delivered chaff), 83 (receipt for the payment for bought textiles), 116 (receipt for the payment of delivered agricultural goods?).

[52] SPP III² 73 (receipt for an advance payment of an inherited loan).

[53] SPP III² 117 (receipt for the compensation for using a deposit).

[54] SPP III² 33 (receipt for money for provisions).

[55] SPP III² 11 (receipt for monetary payment), 19 (receipt for monetary payment), 21 A (receipt for monetary payment), 41 (receipt for monetary payment), 58 (receipt for monetary payment), 62 (receipt for monetary payment to a *nyktostrategos*), 69 (receipt for monetary payment), 94 (receipt for a monthly monetary payment), 104 (receipt for monetary payment and delivery of wheat to a pottery?), 110 (receipt for monetary payment), 114 (receipt for monetary payment).

Currency-related and terminological aspects as well as amounts of sums (see Appendix, fig. 9.6)

Almost all documented sums are mentioned as sums of gold[56] or copper[57] currency or a combination of these two (mainly *nomismata* or *nomismatia* x minus *keratia* y;[58] sums of *solidi* in 24 cases, of *keratia* in 21 cases, mixed in 3 cases and *solidi* minus *keratia* in 19 cases). Whereas the half (*semissis*) and third fraction (*tremissis*) of the *solidus/nomisma* were still minted in gold, the *siliqua/keration* was not used as a proper coin but only as an abstract unit of account.[59] The sums of *keratia* mentioned in the papyri must therefore have circulated as copper coins. Yet only in two of the 70 documents is the nominal value of copper coins, namely *folles*[60] and *nummi/nummia*,[61] explicitly mentioned. In one further document neither the unit nor the sum of the payment is given.[62]

The amount of the sums, given in *solidi*, ranges from half a *solidus*[63] to a maximum of eight *solidi*.[64] The documented deductions, given in *keratia*, range from 2 1/4 to 7

---

[56]   Latin *solidi*; Greek *nomismata* or *nomismatia*: SPP III² 10 (1 *sol.*), 11 (1 *sol.*), 12 (3 1/2 *sol.*), 23 (1 *sol.*), 33 (1 *sol.*), 46 (3 *sol.*), 59 (7 *sol.*), 64 (8 *sol.*), 69 (2 *sol.*), 73 (3 *sol.*), 82 (3 *sol.*), 83 (5 *sol.*), 86 (1 *sol.*), 98 (1 2/3 *sol.*), 104 (1/2 *sol.*), 105 (1 *sol.*), 109 (1 *sol.*), 110 (1 *sol.*), 114 (3 *sol.*), 115 (2 1/2 *sol.*); in the case of SPP III² 7; 37; 100; 112 A the amount of the documented sum paid is not preserved.

[57]   Latin *siliquae*; Greek *keratia*: SPP III² 9 (20 ker.), 15 (jeweils 9 ker.), 19 (10? ker.), 21 A (11 ker.), 22 (20 ker.), 24 B (jeweils 5 ker.), 34 (1 ker.), 35 (4 1/2? ker.), 38 (117 1/8 ker.), 41 (3 1/2 ker.), 42 A (4 ker. und 1 ker.), 47 (6 ker.), 56 (? ker.), 57 (23 ker.), 58 (11 1/4 ker.), 70 (? ker.), 72 (? ker.), 88 (? ker.), 94 (jeweils 12 ker.), 99 (1 1/2 ker.), 116 (7 1/2 ker.). In at least three cases (SPP III² 29; 78; 118) a part of the sum was calculated in *nomismata* or *nomismatia*, the rest in *keratia* (2 *sol.* and ? *ker.*; 2 *sol.* and 3 *ker.*; 1 *sol.* and 22 1/4 *ker.*).

[58]   SPP III² 2 (2 *sol.* minus 10 *ker.*), 5 (2 *sol.* minus 15 1/2 *ker.*), 6 (1 *sol.* minus 4 *ker.*), 8 (2 *sol.* minus 11 *ker.*), 14 (2 *sol.* minus 10 *ker.*), 36 (2 *sol.* minus 10 *ker.*), 40 (2 *sol.* minus 4 1/2 *ker.*), 43 (1 *sol.* minus 6 *ker.*), 44 (each 1 *sol.* minus 7? *ker.*), 62 (3 *sol.* minus 13 1/2 *ker.*), 71 (2 *sol.* minus 15 1/2 *ker.*), 79 (1 *sol.* minus 6 *ker.*), 82 bis (2 *sol.* minus 10 *ker.*), 90 (2 *sol.* minus 10 *ker.*), 91 (2 *sol.* minus 15 1/2 *ker.*), 92 (2 *sol.* minus 10 *ker.*), 95 (1 *sol.* minus 3 *ker.*), 113 (1 *sol.* minus 5 *ker.*), 117 (1 *sol.* minus 2 1/4 *ker.*). The interpretation of these deductions in *keratia* is still a matter of controversy. Maresch 1994, 8–13 assumes that these amounts in *solidi* were not referring to real coins, but used as abstract units of calculation. Banaji 2007, 70–5 understands them as metrological reference to the loss of gold coins in weight and value due to circulation. Zuckerman 2004, 71–91 interprets the amount of the deduction in *keratia* as the basis for the calculation of an additional payment in exchange for the different coin standards.

[59]   See in general Maresch 1994, 1–6.

[60]   SPP III² 112 B. The amount of 40 *folles* mentioned here may correspond to 1 *keration* following Maresch 1994, 73.

[61]   SPP III² 87.

[62]   SPP III² 96.

[63]   SPP III² 104. The receipt in question confirms not only the payment of the sum of half a *solidus* but also the refund of six *artabai* wheat, which the official of a church institution had given for an otherwise unattested pottery. Nothing more is known about the context and the circumstances of this payment.

[64]   SPP III² 64. The document relates to a partial repayment of a monetary loan of 16 *solidi* which a landlord had taken from a clerical estate (*kleros*) in the city of Heracleopolis. The social position

3/4 *keratia* per *solidus*;[65] the possible chronological implications are not discussed here.[66] The remaining sums, given in *keratia*, amount to sums ranging from 1[67] and 23 *keratia*.[68] Thus these texts deal throughout with insignificant amounts and this fact seems to corroborate the hypothesis presented so far concerning the nature of the degree of monetisation.

Resumé of the papyrological evidence

So far the results of the analysis seem to support at least partly Banaji's thesis of a comprehensive monetisation of the rural economical space in Late Antiquity.[69] The papyrological sources analysed in this article present evenly and widely distributed evidence, except for the focus on the area of Medinet el-Fayum which is owed to the circumstances of the discovery. The assumption of a decline of monetisation from the urban to the rural areas is not supported by the papyri. Judging by the specific character of the individual documents, monetary exchange was as widespread in the area of public daily life and local administration as in the area of private business, without any emphasis on one or the other sphere. This analysis also conforms to social observations: based on the degree of monetisation the assumption of social transparency, which is represented by the interconnectedness and interaction of various milieux, social groups, professions, administrative levels, secular and clerical institutions, seems valid for Late Antique Egypt. It cannot be denied, however, that the paying and receiving of large sums was a prerogative of the socially privileged classes.[70] Last but not least, the number and variety of attestations which predominantly document the low-value trade support the assumption of a high degree of monetisation. Within the current discourse of the transition debate it may become necessary to consider the regional-specific differences more strongly when developing future explanatory models.

An outlook for a comparison with the numismatic evidence

A comparison only recently initiated between the archaeological and numismatic evidence yields surprising results, which at first seem to contradict the papyrological evidence and which can at this stage be discussed only briefly and in outline. With

---

of the borrower as well as the person with whom he closed the loan deal, namely the bishop of the same city, explains the extraordinary high amount of the sum.

[65] SPP III² 5; 71; 91.

[66] For this see Frösén 1979, 155–60 and Maresch 1994, 159–71.

[67] SPP III² 34. This sum of money was probably paid to compensate the recipient who is mentioned by name for a service rendered to an official in the local administration (*grammateus*).

[68] SPP III² 57. In this document the sum of 23 *keratia* equals 1 *solidus* (= 24 *keratia*). The text does not state for what kind of work the recipient was paid a wage by the abbot of an unknown institution.

[69] See Banaji 2007, 39–88.

[70] Most obvious is probably the comparison of SPP III² 64 with the other texts.

regard to Byzantine copper coinage of the Alexandrian mint from the sixth to the first half of the seventh century, this area is unusually and remarkably undocumented in the recently published second part of the catalogue of the coin finds in Egypt, which covers all of the Greek/Roman coins known from the Fayum.[71] This is at odds with numerous mentions in papyri. In the preface the editor quotes historical-economic reasons, on which he elaborates no further, to explain the absence of these coins. He also mentions the weak population of the Fayum, for which he also finds support in the absence of early Arabic imitative coinage.[72]

This phenomenon may conversely also be seen as evidence for the continuity of the monetary exchange and of the economic, social and political conditions, in spite of the Sasanian occupation of Egypt at that time. Yet before it may be fully explained, the context of the finds and the numismatic evidence of other areas of Egypt must be taken into consideration.[73] To do so, one has to distinguish systematically between the treasures and hoards which have to be classified as exceptions and the less ambiguous evidence of excavation campaigns. Hoards primarily present a behaviour typical of collective uncertainty in times of political instability or anarchic conditions and may not therefore be taken as a reliable evidence for the degree of monetisation, whereas the stratigraphic analysis of archaeological excavations is in general much more significant. There is also a caveat, as so far only some few – and rather particularly exposed – places and settlements have been systematically excavated and the results are therefore of selective character.

One may further compare the terms referring to the quality and real value – e.g. *arsatikos*,[74] *obryzos*,[75] *rhyparos*[76] – mentioned in the papyri with the metrological data of coin finds. For a chronological assessment both matters must then be assessed in relation to coin reforms and monetary strategies of individual emperors which are historically documented and discussed in detail in the numismatic literature.[77] Knowledge resulting from these comparative studies may be the starting point for much further research focusing on the development of the exchange rate between gold and copper currency and the question of spending power based on a comparison of the level of salary and prices.

---

[71] Noeske 2006. The data documented there comprises more than 100,000 coins, which come from 14 places in the Fayum and from 92 hoards as well as 15 single finds. A fascicle supplementing the catalogue with a detailed analysis and a systematic evaluation of the data is unfortunately still missing.

[72] Noeske 2006, 13–14. The shift in the concentration of settlements from the middle to the outer-most border of the oasis which is mentioned there is, in my opinion, not sufficient for explaining the general absence of copper coin finds from the period between Justin I and the Arab conquest.

[73] Representative material which may be used for comparison can so far only be found in the coin finds of Abu Mina in the west of the Nile delta, on which see Noeske 2002.

[74] SPP III² 59; 69; 86; see in general West and Johnson 1944, 121; Worp 1991, 71–4; Tost 2007, 152.

[75] SPP III² 46, 64; see in general West and Johnson 1944, 132–3; Hendy 1985, 350–6; Maresch 1994, 26–8; Banaji 2007, 75 and note 217.

[76] SPP III² 11; 29; 33; 82; 83; 98; 105; 110; see in general Maresch 1994, 26–8.

[77] The best basis for an analysis of this aspect is still Hahn 1973; 1975; 1981.

REFERENCES

Anderson, P. (1974) *Passages from Antiquity to Feudalism*. London: New Left Books.

Banaji, J. (1998) Discounts, Weight Standards and the Exchange-Rate between Gold und Copper. Insights into the Monetary Process of the Sixth Century. In *Atti dell'Accademia Romanistica Constantiniana. XII convegno internazionale in onore die Manlio Sargenti*, 183–202. Naples: Edizioni Scientifiche Italiane.

Banaji, J. (2000) State and Aristocracy in the Economic Evolution of the Late Empire. In E. Lo Cascio and D. Rathbone (eds), *Production and Public Powers in Classical Antiquity to Byzantium*, 92–99 (Cambridge Philological Society Suppl. 26). Cambridge: The Cambridge Philological Society.

Banaji, J. (2007) *Agrarian Change in Late Antiquity. Gold, Labour, and Aristocratic Dominance*. Revised edition, Oxford: Oxford University Press.

Brown, P. (1971) *The World of Late Antiquity AD 150-750*. London: Thames & Hudson.

Brown, P. (1978) *The Making of Late Antiquity*. Cambridge, MA: Harvard University Press.

Bücher, K. (1893) *Die Entstehung der Volkswirtschaft*. Tübingen: Laupp.

Demandt, A. (1984) *Der Fall Roms. Die Auflösung des römischen Reiches im Urteil der Nachwelt*. Munich: Beck.

Dopsch, A. (1918–1920) *Wirtschaftliche und soziale Grundlagen der europäischen Kulturentwicklung aus der Zeit von Cäsar bis auf Karl den Großen*. Vienna: Seidel.

Eich, P. (2007) Die Administratoren des römischen Ägyptens. In R. Haensch and J. Heinrichs (eds), *Herrschen und Verwalten. Der Alltag der römischen Administration in der Hohen Kaiserzeit*, 378–399 (Kölner Historische Abhandlungen 46). Cologne: Böhlau.

Finley, M. (1973) *The Ancient Economy*. London: Chatto & Windus.

Frösén, J. (1979) Exkurs 3 : Die nicht 'vollgewichtigen' Solidi In H. Zilliacus *et al.* (eds), *Corpus Papyrorum Rainer VII. Griechische Texte IV*, 1–60. Vienna: Saur.

Gascou, J. (1985) Les grands domaines, la cité et l'état en Égypte byzantine. Recherches d'histoire agraire, fiscale et administrative. *Travaux et mémoires* 9, 1–90.

Habermann, W. (1998) Zur chronologischen Verteilung der papyrologischen Zeugnisse. *Zeitschrift für Papyrologie und Epigraphik* 122, 144–160.

Hahn, W. (1973) *Moneta Imperii Byzantini I. Von Anastasius I. bis Justinianus I. (491-565), einschließlich der ostgotischen und vandalischen Prägungen* (Veröffentlichungen der Numismatischen Kommission I, Österreichischen Akademie der Wissenschaften, Philosophisch-Historische Klasse, Denkschriften 109). Vienna: Verlag der Österreichischen Akademie der Wissenschaften.

Hahn, W. (1975) *Moneta Imperii Byzantini II. Von Justinus II. bis Phocas (565-610), einschließlich der Prägungen der Heraclius-Revolte und mit Nachträgen zum 1. Band* (Veröffentlichungen der Numismatischen Kommission IV, Österreichischen Akademie der Wissenschaften, Philosophisch-Historische Klasse, Denkschriften 119). Vienna: Verlag der Österreichischen Akademie der Wissenschaften.

Hahn, W. (1981) *Moneta Imperii Byzantini III. Von Heraclius bis Leo III. - Alleinregierung, mit Nachträgen zum 1. und 2. Band* (Veröffentlichungen der Numismatischen Kommission X, Österreichischen Akademie der Wissenschaften, Philosophisch-Historische Klasse, Denkschriften 148). Vienna: Verlag der Österreichischen Akademie der Wissenschaften.

Hendy, M. F. (1985) *Studies in the Byzantine Monetary Economy c. 300-1450*. Cambridge: Cambridge University Press.

Johnson, A. C. and West, L. C. (1949) *Byzantine Egypt. Economic Studies* (Princeton University Studies in Papyrology 6). Princeton: Princeton University Press.

Jones, A. H. M. (1964) *The Later Roman Empire 284-602. A Social, Economic, and Administrative Survey*. Oxford: Blackwell.

Kreuzsaler, C. (2007) *Griechische Papyrusurkunden kleineren Formats. Neuedition SPP III² 449-552. Quittungen für die Getreidesteuer* (Papyrologica Vindobonensia 6). Vienna: Verlag der Österreichischen Akademie der Wissenschaften.

Maresch, K. (1994) *Nomisma und Nomismatia. Beiträge zur Geldgeschichte Ägyptens im 6. Jahrhundert n.Chr.* (Papyrologica Coloniensia 21). Opladen: Westdeutscher Verlag.

Meyer, E. (1895) *Die wirtschaftliche Entwicklung des Altertums*. Jena: Fischer.

Mickwitz, G. (1932) *Geld und Wirtschaft im römischen Reich des vierten Jahrhunderts n.Chr.* (Commentationes humanarum litterarum 4/2). Helsingfors: Centraltryckeri och Bokbinderi Aktiebolag.

Noeske, H.-C. (2002) *Münzfunde aus Ägypten I. Die Münzfunde des ägyptischen Pilgerzentrums Abu Mina und die Vergleichsfunde aus den Dioecesen Aegyptus und Oriens vom 4.-8. Jh. n.Chr. Prolegomena zu einer Geschichte des spätrömischen Münzumlaufs in Ägypten und Syrien* (Studien zu Fundmünzen der Antike 12). Berlin: Gebrüder Mann.

Noeske, H.-C. (2006) *Münzfunde aus Ägypten II. Die griechisch-römischen Münzfunde aus dem Fayum* (Studien zu Fundmünzen der Antike 22). Berlin: Gebrüder Mann.

Rostovtzeff, M. (1926) *The Social and Economic History of the Roman Empire*. Oxford: Clarendon Press.

Sarris, P. (2006) *Economy and Society in the Age of Justinian*. Cambridge: Cambridge University Press.

Stein, E. (1928) *Geschichte des spätrömischen Reiches I. Vom römischen zum byzantinischen Staate von 284 bis 476 n.Chr.* Vienna: Seidel.

Tost, S. (2007) *Griechische Papyrusurkunden kleineren Formats. Neuedition SPP III² 1-118. Quittungen, Lieferungskäufe und Darlehen* (Papyrologica Vindobonensia 2). Vienna: Verlag der Österreichischen Akademie der Wissenschaften.

Von Reden, S. (2007) *Money in Ptolemaic Egypt from the Macedonian Conquest to the End of the Third Century BC*. Cambridge: Cambridge University Press.

Ward-Perkins, B. (2005) *The Fall of Rome and the End of Civilization*. Oxford: Oxford University Press.

Weber, M. (1891) *Die römische Agrargeschichte in ihrer Bedeutung für das Staats- und Privatrecht*. Stuttgart: Enke.

Weber, M. (1909) Agrarverhältnisse im Altertum. In J. Conrad *et al.* (eds), *Handwörterbuch der Staatswissenschaften* I, 52–188. Jena: Fischer.

Wessely, C. (1904) *Griechische Papyrusurkunden kleineren Formats. Ein Supplement zu den Sammlungen von Ostraka und Überresten griechischer Tachygraphie* (Studien zur Paläographie und Papyruskunde III). Leipzig: Avenarius.

West, L. C. and Johnson, A. C. (1944) *Currency in Roman and Byzantine Egypt* (Princeton University Studies in Papyrology 5). Princeton: Princeton University Press.

Wickham, C. (2005) *Framing the Early Middle Ages: Europe and the Mediterranean 400-800*. Oxford: Oxford University Press.

Worp, K. A. (1991) Two Notes on Byzantine Papyri. *Bulletin of the American Society of Papyrologists* 28, 71–76.

Zuckerman, C. (2004) *Du village à l'empire. Autour du registre fiscal d'Aphroditô (525/526)* (Centre de Recherche d'Histoire et Civilisation de Byzance. Monographies 16). Paris: Association des Amis du Centre d'Histoire et Civilisation de Byzance.

APPENDIX

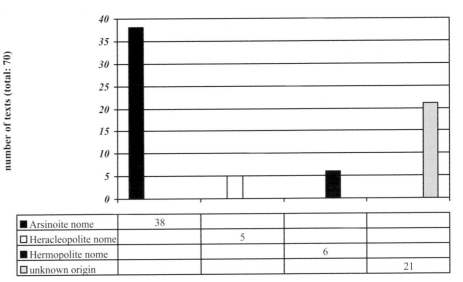

Fig. 9.1 Local-geographical positioning

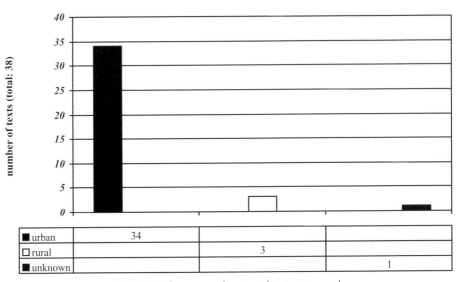

Fig. 9.2a Urban or rural context (Arsinoite nome)

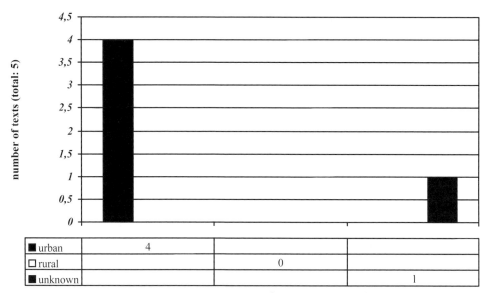

Fig. 9.2b Urban or rural context (Heracleopolite nome)

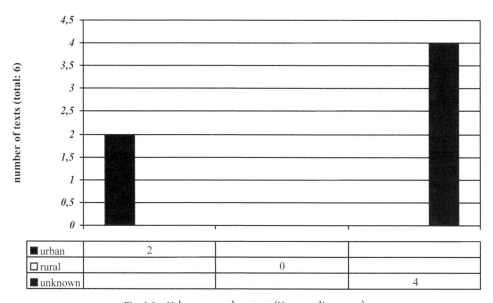

Fig. 9.2c Urban or rural context (Hermopolite nome)

Sven Tost

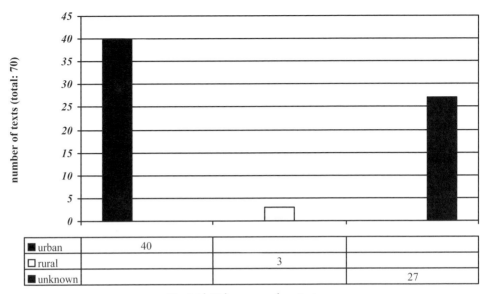

Fig. 9.2d Urban or rural context

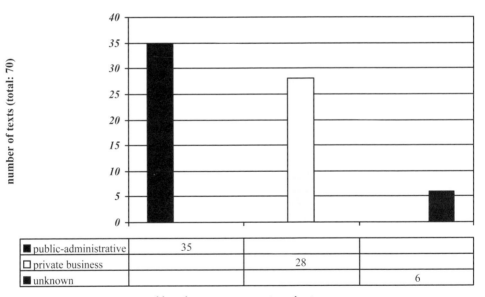

Fig. 9.3 Public-administrative or private business context

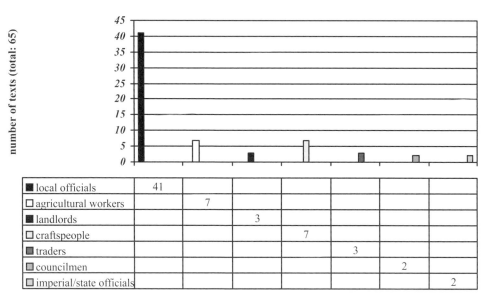

	local officials	41						
	agricultural workers		7					
	landlords			3				
	craftspeople				7			
	traders					3		
	councilmen						2	
	imperial/state officials							2

Fig. 9.4 Social positioning

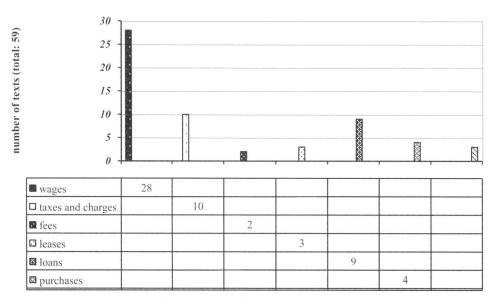

	wages	28						
	taxes and charges		10					
	fees			2				
	leases				3			
	loans					9		
	purchases						4	

Fig. 9.5 Purpose of monetary payment

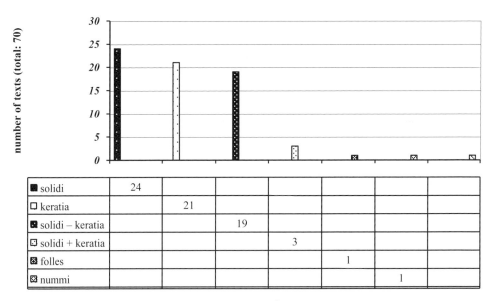

solidi	24					
keratia		21					
solidi – keratia			19				
solidi + keratia				3			
folles					1		
nummi						1	

Fig. 9.6 Amounts of sums

10

Social Network Analysis of Cuneiform Archives – a New Approach

Caroline Waerzeggers

The aim of this paper is to introduce *social network analysis* (SNA) into the field of cuneiform studies. SNA is a method from the social sciences used to describe and analyse human relations; given that relational data abound in cuneiform archives, this approach seems to offer promising avenues of research to Assyriologists.[1] In this paper, I will explore this method using the Babylonian archival material from the mid-first millennium BCE as a test case. For the computational part of this paper, I have received the advice of Ronald Siebes (VU University Amsterdam).

Contents of this paper:
(I) Current approaches to Neo-Babylonian archives and society
(II) Introduction to social network analysis
(III) The network approach in other fields of history
(IV) Social network analysis of cuneiform data: an exploration

---

[1] My discussion of SNA is based on the following handbooks: Scott 2000; Kilduff and Tsai 2003; Carrington, Scott and Wasserman 2005; Wasserman and Faust 1994; Wellman and Berkowitz 1988; Boissevain and Mitchell 1973. For article-length introductions see Mitchell 1974; Wetherell 1989; Wellman 2007, and the online textbook of R. A. Hanneman and M. Riddle at http://faculty.ucr. edu/~hanneman/nettext/ (*Introduction to Social Network Methods*). Mizruchi (1994) evaluates shortcomings and achievements of the network approach in the social sciences. Particularly inspiring are studies that apply SNA in other fields of history. See Wellman and Wetherell 1996; Erickson 1997; Wetherell 1998; Bearman, Moody and Faris 2003; Ruffini 2008, and the section "Historical social network analysis" below. I wish to thank Allon Wagner for advice and feedback on an earlier draft of this article; any remaining mistakes are my own.

NEO-BABYLONIAN ARCHIVES AND SOCIETY: CURRENT APPROACHES

Identifying archives

We are only now getting a grip on our Neo-Babylonian data. The text corpus is large and mostly lacks any archaeological context.[2] Texts say less in isolation, therefore much of the work done in the past decades has been concerned with identifying archives. A method was developed by G. van Driel to do this (1986; 1992), based on a mixture of prosopographical and museological considerations. It leaves room for interpretation, but in practice the method works well: generally, there is no disagreement about the core of reconstructed archives, even if finer delineations are less certain. M. Jursa's recent overview of Neo-Babylonian archives counts at least 132, more than 100 of which are reassembled in said fashion (Jursa 2005). Most of these archives did not exist in modern scholarship 20 years ago and many did not before Jursa's publication nine years ago.

Archive study

The Neo-Babylonian social landscape is now provisionally parcelled up into archives. They cluster in northern Babylonian cities: Sippar, Babylon, Borsippa, Kutha, Dilbat and Kish. The south is less densely covered; it is only thanks to the Uruk and Nippur archives that this area is not entirely underrepresented. Most archives come from a socially homogenous background: the urban elites (priests and more mobile entrepreneurs) and the temple institutions to which some of the former were connected. Rarely have other groups of society left archives: the palace, a governor, an occasional urban artisan, some women, a few agricultural managers of royal estates, a community of Jewish deportees.[3] A large number of archives were left behind as a result of the aftermath of the Babylonian revolts against Xerxes in 484 BCE, which probably accounts for much of the social homogeneity of the corpus.[4] The study of these archives is in full swing. Most problems of handling large data sets are therefore still to come; an effective tool to share and exchange Neo-Babylonian data on a large scale needs to be developed first.

Babylonian society and family archives

Archive studies traditionally approach the Babylonian society piecemeal (by archive) in a topical manner, investigating the genealogies of the archive-holding families, their various properties, priestly offices if any, taxes paid, slaves owned, loans

---

[2] C. 20,500 texts are available to the Vienna START Project according to Jursa 2005; the majority of these remain as yet unpublished.

[3] Jursa 2005 offers an overview.

[4] Waerzeggers 2003/2004.

contracted, etc.[5] This results in lists of attributes characterizing the social groups which left the archives. The lists reveal certain tendencies in elite behaviour. An important breaking point is the involvement – or not – in commercial enterprises of the *harrānu*-type.[6] A correlation with the absence/presence of priestly functions is often observed, which leads to the intuitive conclusion that these activities did not match easily and that we are looking at two social groups.[7] Another essential distinction is the form of slave ownership, again in correlation with priestly activity. Slave-holding on a larger scale and the employment of slave agents as business representatives is not usually found in prebendary families. The presence of either one of these attributes on our checklist will tell us that the persons in question were "likely non-prebendary" and "possibly involved in partnerships" or in some other delocalized activity like tax collecting or agricultural management. The checklist can be further expanded, with for example tax farming, agricultural management, and barley cultivation as activities of the non-priestly milieu. These typologies of elite behaviour are useful but not rigorous categorizations of Babylonian society. Some priestly families engaged in *harrānu* partnerships;[8] this means that kinship ties could cut across categories derived from a topical study of archives. The conclusion must be that this approach fails to grasp the complexities of Babylonian society.

Larger social structures

Archive studies tend to neglect larger social structures, above the archive level. We look through the eyes of the Marduk-nāṣir-aplis, Nabû-ušallims and Bēl-rēmannis who left the archives and study what they did in their lives. This tunnel vision blocks out the larger society: how did Nabû-ušallim and his family connect with other social groups in Uruk and beyond?; did the lives of Marduk-nāṣir-apli in Babylon and Bēl-rēmanni in Sippar intersect in any way, or did they live 'worlds apart'?; what does this kind of information tell us about connectivity in Babylonian society, the distance of kinship networks, the flows in inter-city communication, the potential for mobilizing rebellions?; etc.

The worlds documented by the Neo-Babylonian archives are *not* self-contained units; they touch, intersect and overlap. We are well aware of this fact thanks to certain

---

[5]   The most important studies are: Abraham 2004; Baker 2004; Hunger 1970; Joannès 1989; Jursa 1999; Kessler 1991; Wunsch 1993 and 2000. Studies of the temple archives most often tackle economic, cultural, prosopographical, and legal research questions (e.g. Beaulieu 2003; Bongenaar 1997; Gehlken 1990 and 1996; Holtz 2009; Janković 2004; Jursa 1995; Kleber 2008; MacGinnis 1995; Zawadzki 2006), a society-oriented study is Kümmel 1979.

[6]   The word *harrānu*, literally "road", was used in Babylonian to denote commercial joint ventures. See Lanz 1976 on these enterprises.

[7]   Van Driel 1998, 166; Jursa 2005, 66.

[8]   An example is Marduk-rēmanni, to whom I shall return in the fourth section of this paper.

better-known archive clusters.[9] Later in this paper, I will give examples of how even geographically distant archives sometimes link up, but for now, it is sufficient to point out that there is uncollected evidence in our Neo-Babylonian sources that will enable us to do research into the middle range of social structure: above the individual person and his family and below society as a whole. It is at this point that I want to introduce social network analysis because it connects the micro and macro levels; moreover, it has its own ways of describing the social structure, its own tools to represent and quantify it, and it has been successfully applied to historical societies.

SOCIAL NETWORK ANALYSIS

Social network analysis is a method of carrying out empirical, quantitative research in social structures. It is not a predictive social theory but a "broad strategy for investigating social structure (...) a paradigm (...) a perspective (...) a loose federation of approaches".[10] It developed in the 1960s from three research branches: sociometry, graph theory and organizational anthropology.[11] Since then, SNA grew into one of sociology's 'most promising currents' (Emirbayer 1994), with its own academic journals (*Complexity*, *Social Networks*), textbooks, vocabulary and an increasing degree of sophistication in its technical tools. Today SNA is used to study a wide range of topics, including friendship, factory life, interlocking board memberships, occupational mobility, globalization, sociolinguistics, coalitions and insurgencies, epidemics and computer viruses, virtual communities, social health, criminal organizations, logistics, telecommunications, ... and past societies.[12]

SNA: introduction[13]

The primary unit of observation in SNA is not the individual with his various attributes (i.e. wealth, occupation, age, business profile) but the relations that he maintains with others in the system. An actor is embedded in a web of ties that link him to others.

---

[9]   For instance, in Sippar, the Ebabbar temple archive is so large that it can help us identify the players in other archives from the same city, even if it is only as non-members of the temple household. In this way, M. Jursa discovered that most of Bēl-rēmanni's creditors did not belong to the priesthood like himself (Jursa 1999, 125). Similar connections exist between the private and temple archives from Uruk (Kessler 1991).

[10]   Emirbayer and Goodwin 1994, with a quote from Burt 1980.

[11]   Wasserman and Faust 1994, 10ff.; Scott 2000, 7ff.; Kilduff and Tsai 2003, 13ff.

[12]   See Carrington, Scott and Wasserman 2005, 1f., Wasserman and Faust 1994, 5f., and Rosenthal *et al.* 1985, 1028f. for an overview of topics in social and behavioural sciences that are approached from the network perspective. Applications in history are not so very numerous: see the section "historical social network analysis" below and the appendix.

[13]   This and the following section of my paper are based on the handbooks mentioned in the first footnote unless otherwise specified. Readers who are familiar with SNA are advised to skip both sections.

The 'others' can be *adjacent* actors directly linked to him or actors *removed* by two or more steps.[14] The 'ties' may have any content (e.g. kinship, exchange, patronage, friendship, neighbourhoods), strength (e.g. daily contact, hearsay) or emotional value (e.g. love, indifference). Individuals are not part of just one network, but of many, which are constantly shifting, expanding, overlapping and finally converging with society itself (Mitchell 1974, 280). Action, in the SNA perspective, is always *interactive*: a person's behaviour will affect the context for those with whom he is connected, and *vice versa*, the network context (the pattern of ties around) will affect the choices of persons within (Wellman and Berkowitz 1988). This is explained by the fact that links are routes or channels through which information, resources and emotions can travel (Mitchell 1973, 23). The presence or absence of linkages will facilitate or block communication, exchange, support etc. *Position* or *actor location* determines whether somebody can reach others and be reached by them, which will influence his choices. Network location, therefore, is '*social capital*' and network structures are the routes by which that capital is distributed among the participants or withheld from them (e.g. Scott 2001). A key concept here is the '*bridge over a structural hole*' (an actor who links two otherwise unconnected groups, thereby assuming a position of monopoly in the transfer of knowledge and resources). Network analysts do acknowledge that agency, culture and cognition influence social behaviour, but it is debated how such variables should be combined with the structuralist foundations of network theory.[15]

SNA: methods

Social network analysis comes with its own vocabulary and analytical toolbox. The tools are borrowed from graph theory and matrix algebra and offer the possibility to analyse the properties of networks in a quantifiable manner. In general, SNA first aims to depict the structure of a group (in a graph or matrix) and then to study the influence of this structure on the group or group members (Wasserman and Faust 1994, 9). Two approaches can be discerned in SNA: *whole network* studies try to capture all relations in a social system, while *egocentric network* studies are concerned with the ties that single individuals possess and use (Wetherell 1998, 127f.). Both approaches make observations of the networks at three basic levels: the structure of the entire network, the properties of ties, and the properties of nodes (actors). Each level of observation has its own associated concepts, most of which can be mathematically measured. I will only discuss basic concepts that are relevant to the study of Babylonian social networks. For instance, signed graphs are not very useful because we mostly lack the type of sources that report on positive or negative experiences of a contact (i.e. diaries,

---

[14]   SNA is most commonly used to study human relations, but it can be applied to networks of all types of entities that are interconnected, i.e. rhyming patterns, village networks, trade and travel routes, city traffic flows etc.

[15]   Inter alia Mizruchi 1994; Emirbayer and Goodwin 1994; Emirbayer 1997; Kilduff and Tsai 2003, 79ff; Breiger 2004.

personal letters, treatises). As a matter of fact, for the same reason, certain popular areas of SNA may be out of reach for Assyriologists.[16]

Commonly studied **network properties** are density and centralization. *Density* measures how many ties of all the ones possible are actually realized in a given network. A dense network is indicative of a cohesive world where everybody knows everybody. Ideas, once they find an entrance, are adapted quickly in the collective identity. *Centralization* is the degree to which the network centres around one or more points. This measure enables one to locate the centre of the network as opposed to its periphery. It will identify your most prominent players, or hubs. These are not necessarily the players with the most connections: also those connected to the important ones and those who establish a link between isolated units occupy important positions. *Cliques*, on the other hand, are inward-looking subsections of networks: a group with the maximum number of ties between themselves but only a minimum with outsiders. Other concepts at the network level are *reachability* (the average number of steps between actors) and *balance*. The applicability of this last concept depends on the presence of directed ties, and will be discussed together with tie properties.

Commonly studied **tie properties** are strength, multiplexity, direction and symmetry. Two persons are strongly connected if they meet often, trust each other, are emotionally attached, or offer mutual support. Such ties are important in a person's life experience but rarely productive of new ideas or new horizons. Casual encounters with persons less close to oneself are more likely to create an opening towards other networks or areas of knowledge because we tend to know the friends of our friends and we all share the same ideas. Mark Granovetter was the first to formulate this thesis in a ground-breaking article entitled "The Strength of Weak Ties" that has become one of the most cited in the social sciences (Granovetter 1973). *Multiplexity* has to do with strength; it refers to the number of different relationships that activate the same tie. For instance, workmates who visit the same bar, support the same football team and are members of the same rowing club have a multiplex tie. Such ties are stronger than 'simplex' ones. *Direction* and *symmetry*, finally, are related concepts: a directed tie goes from one person to another but it does not necessarily revert (i.e. supplying financial aid). If it does, that tie is symmetrical. Many network studies are limited to binary measures of relations: either there is a tie or there is none, but what form the recorded tie actually takes is irrelevant. In directed networks, the concept of *balance* becomes relevant. If a network is full of asymmetrical ties, there will be a lot of hierarchy between the actors, and resources, support, resources and so on will travel mainly in one direction. It implies dependency on the givers or senders. If a network is entirely symmetrical, communication patterns will be reciprocal.

Concepts used in describing **node properties** are closely related to those of networks and ties. The *degree* of a node is the numerical measure of its contacts. Actors with a

---

[16]   That is, *cognitive social network analysis*, or, the study of how actors perceive the dynamics in their networks and act accordingly (Kilduff and Tsai 2003, 4f. and 70f.; Wasserman and Faust 1994, 51f.). The cuneiform letter corpora might offer an exception to the rule.

high degree are very active in the network. They occupy a central position and will therefore influence centralization measures on the network level. A high degree measure (many highly active persons) is the same as a high density measure. The concept of degree can be combined with that of tie direction: actors who are chosen by others have an *indegree*, those who chose others have an *outdegree*. If you enjoy a high indegree, you are popular. Finally, a *bridge*, as mentioned earlier, is structurally important because its disappearance will cause the network to disintegrate into two or more pieces. It is a bottleneck in the communication flows that run through the system and vital for its survival. There are ways to calculate just how much of a bottleneck a node is.

SNA: perspectives

The strength of SNA is that it can describe basic structures of social life in precise terms and measure them.[17] It can point out to us which actor functioned as a bridge, who depended from that person in which situations, which groups in society were more inward-looking than others and how much, etc. The visualization tools that come with SNA can certainly be valuable in this respect. 2D representations of social webs consist of dots (actors) connected by lines (ties), a tradition which goes back to Jacob Moreno's sociogram and which has found more fanciful adaptations since then. Many software programs are on offer to generate such pictures and to perform the desired calculations of density, centrality, betweenness, etc.[18]

Can SNA be applied to Neo-Babylonian data? In order to get oriented, I will first discuss some applications of SNA in other fields of history, focusing on the type of sources that were used in these studies, the kind of networks that were reconstructed from them, and the questions that were solved by focusing on the texture of the network rather than on the individual actors.

HISTORICAL SOCIAL NETWORK ANALYSIS

Network analysis has been successfully applied to historical data. Interest in this area dates mostly to the 90s and onwards,[19] but older examples exist.[20] The two major

---

[17] Emirbayer and Goodwin 1994, 1418. The mathematics applied in SNA can be highly complex; e.g. the main publication of a project about the network of French medieval peasants by mathematicians of the university of Toulouse (http://graphcomp.univ-tlse2.fr/index.php?page=accueil) is entitled "Batch kernel SOM and related Laplacian methods for social network analysis", which pretty much sets the tone for the rest of the article (Boulet *et al.* 2008).

[18] Huisman and van Duijn 2005 discuss all the software.

[19] In the 1990s several appeals were made by sociologists to encourage historians to consider the use of SNA methods in their investigations: Wellman and Wetherell 1996; Erickson 1997; Wetherell 1998. These appeals were not directly answered by historians, but many started to engage in historical SNA in that period.

[20] Rosenthal *et al.* 1985; Smith 1979; Rutman and Rutman 1984.

approaches in SNA (whole network and egocentric network, see above) have both found their applications in history, though whole networks are much more demanding in terms of documentary coverage and are therefore less common.[21] In this section, I will discuss five influential publications from different disciplines. More examples can be found in the appendix (Table 10.1).[22]

Rosenthal et al. 1985: the networks of 19th century women reform leaders in New York State

This is one of the earlier examples of historical social network analysis. The authors studied the entire field map of women's organizations in 19th-century NY State. The sources used in this study are biographical dictionaries of the period 1820–1914. From these records, the authors extracted the names of 202 leaders of the women reform movement and their affiliations to 1,015 women's organizations. Many women participated in different organizations or groupings at the same time, which created channels for cross-fertilization, communication, and concerted action. By mapping the connections between the organizations and applying techniques of network analysis,[23] the authors were able to show which organizations were central to the movement, how certain organizations influenced and activated others across time, and which movements remained without effect because of their socially isolated positions.

Padgett and Ansell 1993: the networks of the Medicis in 1400–1434 Florence

This article is most often cited as an example of a successful application of network analysis in history. Padgett and Ansell first show that standard attributional analyses based on wealth (rising vs. declining money), social status (new men vs. old patricians) and neighbourhood (Lion d'Oro vs. Santa Croce) are not enough to explain the composition of the political factions that divided early 15th century Florence between Medici supporters and oligarchic party members (pp. 1268ff.). Next, they set out to show that relational data yield a better understanding of political behaviour in that time and place (pp. 1274ff.). Their central thesis is that factions were mobilized along lines that corresponded to pre-existing social networks. The type of social ties that

---

[21] Erickson 1997; Wetherell 1998.

[22] So far, the earliest network studied with SNA techniques is, as far as I am aware, Cicero's (Alexander and Danowski 1990). Ancient Egypt (before the Byzantine era) and Babylonia have not yet been approached in this manner. McGeough 2007 uses terminology inspired by the network approach to study the economy of Ugarit but does not exploit its quantifying potential. Ruffini 2008 studied elite networks in Byzantine Egypt.

[23] The techniques applied in this study are: centrality (in order to assess the importance of each organization in the network, pp. 1030, 1032ff.), clique detection (in order to locate separate clusters, pp. 1030f., 1036ff.) and directionality (in order to assess the impact of the direction of flows of individuals across organizations on the entire network, pp. 1041ff.).

defined political support were marriages and business associations. Followers of Cosimo de Medici were connected to the Medici family by marriage, partnership, trade and bank ties. Moreover, this faction was both internally fractured (little interaction between Medici supporters) and structurally isolated from the rest of elite society (Medici supporters only reported to the Medicis and not to each other or to the oligarchic party members). This social structure had important consequences for political action as it enabled Cosimo de Medici to control and mobilize his supporters more effectively than did his oligarchic opponents (p. 1279).

The sophistication of this study was possible thanks to the richness of the sources. Padgett and Ansell could rely on many different text types, yielding both panoramic and microscopic views of Florentine elite society: tax censuses, wedding registers, annual censuses of the banking guild, business censuses, account books, chronicles, letters and diaries. From these sources, nine types of interaction between 92 elite families were coded: kinship (incl. marriage), business, joint ventures, banks, real estate ties, patronage, personal loans, friendship and surety ties. These relational data were supplemented with attributional data on the families' wealth, social status, residence, tax assessments, offices and factional membership.

Gould 1991: the networks of communards in 1871 Paris

Gould showed that the level of resistance offered by insurgents during the *semaine sanglante* (21–28 May 1871) depended on the intensity of neighbourhood ties within and across batallions of the National Guard. He thus refuted the commonly held opinion that affiliation to the National Guard is enough to explain commitment to the cause of the Paris commune. Because the recruitment system to the National Guard was to a large extent residential, many neighbours fought alongside each other on the barricades, which sparked solidarity. Volunteer battalions, whose members did not live in the same *arrondissements*, surrendered much more quickly to the French army advancing from Versailles. The data on which Gould based his study were taken from army records, including dispatches of battalion commanders to the commune war ministry that were seized by the army in the last week of fighting.

Carpenter 1994: the networks of the Staffordshire gentry in Medieval England

Carpenter made an enquiry into the degree of localization of the Medieval English gentry, by focusing on the network of one of its members, Philip Chetwynd of Ingestre near Stafford (13th–14th century). The network is reconstructed from data in the Chetwynd cartulary, consisting of charters and legal records. Carpenter found that the network of this person was dense, socially homogeneous, geographically focused and structured along kinship lines and neighbourhoods. Contrary to the expectations from the work of social scientists, the importance of weak ties for generating wider connections could not be confirmed by the author (p. 370). The major advantage of the network approach is, according to Carpenter, that it can replace our intuitions about ancient society with facts.

Mullett 1997: the network of a Byzantine archbishop in Bulgaria (c. 1090–1100)

Mullett reconstructed the personal network of a Byzantine archbishop from his 135 personal letters. In total 301 friends, colleagues, patrons and clients were arranged in zones of descending intimacy, from Theophylact's personal cell to his extended zone of indirect contacts. This map enabled Mullett to visualize the bishop's network and to conduct a number of studies into how he activated that network for different purposes (network*ing*).

SOCIAL NETWORK ANALYSIS OF CUNEIFORM DATA: AN EXPLORATION

This section will address two questions: first, *can* SNA be applied *in theory* to cuneiform data (i.e. are our data right?), and second, how can we proceed *in practice* and what kind of research questions can we envisage tackling with SNA?

The nature and scope of our data[24]

There are certainly plenty of relational data in our cuneiform texts: kinship (including marriage, paternal descent, and affinal relationships), economic relations (occupational interactions, trading partnerships, personal loans, lease of income rights), patronage (institutional ties, master-slave relationships), property (rents, leases, sales), residential connections (city neighbourhoods, village patterns), trust (surety, witnessing, criminal associations), enmity (litigation), etc. A mix of these different types of relationships can be found in any Neo-Babylonian archive.

We should try to get to know as much as we can about all the elements in a network. The bare ID given in the cuneiform texts (name/father's name/family name) is only relevant if that information supplies connections to others. It is possible to differentiate between actor categories by integrating attributes into the analysis. For instance, one can calculate how much of somebody's network was made up of prebendaries if "prebendary" is defined as an actor attribute in the data set. Other categories we could think of are: gender, office (temple or palace), place of main activity, bears a family name, number of slaves owned, dowry wealth, etc. The problem is that we know almost

---

[24] In the handbooks, the data requirements of SNA are not discussed in ways useful for the historian. The focus lies mostly on data collected from questionnaires. That data can be collected from archival texts is mostly acknowledged with a reference to Padgett or Rosenthal or some other article in historical SNA, but these articles do not discuss data requirements from a methodological point of view. Most studies limit the number of actors under observation so as to make the data set more manageable. E.g. Padgett and Ansell look at important Florentine *families*, not at *individuals*. In this way, a dataset of tens of thousands of people is reduced to 92 'actors'.

nothing of persons who do not interact regularly with the archive's core and do not appear in other archives. We should expect, therefore, that most persons in our networks will fill up space without revealing anything more about the persons with whom they interacted. It will be a challenge to remove those unproductive persons from our dataset without missing the weak ties that are bridges to other archives.

The biggest problem is that we lack panoramic sources: tax and population censuses, marriage registers, cadastres and the like. Such sources would offer comparative material about large sections of society and establish links within and between them – think of Padgett and Ansell's Florentine families. Most of the time, our data come from myopic archives. In Uruk and Sippar, the temple archives offer the possibility to venture beyond the micro-cosmos of the family and look at disparate sections of society from a single source; in the other towns we do not have this advantage. Because of our archive-bound vision, the egocentric network approach will in practice be the self-evident choice.

Fortunately, Neo-Babylonian archives are not all self-contained units. They do overlap, intersect and touch: often enough, persons in one archive re-appear in one or more other archives. Such persons connect the various social networks that are documented in the archives. They move in between, form bridges and pull the worlds of our Marduk-nāṣir-aplis, Nabû-ušallims and Bēl-rēmannis together. In order to break through the tunnel vision on Babylonian society offered by the single archive, we will have to search systematically for such areas of interlock. We can proceed on two levels:

A. INTRACITY RELATIONS

Connections can be most easily found in archives from the same city. It is common practice to mine archive clusters for additional information about certain actors, but if collected systematically, such links will enable us to reconstruct local elite societies more fully than we do now. Following the paths between archives, we can draw social maps that come close to *whole networks*. In Sippar, for instance, the families of Bēl-rēmanni and Marduk-rēmanni can be linked up – with the aid of other Sippar archives – into a continuous genealogical chart of at least 10 ancestral families and over 100 individuals (13 female). In Borsippa, at least two such kinship networks can be reconstructed, one centring around the Iliya and Bēliya'u families, and one around the Rē'i-alpi family. There are similar prospects for the Babylon archives.[25]

B. INTERCITY RELATIONS AND GEOGRAPHICAL DISTANCE

The social networks of Babylonian elites did not end at the city gates. Contacts with tenants and property patterns created social ties not only *between* city and countryside, but also *in* the villages (i.e. tenants of the same landowner) and *in* the cities (i.e. landowners of neighbouring plots). Moreover, persons moving between cities generated networks that could stretch over a considerable geographical distance. I will illustrate

---

[25] I.e. Nabû-ēṭir-napšāti of the Ea-eppēš-ilī B archive was married to the daughter of Ṭābia// Sîn-ilī (Jursa 2005, 64).

this with some examples. They are chosen to show how such networks can present themselves in our sources and how difficult it might be to interpret the value of such intercity contacts.

SCENE 1: A MARRIAGE

On 30 May 493 BCE, Marduk-nāṣir and his future son-in-law Tabnēa reached a dowry agreement. The details were recorded in a contract in the city of Uruk (Roth 1989 no. 6) but the actual text was retrieved from the groom's archive in Sippar (Bongenaar 1997). Marduk-nāṣir and Tabnēa lived more than 200 km apart, yet there was a path connecting them. How did they know one another?

A snapshot of that path can be found in BM 75145:[26] Tabnēa met his in-laws at least once prior to the wedding arrangement. However, their meeting was not the focus of that text; it merely happened in the background of the main event. The tie recorded in BM 75145 is therefore unrepresentative of the closeness we are looking for. Marduk-nāṣir and Tabnēa must have known each other in another way. Both belonged to the brewer's division of their local temples (Jursa 2005, 129) but it is unlikely that they knew each other through their jobs. Priests tended to have limited rather than expanded horizons and there is no evidence that the lower priesthoods of the Eanna and Ebabbar temples joined each other in worship. In conclusion, we can observe that members of the Sippar and Uruk urban elites communicated with each other but we do not know how this channel came about.

SCENE 2: ANOTHER MARRIAGE

Around the same time, another intercity marriage was concluded in northern Babylonia. The groom was Bēl-bullissu, son of Marduk-rēmanni of the Ṣāhit-ginê family, the bride was Bulliṭ-iššu, daughter of Nādin-ahi.[27] Like Tabnēa, the groom was from Sippar but the bride was from Babylon, not as far away as Uruk. This time, we know nothing of a prior encounter between the parties. Worse, we know nothing about the bride's father, Nādin-ahi, because he is not mentioned in other records and appears without a family name in the dowry text. Yet, we *do* know something of the social platform which paved the way for this marriage. This platform can be re-created through a number of indirect linkages.

The dowry consisted among other things of a house in Kullab, a residential neighbourhood in the centre of Babylon.[28] It was located on a street leading to the temple of Bēlet-Bābili. In the same neighbourhood, probably on the same street, Iddin-Marduk//Nūr-Sîn had owned a house.[29] He was the father-in-law of Egibi headman Itti-Marduk-balāṭu and the grandfather of Marduk-nāṣir-apli. Marduk-nāṣir-apli in

---

[26] BM 75145, written in Dar 27, casts Tabnēa in the role of creditor of dates and his future brother-in-law, Bēl-iddina son of Marduk-nāṣir, in the role of scribe.

[27] BM 64177; Waerzeggers 2001.

[28] George 1992, 24.

[29] *Camb* 341 (Wunsch 1993 vol. b, no. 348).

turn was married to a daughter of Kalbā//Nabāya. This Kalbā collected taxes from Marduk-rēmanni – the groom's father – on two occasions.[30] The chain formed by all these ties tells us that the wedding parties were connected to the Egibis and therefore indirectly to each other.[31] Of course, this path is only a possible channel of communication, not necessarily *the* channel through which the marriage negotiations actually took place.

SCENE 3: IN SUSA ...

From about the tenth year of Darius' reign onwards Babylonians travelled regularly to Susa. These travels created occasions for Babylonians from all over the country to meet each other in special circumstances, far away from home and in close proximity to the king. Ties forming under such circumstances are likely to have been of some strength. These networks connect large sections of Babylonian elite society, for example:

- Babylon/Sippar/Uruk: Bēl-aplu-iddin/Niqūdu/Ašgandu was in Susa with Marduk-nāṣir-apli//Egibi at the end of Dar 16 (*Dar* 437). He had a brother, Sîn-ili, who witnessed a tablet of Tabnēa//Šangû-Šamaš written in Babylon in Dar 27 (ArOr 33 no. 1). Tabnēa in turn travelled to Susa with Marduk-rēmanni in Dar 17 (BM 63806). These ties are confirmed by Nidintu/Bēl-zēru-ibni/Egibi, who witnessed BM 41440 (an Egibi tablet written in Susa in Dar 23) and wrote the tablet *ArOr* 33 no. 1 of the aforementioned Tabnēa. This Tabnēa is none other than the groom from Sippar who married an Urukean bride in scene 1, discussed earlier.

- Sippar/Bāṣ/Babylon/Borsippa: the *qīpu* of Esagil was part of a travel party arriving in Susa from Borsippa in Dar 29 (VS 6 155); in the same period, he was addressed about matters concerning Šušan by Bēl-bullissu, the son of Marduk-rēmanni who married the bride from Babylon in scene 2 (CT 22 59). In Dar 16, Marduk-nāṣir-apli travelled to Susa in the company of Nidintu/Bēl-kāṣir/Ea-eppeš-ilī, the priest of Bāṣ. The father and uncle of this priest were connected to the Ea-ilūta-bāni family, who left one of the larger archives from Borsippa.[32]

Each of these networks had deeper ramifications in Babylonian society. In an earlier period, Iddin-Marduk (the Egibi father-in-law) provided a link between Uruk, Borsippa and Babylon. During his activities in Borsippa, he met many people who were part of the personal networks of the large, inter-connected web of local priestly families who have left the biggest cluster of private archives from the Neo-Babylonian period. Some of these families in turn were linked up to Uruk, Dilbat and other cities (notably Kish).

These random examples of inter- and intra-city relationships show that we have

---

[30]   BM 74638 (Dar 04) and BM 74601 (Dar 06), both written in Babylon.

[31]   Marduk-rēmanni and the Egibis linked up much more intensely than via Kalbāya alone (Waerzeggers 2001). Nādin-ahi, on the other hand was only weakly connected to the Egibis; we might see the marriage between Marduk-rēmanni's and Nādin-ahi's children as an effect of Granovetter's strength-of-weak-ties theory.

[32]   Abraham 1997; Abraham 2004, 136; Joannès 1989.

plenty of uncollected data about social structures surpassing the archive level. They also show that such data easily become unmanageable if the descriptive method is used. Does SNA make it easier?

Visualization as research tool

Existing SNA software can be used to detect and display ties between persons. This makes the description of interactions less cumbersome and more attractive, while offering at the same time a practical research tool. Before illustrating this point, a few words have to be said about how to prepare (cuneiform) data for this kind of application, taking UCINet as an example.[33] The first step is to assign unique numbers to unique historical persons. Babylonian names are too long and the software too sensitive for spelling variations. Once the numbers are assigned, the information about relations must be prepared. This takes the form of a matrix, either square or rectangular.[34] A square matrix is used to enter information about actor-actor relations. The rows and columns will contain the same set of actors, and at their intersections the existence of a tie ("1") or not ("0") will be marked. Such matrices are also called "adjacency" or "co-occurrence matrices" because they tell us which actors have direct links and are thus adjacent to one another. A rectangular matrix records relations between different elements; in our case this will be actors and texts. At the intersections of rows (actors) and columns (texts), a "1" will tell you that that person occurs in that text, a "0" that he does not. Such matrices are also called "incidence matrices" because they tell us which persons were present at the same occasions. From such matrices information about actor-actor relations can be derived (who was present on the same occasion?) as well as information about connected texts (which occasions had the same participants?).

The data used in my example are taken from Kathleen Abraham's study of the late Egibi archive (Abraham 2004, 106f.). Arguing that Marduk-nāṣir-apli//Egibi's transactions involving boats and the state were conducted in a closed group of acquaintances (p. 106 n. 429), the author presented a four-page table listing the actors (numbered 1 to 27) and the texts in which they appear (pp. 106–109). This dataset can be converted into an incidence matrix (with UCINet, for example), by first entering them into a two-column dl file, the first column for the actor, the second for the text in which he is attested, e.g.

dl nr=27 nc=28 format=nodelist2
row labels embedded

---

[33]   UCINet is an older software program for social network analysis, that was developed by the University of Irvine, California, and is still widely used by historians because of its user-friendliness; for an introduction to UCINet and the visualization program that comes with it (Netdraw), see Huisman and van Duijn 2005.

[34]   Matrix formats and their uses are explained clearly by Scott 2000, 38ff.

column labels embedded
data:

1	BM32883
1	Dar215
2	TCL13196
2	BM31891
2	BM31347
2	BM32873
3	BM31572
3	BM31690

(etc.)

UCINet uses these data to generate an incidence matrix, recording who occurs in which text. From that matrix, an actor-by-actor and a text-by-text matrix can be derived. The text-by-text matrix looks like this (Fig. 10.1):

```
                             1 1 1 1 1 1 1 1 1 1 2 2 2 2 2 2 2 2
               |   1 2 3 4 5 6 7 8 9 0 1 2 3 4 5 6 7 8 9 0 1 2 3 4 5 6 7
                   B B B B B B B B B B B B B B B B B B B B B B D D D O T
                   - - - - - - - - - - - - - - - - - - - - - - - - - - -
    1   BM30256    1 1 1 1 0 0 0 0 1 0 0 0 0 0 0 0 0 0 0 1 0 0 0 0 0 0 0
    2   BM30270    1 4 1 4 0 0 0 0 1 0 0 0 0 0 0 0 0 0 0 1 0 0 0 0 0 0 0
    3   BM30370    1 1 3 1 0 0 0 0 3 0 0 0 0 1 1 0 0 1 0 1 0 0 0 0 0 1 1
    4   BM30490    1 4 1 5 0 0 0 0 1 0 0 0 0 0 0 0 0 0 0 1 0 0 0 0 0 0 0
    5   BM30639    0 0 0 0 2 0 0 0 0 0 2 0 0 0 0 0 0 0 0 0 0 0 0 0 0 0 0
    6   BM30747    0 0 0 0 0 1 0 0 0 0 0 0 0 0 0 0 0 0 0 0 0 0 1 0 0 0
    7   BM30764    0 0 0 0 0 0 3 0 0 1 1 0 2 0 2 0 0 0 1 0 0 0 0 0 0 0
    8   BM30799    0 0 0 0 0 0 0 1 0 0 0 0 0 0 0 0 0 0 0 0 0 0 1 0 0 0
    9   BM30961    1 1 3 1 0 0 0 0 3 0 0 0 0 1 1 0 0 1 0 1 0 0 0 0 0 1 1
   10   BM31347    0 0 0 0 0 0 1 0 0 3 0 0 0 0 1 1 0 0 0 0 0 0 0 0 0 1
   11   BM31393    0 0 0 0 2 0 1 0 0 0 4 0 1 0 1 0 0 0 1 1 0 0 0 0 0 0
   12   BM31554    0 0 0 0 0 0 0 0 0 0 0 1 0 0 0 0 0 0 0 0 0 0 0 0 0 0
   13   BM31572    0 0 0 0 0 0 2 0 0 0 1 0 4 1 2 0 0 0 3 0 0 0 0 0 0 0
   14   BM31690    0 0 0 0 0 0 0 0 0 0 0 0 1 1 0 0 0 0 1 0 0 0 0 0 0 0
   15   BM31786    0 0 1 0 0 0 2 0 1 0 1 0 2 0 3 0 0 0 1 0 1 0 0 0 1 1
   16   BM31891    0 0 1 0 0 0 0 0 1 1 0 0 0 0 3 2 0 0 0 0 0 0 0 0 0 1
   17   BM32873    0 0 0 0 0 0 0 0 0 1 0 0 0 0 2 2 0 0 0 0 0 0 0 0 0 1
   18   BM32883    0 0 0 0 0 0 0 0 0 0 0 0 0 0 0 0 2 0 0 0 0 1 1 0 0
   19   BM32891    1 1 1 1 0 0 1 0 1 0 1 0 3 1 1 0 0 0 4 0 0 0 0 0 0 0
   20   BM39639    0 0 0 0 0 0 0 0 0 0 1 0 0 0 0 0 0 0 0 1 0 0 0 0 0 0
   21   BM41443    0 0 1 0 0 0 0 0 1 0 0 0 0 0 1 0 0 0 0 0 1 0 0 0 1 1
   22   BRM181     0 0 0 0 0 0 0 0 0 0 0 0 0 0 0 0 0 0 0 0 2 0 0 0 0 0
   23   Dar158     0 0 0 0 0 0 0 1 0 0 0 0 0 0 0 0 0 0 0 0 0 0 1 0 0 0
   24   Dar215     0 0 0 0 0 1 0 0 0 0 0 0 0 0 0 0 1 0 0 0 0 2 0 0 0
   25   Dar268     0 0 0 0 0 0 0 0 0 0 0 0 0 0 0 0 1 0 0 0 0 0 3 0 0
   26 OECT10234    0 0 1 0 0 0 0 0 1 0 0 0 0 0 1 0 0 0 0 1 0 0 0 0 1 1
   27  TCL13196    0 0 1 0 0 0 0 0 1 1 0 0 0 1 1 1 0 0 0 1 0 0 0 0 1 2
```

Fig. 10.1 Text-by-text matrix of Marduk-nāṣir-apli's boat file.

How to read this matrix? The first row shows the connections between BM 30256 and the other texts in the sample. The connections are made by one person only (first cell). That one person occurs, in addition to BM 30256 itself, also in BM 30270, BM 30370, BM 30490, BM 30961 and BM 32891. The identity of the connecting person cannot be read from this matrix. For this we must return to the dl file, or consult the actor-by-actor matrix (Fig. 10.2). The connecting person is number "4", who has received the internal number 22 of the matrix. At the intersection of row 22 and column 22 we find the total number of occurrences of person "4" in our sample: 6 times. In these 6 texts, he occurs twice with person 14, twice with person 23, once with persons 25, 27 and 3, twice with 5, once with 7 and twice with 8 and 9. In total, he is connected to 9 persons of the sample.

One gets the impression that person 4 must be a central person in the network, because he is connected to 9 out of 26 persons and occurs in 6 out of 28 texts. The advantage of using network software is that intuitions can be confirmed or refuted.

```
                                   1 1 1 1 1 1 1 1 1 2 2 2 2 2 2 2
                       1 2 3 4 5 6 7 8 9 0 1 2 3 4 5 6 7 8 9 0 1 2 3 4 5 6 7
                       1 1 1 1 1 1 1 1 1 1 2 2 2 2 2 2 2 2 2 3 4 5 6 7 8 9
                       - - - - - - - - - - - - - - - - - - - - - - - - - - -
   1   1   2 0 0 0 1 0 0 0 0 0 0 0 0 0 0 0 0 1 0 0 0 0 0 0 0 0 0
   2  10   0 2 0 0 0 0 0 0 0 1 0 0 0 0 1 0 0 0 0 1 0 0 0 0 0 0 0
   3  11   0 0 3 0 0 0 1 0 0 0 0 0 0 0 1 0 1 0 3 1 0 0 0 0 0 0 0
   4  12   0 0 0 1 1 0 0 0 0 0 1 0 0 0 0 0 0 0 0 0 0 0 0 0 0 0 0
   5  13   1 0 0 1 2 0 0 0 0 0 0 0 1 0 0 0 0 0 0 0 0 0 0 0 0 0 0
   6  14   0 0 0 0 0 3 0 0 0 0 0 1 0 0 0 2 0 0 1 0 0 2 0 0 0 0 0
   7  15   0 0 1 0 0 0 2 0 1 0 0 1 0 0 0 0 0 0 1 0 0 0 0 0 0 0 0
   8  16   0 0 0 0 0 0 0 1 0 0 0 0 0 0 0 0 0 0 0 0 0 0 0 0 0 0 0
   9  17   0 0 0 0 0 0 1 0 1 0 0 1 0 0 0 0 0 0 0 0 0 0 0 0 0 0 0
  10  18   0 1 0 0 0 0 0 0 0 2 0 0 0 0 2 0 0 0 0 1 0 0 0 0 0 0 0
  11  19   0 0 0 0 0 0 0 0 0 0 1 0 0 1 0 0 0 0 0 0 0 0 0 0 0 0 0
  12   2   0 0 0 0 0 1 1 0 1 0 0 4 0 0 0 1 0 0 2 0 0 0 0 0 0 0 0
  13  20   0 0 0 1 1 0 0 0 0 0 0 0 1 0 0 0 0 0 0 0 0 0 0 0 0 0 0
  14  21   0 0 0 0 0 0 0 0 0 0 1 0 0 1 0 0 0 0 0 0 0 0 0 0 0 0 0
  15  22   0 1 0 0 0 0 0 0 0 2 0 0 0 0 2 0 0 0 0 1 0 0 0 0 0 0 0
  16  23   0 0 1 0 0 2 0 0 0 0 0 1 0 0 6 0 0 0 1 0 2 0 0 0 0 0 0
  17  24   1 0 0 0 0 0 0 0 0 0 0 0 0 0 0 0 2 0 0 0 0 0 0 0 0 0 0
  18  25   0 0 1 0 0 0 0 0 0 0 0 0 0 0 0 0 0 2 0 2 2 1 0 0 0 0 0
  19  26   0 0 0 0 0 1 0 0 0 0 0 2 0 0 0 0 0 0 2 0 0 0 0 0 0 0 0
  20  27   0 1 3 0 0 0 1 0 0 1 0 0 0 0 1 1 0 2 0 5 2 1 0 0 0 0 0
  21   3   0 0 1 0 0 0 0 0 0 0 0 0 0 0 0 0 0 2 0 2 3 1 0 0 0 0 0
  22   4   0 0 0 0 0 2 0 0 0 0 0 0 0 0 0 2 0 1 0 1 1 6 2 0 1 2 2
  23   5   0 0 0 0 0 0 0 0 0 0 0 0 0 0 0 0 0 0 0 0 0 2 2 0 1 2 2
  24   6   0 0 0 0 0 0 0 0 0 0 0 0 0 0 0 0 0 0 0 0 0 0 0 2 0 0 0
  25   7   0 0 0 0 0 0 0 0 0 0 0 0 0 0 0 0 0 0 0 0 0 1 1 0 1 1 1
  26   8   0 0 0 0 0 0 0 0 0 0 0 0 0 0 0 0 0 0 0 0 0 2 2 0 1 2 2
  27   9   0 0 0 0 0 0 0 0 0 0 0 0 0 0 0 0 0 0 0 0 0 2 2 0 1 2 2
```

Fig. 10.2 Actor-by-actor matrix of Marduk-nāṣir-apli's boat file.

When we feed the actor-by-actor matrix into Netdraw, we get the following result (Fig. 10.3). Actor 4 is indeed a central person. But surprisingly, there is not a single network, but three unconnected ones. Moreover, there are 2 isolated actors who have ties with nobody else in the sample. This means that Marduk-nāṣir-apli's boat texts were not drafted a 'closed circle of acquaintances', pace Abraham. The software enables us to identify connections more quickly and securely than by traditional means of presentation.

This example is a most basic application of SNA. It simply tells us which persons co-occur and are therefore connected. It does not tell us anything about the type of relationship, or the direction of the tie; it only has binary measures of relationships. In fact, it is a personal name index translated into a network. Such networks create a lot of white noise; for instance, one text with 7 persons (i.e. a creditor, debtor, surety, three witnesses and the scribe) will yield a perfect clique of 7 members connected by 21 ties. Such cliques are a by-product of our textual sources, they do not reflect cliques in society. A better way to build up a network is from a dl file with actor-by-actor relations. In that case you can add information about the property of the tie (i.e. kin, credit, property etc.). This will enable much more detailed research (i.e. credit operations between kin), but the preparation of the dataset will also be more time-consuming because information about the nature of such actor-actor ties can probably not be generated automatically by the prosopographical database that you are using.

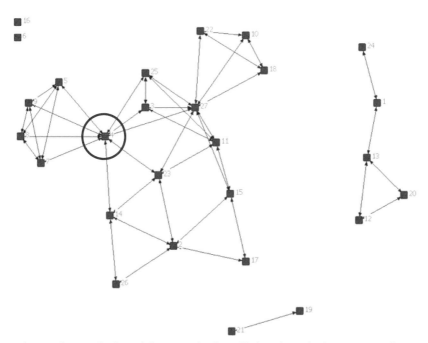

Fig. 10.3 The social network of Marduk-nāṣir-apli's boat file based on Abraham 2004, 106ff; person 4 is encircled. Created with Netdraw.

Things get more complicated if information about actor attributes (i.e. person "100" is a priest, a state official, an inhabitant of Sippar, a house owner, of Judean descent etc.) is added; such attributes are crucial for the correct interpretation of the relationships revealed and the ancient society from which such ties emerged.

Measuring relational data

The possibility of quantifying (inter)actions opens up promising avenues of research into aspects of Babylonian society that are difficult to access at the present moment. I will illustrate this by means of two examples, one relating to the concept of network *density*, the other to network *position*. As explained above, based on attributional data, two groups seem to be represented in the society that produced the majority of the Neo-Babylonian private archives preserved today. The first is characterised by an entrepreneurial profile, the second by a priestly (i.e. prebendary) profile. A number of economic activities can be connected to the first group that are (mostly) absent in members of the second. It is this latter group of prebend-owning priests which carried Babylonian culture into the Persian, Seleucid and Parthian age, making the temples, with their cults, their personnel, and their libraries, into the last bastions of cuneiform heritage. It would be an interesting test case to see whether this 'conservative' mentality somehow translated into the affiliation networks of these people, as SNA establishes a link between the density of a network and the inward-looking attitude of the group members. I have conducted this test by measuring the density of the networks of two members of either group: Bēl-rēmanni, a priest at the local temple of Sippar in the early Persian period, and Marduk-rēmanni, a man from the same town and age who combined a priestly profile with more entrepreneurial business interests.[35] Based on traditional prosopographical data collected from both men's archives, I have calculated the density measures for each of their networks. This measure tells us how many of all possible ties in each of these men's networks were actually realized and how often they were activated. The results are ambivalent: with a measure of 0.024, Bēl-rēmanni's network was more dense than Marduk-rēmanni's with 0.014, but the difference is extremely minimal. There are other indications, however, that Bēl-rēmanni interacted differently with his environment than Marduk-rēmanni did. For instance, while both men met most of their contacts only once, Bēl-rēmanni did so less often than Marduk-rēmanni (74%, as opposed to 84%, of his contacts are unique attestations). Moreover, Bēl-rēmanni established strong and long-lasting relationships with 4% of his contacts, whereas Marduk-rēmanni did so with only 2% of his contacts. Although

---

[35] He was the father of the groom in the second case of intercity marriage discussed above; he belongs to the minority of attested persons who combine characteristics from both groups in their business profiles. See Jursa 1999 for the archive of Bēl-rēmanni and Waerzeggers 2001 for the archive of Marduk-rēmanni. Note that there are some problems involved in comparing the density of networks of unequal size (Scott 2000, 63ff.). One of the reasons why the archives of Bēl-rēmanni and Marduk-rēmanni are chosen as a test case in this article is their roughly equal size.

more research needs to be done on Babylonian ego-networks in order to understand the significance of these figures, they do suggest that some men's networks were more diverse and open than others, and in this case at least, this is correlated to exhibiting a priestly, as opposed to a non-priestly, profile.

The case of Marduk-rēmanni allows us to explore another network property as a category of analysis in cuneiform studies: network position. The most remarkable aspect of Marduk-rēmanni's life is that he rose quickly in the temple community of Sippar, collecting the most impressive prebendary portfolio assembled by one man that we know of, and entering the closed social circle of college scribes of Ebabbar as the only non-member of the Šangû-Ištar-Bābili family in 56 years.[36] Marduk-rēmanni was one of few people from Sippar who was not only a prebend owner at the local temple, but who also entertained regular contacts with persons who lived in the capital and belonged to the personal network of the king.[37] In SNA jargon, one could say that he enjoyed a powerful position, commanding two networks that had little occasion to communicate with each other except through him. As a bridge, he owned substantial social capital; an asset that might have helped him to rise quickly in Sippar's temple community, while Bēl-rēmanni who lacked such connections led a socially stagnant life.

Problems

As I have shown in the previous pages, the application of SNA to cuneiform data is certainly promising, but some problems may be expected. These problems have to do with large data sets and with missing data. First, identifying individuals is fairly easy if we limit ourselves to one archive, but if we want to reconstruct as many snapshots of interregional networks as possible, it will take a long time before we can even dream of turning to the network software. First there needs to be a central database of all Neo-Babylonian texts. At present, this situation is utopian. Then, unique numbers must be given to unique persons. Countless problems will crop up: the identity of homonymous persons, the identity of persons with two names or with a long and short name, the identity of persons mentioned without a family name or father's name, missing links in genealogical trees. Once all actors have been identified, the relational data must be gathered. As argued in the previous section, it is best not to work solely from actor-by-text matrices, even though these are the easiest to generate from traditional prosopographical data. In addition to the problems involved with collecting and handling the relational data that we *do* have, there will also be problems with the data that we *do not* have. This piece of advice of a network specialist to historians is worrying:

"(...) one should (...) try to get data for all pairs of actors, or reach as close to this goal as possible. Missing data can be more problematic for network analysis than for

---

[36] Bongenaar 1997, 58.

[37] Some of the connections between Marduk-rēmanni and the Egibis were discussed above.

attribute analysis. Suppose, for example, that you are studying two factions and your data are 90 procent complete. With that much of the attribute data, you can probably do a good job of comparing the wealth, status, and so on of members of the two groups. But even 90 procent of the network data may lead to a misleading result if the missing ties are structurally crucial ones, such as ties between the two factions." (Erickson 1997)

As our data are always incomplete, does this mean that SNA is always out of reach for us? Certainly not, it means that we have to be careful in drawing conclusions from network structures documented by the texts that we happen to have. It is not different with any other approach to historical data.

Prospects

The type of relational data available in cuneiform texts will allow us to apply both SNA approaches (egocentric and whole network). Egocentric networks are the most obvious choice, because one can stay within archive boundaries. Such studies would focus on the archive's *ego*, his ties to other actors and the ties among these actors. Network software could help us to describe the network properties and add them to our checklists of attributes. As explained above, it would be useful to compare the density of the networks of certain population groups, as it could tell us something about their in- or outward-looking mentality (i.e. priests vs. entrepreneurs). Moreover, visualization tools help to uncover links between certain participants in the network that would otherwise be difficult to see. A text-by-text network would also be helpful in the early stages of research, because it can point out quickly which text clusters are connected by the same persons. In short, SNA can be an important support tool for Assyriologists; it will also help to tackle research questions that cannot be answered with standard methods.

Most challenging and most rewarding are whole networks. We can never hope to get information on all elements in a network, but by stacking up interconnecting egocentric networks we might come a step closer to this ideal. The best prospects are for the urban elites of certain well-documented cities (in particular, Sippar, Babylon, Borsippa, and Uruk). Another avenue of research would be a systematic investigation of intercity relations and geographically spread-out networks. In order to get there, we will first need to have a central database of all Neo-Babylonian texts, so that we can identify the persons whose ties form the paths of such interregional structures. Once this is done, there are potentially many interesting questions to ask and answer, for example: were certain areas of Babylonia more closely connected than others? who supplied those links and through which kind of activity? what role did kinship patterns play in this respect? did such social structures correspond to political fractures (i.e. during the revolts against Xerxes)? etc.

In the end it is perhaps not always desirable or feasible to go through the demanding process of data preparation for network software. The appendix contains many examples of fresh approaches to old data that were merely *inspired* by the network approach and the particular perspective on society that it offers, without making use of the software and complicated mathematical calculations. As Christine Carpenter remarked with regard to the use of network analysis in medieval studies: "Where the theory of networks can help is in focusing the questions to be asked and the means of asking" (Carpenter 1994, 366). The recently renewed interest in prosopographical studies among Assyriologists[38] will certainly benefit from the perspectives and methods offered by SNA, taking the study of Babylonian society to its next level of sophistication.

Note

This article reflects the state of scholarship at the time of its submission in September 2009; it has not been possible to incorporate references to the more recent literature concerning SNA.

REFERENCES

Abraham, K. (1997) TCL 13 193: Šušan and Bāṣ. *Nouvelles Assyriologiques Brèves et Utilitaires* 1997/53.

Abraham, K. (2004) *Business and Politics under the Persian Empire. The Financial Dealings of Marduk-nāṣir-apli of the House of Egibi (521-487 B.C.E.)*. Bethesda, MD: CDL Press.

Alexander, M. C. and Danowski, J. A. (1990) Analysis of an Ancient Network: Personal Communication and the Study of Social Structure in a Past Society. *Social Networks* 12, 313–335.

Baker, H. D. (ed.) (2000–2011) *The Prosopography of the Neo-Assyrian Empire*, 2/I: Ḫ–K (2000); 2/II: L–N (2001); 3/I: P–Ṣ (2002); 3/II: Š–Z (2011). Helsinki: The Neo-Assyrian Text Corpus Project.

Baker, H. D. (2004) *The Archive of the Nappāḫu Family* (Archiv für Orientforschung Beiheft 30). Vienna: Institut für Orientalistik der Universität Wien.

Barkey, K and Van Rossem, R. (1997) Networks of Contention: Villages and Regional Structure in the Seventeenth-Century Ottoman Empire. *American Journal of Sociology* 102, 1345–1382.

Bearman, P., Moody, J. and Faris, R. (2003) Networks and History. *Complexity* 8, 61–71.

Beaulieu, P.-A. (2003) *The Pantheon of Uruk during the Neo-Babylonian Period* (Cuneiform Monographs 23). Leiden: Brill/Styx.

Boissevain, J. and Mitchell, J. C. (1973) *Network Analysis. Studies in Human Interaction*. The Hague: Mouton.

Bongenaar, A. C. V. M. (1997) *The Neo-Babylonian Ebabbar Temple at Sippar: Its Administration and Its Prosopography* (PIHANS 80). Istanbul: Nederlands Historisch-Archaeologisch Instituut te Istanbul.

Boulet, R. *et al.* (2008) Batch kernel SOM and related Laplacian methods for social network analysis. *Neurocomputing* 71, 1257–1273.

Breiger, R. L. (2004) The Analysis of Social Networks. In M. Hardy and A. Bryman (eds), *Handbook of Data Analysis*, 505–526. London: SAGE.

Burt, R. S. (1980) Models of Network Structure. *Annual Review of Sociology* 6, 79–141.

---

[38] E.g. *The Prosopography of the Neo-Assyrian Empire* (Radner ed. 1998–1999; Baker ed. 2000–2011); Hellenistic Babylonia Texts Images and Names (http://cdl.museum.upenn.edu/hbtin/).

Carpenter, C. (1994) Gentry and Community in Medieval England. *Journal of British Studies* 33, 340–380.

Carrington, P. J., Scott, J. and Wasserman, S. (2005) *Models and Methods in Social Network Analysis* (Structural Analysis in the Social Sciences 27). Cambridge: Cambridge University Press.

van Driel, G. (1986) Neo-Babylonian Texts from the Louvre. *Bibliotheca Orientalis* 43, 5–20.

van Driel, G. (1992) Neo-Babylonian Texts from Borsippa. *Bibliotheca Orientalis* 49, 28–50.

van Driel, G. (1998) Care of the Elderly: The Neo-Babylonian Period. In M. Stol and S. P. Vleeming (eds), *The Care of the Elderly in the Ancient Near East*, 161–197. Leiden: Brill.

Emirbayer, M and Goodwin, J. (1994) Network Analysis, Culture, and the Problem of Agency. *American Journal of Sociology* 99, 1411–1454.

Emirbayer, M and Goodwin, J. (1997) Manifesto for a Relational Sociology. *American Journal of Sociology* 103, 281–317.

Erickson, B. H. (1997) Social Networks and History. *Historical Methods* 30, 149–157.

Ericsson, T. (2006) Integration and social networks: Lutherans in revolutionary Paris, 1789–1797. *History of the Family* 11, 161–170.

Gehlken, E. (1990) *Uruk. Spätbabylonische Wirtschaftstexte aus dem Eanna-Archiv. Teil I. Texte verschiedenen Inhalts* (Ausgrabungen aus Uruk-Warka, Endberichte 5). Mainz: Verlag Philipp von Zabern.

Gehlken, E. (1996) *Uruk. Spätbabylonische Wirtschaftstexte aus dem Eanna-Archiv. Teil II. Texte verschiedenen Inhalts* (Ausgrabungen aus Uruk-Warka, Endberichte 11). Mainz: Verlag Philipp von Zabern.

George, A. R. (1992) *Babylonian Topographical Texts* (Orientalia Lovaniensia Analecta 40). Leuven: Peeters.

Gould, R. V. (1991) Multiple Networks and Mobilization in the Paris Commune, 1871. *American Sociological Review* 56, 716–729.

Gould, R. V. (1996) Patron-Client Ties, State Centralization, and the Whiskey Rebellion. *American Journal of Sociology* 102, 400–429.

Granovetter, M. S. (1973) The Strength of Weak Ties. *American Journal of Sociology* 78, 1360–1380.

Hanneman, R. A. and Riddle, M. (2005) *Introduction to Social Network Methods*. Riverside, CA: University of California, Riverside (published in digital form at http://faculty.ucr.edu/~hanneman/).

Holtz, S. E. (2009) *Neo-Babylonian Court Procedure* (Cuneiform Monographs 38). Leiden/Boston: Brill.

Huisman, M. and van Duijn, M. A. J. (2005) Software for Social Network Analysis. In: Carrington, Scott and Wasserman (eds), 270–316.

Hunger, H. (1970) Das Archiv des Nabû-ušallim. *Baghdader Mitteilungen* 5, 193–304.

Janković, B. (2004) *Vogelzucht und Vogelfang in Sippar im 1. Jahrtausend v. Chr.* (Alter Orient und Altes Testament 315). Münster: Ugarit-Verlag.

Joannès, F. (1989) *Archives de Borsippa. La famille Ea-ilûta-bâni. Étude d'un lot d'archives familiales en Babylonie du VIIIe au Ve siècle av. J.-C.* Geneva: Droz.

Jursa, M. (1995) *Die Landwirtschaft in Sippar in neubabylonischer Zeit* (Archiv für Orientforschung Beiheft 25). Wien: Institut für Orientalistik der Universität Wien.

Jursa, M. (1999) *Das Archiv des Bēl-rēmanni* (PIHANS 86). Leiden: Nederlands Historisch-Archaeologisch Instituut te Istanbul.

Jursa, M. (2005) *Neo-Babylonian Legal and Administrative Documents. Typology, Contents and Archives* (Guides to the Mesopotamian Textual Record 1). Münster: Ugarit-Verlag.

Kessler, K. (1991) *Uruk. Urkunden aus Privathäusern. Die Wohnhäuser westlich des Eanna-Tempelbereichs.*

Teil 1: Die Archive der Söhne des Bēl-ušallim, des Nabû-ušallim und des Bēl-supê-muhur (Ausgrabungen aus Uruk-Warka, Endberichte 8). Mainz: Verlag Philipp von Zabern.

Kilduff, M. and Tsai, W. (2003) *Social Networks and Organizations*. London: Brassey's.

Kleber, K. (2008) *Tempel und Palast. Die Beziehungen zwischen dem König und dem Eanna-Tempel im spätbabylonischen Uruk* (Alter Orient und Altes Testament 358). Münster: Ugarit-Verlag.

Kümmel, H. M. (1979) *Familie, Beruf und Amt im spätbabylonischen Uruk*. Berlin: Mann.

Lanz, H. (1976) *Die neubabylonischen harrânu-Geschäftsunternehmen*. Berlin: Schweitzer.

MacGinnis, J. (1995) *Letter Orders from Sippar and the Administration of the Ebabbara in the Late-Babylonian Period*. Poznań: Bonami Wydawn.

McGeough, K. M. (2007) *Exchange Relationships in Ugarit* (Ancient Near Eastern Studies Suppl. 26). Leuven: Peeters.

Mitchell, J. C. (1973) Networks, norms and institutions. In J. Boissevain and J. C. Mitchell (eds), *Network Analysis. Studies in Human Interaction*, 15–35. The Hague: Mouton.

Mitchell, J. C. (1974) Social Networks. *Annual Review of Anthropology* 3, 279–299.

Mizruchi, M. S. (1994) Social Network Analysis: Recent Achievements and Current Controversies. *Acta Sociologica* 37, 329–343.

Mullett, M. (1997) *Theophylact of Ochrid. Reading the Letters of a Byzantine Archbishop* (Birmingham Byzantine and Ottoman Monographs 2). Aldershot: Variorum.

Padgett, J. F. and Ansell, C. K. (1993) Robust Action and the Rise of the Medici, 1400–1434. *American Journal of Sociology* 98, 1259–1319.

Padgett, J. F. and MacLean, P. D. (2006) Organizational Invention and Elite Transformation: The Birth of Partnership Systems in Renaissance Florence. *American Journal of Sociology* 111, 1463–1568.

Polden, A. (2006) The social networks of the Buckinghamshire gentry in the thirteenth century. *Journal of Medieval History* 32, 371–394.

Radner, K. (ed.) (1998–1999) *The Prosopography of the Neo-Assyrian Empire*, 1/I: A (1998); 1/II: B–G (1999). Helsinki: The Neo-Assyrian Text Corpus Project.

Rosenthal, N., Fingrudt, M., Ethier, M., Karant, R. and McDonald, D. (1985) Social Movements and Network Analysis: A Case Study of Nineteenth-Century Women's Reform in New York State. *American Journal of Sociology* 90, 1022–1054.

Roth, M. T. (1989) The material composition of the Neo-Babylonian Dowry. *Archiv für Orientforschung* 36/37, 1–55.

Ruffini, G. R. (2008) *Social Networks in Byzantine Egypt*. Cambridge: Cambridge University Press.

Rutman, D. B. and Rutman, A. H. (1984) *A Place in Time: Middlesex County, Virginia 1650–1750*. New York: Norton.

Scott, J. (2000) *Social Network Analysis. A Handbook*. London: SAGE.

Scott, J. (2001) *Power*. Cambridge: Polity Press.

Shaw, D. G. (2005) Social networks and the foundations of oligarchy in medieval towns. *Urban History* 32, 200–222.

Smith, R. M. (1979) Kin and Neighbours in a Thirteenth-Century Suffolk Community. *Journal of Family History* 4, 219–256.

Waerzeggers, C. (2001) *Het archief van Marduk-rēmanni. Studie van de familie Ṣāhit-ginê in Nieuwbabylonisch Sippar (548-484 v. Chr.)*. PhD thesis, University of Ghent.

Waerzeggers, C. (2003/4) The Babylonian Revolts Against Xerxes and the 'End of Archives'. *Archiv für Orientforschung* 50, 150–173.

Wasserman, S. and Faust, K. (1994) *Social Network Analysis. Methods and Applications* (Structural Analysis in the Social Sciences 8). Cambridge: Cambridge University Press.

Wellman, B. (2007) The network is personal: Introduction to a special issue of Social Networks. *Social Networks* 29, 349–356.

Wellman, B. and Berkowitz, S. D. (1988) *Social Structures. A Network Approach* (Structural Analysis in the Social Sciences 2). Cambridge: Cambridge University Press.

Wellman, B. and Wetherell, C. (1996) Social Network Analysis of Historical Communities: Some Questions from the Present for the Past. *History of the Family* 1, 97–121.

Wetherell, C. (1989) Network Analysis Comes of Age. *Journal of Interdisciplinary History* 19, 645–651.

Wetherell, C. (1998) Historical Social Network Analysis. *International Review of Social History* 43, 125–144.

White, L. M. (1991) Finding the Ties that Bind: Issues from Social Description. *Semeia* 56, 3–22.

Wunsch, C. (1993) *Die Urkunden des babylonischen Geschäftsmannes Iddin-Marduk. Zum Handel mit Naturalien im 6. Jahrhundert v. Chr.*, 2 vols. (Cuneiform Monographs 3a–b). Groningen: Styx Publications.

Wunsch, C. (2000) *Das Egibi-Archiv, I. Die Felder und Gärten*, 2 vols. (Cuneiform Monographs 20A–B). Groningen: Styx Publications.

Zawadzki, S. (2006) *Garments of the Gods. Studies on the Textile Industry and the Pantheon of Sippar according to the Texts from the Ebabbar Archive* (Orbis Biblicus et Orientalis 218). Fribourg: Academic Press.

APPENDIX[39]

Table 10.1 (see next three pages)

---

[39] This appendix is intended as an addition to the section "Historical social network analysis" above.

Table 10.1 Some examples of historical social network analysis.

Author(s)	Time + Place	Source type	social group studied	NW type[1]	NW information gathered in study	Aim of study
Smith 1979	Medieval England (c. 1260–1293)	court records	villagers and landholders	WN	After a statistical study of the number of kinship ties in 13,592 recorded contacts among villagers and landholders, the author proceeds to the reconstruction of the egocentric networks of 425 landlords with regard to kinship, propinquity and economic ties	The author uses a statistical and network-approach to measure the relative importance of kinship and neighbourhood ties among the villages of a Suffolk manor
Polden 2006	Medieval England (c. 1180–1320)	charters	gentry	WN	contacts of 20 small and middling knightly families in Buckinghamshire (legal, marriage, monastic patronage, feudal ties, neighbourhood, credit operations)	The horizons of the families studied were fairly localized but not entirely so; certain types of interaction took place outside the county, notably marriage negotiation by wealthy families
Shaw 2005	Medieval England (c. 1377–1429)	court records	burgesses	WN	contacts between 98 people in a 50-yr timespan during arbitration	The urban oligarchs interacted in a tight and dense social web.
Gould 1996	18th C. United States	Pennsylvania state government records	county elites	WN	Gould measures the strong ties between 44 elite persons of 3 Pennsylvanian counties based on the existence or absence of surety bonds between them	Elite support or dismissal of the Whiskey Rebellion (a popular movement against a new federal tax in 1794) was determined by a person's position in the larger network of patronage relations that tied the regional elites together

[1] NW = network; WN = whole network; PN = egocentric or personal network.

Author(s)	Time + Place	Source type	social group studied	NW type[1]	NW information gathered in study	Aim of study
Rutman & Rutman 1984	Early modern America (1650–1750)	tax, court and church records, registers of marriages, births and deaths	inhabitants of Middlesex county, Virginia	WN	contacts between 12,000 persons who resided in Middlesex county between 1650 and 1750	Kinship and friendship ties overlapped less strongly after more people settled the county; there was a noticeable difference between the county's elite and commoners as to the balance between local and provincial ties in their networks
Ericsson 2006	revolutionary Paris (c. 1789–1797)	wedding registers	Lutheran immigrants	WN	the networks of immigrant Lutherans in revolutionary Paris are studied on the basis of witness-appearance in wedding registers	Occupation, geographical origin and residential proximity were the most important ties in the networks of Lutherans who immigrated to Paris
Padgett & McLean 2006	Renaissance Florence (14th–15th C.)	tax censuses, wedding registers, annual censuses of the banking guild, business censuses, account books, chronicles, letters, diaries	Florentine elites	WN	Analysis of partnership networks among the Florentine elites in combination with marriage ties and other social structures	The authors show that the birth of financial capitalism in Renaissance Florence was partly rooted in elite responses to class revolt in the 14th century.

Author(s)	Time + Place	Source type	social group studied	NW type[1]	NW information gathered in study	Aim of study
Barkey & Van Rossem 1997	Ottoman Anatolia (mid-17th C.)	190 court cases in three court registers	peasants of the Manisa region (near Izmir)	WN	1,121 ties of kinship, friendship, acquaintanceship, trade and patronage between peasants from the villages around Manisa; these ties were coded as to their value (cooperative, conflicting, neutral) and set against the geographical pattern of the villages in order to evaluate the social integration of the countryside	Regional structure is an important factor in explaining contention among villagers.
White 1991	Rome (4th C.)	various	Christian and pagan Roman aristocracy	PN	kinship, marriage, high imperial office, membership of priestly colleges and neighborhood connections of Aurelius Symmachus' faction in pagan vs. Christian debates in 382–382 CE	Existing social networks influenced the process of diffusion of Christianity, and the revival of paganism, among the 4th Century CE Roman aristocracy.
Alexander & Danowski 1990	Rome (1st C. BCE)	280 letters written by Cicero	Cicero's corresponden ts	PN	1,914 contacts between 524 individuals; neither direction nor content of contact was taken into consideration, but the individuals were ranked in a power structure of 7 levels	the authors measure the level of social interaction between senators and knights in Cicero's letters

The Volatility of Prices of Barley and Dates in Babylon in the Third and Second Centuries BC[1]

R. J. van der Spek

1. THE DATA: PROBLEMS OF METROLOGY AND METHODOLOGY IN PRESENTING AND COMPARING PRICES

1.1. The sources

First millennium Babylonia has produced a dataset of prices which has no equivalent in the ancient world. In the Neo-Babylonian (612–539 BC) and Achaemenid (539–331 BC) periods these prices are recorded in all kinds of transaction such as sale contracts, loans and administrative documents. Another peculiar dataset is contained in the Astronomical Diaries from Babylon (Sachs and Hunger 1988; 1989; 1996; abbreviated AD I, II and III). This dataset is especially relevant for the Hellenistic period (from 331 BC to 30 BC) as the data from other sources are very scarce. These astronomical diaries are a dataset for research in the field of divination, a type of scholarship for which Babylonia was well known (praised as well as condemned) in antiquity. These diaries contained a notation of celestial phenomena followed (to an increasing degree over time) by information on other ominous events such as monstrous births, wind direction, the weather, and the level of the Euphrates, but also more mundane occurrences such as deeds of kings, important events in Babylon and the level of the prices of six commodities: barley, dates, cuscuta, watercress, sesame and wool. The basic premise

---

[1] This paper is part of the project 'On the efficiency of markets for agricultural products in pre-industrial societies: The case of Babylonia c. 400–c. 60 BC,' funded by the Netherlands Organization for Scientific Research (NWO); for the results see van der Spek, van Leeuwen and van Zanden 2014. Section 5 was written by Bas van Leeuwen, postdoctoral researcher in the team.

of this scholarship of divination is that the gods give information concerning the fickle future via capricious movements of oil on water, the flight of birds, the wind, the movements of the planets, the occurrence of eclipses of sun and moon, the form of the livers of sacrificial animals. The birth of exceptional creatures (animals or people with deviant forms), the entrance of (strange) animals into the city or temple, sudden collapses of temple doors, and weather phenomena could all contain information concerning the future. As the Babylonians believed that all these phenomena were part of a coherent whole, developments in one field were related to changes in other phenomena. The basic purpose of Babylonian scholarship was to find out regularities in these relations. In one field they were very successful: after centuries of scientific research the Babylonian astronomers were able to predict the constellation of the planets and the stars, and lunar and solar eclipses. It has been argued that by these very successes the study of the celestial phenomena made these phenomena too regular and predictable to be acceptable as a means of conveying divine messages concerning the future. This may be a reasonable way of thinking (the role of the gods would be minimised), but it did not deter the astronomers/astrologers from continuing with their work, nor does it deter astrologers nowadays. Conversely, it may have given the scholars something to go on. If there is regularity in celestial phenomena, one might one day also find regularities in other phenomena which seem irregular but which may not be so, such as the death of kings, the level of the Euphrates and the volatility of prices. It would give them a real grip on the future. The study of omens and of earthly and heavenly phenomena in a coordinated approach would help them since they believed that the signs in heaven concur with the signs on earth.[2]

The very fact that prices are recorded in the astronomical diaries shows they were regarded as volatile and unpredictable. It would be senseless to record these prices if they were set by the king. Prices were, in principle, like the whims of the weather, but (this was to be researched) some correlation with other events could be detected and hence convey information on the future. For us it is strange to see the results of this science in one document: "if the sun is surrounded by a halo, it will rain the next day" (which is a correct observation) and "if the sun is eclipsed on the western part on day x of month y, the king of Westland will die" (for which I see no scientific ground). From other sources we know that the Babylonians were aware of the fact that prices are higher before harvest than after harvest and that warfare could increase prices. But other factors were at stake as well in their minds, such as a relationship to the constellation of the stars.

One might question the reliability of the prices, and this has been done, but from the very fact that the information in the diaries that we can check (e.g. on the orbit of the planets and the death of kings) is correct, we may assume that the information on the prices is also basically correct. We may assume a margin of error. It was the method of the astronomers to go into the streets of Babylon and see what they could

---

[2] The best study on Mesopotamian scholarship in this field is Rochberg 2004.

buy for one shekel of silver. Of course they will not have checked all shops and computed an average and hence it occasionally occurs that we have different prices from different tablets, but the differences are not significant.

Recently a new corpus of texts has been published: documents containing just series of prices, hence without astronomical observations or other information (Slotsky and Wallenfels 2009). The compilers of these lists seem to have had a real scientific interest in the development of prices. One tablet (no. 7), for instance, collects the prices of dates of months VIII (harvest month) of the Seleucid years 178–185 (134–127 BC), but others try to give a complete overview of all months (no. 8) of the years SE 185–190. While the astronomical diaries give the exchange value of one shekel of silver, these texts often have two shekels as a point of reference, and in two cases even 1 mina of silver (60 shekels). Where we can compare the prices with the astronomical diaries it is striking that the prices of these price lists confirm the prices of the diaries, sometimes precisely, although sometimes one document has average prices of a month where the diary has more detailed information (beginning, middle and end of the month). As in the diaries, the price lists convey more and more detailed prices for smaller parts of the month (days or cluster of days). The price lists have enhanced our knowledge of the prices considerably.

One text is of extreme interest: text 6 r. 12′–15′. It gives two distinct exchange values of barley (for two shekels of silver) for month III 175 SEB = 27 May–25 June 137 BC: 2 *pan* 2 *sut* (= 84 litres) in staters of Demetrius and 2 *pan* (= 72 litres) in staters of Arsaces. Wallenfels makes the interesting observation (p. 94, n. 65): "The increased purchasing power (+6%) of the Demetrius staters is almost identical to the greater average weight of silver tetradrachms minted at Seleucia on the Tigris by Demetrius II (+6.7%) over those of Mithradates." The document refers to the time shortly after the abortive attempt in 138 BC to reconquer Babylonia from the Parthians. In his short reign of a few months he apparently was able to introduce new coins, which had a higher weight than the Parthian coins. After the demise of Demetrius (he was captured), his coins apparently remained in use. We can draw some conclusions: 1. The Babylonians were well aware of the (intrinsic?) value of the coins; 2. The shekels mentioned in the astronomical diaries do not refer to the precise silver content of the coins, but to the coins as such. This may also confirm my earlier suggestion that by this time one shekel stood for two drachmas, hence two shekels for a tetradrachm: two shekels of Arsaces had a lower value than two shekels of Demetrius.

1.2. The commodities

As stated above, the diaries record the prices of six products. For comparative price research the prices of grain (barley), dates and wool are most useful. Barley and dates were the most common staples of Babylonian food consumption. We can regard Babylonia as a dual-crop economy, in which the importance of dates grew over time. It was a good alternative to grain, and so high grain prices could fall not only after the barley harvest in April/May, but also after the date harvest in October (Vargyas 2001, 97, 178–82). Dates were increasingly used as a raw material for the processing of beer. We have no prices for wine: the Babylonians hardly drank wine. Unfortunately we have no prices of meat, which must have remained a luxury product.

1.3. Problems of metrology

What is recorded in the diaries are in fact not prices, but a record of the purchasing power of one shekel of silver. The foodstuffs are quantified in measures of capacity according to the following table:

1 kor (GUR, *kurru*)	= 5 bushel = 30 seah = 180 qa = **180** litres.
1 bushel (PI, *pānu*)	= 6 seah = 36 qa = **36** litres.
1 seah (BÁN, *sūtu*)	= 6 qa = **6** litres.
1 litre (SÌLA, *qû* or *qa*)	= **1 litre** (or: 0.84 or 0.97 litre) = 2 minas of water
1 mina (MA.NA, *manû*)	= 1 pound (500 gr.)

In the tables I have converted the exchange values in litres, maintaining an equivalent of 1 *qa* as 1 litre. Wool was measured using a weight measure, the mina, being one metrical pound. I follow in this the convenient advice of Marvin Powell (1989/90). The shekel is best reckoned as 8.33 grams of silver, again in accordance with Powell.[3]

While in antiquity prices are mostly given according to measures of capacity of the commodities in question, in modern historical studies grain prices are often given in kilograms or tonnes. This presents a great problem. It is very difficult to find a reliable rate for converting litres of barley into kilograms. In this paper I have chosen the rate 1 litre of barley = 0.62 kg of barley. I assume that the prices of barley were for un-milled grain. It is difficult to know whether the barley was expected to be winnowed and cleaned of husks. In Greek sources barley prices are often given as prices of *álphita* = barley flour. When barley is milled it does not lose much weight, but it increases in volume. The volume of barley flour is 50% more than the volume of whole grain (Foxhall and Forbes 1982, 78).[4] For dates I have chosen the conversion rate of 1 litre = 0.75 kg (Jursa 1995, 150, n. 302).

1.4. Problems of methodology

Statistical analysis is useful and possible with a considerable amount of data. The number of barley prices we have is impressive, so it seems that statistical analysis is

---

[3] For further considerations concerning metrology: see the website on www.livius.org or http://www.livius.org/w/weights/weights.html and the introduction to my price tables on the website of the International Institute for Social History in Amsterdam (Internationaal Instituut voor Sociale Geschiedenis) www.iisg.nl or http://www.iisg.nl/hpw/data.php#babylon.

[4] For more information see Foxhall and Forbes 1982; Powell 1989/90; van der Spek 1998, 246–53.

possible. In fact it has been done by Alice Slotsky (1997) and Peter Temin (2002). Yet there are a number of problems to be solved. Firstly, **the number of data**. It is actually impossible to count the number of data, as can be shown by the following example. For some months we have one price for the whole month, and so we have one datum. In some instances a distinction is made between the beginning, the middle and the end of the month, hence we have three data. But we can also argue that we had three data in the first instance, in that all the prices were probably the same for the beginning, middle and end of the month. In the later diaries, however, we often have a record of the prices day by day, in two instances even prices in the morning and the afternoon. Then we have 30 or even 60 data per month. If we discard the exceptional cases of two prices per day, we might construe a dataset of 365 prices per year. It is a time-consuming task, but it can be done—in fact, this is what our research team at the VU University has done.

The problem, however, is that the dataset is incomplete. We simply do not possess all the astronomical diaries, and many are damaged at crucial places. Hence for many years we have no data at all, and for the other years we have information for only a few months. Thus it is possible to count the data as given in the diaries, but it presents a distorted picture. Instead of counting the number of prices it seems advisable to count the years for which we possess prices. For the period 299–61 BC (i.e. 239 years) we have 138 years in which at least one barley price is recorded, hence 101 are blank.[5] For dates the figures are 119 years with data, hence 120 blank.[6] Prices tended to fluctuate within one year owing to seasonal and other influences. Hence it is dangerous to compare a price from November in one year with a price from June in another year. For statistical analysis it is necessary to have an idea of average and median prices. It is, however, a dubious procedure to combine the average price of, say, four prices from month I with one price from month VI. Such an average gives a distorted picture.[7] Therefore it is advisable to try to establish the **range** within which the prices move: the highest and lowest prices in a certain period. As the highest and lowest prices may be exceptional, these may also distort the picture. To refine our picture it is then helpful also to look at the second highest and second lowest prices, provided that these prices are not from the same economic year (harvest to harvest). To get a better

---

[5] One might have a somewhat better picture if we would reduce the period from 295–74 (i.e. 222 years) which contains 137 and 117 years respectively with price information and leaves 85 and 105 respectively blank. The new pricelists have increased the number of years with price attestations by 11. For a method of coping with missing data, see Persson 1999, 114–15; Földvári and van Leeuwen 2009, and n. 5.

[6] Here the price lists provided us with 9 extra years with data.

[7] The distortion is somewhat reduced thanks to the fact that the greatest volatility exists *between* the years, not *within* one year. Furthermore, Földvári and van Leeuwen 2009, in their study of a "partial equilibrium model," found out that the data are not "missing completely at random," which means that there is a certain bias. However, the data can be qualified as "missing at random," which indicates that the bias is not important in respect to variables which are important for our study, such as famines and wars.

idea of the prosperity and price level of a certain period one may then compute the number of years in which prices stayed below a certain level that is expected to be acceptable for subsistence in relation to wages (cf. van der Spek 2005).

2. WHAT ECONOMIC HISTORY CAN WE WRITE FROM PRICES?

In this paper I shall focus on market integration. Two aspects will be considered: the volatility of the prices and the purchasing power of silver.

Volatility of prices is an indicator of market integration. When there is a scarcity of grain, prices will rise, but thanks to grain imports prices may return to a more favourable level after some time. The same is true for periods of superabundance. Prices will be low in such a case, which makes export to countries with higher prices profitable. The superabundance will diminish and prices will rise again. This process will mitigate price fluctuations. Hence a high volatility of prices is an indicator of low market integration (cf. Persson 1999 *passim*).

Mutatis mutandis the same is true as regards silver. In an integrated market situation it will be profitable to invest silver in a region where the purchasing power is high. However, owing to the import of silver the purchasing power will gradually diminish and so the market will equalise the value of silver in different regions. Hence the continuation of strongly different exchange values of silver in neighbouring regions is an indicator of low market integration.[8]

3. THE VOLATILITY OF PRICES

3.1. The volatility of barley prices in the city of Babylon, 299–61 BC

According to the Babylonian standard, 1 shekel (= 8.33 gr.) of silver was a reasonable monthly wage for which one could buy one *kor* of grain = 180 l. This amounts to **75 grams of silver** for a tonne of barley. This is an **iconic** price. The **midpoint** (mode) in the range of the exchange values for one shekel of silver in the Seleucid period was **120 litres of barley = 112 grams of silver** for a tonne of barley (Aperghis 2004, 79–80). At this price level, and with a wage of 2 shekels per month (wages between 2/3 and 4 shekels are recorded, but the number of data is extremely small), it was possible to feed a family of 5 persons (van der Spek 2006, 293). It is important, though, to recognise that this only concerns 5.6% of all price quotations (or, if we set it between 110 and 130 litres, 10.6%). The median (78 litres) and mean (94 litres) are lower (hence, the prices are higher: median 172 and mean 241[9] grams of silver per tonne), suggesting

---

[8]   See Flynn 2009 for a study on the role of silver as both commodity and means of exchange.

[9]   The mean is, of course, not 94 litres converted into grams of silver per tonne—such a procedure is unacceptable (cf. van der Spek and Mandemakers 2003, 523–4); van der Spek http://www.iisg.nl/hpw/babylon.php §3.2)—but the mean of the real prices in grams of silver; in actual fact it is the

that the iconic price is a minimum price, hardly current anymore. We may also notice
that the median price is lower than the mean price, which, as argued by van der Spek
and Mandemakers (2003, 4), is to be expected, as "this is caused by the very inelastic
nature of the demand for basic foodstuffs: people do not eat much more when
the supply of grain is vast, but they pay a lot more, when supply is scarce."
Indeed, when we look at the price data in the astronomical diaries we see famine
occurring at 36–39 litres per shekel = 345–373 grams of silver for a tonne of barley.

Let me first give a general overview of the prices of barley 480–60 BC (fig. 11.1). It
is a collection of all data from the astronomical diaries without reduction or

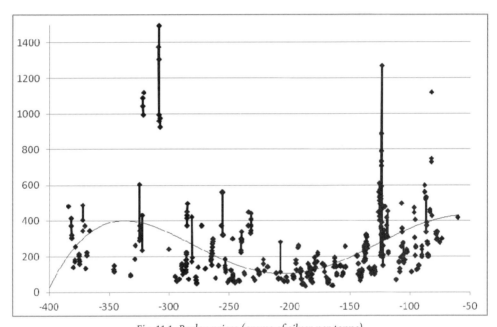

Fig. 11.1 Barley prices (grams of silver per tonne)

manipulation. The only manipulation is that the prices are given in grams of silver
per tonne of barley (instead of litres per shekel). I plotted the price series with a
sixth-order polynomial in order to capture all possible trend changes.

A first glance at the graph presents an impression of highly fluctuating prices and
an uneven density of data. Hence, I have made some other models to look at the prices.
In fig. 11.2 I have collected the highest and lowest prices of the period 299–70 BC in
the hope of presenting a more balanced picture. I have chosen this period in order to
skip the extreme high prices of the period of Alexander the Great and his early

mean of monthly averages. The problem of the missing months did not appear to be too problematic
for the present study (cf. n. 5).

successors, a very unstable period with very destructive warfare. Furthermore, from 321–311, a whole decade, we have no diaries at all! In the second place these tables present an overview of the ranges between high and low prices per decade and give us an equal number of price data in every decade. As from some years we have six prices and from other years only one or nothing, it would give a distorted picture to lump all these prices together and base calculations on this. For the same reason I always took a second highest and lowest price from a *different economic year*. It would make little sense to present a second highest price from a month following or preceding

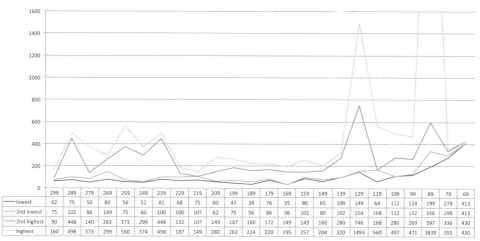

	299	289	279	269	259	249	239	229	219	209	199	189	179	169	159	149	139	129	119	109	99	89	79	69
lowest	62	75	50	80	56	52	81	68	75	60	47	34	76	35	90	65	100	149	64	112	124	199	278	413
2nd lowest	75	102	86	149	75	60	100	100	107	62	75	56	86	36	102	80	102	154	168	112	132	336	299	413
2nd highest	90	448	140	263	373	299	448	132	107	149	187	160	172	149	149	160	280	746	168	280	269	597	336	430
highest	160	498	373	299	560	374	498	187	149	280	263	224	220	195	257	204	320	1493	560	497	471	3839	355	430

Fig. 11.2 Prices of barley per decade per tonne, 299–70 BC The shekels are converted into grams of silver at the rate of 8.33 grams per shekel. The decades are arranged as follows: 299–290, 289–280 BC, etc.

the highest. In the first place this would give hardly new information, and in the second place it would distort the picture since from some years we have prices from consecutive months and from other years only one price.

This table should be consulted with caution. In some cases the information is based on 2 or 7 data per decade, in other cases, especially in the Parthian period, we have 44 or 48 prices at our disposal.

What can we deduce from these figures? The figures exhibit a large degree of volatility between the highest and lowest prices within a decade. The range is between 74 and 3640 grams of silver. The average range is 418 grams. The second striking observation is that prices were higher in the Parthian period, and that the range between highest and lowest prices was larger too. Evidently the figure for 89–80 BC is very much distorted by one extremely high price. When we treat the Seleucid period (299–140) and Parthian period (139–61) separately, we encounter a more nuanced picture. The average range between highest and lowest was 215 in the Seleucid period

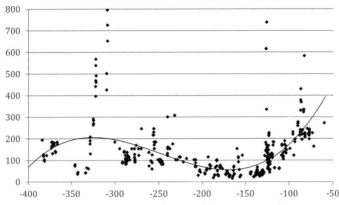

Fig. 11.3 Date prices (grams of silver per tonne)

and 825 in the Parthian period. In the entire period the highest price was on average 5.68 times the lowest price (under the Seleucids 4.99 times, under the Parthians 7.25 times).[10]

3.2. The volatility of date prices in the city of Babylon, 299–61 BC

We can do the same for **date prices**. First, I give a graph with all prices from the period 400–60 BC, and then graphs of the prices of dates per decade (figs. 11.3 and 11.4).

What can we deduce from the figures for **dates**? These figures also exhibit a large degree of volatility between the highest and lowest prices within a decade, but far less than in the case of barley. The range is between 22 and 699 grams of silver. The average range is 127 grams. The second clear observation is that prices were higher in the Parthian period and that the range between highest and lowest prices was larger too. Evidently, the figure for 89–80 is much distorted by one extremely high price, just as for barley, though the highest barley price was much more extreme. When we treat the Seleucid (299–140 BC) and Parthian (139–61 BC) periods separately, we encounter a more nuanced picture. The average range between highest and lowest date price was 81 in the Seleucid period and 232 in the Parthian period. Yet it is interesting to note that the range between highest and lowest prices was much more stable for dates than for barley.

---

[10] This paper focuses on the absolute deviations of the price. Although that is informative about actual volatility, it makes it difficult to compare with other regions and time periods. For a comment on comparison with other regions and alternative measures of volatility see Földvári and van Leeuwen 2011.

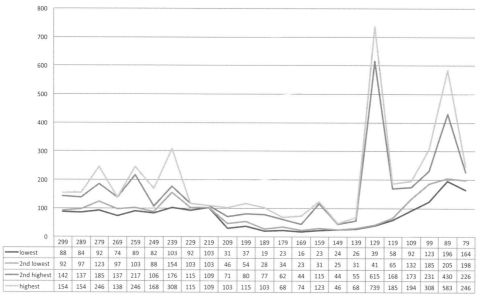

	299	289	279	269	259	249	239	229	219	209	199	189	179	169	159	149	139	129	119	109	99	89	79
lowest	88	84	92	74	89	82	103	92	103	31	37	19	23	16	23	24	26	39	58	92	123	196	164
2nd lowest	92	97	123	97	103	88	154	103	103	46	54	28	34	23	31	25	31	41	65	132	185	205	198
2nd highest	142	137	185	137	217	106	176	115	109	71	80	77	62	44	115	44	55	615	168	173	231	430	226
highest	154	154	246	138	246	168	308	115	109	103	115	103	68	74	123	46	68	739	185	194	308	583	246

Fig. 11.4 Date prices in decades (grams of silver per tonne)

	Barley	*Dates*
Range lowest–highest prices within one decade	74–3640	22–699
Average range	**418**	**127**
Range lowest–highest prices **Seleucid** period	74–504	22–205
Average range **Seleucid** period	**215**	**81**
Range lowest–highest **Parthian** period	220–3640	42–699
Average range **Parthian** period	**825**	**232**
Factor average lowest > highest price	5.68	3.41
Factor **Seleucid** period	4.99	2.80
Factor **Parthian** period	7.19	4.81

Fig. 11.5 The range between highest and lowest prices (prices in grams of silver per tonne)

3.3. Barley and dates combined

In order to make possible a comparison between highest and lowest prices of barley and dates I have combined them in one graph, in prices per tonne (figs. 11.6 and 11.7). The most interesting finding is that the volatility was indeed particularly high in the period after c. 139 BC. Furthermore, this volatility was especially high for barley. Indeed, if we compare the difference in the highest prices of barley and dates and the

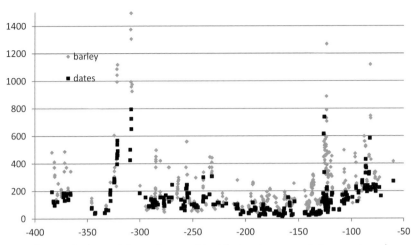

Fig. 11.6 Barley and date prices combined (prices in grams of silver per tonne)

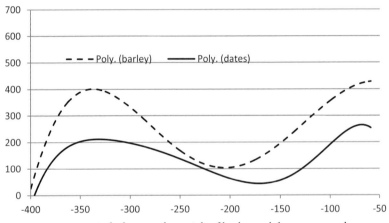

Fig. 11.7 Sixth-degree polynomials of barley and dates compared

lowest prices, we find that the difference between barley and dates in the highest prices is considerably bigger than in the lowest prices. This seems to indicate that volatility for barley is considerably higher than for dates in the Parthian period (but see § 7 for a more nuanced view).

3.4. Some tentative conclusions

On the basis of these graphs we can make the following observations:

1. The **range** of highest and lowest prices of barley is higher than that of dates. The explanation is that the date harvest is less susceptible to the vagaries of the

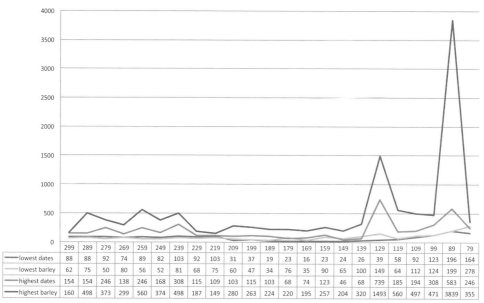

	299	289	279	269	259	249	239	229	219	209	199	189	179	169	159	149	139	129	119	109	99	89	79
lowest dates	88	88	92	74	89	82	103	92	103	31	37	19	23	16	23	24	26	39	58	92	123	196	164
lowest barley	62	75	50	80	56	52	81	68	75	60	47	34	76	35	90	65	100	149	64	112	124	199	278
highest dates	154	154	246	138	246	168	308	115	109	103	115	103	68	74	123	46	68	739	185	194	308	583	246
highest barley	160	498	373	299	560	374	498	187	149	280	263	224	220	195	257	204	320	1493	560	497	471	3839	355

Fig. 11.8 Highest and lowest date and barley prices combined (in grams of silver per tonne)

climate. The stability in the relationship between high and low prices of dates is much stronger than that of barley, in the entire period.

2. In the second half of the Seleucid period (220s to 140s BC) the **volatility** of both products is smaller than in the preceding and following periods. The **level** of the prices themselves is also lower. The higher volatility and price level of the following period (= the Parthian period) is easily explained by the fact that the Parthian period was politically very unstable. Warfare, insurrections, and invasions of Arabs were the order of the day. The preceding period is more difficult to explain. At first glance it is not evident that the stability was much lower, although in 246/5 Babylon was invaded by Ptolemy III[11] and the 230s saw dynastic struggles and unrest in Babylon.[12] Further detailed historical research should elucidate this.

Note that lower prices may also be the consequence of a scarcity of silver.

3. In roughly the same period (210s–110s) the lowest date prices are lower than the lowest barley prices, while the situation was consistently the opposite in the preceding period. While lower prices in general may be caused by a scarcity of silver, this is not true for a *relative* decrease in prices of dates in relation to barley. The most plausible explanation is that the supply of dates increased in respect to barley. This may have been the effect of a royal law, attested in the reign of Antiochus III (222–187 BC) which promoted the planting and cultivation of dates (van der Spek 1995, 232).[13] Another

---

[11] Cf. Appian, *Syriaca* 65; BCHP 11.

[12] See the relevant Astronomical Diaries and a discussion in van der Spek 2006, 296–302.

[13] The evidence is a lease contract in perpetuity of a tract of temple land in Uruk to be planted

explanation would be that it was caused by a fall in the demand for dates, but that would be contrary to the trend towards increasing date cultivation because the nutritional value of dates was higher than that of barley. Aperghis, hypothetically, attributes the fall in prices to a tax reduction by the king.[14]

4. The price trends do not differ very much. This is especially evident from the graphs showing the normalised prices of barley and dates. As both products are basic they are a substitute for one another. When the price of one product rises, the demand for the other product will increase. Both crops were widely available in Babylonia. The relative change after c. 220 BC seems best explained by a long-term increase in the supply of dates relative to barley.

4. PEAK PRICES

4.1. Periods of high prices of barley

As I remarked before, the stability of the economy and of price levels is not only measured by the *range* between high and low prices, but also the *duration* of the period of high prices. In other words: was the Babylonian economy able to recover quickly from a period of high prices, or did high prices have a lasting effect? Let us now take a special look at the **highest prices**. Note that prices of about 370 gr. of silver per tonne meant famine. In three instances famines were recorded at these price levels. The question to be addressed is how far-reaching these prices were. Did they really upset the Babylonian economy, or were these high prices owed to special circumstances and was the Babylonian economy able to counterbalance these shocks and return to more normal price levels?

Let us first take a look at the Seleucid era which was the more stable period. The Seleucid period as a matter of fact contains ten periods of high prices in 160 years (Tables 11.1–11.16). The years of high prices are shaded in gray:

Table 11.1 *October 286–February 285 (min. 10 months; max. one year more; recovery max. 1 year)*

October 287–May 286	General rise from 112 to 224 gr. per tonne.
October 286–February 285	373–498
February 284	75

Note: No exogenous shocks are known which can explain these high prices, but they must have been present, as the prices start to rise after(!) the harvest. We only know that Seleucus I was campaigning in Cilicia and Antiochus, his son, in Media (Will 1979[2], 94–7; Plut. *Dem.* XLVII-XLIX; Diod. XXI 20).

---

with dates "according to the decree (*diagramma*) of the king," dated to 221 BC. The content of the decree is not known (van der Spek 1995, 227–34, no. 7 r. 34 and 38).

[14] Aperghis 2004, 84 observes a dramatic rise of from c. 120 to 240 litres of dates per shekel between 208 and 205 BC. "This cannot be explained by a single good harvest, because date prices seem to have oscillated about this new level for the next seventy years or so." In a lecture at the Francqui Conference in Brussels, October 2009, he attributed it to a royal tax measure.

Table 11.2 December 282 BC (1 month; recovery in days – if correct)

February 284	75 grams per tonne of barley
5 November–3 December 282	172 (78 l. p. shekel)
4 December 282–1 January 281	448 (30 l. p. shekel)
2–31 January 281	186 (72 l. p. shekel)

Note: If this high price is correct it may be due to preparations for Seleucus I's last campaign. At the beginning of 281 BC he invaded Asia Minor. However, one might speculate that a scribal error is at work here.

Table 11.3 October 274–March 273 (min. 6 months; max. 5 years; recovery max. 30 months)

Feb. 276	140
October/November 274	373
March 273	373
October 271	132

Note: This high price may be due to preparations for Antiochus I's First Syrian War. Cf. van der Spek 2000, 305–7.

Table 11.4 December 266–May 264 (min. 5 + 7 months; max. 45 months; recovery max. 1 and 28 months)

March 270	136
October–December 266	172–187 (fluctuating)
27 December 266	201
April 265	249
May 265	204
June 265	149
17 October 265	204
April 264	299
3–12 May 264	280
October 262	80

Note: Not much is known about the political situation. In March 268 Antiochus I laid the foundation of the Ezida temple in Borsippa (Antiochus Cylinder I 14). He also ordered restorations in Esagila (*ibid.* I 7). The work may have continued for years after this. On 30 April 267 debris was removed from the "small courtyard" in Babylon (AD I No. -266A: 13'). In September-November 267 there were "many sick people" in Babylon, of which many died (AD I No. -266B: 4' and 15'). A message about the king (content broken off) was heard by the astronomer in September 265. The brief recovery in June 265 can be attributed to the harvest, but in October the prices were high again. Unfortunately we have no information on date prices in this period.

Table 11.5 June 257–Oct. 256 (min. 1.5 years; max. 5 years; recovery max. 18 months)

Jan. 259	149
June 257	373
January 256	560
April 256	560
May 256	320
21 August–17 October 256	320
May 254	187
October 254	111

Note: It is the reign of Antiochus II (261–246 BC). The period in question is that of the 2nd Syrian War (260–256). According to Jerome *Comm. In Danielem* XI 6, Antiochus campaigned extensively against Ptolemy II using all the armies of Babylonia and the East. After this war Antiochus donated land to his wife Laodice and his sons, who in turn gave it to the "Babylonians, Borsippeans and Cutheans" ["Lehmann text" CTMMA 5, 147; van der Spek 1993, 74-6]. The diaries do not give much information on Babylon, except that in September /October 256 BC "people of the land" did battle in the temple district of Babylon (AD II, p. 23, No. -255 r. 15). Hence local unrest may have caused high prices as well, although the unrest may also have been a consequence of prevailing high prices.

Table 11.6 October 248 (min. 1 month; max. 1.5 years; recovery max. 2 months)

March/April 249	124 (108 l. p. shekel)
29 September–19 October 248	299 (45 l. p. shekel)
18 December 248–15 January 247	89 (89 l. p. shekel)

Note: It is still the reign of Antiochus II. Antiochus was in Asia Minor according to the classical sources. The Diaries tell us that Antiochus "departed from Seleucia" in February/March 252 (AD I, p. 43, No. -251 upper edge 3). In July/August 250 he launched a campaign from Antioch: "[Antiochus] levied his [troops] and his chariots and [departed] from Antioch" (AD I, p. 45, No. -249 A r. 6). In the month of our high price, Sept./Oct. 248 BC) a letter arrived with a message concerning Laodice, the wife of the king (AD I, p. 55, No. -247 B 4). Not much can be deduced from all this.

June 242	60
August 241	224
1–10 November 241	299
11–20 November 241	373
21–29 November 241	345
December 241	299
30 December 241–8 January 240	280
9–7 February 240	299
8–17 February 240	373?
27 February–8 March 240	299
4–13 June 238	112

Table 11.7 August 241–March 240 (min. 8 months; max. 4 years; recovery max. 26 months)

Note: Winter 246/5 was a very difficult period for the city of Babylon. It was the period of the Third Syrian or Laodicean War (246–241). Ptolemy III invaded Babylon in person and heavy street fighting and slaughter took place in the city (see Babylonian Chronicle BCHP 11). It must have had an effect on prices, but unfortunately we have no data. The prices before and after the event, however, were quite low: 52 grams of silver in September 246 and 66 grams in January 242. So if the prices had been high, the situation went back to normal rather soon. I have no idea why the prices in 241/240 were so high. It may have nothing to do with war, but rather with crop failure.

26 June–3 July 238	100
September–October 235	373
January–February 234	448
4–13 October 233	280
14–23 October 233	344
24 October–1 November 233	373
2–11 December 233	448
12–21 December 233	407
22–31 December 233	373
1–10 January 232	407
11–20 January 232	498
30 January–28 February 232	345
September–October 231	81

Table 11.8 September 235–February 232 (min. 2.5 years; max. 7 years; recovery max. 17 months)

Note: This is a longer period of high prices. Actually it is surprising that these high prices did not start earlier, as we read in the diaries:
* June/July 238 BCE: "That month there were many deaths; per house two or three died. | That [month]: there was a battle in the district of the palace, which is in Babylon [...]. That month, the 29th (and) the 30th (2 and 3 July): when the troops from the palace had moved out, with the royal troops of the garrison | [they did battle]. That month, from [day x to day y] there were constantly locusts" (AD I, p. 89, No. –237 Obv. 12′–14′).
The struggle may have had connections with the land donation of Antiochus II. We possess two copies of a document mentioning a decree of the *shatammu* (temple dean) concerning it and mentioning the wish that the land should remain property of the Babylonians, each in their individual tract ("Lehmann Text", CTMMA 5, 147; cf. van der Spek 1993, 66, 69, 76).
The high prices of October 235 are in line with what we know of this period. It was a period of internal warfare:
* October 235 BCE: "That month, the 17th (13 October), a huge stroke of lightning occurred in the [...] at the side of the Enamtila temple (temple of Enlil on the West Bank). That month, [the xth], | the [strat]egos [gathered] many troops for a battle with the garrison commander [who was] in the palace, who rebelled against Seleucus (II), the king." (AD I, p. 95, No. –234 Obv. 12–13).
The relationship between political events and prices, however, is not always so clear. In October 231 and January/February 229 the broken diaries again mention troops and battles, but the prices in these months were quite low. It is sobering to note that the diaries of year 235/4 (SEB 77) tell that "That year, rains most of the times kept off." (AD I, p. 101, No. –234 r. 37′).

Table 11.9 April 208 (min. 1 month; max 1 year; recovery max. 1 month)

14–23 June 210	80
3 April–1 May 208	280
2–11 May 208	149
12–21 May 208	80
22–31 May 208	93
19–27 September 208	77

Note: The diaries of this month have the remark: "[...] the peak flood came. That month, five dogs approached one bitch." (AD II, p. 193, No. -207A: 17). For the rest we have hardly any information. Antiochus III was on his *Anabasis* towards the east marching from Parthia to Bactria.

Table 11.10 October 194–February 193 (min. 5 months; max. 3 years; recovery max. 17 months)

13–22 December 196	187
23 December 196–1 January 195	172
2–11 January 195	160
8 June–6 July 195	124
23 September–22 October 194 (month VII)	249
20 January–17 February 193	263
18 – 27 February 193	244
3 August–1 September 192	112

Note: The diaries present hardly any information: the broken diary of month VII SEB 118 suggests that the satrap of Babylonia entered Babylon and sacrificed in Esagila (AD II, p. 281, No. -193B: 29′). 194 BC saw preparations for the war of Antiochus III with Rome, but it is very questionable whether this had any effect on prices in Babylon.

Table 11.11 February 180–October 172 (period of relatively high prices with two peaks with maximum recovery periods of 1 and 46 months respectively)

July–August 182	56
4–13 February 180	187$^?$ (max. possible price)
14–23 February 180	**224**
24 February–5 March 180	149
March 180–March 178	Fluctuating between 124 and 172
December 178–January 177	**210–220**
November 174	160
July–October 172	150–102–124–148
October 171	86

Note: It covers the reigns of Seleucus IV (187–175 BC) and Antiochus IV (175–164 BC). It is a period of eight years of relatively high prices with two peaks. It is hardly possible to detect exogenous shocks causing these price fluctuations.

Table 11.12 August 155 (min. 10 days; max. 1 year 6 months; recovery max. 5 months)

16–25 July 156	139
4–13 August 155	257
7–16 February 154	72

Note: reign of Demetrius I (162/1 –150). No historical information in the diaries.

Table 11.13 August–September 145 (min. 2 months; max. 10 years; recovery max. 11 months)

March 154	144
August–September 145	204–195–204
August 144	160

Note: In the summer of 145 BC Ptolemy VI invaded the Seleucid empire, defeated king Alexander Balas and took Antioch, but was driven back to Egypt by Demetrius II (145–141 BC in Babylonia) by August 145 BC. Note that the date prices were not high in 145.

July 141-August-November 139	Gradual rise 80 > 172 > 224
February 138	258
May 138	160
August 138	179
September 138	187
October 138 > April 137	217 > 320
April 137 > July 137	320
July 137 > March 136	320 > 263
September 135	136

Table 11.14 August 139-March 136 (c. 2-4 years; recovery max. 17 months)

Note: Spring 141 BC: the Parthians conquer Babylonia. The Parthian period is a period of higher barley prices in general. In July 138 BC Demetrius II tried to reconquer Babylonia, but was defeated near Babylon by Mithradates I and taken captive. In December 138 royal troops were encamped near Seleucia. There was warfare against an Elamite invasion, especially in the southern marshes.

October 130	112
June 127	448
September 127	560
29 March–26 April 126	672 > 448 > 672
27 April–6 May 126	746 > 672 > 746
7–25 May 126 (old barley)	640
c. 13 May–25 May 126 (new barley)	448 > 373 > 299 > 373 > 407 > 336
28 May 126–3 January 125	345 fluctuating to 597
February–June 125	Falling to 154
June–November 125	Rising to 597
November 125–March 124	655 (Nov/Dec. 345) > 896 > 517
5 April–4 May 124	707
5 May–8 May 124	**1493**
9 May–14 May 124	**1414**
18 June–1 July 124	489
August 124 to April 123	427 falling to 179

Table 11.15 June 127-August 124 (min. 3 years 1 month; max. 6.5 years; extreme high prices one month only; recovery of long period of high prices in 8 months)

Note: This is a period of severe unrest in Babylonia. Antiochus VII invaded Babylonia in 130 BC but was defeated already in 129 BC. Before May 127 BC Hyspaosines of Characene was recognised as king in Babylon but already by November 127 he had been driven out. The high prices of spring 126 BC must be related to unrest again. The astronomical diary AD III, p. 261, no. -125A reports that in month I all crops were expensive, including garlic and leek (no. -125A: 12). Warfare, massacres, destruction of fields and raids of Arabs are reported (ll. 13–21). In spring 125 BC, month I, April-May, the situation was not much better. Mention is made of collapsing walls, incursions of Arabs, who are bought off, and traffic (?) being cut off to Borsippa and other cities (AD III p. 265, no. -124A: 8′–9′). In month II (May-June) there was a fire in the royal palace (l. 23′), in month III (June-July) Arabs were probably again bought off with presents (l. 37′), in month IV (July-August) there was again fire in the palace, the Arabs broke a hole into the wall of Babylon, trade (?) was again cut off and Arabs were given presents "as before" (r. 4′-7). In month V (August-September) the general of Babylonia entered Babylon and announced the appointment of a Greek as *shatammu* (highest temple official) of Esagila (cf. Sciandra 2012); not much about warfare in this damaged diary, but sick people are mentioned (r. 18′-24′). We shall not discuss every detail here, but raids of Arabs continue: "that month (= IX = December 125), the Arabs plundered as before; panic of the Arabs as before was much in the land," while the king started war with Pitthides, king of Elam (AD III p. 275, no. -125B 19′- 21′). A long report about the war with Pitthides is given in the diary concerning month X (January 124) (r. 12′-20′); cf. van der Spek 2001, 451-3). The high prices of May 124 BC (month II 188 SEB) can be explained by troubles caused by the Arabs ("[traffic(?)] was cut off because of the Arabs," AD III, p. 281, No. -123A: 4′-5′). The news of one month later was the death of king Hyspaosines of Mesene (18′-21′).

Table 11.16 April 83–January 82 (min. 10 months; max. 1 year 2 months - of extreme high prices; recovery in 3 months)

July 84	467
$2^?$–8 April 83	2067
9–11 April 83	2239
$12^?$–$14^?$ April 83	3839
18–25 October 83	1120
$24^?$ December 83–7 January 82	746
1 April 82	430

Note: The historical sections are much damaged, but mention is made of a revolt in April 83. The high price of 3839 grams of silver (3.5 litres for a shekel) is said to be for "barley on the way?; ŠE.BAR *ina ma-lak*). Before it mention is made of the fact that something (supply?) was in arrears ... *im?-]/meš\-ku-ú* from *namarkû*, "to be in arrears, to lag behind" (Cf. van der Spek and Mandemakers 2003, 529–30). The high prices may well be due to the insecure position of the Parthian dynasty under Orodes I. Unfortunately we have no detailed information. The historical section of the diary is much damaged, but mention is made of a revolt (*sīhu*: AD III, p. 476, no. -82A: 21).

It is unfortunate that, owing to the gaps in our evidence, the exact duration of the price peaks often cannot be established. It may be argued that extreme prices by definition did not last long, since a long-lasting famine implies massive mortality. Also, there is evidence from other times and places that after a long period of high prices, it took only one or two months for them to return to normal. If we compare the data above with extreme barley prices in Pisa (1548–1590) and extreme rice prices in Jakarta (1824–1850), where extreme prices are defined as at least 30% above average and the duration is calculated as the period when the prices are at least 20% above average, we find that the average duration of high prices (i.e. prices at least 20% above average) is 8.9 and 9.4 months respectively.[15] Hence, the duration in Babylon seems to be on the high side. Even if the minimum duration of the periods of extreme high prices were correct, Babylonia did not fare better, despite the fact that Babylonia was a dual-crop economy (barley and dates), which has a mitigating effect on prices. In some cases the high prices could be interpreted as caused by exogenous shocks such as military campaigns or internal conflicts. It looks as if a period of crisis could be followed by quick recovery only when there was a brief intermezzo with high prices, possibly because of a siege of the city or other disturbances that did not affect the availability of dates and barley in the medium run. Thanks to the dense canal system, grain could be imported from the Diyala region or from southern Babylonia (Uruk region). Unfortunately, we have only prices from the city of Babylon, not from other cities. It is unlikely that barley was imported from more distant regions, like Syria. Storage facilities in Babylon might help, so that even in times of scarcity enough seed-corn was available. Yet storage did not extend much longer than the economic year, as was argued on different grounds by Jursa (2010, 591–2) and by van Leeuwen, Földvári, and Pirngruber (2011). Hence, it seems that short-term shortages in Babylon could be countered with regional trade, while long-term shortages caused by harvest failures were carried over to the next

---

[15] Calculations made by Bas van Leeuwen on the basis of Jan Luiten van Zanden, *Monthly rice prices on Java (Batavia, Semarang, and Surabaya) 1824-1855* (downloaded from: http://www.iisg.nl/hpw/data.php#indonesia); Paolo Malanima, *Grain prices and prices of olive oil in Pisa, 1548-1818 (monthly averages)* (downloaded from: http://www.iisg.nl/hpw/data.php#italy).

year because of lack of seed grain. Further research on periods of medium-high prices would be profitable.

The Parthian period experienced longer periods of high prices. This is easily explained by the very unstable political situation. The Parthian take-over (spring 141) occurred quite peacefully without much war and bloodshed, but later incursions of Elamites, Arabs, Seleucids (Demetrius II in 138), Mesene (Hyspaosines, who took the throne for a few months in 127 BC), and rebellious generals like Mitrates and Gotarzes were very harmful.

4.2. Periods of low prices of barley

I have not studied the periods of low prices in great detail, but I point to two periods of extreme low prices. In October/November 188 BC a shekel of silver could buy 390 litres of barley, so that a tonne of barley could be bought for 35 grams of silver (= 4.2 shekels = 8 or 9 drachmas, a good monthly wage). It is good to let these figures sink in. If a Babylonian wanted to buy a kilo of barley on the market in Babylon, he needed 0.035 grams of silver = 0.042 shekel = 0.084 drachmas = 0.252 obol. It is next to nothing. In a modern market economy the barley would have been withdrawn from the market.

A similar price was current in 166 and 165 BC. In August/September 166 BC a shekel could buy 372 litres (= 36.12 grams of silver for a tonne) and in October 165 even 372.5 litres (35.5 gr. per tonne). The last instance is a good example of how events could take a sudden turn. On the 25th and 26th of the month Adar (XII) 147 Seleucid Era Babylonian calendar (SEB) = 22 and 23 March 164 BC "there was no exchange of barley," KI.LAM *še-im* TAR-*as*. Apparently all of a sudden an extreme scarcity of grain prevailed. A month later, April/May 164 BC, a shekel could buy only 96 litres (140 grams of silver for a tonne), falling to 69 litres in November 164 (195 grams of silver). All this may be connected with the advance of the army of Antiochus IV. The damaged astronomical diaries of month VII 147 SEB = October 165 seem to report that Antiochus departed from Antioch on the Orontes to Armenia (AD II, p. 497, No. -164B: 15′–C: 14′). The army of Antiochus IV, who was preparing a campaign against the east, may have entered Babylonia in the summer of 164. He may have taken the grain from the market to feed his soldiers in March, resulting in much higher prices in the summer.

As regards the very low prices, we must take into account the possibility that these low prices were not (only) caused by an abundant harvest, but also by a scarcity of silver. Antiochus III may have levied so much silver that the purchasing power of the remaining silver was high. The same may be adduced from the low prices in 188 during Antiochus' campaign against Greece and the Romans, resulting in the Peace of Apamea (188) where it was decided that the Seleucid king had to pay an indemnity of 15,000 talents of silver to the Romans. Le Rider and De Callataÿ, however, argue that the Seleucid empire was rich enough to pay this (Le Rider and De Callataÿ 2006, 199–202). Be that as it may, in the course of time the Romans increasingly drained the east of its resources, including silver.

4.3. Periods of high date prices

The date prices also exhibit short periods of high prices. The number of these periods is smaller than for barley and the prices show fewer extremes. The reason must be that date palms are less vulnerable to changes in the climate, damage to the irrigation system and destruction through warfare.

Table 11.17 1–29 March 270 (min. 1 month; max 5 years; recovery max. 52 months)

October 271	154
1–29 March 270	246
October 266	138

Note: Unfortunately, there are no data from March 270 to October 266, so one cannot tell whether or not the price of dates was on a high level for long. Unfortunately we hardly have any information concerning events which might have led to these high prices.

Table 11.18 April–May 258 (min. 1 month; max 15 months; recovery within a few days); June 257–May 256 (min. 1 year; max 26 months; recovery max. 3 months)

January 259	97
27 April–6 May 258	211
7 May–15 May 258	132
16 May–13 June 258	89
3 June–2 July 257	217
25 January–13 February 257	246
26 March–23 May 256	246
20 August–17 September 256	185
18 September–17 October 256	154
5 December 255–3 January 254	185
2–30 May 254	185
27 September–25 October 254	No dates on the market (barley 112)
4 October 252–2 November 252	103

Note: Note the quick recovery from a high price in May–June 258. A plausible explanation will be the arrival of the barley harvest on the market. Unfortunately we have no barley prices from this year. Prices are again high in 257 and 256, but from about September 256 the prices fall, possibly owing to the date harvest (though it is a little early for that). The explanation may be that a good harvest could be expected. In October–November 254 there were no dates on the market. This may have been caused by scarcity just before the new harvest. Unfortunately we do not know whether the prices were high in the previous months, nor in the two years after.

Table 11.19 November 233–January 232 (min. 3 months; max. 3.5 years; recovery max. 14 months)

October 235	176
2 November 233–29 January 232	308
April 231	103

Note: The maximum duration of the high prices may have been 3.5 years, but note that the price could fall back to 1/3 within one year.

Table 11.20 August–September 159 (min. 2 months; max. 2.5 years; recovery max. 12 months)

February 160	44 (?)
29 July–26 August 159	115
27 August–25 September 159	92
8–16 August 158	57
9 April–8 May 157	23

Note: A peak in August 159, recovery starts already in September (impending harvest?); a year later the price is much lower.

Table 11.21 February 154 (min.
1month; max. 11 years; recovery
max. 112 months)

July 156	31
7 February–7 March 154	123
August 145	44

Note: Hardly anything can be derived
from this chart. It is sobering to note
that we have no prices of barley and
dates from the years 153–146 BC!
Compare the pattern of barley: July 156
BC: 139 gr., August 155: 257 gr.,
February 154 72 gr. of silver per tonne.

Table 11.22 November 127–April 126 (High prices about 2 years; extreme
high prices c. 3 months; recovery max. 4 and 1 month; max. 3.5 years;
gradual recovery 1 year)

7 September–5 October 130	46
5 November–4 December 130	41.03 > 42.45 > 41.57
24 October–21 November 129	41 > 46 > 50 (?)
12 November–11 December 128	137 > 154 > 185
7 May–5 June 127	615
1–30 November 127	123 > 137 > 154
1–29 December 127	336
29 January–26 February 126	739
29 March–c. 7 April 126	185
c. 7–21 April 126	168 > 154 > 137 > 123 > 119 > 112
22 April–30 September 126	Fluctuating around 154 (137–168)
1 October–31 December 126	Fluctuating between 103 - 142
16–25 April 125	62

Note: A similar fall in the date price is visible here as in the previous sample of
prices. It is notable that the date prices only started to rise after 130 BC, eleven
years after the invasion of the Parthians, while the barley prices started to rise
immediately. After the 120s both commodities experienced a steady rise in prices

Table 11.23 April 83
(min. 1 month; max 1
year; recovery max. 7
months)

August 84	336
2–7 April 83	583
December 83	226

Note: April 83 was also the
month of extreme high
barley prices (see above).
Note that this extreme
prices is not so extreme as
the barley price in the same
month. It was a period in
which prices were
generally high.

5. MEASURING VOLATILITY (by Bas van Leeuwen)

This paper focuses on the *unconditional* (i.e. not removing any factors that may affect
the variance, but not the market performance) variance of the prices. This precludes
an analysis of the prices in terms of market performance, since that requires an analysis
of the *conditional* price volatility since factors such as the existence of a dual crop
structure, even though affecting price volatility, do not affect market performance.
This will be done within our project on the performance of markets in Babylonia as
indicated in footnote 1. Yet it is useful to make some comments on conditional volatility
and its relation with unconditional volatility in order to show the limits of this paper.

   The basic underlying argumentation is that greater price volatility indicates that
the market is less able to cope with unexpected shocks. Hence, the greater the volatility,
the less the market performs (Persson 1999). One often-used way in which this
unconditional variance is calculated is using the Coefficient of Variation (CV). Since

country	period	product	CV	
Babylon	300–60BC	dates	1.144	shekel/100 l
Babylon	300–141BC	dates	0.691	shekel/100 l
Babylon	140–60BC	dates	1.046	shekel/100 l
Babylon	300–60BC	barley	0.733	shekel/100 l
Babylon	300–141BC	barley	0.706	shekel/100 l
Babylon	140–60BC	barley	0.691	shekel/100 l
England	1209–1347AD	barley	0.378	shilling/bu
England	1350–1500AD	barley	0.347	shilling/bu
Florence	1325–1347AD	barley	0.322	denier/setier
Modena	1650–1700AD	barley	0.263	soldi/staro
Vienna	1650–1800AD	barley	0.464	kreuzen/metzen

Table 11.24 Coefficient of variation (CV) of barley per period and country

Source: Földvári and van Leeuwen 2010; 2011

this is the standard deviation divided by the mean, it is independent of the level of the prices. This is important since an increase in prices from 1 shekel to 2 is a rise of 100%, but a rise from 101 to 102 is a rise of only 1%.

Therefore, most studies use the Coefficient of Variation (CV). The result of several of these estimates is given in Table 11.24.

The above table shows two important things. First, Babylonia seems, in general, to have a far higher CV than other countries/cities. This implies that market performance was much lower in Babylonia than elsewhere. This does not seem to correspond with the existing evidence of working markets in Babylon (Vargyas 2001; Temin 2002; van der Spek and Mandemakers 2003). Second, the CV over the entire period is higher than that of each of the sub-periods. Given the assumption that the CV reflects market performance, this cannot be the case. After all, market performance over the entire period cannot be higher or lower than an average of the sub-periods. Consequently, other factors than mere market performance must be embedded in the CV, as is also argued by Persson (1999, 107–8). This makes *unconditional* volatility at best an impaired indicator of market performance.

Földvári and van Leeuwen (2011) and van Leeuwen *et al.* (2011) used a model to separate the region-specific factors influencing volatility, such as the agricultural structure, from the unexplained shocks such as war and weather. Since the performance of a market is determined by the speed with which markets react to an unexpected shock, removing explained volatility will lower the CV resulting in only the conditional volatility (i.e. volatility conditional on removing the explained part). Indeed, Table 11.25 shows the corrected CV (or, equivalently, the standard error of the regression on first differences).

Table 11.25 Standard error of the regression of first differences

	barley	dates
300–60 BC	0.20	0.19
300–141 BC	0.23	0.23
140–60 BC	0.11	0.14

As you can see, the picture changes strongly compared with Table 11.24, when we use this new volatility measure. First, we find that the overall volatility estimates are located in between the estimates for the sub periods, as can be expected on the basis of the theory. Second, both barley and dates now have almost equal market performance. This is much more likely than having a far less well performing market in Babylon for barley than dates during the Parthian period, as found in Table 11.24. Thirdly, we find that market performance remains more or less stable (or increases slightly) during the Parthian period. This is true even though we have shown several times in this paper that absolute volatility increases in the Parthian period. This suggests that predictable factors unrelated to market performance caused an increase in volatility during the Parthian period. A possible explanation may be that the general rise in prices found in that period increased the general price level, which caused the variance to go up (see Földvári and van Leeuwen 2011). Comparison with other economies of later periods has to be made on this basis.

6. SOME CONCLUDING REMARKS

It is flatly impossible to arrive at firm conclusions at this stage of our research. Research into the volatility of the prices has to be conducted using a range of statistical methods. In addition, careful notice must be taken of the historical circumstances, so that one can judge the situation in different periods. Many aspects remain to be examined, such as the role of transport, climate, war, comparisons of prices of barley with those of other agrarian products. It is also necessary to study other available prices, such as the prices of slaves, houses and arable land. The purchasing power of silver also needs more delicate study. Many questions remain concerning the role of silver in the economy in relation to trade and wages in kind, the circulation of money, the purity of the silver coins, fiduciary money (bronze), the amount of silver in circulation.

A first glance at the evidence presented in this paper seems to reveal a rather volatile course of the prices. Yet this is absolute volatility. For example, the range between high and low prices was higher for barley than for dates, yet the coefficient of variation was higher for dates. This suggests that the absolute volatility is higher for barley because of its higher price. After all, if two series have 10% volatility, but one series has a lower average (say 10) than the other series (say 100), then the absolute deviation of the latter series is 10 times higher than for the former (1). But, as argued by Földvári and van Leeuwen (2011), even making the volatility level independent is not enough. They argued that, after removing country- and time-specific effects, in actual fact the market performance of both products was about the same.

Indeed, prices of barley were on average higher than prices of dates. It is also remarkable that prices of dates continued to fall at the end of the Seleucid period, while the barley prices rose. For an explanation we can look both at the supply and the demand side. A determined effort to promote the growing of dates in the 220s/210s by Antiochus III may have been successful. It may also have been the case that the demand for grain grew more than the demand for dates, for example by the preference of the Greek colonists established there under Antiochus III or IV. Aperghis attributed the decrease in date prices around 205 BC to a tax reduction. All this is, however, not indicative of a lower market performance.

Although the *average* prices of barley were consistently higher than those of dates, in the period 210s–110s BC the *lowest* date prices were lower than the lowest barley prices. I have not found so far any explanation for this phenomenon.

The Seleucid period was more stable than the following Parthian period in terms of absolute volatility. The Parthian period was also a period of higher prices. This may give support for Heichelheim's (1930; 1954/5) picture of an economic crisis in the second part of the second century, although Földvári and van Leeuwen (2011) find that actual market performance remained about the same as in the Seleucid period. It is questionable, though, whether this crisis has anything to do with a worldwide economic crisis, or whether it is simply to be explained by the local political and military instability of the Parthian period. On the other hand, as the political situation was insecure in the Seleucid and Ptolemaic empire as well, this general unrest may have caused economic crisis, or perhaps vice versa.

BIBLIOGRAPHICAL ABBREVIATIONS

AD I, II, III	Sachs and Hunger (1988, 1989, 1996)
BCHP	I. Finkel, R.J. van der Spek, Babylonian Chronicles of the Hellenistic Period (to be published; online: www.livius.org > Mesopotamia
CTMMA 5	R. Wallenfels (ed.) (in press), *Cuneiform Documents from the Metropolitan Museum of Art*, vol. 5. New York.

REFERENCES

Aperghis, M. (2004) *The Seleukid Royal Economy. The Finances and Financial Administration of the Seleukid economy*. Cambridge: Cambridge University Pres.

Flynn, D. O. (2009) *A Price Theory of Monies. Evolving Lessons in Monetary History. Collected Papers* (Collection Moneta 98). Wetteren: Moneta.

Földvári, P. and van Leeuwen, B. (2009) *The structural analysis of Babylonian price data: a partial equilibrium approach.* Paper presented at the World Economic History Congress Utrecht, 7 August 2009, http://www.wehc2009.org/programme.asp .

Földvári, P. and van Leeuwen, B. (2010) *The evolution of market related institutions in Babylon in a regional perspective*. Unpublished paper.

Földvári, P. and van Leeuwen, B. (2011) What can price volatility tell us about market efficiency? Conditional heteroscedasticity in historical commodity price series. *Cliometrica 5/2, 165–186.*

Foxhall, L. and Forbes, H. A. (1982) Sitometreia: the role of grain as a staple food in classical antiquity. *Chiron 12, 41–90.*

Heichelheim, F. (1930) *Wirtschaftliche Schwankungen der Zeit von Alexander bis Augustus*. Jena: Fischer Verlag.

Heichelheim, F. (1954/5) On ancient price trends from the early first millennium B.C. to Heraclius I. *Finanzarchiv* 15, 498–511.

Jursa, M. (1995) *Die Landwirtschaft in Sippar in neubabylonischer Zeit* (Archiv für Orientforschung, Beiheft 25). Vienna: Institut für Orientalistik.

Jursa, M. *et al.* (2010) *Aspects of the economic history of Babylonia in the first millennium BC. Economic geography, economic mentalities, agriculture, the use of money and the problem of economic growth* (Alter Orient und Altes Testament 377). Münster: Ugarit-Verlag.

Le Rider, G. and De Callataÿ, F. (2006) *Les Séleucides et les Ptolémées. L'héritage monétaire et financier d'Alexandre le Grand*. Paris: Éd. du Rocher.

Persson, K. G. (1999) *Grain Markets in Europe 1500-1900*. Cambridge: Cambridge University Press.

Powell, M. A. (1989–90) Masse und Gewichte. *Reallexikon der Assyriologie* 7, 457–517.

Rochberg, F. (2004) *The Heavenly Writing. Divination, Horoscopy, and Astronomy in Mesopotamian Culture*. Cambridge: Cambridge University Press.

Sachs, A. and Hunger, H. (1988) *Astronomical Diaries and Related Texts from Babylonia*. I: *652-262 BC*. Vienna: Verlag der Österreichischen Akademie der Wissenschaften.

Sachs, A. and Hunger, H. (1989) *Astronomical Diaries and Related Texts from Babylonia*. II: *261-165 BC*. Vienna: Verlag der Österreichischen Akademie der Wissenschaften.

Sachs, A. and Hunger, H. (1996) *Astronomical Diaries and Related Texts from Babylonia*. III: *164-61 BC*. Vienna: Verlag der Österreichischen Akademie der Wissenschaften.

Sciandra, R. (2012) The Babylonian correspondence of the Seleucid and Arsacid dynasties: new insights into the relations between court and city during the Late Babylonian period. In G. Wilhelm (ed.), *Organization, Representation and Symbols of Power in the Ancient Near East. Proceedings of the 54th Rencontre Assyriologique Internationale at Würzburg, 20-25 July 2008*, 225–248. Winona Lake, IN: Eisenbrauns.

Slotsky, A. L. (1997) *The bourse of Babylon. Market quotations in the Astronomical Diaries of Babylonia*. Bethesda, MD: CDL Press.

Slotsky, A. L. and Wallenfels, R. (2009) *Tallies and Trends. The Late Babylonian Commodity Price Lists*. Bethesda, MD: CDL Press.

Temin, P. (2002) Price behavior in ancient Babylon. *Explorations in Economic History* [online] 39, 46–60.

van der Spek, R. J. (1993) New evidence on Seleucid land policy. In H. Sancisi-Weerdenburg *et al.* (eds), *De Agricultura. In Memoriam Pieter Willem de Neeve (1945-1990)*, 61–77. Amsterdam: Gieben.

van der Spek, R. J. (1995) Land ownership in Babylonian cuneiform documents. In M. J. Geller and H. Maehler (eds), *Legal Documents from the Hellenistic World. Papers from a Seminar*, 173–245. London: Warburg Institute, University of London.

van der Spek, R. J. (1998) Cuneiform documents on Parthian history: the Rahimesu archive. Materials for the study of the standard of living. In J. Wiesehöfer (ed.), *Das Partherreich und seine Zeugnisse*, 205–258 (Historia Einzelschriften 122). Stuttgart: Steiner.

van der Spek, R. J. (2000) The effect of war on the prices of barley and agricultural land in Hellenistic Babylonia. In J. Andreau, P. Briant, and R. Descat (eds), *Économie Antique. La guerre dans les économies antiques*, 293–313 (Entretiens d'archéologie et d'histoire 5). Saint-Bertrand-de-Comminges: Musée archéologique départemental de Saint-Bertrand-de-Comminges.

van der Spek, R. J. (2001) The theatre of Babylon in cuneiform. In W. H. van Soldt *et al.* (eds),

Veenhof Anniversary Volume. Studies presented to Klaas R. Veenhof on the occasion of his sixty-fifth birthday, 445–456. Leiden: Nederlands Inst. voor het Nabije Oosten.

van der Spek, R. J. (2005) Palace, temple and market in Seleucid Babylonia. In V. Chankowski and F. Duyrat (eds), *Le roi et l'économie. Autonomies locales et structures royales dans l'économie de l'empire séleucide. Actes des rencontres de Lille (23 juin 2003) et d'Orléans (29-30 janvier 2004)*, 303–332 (Topoi Suppl. 6). Lyon: Maison de l'orient méditerranée.

van der Spek, R. J. (2006) How to measure prosperity? The case of Hellenistic Babylonia. In R. Descat (ed), *Approches de l'économie hellénistique*, 287–310 (Entretiens d'archéologie et d'histoire 7). Saint-Bertrand-de-Comminges: Musée archéologique départemental de Saint-Bertrand-de-Comminges.

van der Spek, R. J. and Mandemakers, C. A. (2003) Sense and nonsense in the statistical approach of Babylonian prices. *Bibliotheca Orientalis* 60, 521–537.

van der Spek, R. J., van Leeuwen, B. and van Zanden, J. L. (eds) (2014), *A History of Market Performance from Ancient Babylonia to the Modern World* (Routledge Explorations in Economic History). London: Routledge.

van Leeuwen, B., Földvári, P. and Pirngruber, R. (2011) Markets in pre-industrial societies: storage in Hellenistic Babylonia in the medieval English mirror. *Journal of Global History* 6/2, 169–193.

Vargyas, P. (2001) *History of Babylonian Prices in the First Millennium BC. 1. Prices of the Basic Commodities* (Heidelberger Studien zum Alten Orient 10). Heidelberg: Heidelberger Orientverlag.

Will, É (1979[2]) *Histoire politique du monde hellénistique (323-30 av. J.-C.). 1. De la mort d'Alexandre aux avènements d'Antiochos III et de Philippe II*, 2nd edition (Annales de l'Est; mémoire 30). Nancy: Presses universitaires de Nancy.

12

Wheat Prices in Ptolemaic Egypt

Sitta von Reden

1. THE SELECTION OF THE DATA

Only wheat prices have survived in sufficient quantity to make possible comparison over time and place.[1] Prices for oil and barley are rare, while the material on wine is complicated by the fact that both the quality of, and measures for, wine varied more considerably than in the case of grain and oil.[2] Daily wages can be calculated in a fair number of circumstances, but once again the varying conditions of employment, additional payments in kind, and the overall pay status of the employee add unknown factors to the data we have.[3] Silver and land in Egypt are the only other items that are likely to render useful price information, but their interpretation bears its own problems and must await independent treatment.[4]

The corpus of wheat prices from Ptolemaic Egypt comprises some 100 figures (see Tables 12.1 and 12.2, Appendix). Most belong to the period from c. 275 to c. 80 BC, that is, from the reign of Ptolemy II Philadelphos to the death of Ptolemaios XII Soter II. Important periods of possible economic change in the first years of Ptolemaic rule on the one hand and the reign of Kleopatra VII on the other are not represented in these data. Not all information, moreover, is equally useful for economic analysis, and several

---

[1]   A version of this paper has now appeared in von Reden 2010. Its publication in this volume for which it was originally prepared is to allow, as was planned, comparison at a 'world' level with the papers of van der Spek and Rathbone. I wish to thank the organizing committee of the conference as well as Alan Bowman, our respondent, for helpful comments and suggestions.

[2]   For recent lists of prices of all these commodities, see Maresch 1996, 181ff. For the greater variation in wine measures, ibid. 187.

[3]   I have discussed the varying conditions and payment of dependent labour in von Reden 2007, 130–52, 205–26.

[4]   Maresch 1996, 195–8 for silver prices; Maresch 1996, 206–8 and Cadell 1994 for land prices.

prices just reduplicate each other. What is more, despite the relative wealth of information by the standards of Greco-Roman history, we have to bear in mind some fundamental questions that are not easily answered by the evidence itself. Although there are reasons to believe that markets, money and coinage in the less Hellenised areas of Upper and Middle Egypt were not totally absent, urbanisation, population density, and economic organisation varied considerably between Upper and Lower Egypt.[5] Especially the southern regions of the Nile valley continued to be dominated by an old land tenure regime where the distribution mechanisms of surplus grain are likely to have been different from the practices we know through Greek papyri. Even within the areas of Greek occupation our evidence tends to concentrate on the activities of a few groups of people (Greek land owners and their agents, local administrative offices, and the military).

The first is whether our material is representative of price behaviour in Egypt as a whole. As we shall see, the evidence comes mostly from the areas of dense Greek occupation in the Fayum and the adjacent areas of the Oxyrhynchite and Herakleopolite nomes. Given the nature of the evidence and its uneven distribution we have to ask, secondly, what price variation in our sample might mean. Rarely can we tell whether a cluster of high or low prices represents short or long-term change as it is mostly isolated and disparate in time and place. Accidents of the evidence that we are unaware of, or some monetary change that is not known, add further uncertainties to the analysis of change. Prices, moreover, were subject to individual negotiation, conditions of sale and its location. Market prices were higher than farm gate rates where the buyer carried the costs of transport and risk of the journey. So-called penalty prices which were fixed by the government in compensation for unfulfilled rental obligations in kind are likely to reflect prices conceived of as normal or typical. Yet their variation in private contracts over time may not reflect just changing price levels, but varying degrees of state control over private contracts. Contractors at different times might have felt not equally compelled to follow government regulations.

Related to the question of how to evaluate change is the problem of what factors we regard as having influenced variation and change. Short or long-term economic factors reaching from variable harvests due to unforeseen incidents and the Nile inundation to changes in patterns of production and consumption may be as relevant as extraneous factors such as political change in Egypt and the Mediterranean, changing social conditions, or long-term demographic development. One of the major reasons why Heichelheim and Reger differ so dramatically in their interpretation of Delian price developments is that they have privileged different political events in the history and economic context of the island.[6]

A third factor that affects our data is the question of the relationship between the money supply, both regional and local, and the level of prices. We know that Egypt

---

[5] Manning 2003; 2007; Muhs 2006 for the degree of monetization in Upper Egypt; Monson 2012 for uneven urbanisation in different parts of Egypt.

[6] Most notably, Reger 1994, 163; compare Heichelheim 1930, 55–6.

was heavily dependent on imported silver and bronze for the supply of monetary metal, which strongly influenced mint policy from the early years of Ptolemaic rule onwards (see below). By the late third century BC, very few transactions in silver are attested in the countryside, while the state rendered internal and external payments in bronze coinage.[7] Coin hoards and numismatic change suggest several fundamental manipulations to the value of bronze coinage during the late third and second centuries, and eventually the state minted debased silver coinage. The fact that the Romans did not mint new silver coinage in the imperial mint of Alexandria until the reign of Tiberius, and thereafter in rarer intervals than elsewhere, suggests that, since provincial mints were left to their own metal supplies, the Egyptian coin supply remained constrained by the lack of local metal resources.[8] The question of how varying supplies of monetary metal, quantities of coins in circulation and debasement of coinage influenced economic behaviour and thus prices is a highly controversial issue, but it must be fairly certain that both metal supply and the supply of coinage affected local price formation, if to an unknown extent.[9]

Leaving these questions aside, the range of price information that can be used for preliminary study is smaller by 40% than the sample suggested by Heichelheim in 1930, despite the fact that more material has come to light since. Heichelheim identified about 135 wheat prices, some of them derived directly from the texts, others indirectly through proxy data.[10] His list may be divided into the following categories:

1   Wheat prices recorded in accounts or letters in relation to sale
2   Conversion rates of cash into wheat and wheat into cash, recorded in contracts or accounts
3   Monetary penalty prices that were payable in lieu of grain for un-fulfilled rental obligations in kind, recorded in tenancy contracts
4   Sales prices and penalty prices of barley and olyra (Egyptian emmer) converted into wheat at the rate of 5:3:2, recorded in contracts
5   Conversion rate of taxes paid either in wheat or in cash, recorded in accounts and tax receipts

For my own database I have used categories 1 to 3, but excluded 4 and 5.[11] The conversion rate of 5:3:2 for wheat, barley and olyra was standard both in official and interpersonal transactions throughout the Hellenistic period, but this does not mean that there was a fixed relationship of value between the three crops in the market.[12] For Egypt we are lacking the data to test this question, but on Delos prices of different

---

[7]   Maresch 1996; Noeske 2000.

[8]   Huston and Lorber 2001; Harl 1996, 117–24; and below.

[9]   Howgego 1995; Beyer 1995; Rathbone 1996 for the general issues; Cadell and Le Rider 1997, 77ff and Bagnall 1999 for Egypt.

[10]   Heichelheim 1930, 118–22.

[11]   I have used, however, the price series known for olyra of the year 158 BC (Table 12.1 (24)) in order to establish a median price of olyra for that year, and thus a corresponding price for wheat at the conversion rate of 2:5.

[12]   For standard conversion rates, Maresch 1996, 182–3.

cereals did not move in tandem. For example, the price of wheat in 282 rose by almost 50% between August and September, staying at the same level up to December, while the price of barley rose by c. 25% between October and November, reaching then 200% of the normal summer price (Tables 12.4 (1)–(7) and 12.5 (1)–(3)). Although both prices rose in the winter months, that of barley increased more gradually over a greater number of months and (in that year) to a relatively higher level in comparison to the summer price.

As far as tax payments are concerned, a number of taxes are attested as being paid either in cash or in kind (e.g. a doctor's tax (*iatrikon*), the tax for guarding property (*phulakitikon*), or the dyke tax (*chomatikon*)) depending either on the nature of the property on which the tax was levied, or on the right of certain tax payers to commute their taxes.[13] But we have no information about how these taxes were calculated, nor do we know what rate of conversion was applied for payment in wheat or cash. Heichelheim simply took two contemporary figures and, assuming that the tax was paid always at the same rate, took their value relationship as the current price of grain.

Penalty prices (*epitima*), moreover, are a special kind of price and need to be listed independently. If a debtor in a loan, tenancy or sales contract with deferred delivery defaulted with the payment of his obligations in kind, the creditor could execute the contract.[14] Written contracts specified the conditions of the right of execution. The parties could agree either that the creditor should have the right to increase the debt in kind by a specified amount, or ask for compensation in cash. In the case of the latter, contracts specified that the conversion rate should either be the future price of grain in the market of the place of fulfilment or the future highest market price. A third option was to ask for the official penalty price set by the government in contracts with the state. This price seems to have been twice the amount of the official conversion rate of wheat into cash, which in the mid-third century BC was 2 drachmas per artaba of wheat (P. Col. I, 54 (250 BC)). It is important to realise, however, that the official penalty price was not the only form of penalty payment that was applied to private contracts, but was adopted in those contracts where the parties had agreed that execution should be 'according to the rules of the king' or 'as in contracts with the king' (*praxis kata to diagramma*, or *hos pros basilika*).[15] As we see from Table 12.2 in the Appendix, penalty prices varied from time to time, but they may not in all cases represent the official penalty price set by the *diagramma* of the king.

Sales prices, conversion rates and penalty prices thus represent three different kinds of price that have a different relationship to the market. Although all may be seen as depending on market prices, they are likely to have responded differently to short-, mid- or long-term change.[16]

---

[13] Von Reden 2007, 92–4; Préaux 1939.

[14] Weber 1932, 154–62; Seidl 1962, 99ff; Westerman *ad* P. Col. I 54.

[15] Seidl 1962, 100–2 suggests that this was a particularly quick form of execution not involving a court.

[16] Cadell and Le Rider 1997, 78f. for a possible explanation of the rise of the penalty price by

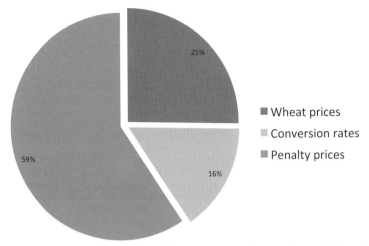

Fig. 12.1 Relative proportion of attested price information

2. DIFFERENTIATING THE DATA

2.1. Sale prices

The category of sales prices at first seems to be the most relevant for the question of market integration. Of the entire sample of price information taken into consideration, they form just one quarter of our total of prices, or 23 data (fig. 12.1). Unfortunately we lack sufficient information to differentiate the data of this group. In particular we would like to know surrounding factors to eliminate variation for other than economic reasons. Grain prices vary according to season, location, and conditions of sale, that is, variables that need to be corrected before comparison over time. Moreover, we do not know whether sales prices reflect market prices in all instances. Heichelheim differentiated his price data according to the following principles, without, however, considering how this might affect his comparative time series:

1 pre-harvest prices
2 post harvest prices
3 prices paid by the administration
4 market prices
5 farm-gate prices

We can adopt these categories but add a further one considering regional variation. Different market conditions and transport costs determined prices, for example, in the capital of Alexandria as opposed to the *chora*; and possibly different degrees of monetization and market development affected price formation in Upper as opposed to Lower Egypt.

25% (independent of currency changes) in the reign of Ptolemy IV.

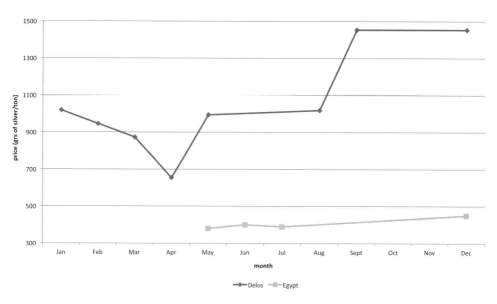

Fig. 12.2 Inter-annual variation of cereal prices on Delos and in Egypt

SEASONAL VARIATION

We have two documents indicating seasonally specific sales prices in Table 12.1 (5) and (28). The harvest in Egypt started in late March/early April; thus the prices of these documents are likely to represent higher than average prices within the agrarian year. However, the same document as (28) mentions payment for 'this year's grain' (*puros eniausios*, P. Tebt. I 112, 57 and 118) which suggests that new grain already was, or would soon become, available.[17] In Egypt, moreover, seasonal variation of cereal prices seems to have been relatively low. If similar rules applied to wheat as to olyra, the degree of variation of cereal prices in Egypt within one year can be taken from Table 12.3.[18] In comparison with the seasonal variation of cereal prices on Delos (Table 12.6), it was moderate.

REGIONAL VARIATION

We have two documents relating to Alexandria (3 and 13) that indicate significantly higher wheat prices in the capital than in the *chora*. We have also one price from Thebes in Upper Egypt (30), showing no particular difference from price levels in the Fayum and adjacent areas. This is somewhat surprising, since in Duncan-Jones's analysis of wheat prices in Roman Egypt, the median average in Lower Egypt is twice the

---

[17] Verhoogt 2005 *ad loc.* for the expression. Possibly the expenditure at that time of the year represented an option on grain that was soon coming in.

[18] Since olyra in contrast to wheat was not exported from Egypt, seasonal variation of prices was strictly determined by agricultural factors.

median average of wheat prices in Upper Egypt.[19] Such price discrepancy might be regarded as being reflected in the lower penalty price attested in Thebes for the years 109 and 108 BC (Table 12.2 (39) and (40)); but yet lower penalty prices are attested in the Arsinoite, Herakleopolite and Hermopolite nomes (Table 12.2 (22) and (24)–(26)). There is thus no positive evidence for regional price variation between Upper und Lower Egypt in our sample.

OFFICIAL GRAIN PRICES?

We have two documents representing grain purchases by a local tax office (26–28). But both belong to the same dossier representing the activities of Menches, a village clerk in Kerkeosiris in the Arsinoite nome. It may be significant that the price of 2 drachmas per artaba comes from a time when official penalty prices oscillated around 3 to 5 drachmas (Table 12.2 (22–31)). So 2 drachmas might reflect the 'normal' price that the government set for the conversion of debts in kind into cash. But the documents reveal nothing about special conditions under which grain was purchased by public officials.[20]

LOCATION OF SALE

How can we distinguish between market prices and prices negotiated between individuals on the farm? In very few cases is it clear from the context that market prices are mentioned. (3) and (13) explicitly refer to current prices in Alexandria, while (5), (14) and (35–37) relate quite unequivocally to market prices in the *chora*. But for the rest it is impossible to draw the distinction. Does the fact that an individual is named as recipient of the purchase price point to the fact that the grain was not transacted in the market? This would be quite an untenable assumption. Do prices attested in the Zenon archive, an archive compiled in connection with the management of a large estate, indicate farm-gate prices? This would be an equally untenable assumption. To take, furthermore, lower than usual prices as farm-gate prices would lead us into tautologies. We must come to the conclusion that there is simply no way of identifying different kinds of sales condition within the sample of prices we have.

2.2. Conversion rates

A fair number of our prices are not real prices but conversion rates of wheat into cash, or cash into wheat (15%, or 14 in total).[21] Conversion rates between cash and kind were used in a great variety of circumstances. Employees on large agrarian estates or the local administration could commute their cash wages into wheat payments, or

---

[19]   Duncan-Jones 1976, 243.

[20]   Accounts of local offices or tax offices frequently refer to *sitos agorastos* (purchased grain), which suggests that the local administration had no privileged access to the royal grain stores in which tax grain was stored; see von Reden 2007, 87.

[21]   Conversion rates are integrated into Table 12.1, but differentiated in fig. 12.5.

vice versa, either to buy food for themselves or sub-employees. Landlords who had provided monetary loans to their tenants for financing additional agrarian labour (so-called *katerga* loans) also commuted these into kind when adding them to the rent at the end of the rental period. Moreover, certain tenancy contracts (termed 'prodomatic' by modern scholars) foresaw a full or part pre-payment (*prodoma*) of the rent as a loan in cash which was offset against the rent in kind at the end of the agrarian year (e.g. Table 12.1 (18)). Once again, a rate of conversion by which the loan in cash was to be offset against the rent in kind was agreed in the tenancy contract.[22] A similar construction was the sale of a commodity (such as grain) against advance payment of money repayable with interest in form of the commodity purchased (e.g. Table 12.1 (25)). Legal scholars have termed this transaction a 'sale with deferred delivery'. Although this was one reason for making the contract, it could also be used as a way of borrowing money to be repaid in kind. So the 'price' of the commodity purchased was the loan to be repaid plus interest.[23]

Finally, there was an official rate of conversion between cash and kind that applied to the commutation of rental debts on royal land into cash penalties, and there might have been further such rates for commuting cash taxes into kind and vice versa.

Documents (7) to (8) and (16) in Table 12.1, belonging to the Zenon archive, represent the practice of private employees converting their monetary salary into payments in kind at an 'internal' rate (see also (15), (34) and (35)). Documents (6) and (10), belonging to the same archive, represent the rate at which Zenon himself converted *katerga* loans into grain rents payable by his tenants. Documents (27) and (29) represent cash salaries converted into wheat by a local tax office. It is notable that the conversion rates of the tax office are very close to those used by Zenon for his tenants. Moreover, they remained remarkably similar over a period of 150 years. No distinction, furthermore, seems to have been made as to whether a landlord commuted his own cash advances into kind or an employee his wage into grain handouts. It should also be noted that interpersonal conversion rates tended to be lower than the official rate applied to unfulfilled contracts, as well as market prices.

2.3. Penalty prices

Penalty prices (so-called *epitima*) form the largest category of attested prices (60%, or 54 in total). During most of the third century BC *epitima* remained stable at 4 drachmas per *artaba*, representing double the official conversion rate of 2 drachmas per *artaba* of wheat (Table 12.2). In about 220 BC, however, the official penalty price that had been valid for at least 80 years increased to 5 drachma, representing an official conversion rate of grain into cash of 2 1/2 drachmas. Soon afterwards penalty prices rose further to 10 drachmas. However, as will be suggested in the next section, this increase does not reflect real price rise, but a nominal increase due to a currency

---

[22]   Von Reden 2007, 186–91.
[23]   Bagnall 1977.

change in which the value of the bronze drachma was halved against the silver drachma in which penalty prices were assessed. Assuming further the currency changes I shall suggest below, *epitima* remained stable at this level for the next one and a half centuries, although oscillating around that level temporarily.

The fluctuation of the official penalty price suggests several aspects in relation to market prices. First, penalty prices may have been oriented at current market prices and responded, if slowly, to changes of this price (e.g. in 220 BC and possibly in the middle of the second century when various rates appear in the sample). An alternative, and in my view more likely, explanation would be that market prices were oriented towards official prices which were regarded as reflecting a normal or customary price. Secondly, they suggest in principle great stability of wheat prices over a period of two and a half centuries. Once again, the stability might be regarded as due to market conditions, or to the fact that official penalty prices and conversion rates stabilized the market price. However, one might perceive a slightly greater volatility in the mid to late second century, although such variation might be due to our lack of knowledge of short-term currency changes, or lesser state control over *epitima* in private contracts. Thirdly, the movement of penalty prices might suggest an increase of market prices by about 25% by the late third century BC.

3. CREATING A TIME SERIES OF PRICES

3.1. Measures

In order to compare prices over time and place, local weight and currency systems must be translated into comparable units. One way of comparing variable ancient units of weight and capacity is by converting them all into modern metrological units. In the case of cereals, however, this bears the problem of translating measures of capacity into measures of weight, as we tend to weigh cereal products on a scale rather than filling standard baskets or sacks. Yet different varieties of grain as well as grains of different regions have a different weight per volume, and we need to make modern experiments to get an idea of the variability.[24] Cereals also have a different weight/volume relationship depending on whether they are sold before or after sifting and winnowing. In Egypt cereals could be sold and purchased in both conditions. In P. Lond. VII 1996, for example, 2 1/2% are added to the price for the fact that the grain was sifted before sale.[25] There were also different measures used in different parts of Egypt and its foreign possessions. The artaba used most commonly in the Arsinoite nome was that of 40 choinikes (roughly 40 litres), but different artabas are attested in other texts. The fact that oil crop was measured in an artaba of 30 choinikes both

---

[24]   Thus done in the pioneering exercise by Foxhall and Forbes 1982 based on modern Greek cereals.

[25]   Skeat *ad* P. Lond. VII 1996, 40.

in the Arsinoite nome and beyond (e.g. P. Rev. 39, 2 and 19, P. Cair. Zen. IV 59717, P. L. Bat. XX, 12 and 13) does not have to concern us here, although scholars have used these texts for discussing the artaba of wheat.[26] Yet P. Cair. Zen. I 59004, 16 does mention an artaba of 30 choinikes in the Ptolemaic province of Syria-Palestine, and the demotic contract of P. Loeb. dem. 3, 11, drawn up in the Hermopolite nome, specifies that the rent in wheat be measured out in an artaba of 28 choinikes.[27] Contracting partners sometimes also distinguished whether payment was to be made in the 'receiving' (*dochikon*) or 'paying' (*anelotikon*) measure, the former containing 42 as opposed to 40 choinikes of grain (e.g. P. Tebt. I, 11 and P. Lond. VII 1996, 40; cf. Table 12.2 (25); Table 12.1 (19)). Rents in kind were usually assessed by the landlord in the *dochikon* measure, and may then not have influenced the rate of conversion into cash, but when grain was purchased or sold in the *dochikon* measure the 'difference in measure' (*metrou diaphoron*) was accounted for in terms of a 5% surcharge on the price.[28] In order not to complicate things too much, and since the majority of our prices come from the Arsinoite nome, I shall assume for all prices an artaba of 40 choinikes representing roughly 40 l or 30 kg of Egyptian wheat (note, however, the exceptions in Table 12.1 (11); and Table 12.2 (1) and (25)!).

According to conventional understanding, the Egyptian artaba was c. 20% lighter than the Attic/Delian medimnos containing 48 choinikes of the same size as the Egyptian choinix. Thus Foxhall and Forbes (1982), following Hultsch (1862), calculated the medimnos of wheat at 40 kg with a choinix of 1.09 l equivalent to c. 840 grs of wheat. This calculation, however, seems to be rendered obsolete by an inscription that came to light in the Athenian agora in 1986.[29] According to this Athenian grain-tax law, the choinix was equivalent to 623 grs of wheat, and thus the medimnos of wheat, quite similar to the Egyptian artaba, equivalent to just over 30 kg.[30] Since, however, it is assumed that Egyptian wheat was bulkier than the varieties consumed in Attica and the Aegean, an Egyptian artaba was still not equivalent to an Athenian/Delian medimnos of wheat. The difference was, on current understanding, within the range of 25%.

3.2. Currency

Translating different currency systems into comparable units is even more complicated. In order to create a cross-cultural system we have to convert ancient monetary units

---

[26] E.g *LÄ* III, p. 1212 s.v. Maße und Gewichte; also Pestman in P. L. Bat. XXI, vol. 2, p. 549; see, by contrast Shelton 1977.

[27] Shelton's 1977 argument that there was only one artaba of 40 choinikes for the measurement of grain throughout Egypt is therefore not entirely convincing. For an overview of measures used in the Zenon archive, see P. L.. Bat. XXI, vol. 2, p. 549.

[28] Rowlandson 1996, 242–3 for the practice in tenancy contracts (P. Tebt. I 11 for a Ptolemaic example); Skeats *ad* P. Lond. VII 1996, 40 for accounting practice.

[29] Agora inv. I 7557; Rhodes and Osborne 2003, no. 26 (374/3 BC).

[30] Rosivach 2000 for discussion.

Ptolemaic currency standard (third century BC)

1 *Stater* (4 drachms)	14. 3	(x 1.25 = Attic)
1 Drachma (6 obols)	3.6 g.	(x 1.15 = Attic)
1 Obol (8 chalkoi)	(0.6 g)	(bronze coin)
1 Mna (100 dr)	(357 g = 27.8 g gold)	(gold coin; s/g 1:13)
1 Talent (6000 dr)	(22.42 kg)	(unit of account)

Attic currency standard (fourth to first quarter of the second century BC)

1 *Stater* (4 dr)	17.4 g	(5 dr of Ptolemaic currency)
1 Drachma (6 ob)	4.36 g	(1 dr 1 ob of Ptolemaic currency)
1 Obol (8 chal)	0.728 g	(bronze coin)
1 Mna (100 dr)	(436 g)	(unit of account)
1 Talent (6000dr)	(26.196 kg)	(unit of account)

Fig. 12.3 Ptolemaic and Attic currency standards

into the amount of grams of silver represented by the tetradrachm (stater), shekel or denarius used in the texts. We are aware that this is a tool for comparison only, since the real value of silver itself was subject to variation. In Egypt, moreover, during the late third to late second centuries BC no silver currency was used at all in payment for grain. Some prices were reckoned in silver, but all payments were made in bronze, and bronze denominations had a flexible rather than fixed relationship to the value of silver coins.[31]

Because of their need of money and lack of silver resources, the Ptolemies soon after the conquest of Egypt minted a silver currency that was 25% lighter than coinages in the Attic standard that dominated the eastern Mediterranean during the Hellenistic period (fig. 12.3). In order to earn silver, the Ptolemies exchanged all heavy-weight silver coins against their own lighter one at a rate of 1:1, and prohibited the use of foreign coins in their country as well as their closer possessions of Syria-Palestine, Cyrene and Cyprus.[32] Outside of Egypt and these provinces, the Ptolemaic currency was exchanged according to its real weight, that is, 5 Ptolemaic silver drachmas against one Attic-weight tetradrachm and 1 drachma 1 obol of Ptolemaic coinage for 1 Attic-weight drachm. Early Ptolemaic Egypt had a tri-metallic currency system of silver drachmas and tetradrachms (the *stater*), bronze obols, half-obols and *chalkoi*, as well as gold *chrusoi* and *trichrusa* valued at 20 and 60 silver drachmas respectively.

Because of the increasing demand for coinage within Egypt, Ptolemy II increased the size of the bronze coinage in around 265 BC by minting pieces of up to one drachma. Bronze denominations of such value had been unusual in the Greek world where bronze had been minted for denominations not above one obol. The Ptolemaic bronze drachma within Egypt was traded as equal to one drachm in silver, although in certain

---

[31]   The price of silver increased by 100–150% in the course of the second century, while the bronze currency was pegged to silver according to a value relationship by weight. See below and Maresch 1996, 195–8.

[32]   Jenkins 1967; Cadell and Le Rider 1997, 9–21; von Reden 2007, 29–78.

cases an agio of c. 10% was charged on exchange. In most payments to the state (taxes, penalties or rents), but also in some private transactions, payment *pros argurion* ('towards silver') was requested, which meant that the agio was to be paid on top.

The system worked until the end of the reign of Ptolemy III (c. 223/2 BC) when silver currency seems to have become increasingly rare in the *chora*. Although tax, rent and other liabilities were still charged in the silver standard (*pros argurion*), in practice no payments were made in silver coins any longer. While for a few more years bronze drachms were still virtually equivalent to silver ones, by the end of the 220s the currency system of Ptolemy II was reformed.

The first step seems to have been to reduce the value of the bronze drachma against its silver equivalent by 50%, so that 2 drachms of bronze had to be paid for 1 drachm in *pros argurion* payments. The change is reflected in the change of penalty prices from the former 5 drachmas (in silver) to 10 drachms in bronze.

The subsequent currency changes in Egypt are hard to understand and highly controversial.[33] No ancient author has commented on the changes, and the rhythmical price increases that we can observe in the papyrological documents are the only guide to the development. This has created the great methodological problem of separating real changes of price from changes of nominal prices.

A fairly independent source for the nature of the currency change are certain governmental *epitimia* which, rather than being related to commodity prices, represent fines imposed by the state for the breach of contract.[34] These fines remained payable in silver and thus offer some idea of the variable amounts of bronze drachmas payable towards a sum of silver.[35] There is no room here for detailed discussion of the evidence and the model of currency transformation derived from it.[36] Suffice it to give a brief outline of a possible scenario in order to understand the translation of prices into the silver standard of the third century. This will form the basis for our conversion of late third to first-century prices into grams of silver.

Towards the late third century BC the amount of bronze coinage paid for a silver stater (a tetradrachm) steadily increased. In 209 BC 16 bronze drachmas were paid for one silver tetradrachm plus the agio of c. 10% (UPZ I149, 32).[37] Probably as a result of the increasing discrepancy of the valuation of silver and bronze coinage in everyday

---

[33] Reekmans 1951; Maresch 1996; Cadell and Le Rider 1997.

[34] These penalty charges need to be distinguished from the penalty prices explained in the previous section, as they were independent of the nature of the commodity or money owed by contract. Although the Greeks called them both *epitima* the one set a cash price (in silver and later bronze) for the commodity owed in kind, the other represented a fine dependent on the value but not the nature of the commodity or money owing. The fines were always payable in silver, but when paid in bronze (which was the norm) the conversion rate immediately reflected the current silver price. Therefore *epitima* give a better picture of the currency changes of the second century BC than models based on changing commodity prices; see Maresch 1996, *passim*.

[35] In the following I use the italicized term *drachmai* to distinguish the drachma weight from the monetary unit.

[36] I am following Maresch 1996, whose model I have discussed in von Reden 2007, 70–8.

[37] Cadell and Le Rider 1997, 52–6 for discussion and dating of this text.

practice, a governmental reform of the monetary system became necessary at the end of the third century.[38] It seems that bronze coins were no longer valued against the silver stater as had been usual in the tri-metallic monetary system, but according to the customary real relationship of value between silver and bronze, which was 1:60.[39] As a result, there appears a nominal jump of prices by a factor of 60 in our evidence. In principle, the fiduciary element of the bronze coinage was given up; in practice, however, it is unlikely that 60 bronze drachmas (weight) were given in payment of a sum expressed in these terms. More likely, coins of a certain size and weight represented a certain quantity of bronze drachmas (like inflation money of the twentieth century) and coins thus continued to have a fiduciary element. [40]

The consequence of this monetary manipulation was that coins could be manipulated almost arbitrarily in the future. In the course of the second century, once around 180 BC and another time at around 160 BC, the number of bronze drachmai represented by certain coins was doubled again.[41] As a result, nominal prices increased further, reaching 120 and 240 times the level of former prices reckoned in silver currency.

Around 130 BC the monetary system underwent further change. Silver currency reappears in the papyri. But from demotic texts and the level of *epitima* we can assume that no longer 4 but 20 monetary drachms were reckoned to the stater (the tetradrachm), while the bronze drachma continued to be reckoned either at 1/120 or 1/60 to the silver drachma.[42] Thus a silver stater came to be represented by 1200 or 2400 bronze drachmas. Under Kleopatra VII the currency system gradually returned to its third-century model, but the silver coinage was massively debased to about 30% of its former silver content, probably in the attempt to find a new solution to continuing silver shortage.[43] Unfortunately, no price data for wheat are attested for this period to allow insights into how consumers responded.

---

[38]   Huston and Lorber 2001 for the visibility of this reform in the hoard evidence.

[39]   For this ratio, see Menu 1982, 169.

[40]   Maresch 1996, 60–1 with Weiser 1995, although the latter's attribution of extant coins to monetary values is controversial.

[41]   Various political reasons may be adduced for explaining these changes, which has led scholars to date the currency changes to 183 and 163 BC precisely; see Maresch 1996, *passim*, and Reekmans 1951. I regard the reconstruction of political contexts for monetary changes in Egypt as fairly arbitrary. The reform of c. 180 BC may have been the result of Ptolemy VI acceding to the throne and the inauguration of his dynastic cult. The reform of c. 164/3 may be connected with the expulsion of Ptolemy VI from Egypt and the establishment of the single rule of Ptolemy VIII, celebrated by the inauguration of his dynastic cult in 180 BC; further examples of the possible connection between dynastic change and monetary reform in von Reden 2007, 48ff and 62ff.

[42]   The changes of Period 5 appear first in, and can be taken from, demotic papyri which followed different conventions of noting monetary sums and prices; Maresch 1996, 34–51 and 80–4. Several systems seem to have existed contemporaneously, as is reflected in the level of *epitima* and land prices, which were not only reckoned but also paid in silver currency. In the case of commodity and penalty prices we can only glean from their level which monetary values were applied; see Table 2 (45) and (52).

[43]   Hazzard 1990.

Period 1: (c. 220–c. 200; Ptolemy IV)
1 silver drachma = 2 bronze drachmas

Period 2: (c. 200–c.180 or later; Ptolemy V)
Bronze currency is tariffed at the relationship of the metal value between bronze
and silver of 1:60:

  60 bronze drachma = 1 drachm of former silver drachma

Period 3: (c. 180 – 164/3; Ptolemy VI)
Relationship of metal value between bronze and silver, or nominal value of bronze
coins, doubles once again:

  120 bronze drachmai = 1 third-century silver drachma

Period 4: (164/3- c.130; Ptolemy VIII)
Value of bronze coins further decreases by 100 per cent:

  240 bronze drachmai = 1 third-century silver drachma

Period 5: (c. 130- 30; Ptolemy VIII – Kleopatra VII)
Bronze currency is possibly linked to silver currency again, but in a new
relationship of value:

  1 bronze drachma = 1/120 of silver drachma (occasionally also 1/60 of silver drachma)
  1 drachma (bronze or silver) no longer 1/4 of the stater ('tetradrachma') but 1/20.

Fig. 12.4 *Currency changes from the late third to first centuries BC*

The various phases of change that I have outlined in this section are summarised
in fig. 12.4.

For our price series in Table 12.1 this leads to the following equivalencies between
the prices attested in our documents and the prices in the Ptolemaic silver standard
of the third century BC (fig. 12.5).

Period 1. (c. 220–c. 200): × 2
Period 2: (c. 200–183/168): × 60
Period 3: (183–130): × 120
Period 4: (163–130): × 240
Period 4: (c. 130–30): × 600 or × 300

Fig. 12.5 *Suggested equivalencies of bronze currency with third-century silver standard*

On this basis we arrive at a surprisingly plausible price series from the late third to the first century BC (figs. 12.6–12.8, below).

4. EGYPTIAN PRICES IN THE LIGHT OF OTHER MEDITERRANEAN PRICE INFORMATION

The price series from Hellenistic Egypt may be compared with the prices of wheat and barley we have from classical Athens and Hellenistic Delos (Tables 12.7 and 12.8 [Athens], 12.4 and 12.5 [Delos]). As very few data have survived under very different circumstances, only the most general observations can be made. In Athens, both price data and explicit statements about price developments convey a firm notion of a 'normal' wheat price that government and benefactors aimed to maintain, or re-establish, at times of crisis (Table 12.7 (6), (8) and (13)). Thus both honorary decrees and Attic orators praise individuals who imported grain at times of scarcity in order to achieve a return to the normal or the 'established' price.[44] Such a normal price seems to have ranged between 5 and 6 drachms per medimnos of wheat. These prices lie above those attested in the Egyptian *chora* during the Hellenistic period, but only about 15 to 20% above those attested for Alexandria (Table 12.1 (3) and (13)). The prices are comparable to Delian summer prices, but the inter-annual variation of the Delian price material also puts into perspective the Athenian emergency price of 335 BC (Table 12.7 (6)) which is just a little over 50% above the Delian winter price (Table 12.4 (7)–(10)). Still, it is noteworthy that in Athens rather dramatic deviations from the normal price occurred, reaching up to three times the normal price. In the Egyptian papyri, price variation of no more than 20 to 30% is attested. However, comparison with Athens may render more plausible the story of Kleomenes tampering with a grain price that had reached three to five times the level of average prices in the *chora* during the third century (Table 12.1 (1)). Equally noteworthy, however, is that the 'normal' price of Athenian wheat remained as stable as average prices in Egypt between the third and first centuries.

The data from Delos show above all the extent of inter-annual variation of wheat prices in what might have been a market of imported grain.[45] An increase by as much as 60% of the summer price during the winter months may have been quite normal in any given year. In Egypt no more than a 20% price difference between summer and winter prices is attested. The Delian inter-annual price range, incidentally, may once again explain why a benefactor could be praised for selling imported grain at 50% above the 'normal' rate (Table 12.7 (8)). But beyond the crude observation that prices in Athens, Delos and Alexandria were fairly comparable, there is no indication that grain prices in the Greek cities of the Mediterranean were dependent on each other.

---

[44]   Such established prices (*kathestekuia time*, Dem. 34, 39; cf. 56, 8 and 10) cannot be regarded as a fixed or 'regulated' price, as Migeotte 1997 has argued; the term *kathestekuia time* rather refers to the level that had been negotiated in the harbour and was then regarded as 'established', see Eich 2006, 218–38, esp. 235.

[45]   Reger 1994, 83–116 for the conditions of the Delian grain supply.

5. CONCLUSIONS

Heichelheim argued that there was an increase of purchasing power of the Greek drachm in the first half of the third century causing prices all over the Mediterranean to fall. Towards the end of the century purchasing power decreased, either because of an increase in production or a decrease of liquid capital caused in turn by the movements of capital beyond Egypt, or the hoarding of money within the country (for which, incidentally, there is no numismatic evidence). The dynastic crises and local revolts in the second century, moreover, destabilized prices even further.

In light of the foregoing discussion and the qualification of the material produced in Tables 12.1 and 12.2, one must be more moderate in drawing conclusions for economic history. There are simply too few *comparable* data for creating a general model of long-term price development in Hellenistic Egypt. Still, one might wish to point out that both real prices of wheat and conversion rates remained quite stable over a period of over 200 hundred years. This price stability can be confirmed by the level of wages which remained equally stable in relation to contemporary prices of wheat. In 257 BC, for example, an *ergates* (worker) earned 1 obol a day buying 2 choinikes of wheat at 2 drachmas 2 obols per artaba. In 182 BC an *ergates* earned 20 drachmas daily, again buying 2 choinikes of wheat at 160 drachmas per artaba. In 94 or 61 BC an *ergates* earned 120 dr as daily wage, buying 2 1/2 choinikes of wheat at 2000 drachmas.[46] Tentatively I have suggested that price stability was influenced by governments setting prices for their own penalty payments involving conversion of grain into a cash value, and conversion rates of cash into kind and *vice versa* in case of other payments to and from the state. Market prices, in other words, were not regulated by the government, but in practice followed price setting according to conventional or customary rates.

If between the third and first centuries BC there was some population increase, as it is arguable in light of the growth of the capital of Alexandria, Greek immigration, and agricultural extensification,[47] price stability over two centuries might mean an increase in economic performance during that period. Increasing aggregate consumption was met by an increase in aggregate production that kept supply and demand at a stable level. Price stability might be taken as an indication for a high degree of internal market integration. But the data from Egypt are too few to distinguish market forces from other forces that stabilized prices.

One might further observe that there was a slight but general increase in price of about 25% by the end of the third century, reflected in the long-term increase of the penalty prices set in contracts from the 2nd century BC onwards. The most significant change observable in the price series is an apparently greater volatility of prices in the second as compared to the third century. This might be just a reflection of the troubled currency, or of our lack of understanding of it. But it is also possible that the greater variation of wheat prices is a reflection of increased monetization and an increase of market exchange that predictably leads to a greater volatility of prices

---

[46] E.g. PSI IV 332, 10 and *passim* (257/6 BC); P. Tebt. III 2, 22.40 (c. 182 BC); P. Tebt. I 108 descr. (95/4 or 61/3 BC); further examples in Maresch 1996, 191–4.

[47] Monson 2012.

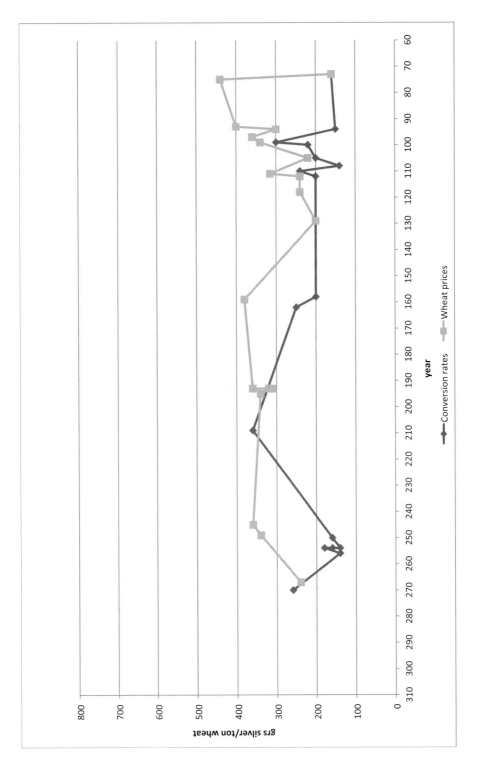

Fig. 12.6. Wheat prices and conversion rates

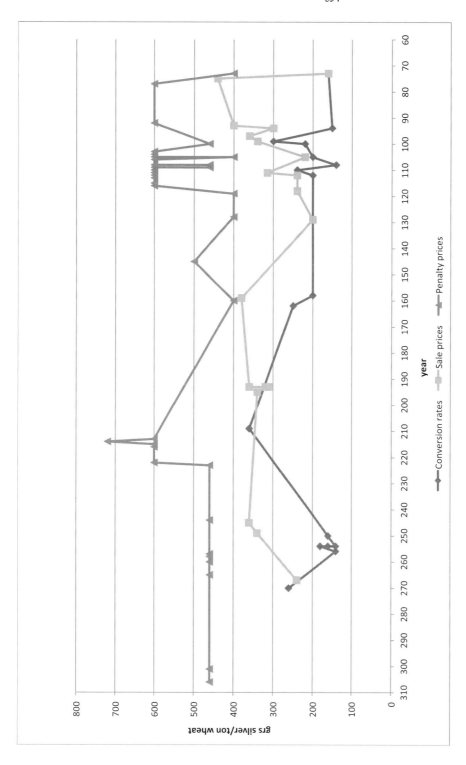

Fig. 12.7. Wheat prices differentiated by category

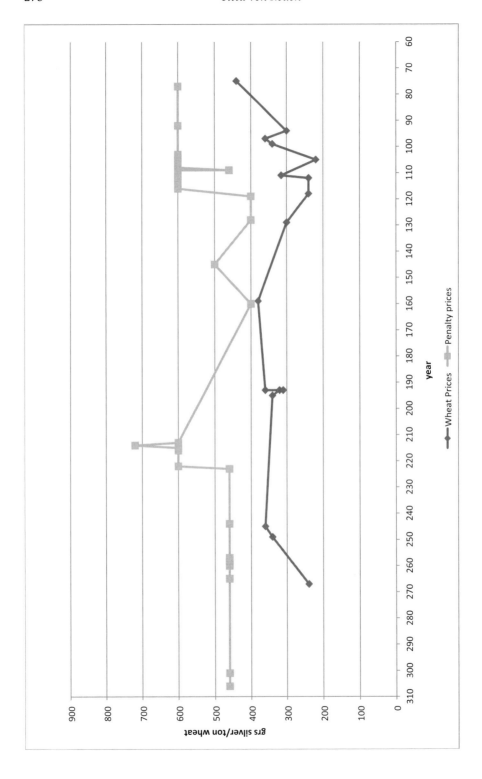

Fig. 12.8. Wheat prices (including conversion rates) in comparison to penalty prices

affected increasingly by supply and demand rather than notions of customary price. The problems of the silver currency that arose at the end of the 220 BC need not be interpreted in terms of exceedingly high (or excessive) expenditure of the king—as our moralizing literary sources have it. But they may equally well, and more plausibly, be regarded as the result of an increasing demand for coinage in face of increasing monetization but limited silver resources.

REFERENCES

Andreau, J., Briant, P. and Descat, R. (eds) (1997) Économie antique. *Prix et formation des prix dans les économies antiques.* Saint-Bertrand-de-Comminges: Musée archéologique départemental de Saint-Bertrand-de-Comminges.

Bagnall, R. (1977) Prices in sales with deferred delivery. *Greek, Roman and Byzantine Studies* 18, 85–96.

Bagnall, R. (1999) Review of Cadell and Le Rider 1997. *Schweizerische Numismatische Rundschau* 78, 197–203.

Beyer, F. (1995) *Geldpolitik in der römischen Kaiserzeit. Von der Währungsreform des Augustus bis Septimius Severus.* Wiesbaden: Dt. Universitätsverlag.

Cadell, H. (1994) Le prix de vente des terres dans l'Égypte ptoléma que d'après les papyrus grècs. In S. Allam (ed.) *Grund und Boden in Altägypten. Akten des internationalen Symposiums in Tübingen 18.-20. Juni 1990,* 289–305. Tübingen: S. Allam.

Cadell, H. and Le Rider, G. (1997) *Prix du Blé et Numéraire dans l'Égypte Lagide de 305-173.* Brussels: Fondation Égyptol. Reine Élisabeth.

Duncan-Jones, R. (1976) The price of wheat in Roman Egypt under the principate. *Chiron* 6, 241–262.

Eich, A. (2006) *Die politische Ökonomie des antiken Griechenland (6. - 3. Jh. v. Chr.).* Cologne: Böhlau.

Foxhall, L. and Forbes, H. A. (1982) Sitometreia: the role of grain as a staple food in classical antiquity. *Chiron* 12, 41–90.

Harl, K. W. (1996) *Coinage in the Roman Economy.* Baltimore/London: Johns Hopkins University Press.

Hazzard, R.A. (1990) The composition of Ptolemaic Silver. *Journal of the Society for the Study of Egyptian Antiquities* 20, 89–107.

Heichelheim, F. (1930) *Wirtschaftliche Schwankungen der Zeit von Alexander bis Augustus.* Jena: Fischer.

Howgego, C. (1995) *Ancient History from Coins.* London: Routledge.

Hultsch, F. (1862) *Griechische und römische Metrologie.* Berlin (repr. 1971): Weidmann.

Huston, S. M. and Lorber, C. (2001) A hoard of Ptolemaic bronze coins in commerce, October 1992 (CH 8, 413). *Numismatic Chronicle* 161, 11–40.

Jenkins, G. K. (1967) The monetary system in the early Hellenistic times with special regard to the economy of the Ptolemaic kings. In A. Kindler (ed.) *The Patterns of Monetary Development in Phoenicia and Palestine in Antiquity,* 53–74 (Proceedings of the International Numismatic Convention, Jerusalem, 27–31 Dec. 1963). Tel Aviv: Schocken.

Maresch, K. (1996) *Bronze und Silber. Papyrologische Beiträge zur Geschichte der Währung im ptolemäischen und römischen Ägypten bis zum 2. Jh. n. Chr.* Opladen: Westdeutscher Verlag.

Menu, B. (1982) Le prêt en droit égyptien ancien (Nouvel Empire et Basse Epoque). In B. Menu (ed.) *Recherches sur l'histoire juridique, économique et sociale de l'Ancienne Égypte*, 217–300. I. Versailles: B. Menu.

Migeotte, L. (1997) Le contrôle des prix dans les cités grecques. In Andreau *et al.* (eds), 33–52.

Monson, A. (2012) *From the Ptolemies to the Romans. Political and Economic Change in Egypt.* Cambridge: Cambridge University Press.

Noeske, H.-C. (2000) Zum numismatischen Nachweis hellenistischer Stiftungen am Beispiel ptolemäischer Geldgeschenke. In K. Bringmann (ed.) *Schenkungen hellenistischer Herrscher an griechische Städte und Heiligtümer. Vol. II.1*, 221–248. Berlin: Akademischer Verlag.

Préaux, C. (1937) *L'Économie royal des Lagides.* Brussels: Édition de la Fondation égyptologique reine Élisabeth.

Rathbone, D. (1996) Monetization not price inflation. In C. E. King and D. G. Wigg (eds) *Coin Finds and Coin Use in the Roman World. 13th Oxford Symposium on Coinage and Monetary History*, 321–339 (Studien zu Fundmünzen der Antike 10). Berlin: Mann Verlag.

Reekmans, T. (1951) The Ptolemaic copper inflation. *Studia Hellenistica* 7, 61–119.

Reger, G. (1994) *Regionalism and Change in the Economy of Independent Delos.* Berkeley: University of California Press.

Rhodes, P. and Osborne, R. (2003) *Greek Historical Inscriptions, 404 - 323 BC.* Oxford: Oxford University Press.

Rosivach, V. (2000) Some economic aspects of the fourth-century Athenian market in grain. *Chiron* 30, 31–64.

Rowlandson, J. (1996) *Landowners and Tenants in Roman Egypt.* Oxford: Clarendon Press.

Seidl, E. (1962) *Ptolemäische Rechtsgeschichte* (Ägyptologische Forschungen 22). Glückstadt: Augustin.

Shelton, J. S. (1977) Artabs and Choinikes. *Zeitschrift für Papyrologie und Epigraphik* 24, 55–67.

Verhoogt, A. (2005) *Regaling Officials in Ptolemaic Egypt* (Pap. Lugd. Bat. 32). Leiden: Brill.

von Reden, S. (2007) *Money in Ptolemaic Egypt.* Cambridge: Cambridge University Press.

von Reden, S. (2010) *Money in Classical Antiquity.* Cambridge: Cambridge University Press.

Weber, F. (1932) *Untersuchungen zum gräko-römischen Obligationenrecht.* München: Beck.

Weiser, W. (1995) *Katalog Ptolemäischer Bronzemünzen der Sammlung des Instituts für Altertumskunde der Universität Köln* (Papyrologica Coloniensia 23). Opladen: Westdeutscher Verlag.

APPENDIX

Table 12.1 Wheat prices and conversion rates in Egypt, third to first centuries BC

	Date	Price/artaba in dr.	Silver Price/artaba in dr.	Grs of silver/ton[1]	Reference	Notes
1	c. 330	10 (Attic standard)	10	1200	[Arist]. *Oik.* 1352 b	Emergency price of grain in the *chora*; possibly a stylized figure.
2	270	2 dr 1 ob	2 dr 1 ob	260	P. Hib. I 99, 14	*adaeratio*[2] of wheat rent
3	270	4 dr 5 ob	4 dr 5 ob	580	P. Hib. I 110, 11	Market price in Alexandria
4	267	2	2	240	P. Hib. I 100, 6	Payment for grain
5	256/March	2 dr 5 ob	2 dr 5 ob	340	P. Mich. Zen 28	Bulk sale in harbour
6	256?	1 dr 1 ob	1 dr 1 ob	140	SB XIV 11659, 4	Tenancy contract. Conversion of monetary loans into wheat rent
7	254/Jan and Feb	1 dr 3 ob	1 dr 3 ob	180	PCZ[3] III 59499,*r* 4 and 5	Conversion of monetary payment into wheat
8	254/March	1 dr 2 ob	1 dr 2 ob	160	PCZ III 59499, 7	Conversion of monetary payment into wheat
9	254	1 dr 1 ob	1 dr 1 ob	140	P. Lond. VII 1974, 38	Payment for *sitometria*[4] grain
10	250	1 dr 2 ob	1 dr 2 ob	160	P. Col. Zen. I 54, 16	Tenancy contract. Conversion of monetary loans into wheat rent.
11	c. 250?	3	3	360	P. Lond. VII 1996,41	Sales price of grain in ‚dochikon' measure
12	c. 249?	2 dr 5 ob	2 dr 5 ob	340	P. Lond. VII 2002, 28	Price of grain
13	249	5 dr 2 ob	5 dr 2 ob	640	PCZ III 59320	Price in Alexandria
14	mid 3rd	3	3	360	P. Sorb. 33, 15 f.	Market price
15	mid 3rd	1 dr 3 ob	1 dr 3 ob	180	P. Petr. III, 47 (a) 3	Payment for *sitometria* grain
16	mid 3rd	1 dr 3 ob	1 dr 3 ob	180	PCZ IV 59698, 5	Payment for *sitometria* grain

[1] Calculated as 0.6 [g weight of 1 ob] x (price in obols) x 33.3 [artabas of wheat in kg per ton]

[2] *adaeratio* = payment in cash of a payment calculated in kind

[3] PCZ = P. Cair. Zen.

[4] *sitometria* = grain handout

	Date	Price/artaba in dr.	Silver Price/artaba in dr.	Grs of silver/ton[1]	Reference	Notes
17	3rd	2	2	240	P. Petr. III 80 a ii 16 and 22	Payment for grain
18	209	6	3	360	P. Heid. VI 383, 20	Prodomatic tenancy agreement.[5] Repayment of monetary loan as rent in kind
19	195?	170	2 dr 5 ob	340	P. Köln V 217, 6 ff	Sales price of grain
20	193/87	160	2 dr 4 ob	320	BGU VII 1536,3	Sales price of grain
21	193/87	155	2 dr 3.5 ob	310	BGU VII 1532,12	Sales price of grain
22	193/87	180	3	360	BGU VII 1532, 13	Sales price of grain
23	158	400	1 dr 5 ob	200	SB V 7617, 98	Account. Payment for *sitos* in Serapis temple
24	159	750 [300 olyra]	3 dr 1 ob	379.6	UPZ I 91–93	Median price of *olyra* in that year. Converted into wheat price at the rate of 2:5.
25	c. 129	(400) 600	(1 dr 5 ob) 2 dr 5.5 ob	(200) 300	SB VI 9420,6	Price of wheat in 'sale with deferred delivery'. Loan repayable in kind with 50 per cent interest
26	118	1200	2	240	P. Grenf. I 22, 11	Purchase price of grain bought by local tax office
27	112/March	1000	1 dr 4 ob	200	P. Tebt. I 112, 58	Conversion of wage in kind paid by local tax office (12 March)[6]
28	112/March	1200	2	240	P. Tebt. I 112, 113	Purchase price of grain bought by local tax office (16 March)
29	112/March	800	1 dr 2 ob	160	P. Tebt. I 112, 118	Conversion of wage in kind paid by local tax office (16 March)[7]

[5] *prodoma* = prepayment
[6] For this price representing a conversion rate, Verhoogt 2005, 116 and 127.
[7] See previous note.

	Date	Price/artaba in dr.	Silver Price/artaba in dr.	Grs of silver/ton[1]	Reference	Notes
30	111	1560	2 dr 4 ob	315	Botti, Test dem. 4 r	Price for grain (Thebes)
31	110/9	1200	2	240	P.L. Bat XIX 6, 33	Purchase price of land converted into payment in grain (Pathyris, Upper Egypt)
32	108	720	1 dr 1 ob	140	P. Tebt. I 224 v	Conversion of wage in kind
33	100?	1080	1 dr 4 ob	220	SB XVI 12675, 16	Account. Payment for grain
34	late 2nd c.	1000	1 dr 4 ob	200	P. Tebt. I 116, 2	Payment to individual. Conversion rate of wage in kind?
35	late 2nd c.	1100	1 dr 5 ob	220	P. Tebt. I 116, 32	Payment to named individual. Conversion rate of wage in kind?
36	99	1680	2 dr 5 ob	340	P. Tebt I 117, 10	Purchase of grain
37	99	1500	2 dr 3 ob	300	P. Tebt I 117, 18 note	Purchase of grain
38	99	1680	2 dr 5 ob	340	P. Tebt I 117, 47	Purchase of grain
39	97/64	1800	3	360	P. Tebt I 120, 72	Account. Payment for grain
40	94/61	840	1 dr 1.5 ob	150	P. Tebt I 208 des.	Account. Payment for grain
41	94/61	1500	2 dr 3 ob	300	P. Tebt I 121, 140	Account. Payment for grain
42	93	2000	3 dr 2 ob	400	P. Tebt I 109, 15	Prodomatic tenancy agreement.[8] Prepayment of rent in kind as loan of money
43	1st c.	?800	?1 dr 2 ob	?160	PSI VIII 968, 3	Price of grain. Reading uncertain.
44	1st c.	2200	3 dr 4 ob	440	P. Oxy IV 784 des.	Price of grain

[8] See note 5.

Table 12.2 Penalty prices for wheat in Egypt, third to first centuries BC (continued over the page)

	Date	Penalty price	Penalty price in silver standard	Grs of silver/ton	Reference
1	306	4 dr	4 dr	460	P. Loeb dem. 3, 18 (Tenis, Hermopolite nome)[1]
2	301/300	4 dr	4 dr	460	P. Hib. I 84a 8–9
3	c. 265	4 dr	4 dr	460	P. Hib. I 65, 24
4	260/59	4 dr	4 dr	460	BGU VI 1226, 13
5	258/7	4 dr	4 dr	460	BGU 1228, 13
6	257	4 dr	4 dr	460	P. Sorb. 17 a 15. b 16
7	244/3 or 218/7	?4 dr	?4 dr	460	P. Hib. I 91,11
8	3rd c.	4 dr	4 dr	460	BGU VI 1267, 13
9	223/2	4 dr (silver)	4 dr	460	P. Tebt. III 1, 815 fr 3 ii 14
10	222	5 dr (? Silver)	5 dr	600	P. Hib. I 90, 15
11	216/5	10 dr (bronze)	5 dr	600	BGU VI 1262, 13
12	215/4	10 dr	5 dr	600	BGU VI 1264, 22 f.
13	215/ 4	10 dr	5 dr	600	BGU X 1969, 8
14	215/4	10 dr	5 dr	600	BGU XIV 2383, 12
15	215/4	10 dr	5 dr	600	BGU X 1943, 12-14
16	214/3	10 dr	5 dr	600	BGU VI 1265, 20
17	214/3	10 dr	5 dr	600	BGU X 1944, 12
18	214/3	10 dr	5 dr	600	P. Frankf. I, 23
19	214/3	12 dr	6 dr	720	BGU XIV 2397, 10, 11, 29
20	213/2	10 dr	5 dr	600	BGU X 1946, 12
21	173	500 dr	4 dr 1 ob	500	P. Amh. II 43, 12
22	160/59	400 dr	3 dr 2 ob (1:120)	400	BGU XIV 2390, 34, (Herakleopolite nome)
23	before 145	1000 dr	4 dr 1 ob	500	BGU VI 1271, 8
24	128/7	2000 dr	3 dr 2 ob	400	P. dem. Loeb 55, 13 (?Tenis, Hermopolite nome)
25	119	2000 dr	3 dr 2 ob	400	P. Tebt I 11, 17 (Kerkeosiris, Arsinoite nome)[2]
26	116	2000 dr	3 dr 2 ob	400	P. L. Bat XXII 34, 11 (Tenis, Hermopolite nome)
27	116	3000 dr	5dr	600	P. L. Bat XXII 26, 18
28	c. 115	3000 dr	5 dr	600	P. Fay. 11, 17
29	113	3000 dr	5 dr	600	P. L. Bat XXII 21, 22
30	113/2	3000 dr	5 dr	600	P. L. Bat XXII 27, 19
31	112	3000 dr	5 dr	600	P. L. Bat XXII 13, 24
32	111	3000 dr	5 dr	600	P. L. Bat XXII 22, 21
33	110	3000 dr	5 dr	600	P. L. Bat XXII 14, 25
34	110	3000 dr	5 dr	600	P. L. Bat XXII 1, 16
35	110?	3000 dr	5 dr	600	P. L. Bat XXII 28, 27
36	109	3000 dr	5 dr	600	P. L. Bat XXII 2 dem, 11
37	109	3000 dr	5 dr	600	P. L. Bat XXII 15, 23
38	109	3000 dr	5 dr	600	P. L. Bat XXII 16, 28
39	109	1200 dr	4 dr (1:300)	460	P. Chicago Field Mus. dem.

[1] The rent in kind is specified as payable in artabas of 28 choinikes. This does not seem to have affected the penalty price.
[2] The *dochikon* measure is used for the calculation of the wheat rent, but this may not have affected the penalty price; see previous note.

	Date	Penalty price	Penalty price in silver standard	Grs of silver/ton	Reference
					31323, 14 (Thebes, Upper Egypt)
40	108	1200 dr	4 dr (1:300)	460	P. Turin dem. Suppl. 6086, 16 (Thebes)
41	108	3000 dr	5 dr	600	P. L. Bat XX II 3, 15
42	108	3000 dr	5dr	600	P. L. Bat XX II 4, 16
43	108	3000 dr	5 dr	600	P. L. Bat XX II 23,22
44	late 2nd c.	2000 dr	3dr 2 ob	400	P. L. Bat XX II 32, 17
45	106	1500 dr	5 dr (1: 300)	600	P. L. Bat XX II 5 dem, 20
46	105	3000 dr	5 dr	600	P. L. Bat XX II 19,21
47	104	3000 dr	5 dr	600	P. L. Bat XX II 25,28
48	104/3 or 102/1	3000 dr	5 dr	600	P. Köln VI 275, 11
49	103	2000 dr	3 dr 2 ob	400	P. Louv. dem. 2436 b
50	100	2400 dr	4 dr	460	P. Adler 15, 9
51	92 or 59	3000 dr	5 dr	600	P. Tebt. I 110, 9
52	73 or 44	4000 dr	3 dr 2 ob (1:300)	400	P. Oxy. XIV 1639, 13
53	77	3000 dr	5 dr	600	P. Merton I 6, 24 f.
54	51	3000 dr	5 dr	600	PSI X 1098, 28

Table 12.3 *Inter-annual variation of olyra price in Egypt, 159/8 BC*

Date	Olyra price/artaba	Extrapolated wheat price/artaba[1]	Silver standard [wheat]	Grs silver/ton [wheat]	Reference
1. Pharmouthi (May)	250 dr	625 dr	2dr 4 ob	319.7	UPZ I 91, 7
('from Talus')	300 dr	750 dr	3 dr 1 ob	379.6	UPZ I 91, 9
13 Pharmouthi	320 dr	800 dr	3 dr 2 ob	400	UPZ I 91, 9
17 Pharmouthi	290 dr	725 dr	3 dr	359.6	UPZ I 91, 9
27 Parmouthi	320 dr	850 dr	3 dr 2 ob	469.5	UPZ I 92, III 12 (cf. I 91, 10 = 340 dr)
29 Pharmouthi	320 dr	800 dr	3 dr 2 ob	400	UPZ I 91, 10 with Wilcken ad loc.
1. Pachon (June)	290 dr	725 dr	3 dr	400	UPZ I 91, 15
('from Petesis')	300 dr	750 dr	3 dr 1 ob	379.6	UPZ I 91, 18
(different seller)	300 dr	750 dr	3 dr 1 ob	379.6	UPZ I 91, 19 with Wilcken ad loc.
Pauni (July)	315 dr	788 dr	3 dr 1.5 ob	389.6	UPZ I 93, 6
('from Petesis')	300 dr	750 dr	3 dr 1 ob	379.6	UPZ I 93, 7
Hathyr (December)	360 dr	900 dr	3 dr 4.5 ob	449.6	UPZ I 96, 8

[1] Wheat:Olyra 5:2

Table 12.4 *Wheat prices on Delos, third to first centuries BC*

	Date/month	Price/medimnos	Silver/ton[1]	Reference
1	282/1	7 dr	1013.3	ID 158 A 37–38
2	282/2	6 dr 3 ob	940.8	ID 158 A 39–40
3	282/3	6 dr	868.6	ID 158 A 41–42
4	282/4	4 dr 3 ob	651.4	ID 158 A 42–43
5	282/5	6 dr 5 ob	988.7	ID 158 A43–44
6	282/8	7 dr	1013.3	ID 158 A45–46
7	282/9	10 dr	1447.5	ID 158 A46–7
8	190/12	10 dr	1447.5	ID 401, 22
9	174/12	11 dr	1599.6	ID 440 A69
10	178/12	10 dr	1447.5	ID 445, 13

[1] Calculated as 4.36 g [Attic standard/dr] x (price in drachmas) x 33.2 [medimnoi of wheat in kg per ton]

Table 12.5 Barley prices on Delos, 3rd and 2nd centuries BC

	Date/month	Price/medimnos	Silver/ton	Ref.
1	282/10	4 dr	579.0	ID 158 A 48
2	282/11	5 dr	723.75	ID 158 A 48–49
3	282/12	5 dr	723.75	ID 158 A 49–50
4	258/2	3 dr	434.3	ID 224 A 29
5	250/1	3 dr 2 ob	482.5	ID 287 A 45
6	250/5	3 dr 1 ob 4 ch	470.3	ID 287 A 59–60
7	250/6	3 dr	434.3	ID 287A 64
8	250/7	2 dr 4 ob	385.9	ID 287 A 66
9	250/8	2 dr 2 ob	337.7	ID 287 A 67–8
10	250/9	2 dr	289.5	ID 287 A 71
11	247/8	2 dr 3 ob	361.9	ID 291 b + 55
12	246/7	4 dr	579.0	ID 290,82
13	246/10	4 dr	579.0	ID 290, 97–98
14	224/5	2 dr	289.5	ID 338A a 35
15	179/12	4 dr	579.0	ID 442A220
16	178/12	3 dr 4 ob 4 ch	542.7	ID 445, 4–5
17	177/12	4 dr	579.0	ID 452, 9
18	174/12	4 dr	579.0	ID 440 A 62–63

Table 12.6 Inter-annual variation of wheat price on Delos, 282 BC

Month	Price/medimnos	Grs silver/ton	Reference
January	7 dr	1013.3	ID 158 A 37–38
February	6 dr 3 ob	940.8	ID 158 A 39–40
March	6 dr	868.6	ID 158 A 41–42
April	4 dr 3 ob	651.4	ID 158 A 42–43
May	6 dr 5 ob	988.7	ID 158 A43–44
August	7 dr	1013.3	ID 158 A45–46
September	10 dr	1447.5	ID 158 A46–47
[December (190)]	10 dr	1447.5	ID 401, 22

Table 12.7 Wheat prices in Athens, fifth to fourth centuries BC

	Date	Price/medimnos	Grs silver/ton	reference	Notes
1	415	6 dr 3 ob	940.8	IG I³ 421. 137	Grain sale by auction
2	415	6 dr	868. 6	IG I³ 421. 138	Grain sale by auction
3	415	6 dr 2 ob	916.8	IG I³ 421. 139	Grain sale by auction
4	392	3 dr	434.3	Ar. Ecc. 547-8; cf. Suidas s.v. hekteus	Stylized figure?
5	early 4th c.	6 dr	868.6	IG II/III² 1356. 17.21	Law concerning price of wheat sold by temple
6	335	16 dr	2316.0	Dem. 34. 39	Emergency price
7	334	5 dr	723.75	Dem. 34. 39	"normal" price
8	c. 330	9 dr	1302.8	IG II/III² 408	Benefactor making available grain at 50 per cent more than "normal" rate.
9	330	5 dr	723.75	SIG³ 304	Special price for imported grain
10	329/8	5 dr	723.75	IG II/III² 1672, 282ff.	grain purchase
11	329/8	6 dr	868.6	IG II/III² 1672, 282ff.	grain purchase
12	324	5 dr	723.75	IG II/III² 360	Special price for imported grain
13	300	6 dr	868.6	SIG³ 354	"normal" price

Table 12.8 Barley (krithai) prices in Athens, fourth century BC[1]

	Date	Price/medimnos	Grs silver/ton	Reference	Notes
1	430	2 dr	289.5	Plut. Mor. 470 f.	Evidence not contemporary
2	late 5th c.	3 dr	434.3	Gnom. Vat. 495	Evidence not contemporary
3	400	4 dr	579.0	Stratt fr. 13 (Edmonds)	Basket= medimnos
4	c. 330	5 dr	723.75	IG II/III² 408	See above, Table 12.7 no. 8
5	329/8	3 dr	434.3	IG II/III² 1672, 282	Grain purchase
6	329/8	3 dr 5 ob	554.9	IG II/III² 1672 ,283	Grain purchase

[1] Wheat:Barley 2:1

13

Mediterranean Grain Prices c. 300 to 31 BC: the Impact of Rome

Dominic Rathbone

1. INTRODUCTION

The original aim of this paper was just to present and assess the attested grain prices in the Roman world in the last three centuries BC so as to permit, in conjunction with the papers of van der Spek and von Reden, a unified analysis of grain prices over this long period in the broad area of the ancient Mediterranean and Near Eastern world. After a brief review of Roman and Greek metrology in section 2, this is what I do in section 3.

A fundamental problem is immediately apparent. In the utter absence of the sorts of abundant documentation available for Babylonia and Egypt, the Roman world presents a sorry case of too few data. This can be palliated by comparing prices from the old Greek world in the second century as it was increasingly dragged into the Roman ambit but these too, even including the set of prices from the accounts of the temple officials (*hieropoioi*) of Delos, are pitifully few.

In an attempt to compensate for this deficiency, I experiment in this paper with using other evidence for the possible impact of Rome on the grain market of the Mediterranean. The Roman state created two particular forms of heavy demand which are roughly quantifiable in an unbroken annual series: the supply of its armies from the later third century onwards and the wheat distribution (*frumentatio*) to citizens in Rome instituted in 122 BC. The data for these are presented in sections 4 and 5 respectively. Of course other ancient states supplied their armies and provided grain for their urban centres, but Rome was unique in the regularity and scale of its provision of these supplies. Although it might be objected that the recipients would have had to feed themselves anyway, I assume that their concentration created anomalous vortexes of demand, with a potential Mediterranean-wide impact, in contrast to the mass of the population dispersed among small towns and the countryside, whose surpluses and shortages were usually local and had no discernible effect on the broad picture. At any rate, it seems worth investigating whether variations in the demand of the Roman state for grain find any reflections in the price data from the east Mediterranean and Near East.

There is also much potentially useful data for patterns and variations in the grain supply and demand of the Roman world from notices in ancient historical and other writings of shortages in particular places and years, special levies and transfers of grain, and so on, admittedly a rather random and motley collection, and also from what we can reconstruct about Roman taxation in kind of the provinces it gradually created through this period. To collect all this data for the three centuries would be an enormous undertaking of uncertain usefulness. However, I introduce some of it in section 6 where I combine the trends in the data for prices, army supplies and the *frumentatio*, and attempt to draw some conclusions about the probable pattern of grain prices in the Roman world from the late third to early first century BC. Indeed the general focus of this paper is on this more restricted period for reasons of evidence and history. Almost all the known Roman grain prices come from it, as does the majority of the Greek prices outside Egypt, and the Babylonian price series too ends in 60 BC. It is much better attested in general than most of the third century (for which Livy is not extant). It sits between the extreme cases of the Hannibalic War and the 'global' civil wars of the fall of the Republic, and covers the development of direct Roman intervention in the Greek world.

2. ROMAN AND GREEK METROLOGY

In this paper, as van der Spek and von Reden do in theirs, I convert ancient grain prices into their equivalent in grammes of silver per metric tonne of grain so as to enable comparison between prices expressed in different ancient metrological systems and coinages. The rationale for this procedure and the metrological problems it reveals are discussed in the following 'Preliminary conclusions' paper.

The modern equivalences for Roman measures are secure because Roman weights and measures formed an integrated system like the metric one today, and numismatic research has established reliable values for the Roman coinage.[1] The standard dry measure of the Roman Republic was the *modius*, or *modius Italicus*, equivalent to 8.62 litres. The Roman *libra*, pound weight, was equivalent to 323 grammes. In 212/1 the Romans introduced the silver *denarius*, which in the mid-second century became the

---

[1] This is not the place for a discussion of Roman (and Greek) metrology. The most generally useful and reliable handbook remains Hultsch 1882, supplemented for Roman metrology and coins by various studies by Duncan-Jones and Crawford.

most important Roman coin in circulation, although the principal unit of account to 141 BC was the *as*, and from 140 BC on the *sestertius* (abbreviated as HS). Down to 141 BC there were 10 asses = 4 sesterces to the denarius; from 140 BC there were 16 asses = 4 sesterces to the denarius. From 212/1 down to 157 BC the denarius was minted at an official target weight of 72 to the Roman pound of silver (= 4.49 g), and from 156 BC to AD 64 at 84 to the pound (= 3.85 g).

For prices from the Roman world given by Greek writers using Greek equivalents, and for the prices from the Greek world which I compare, I use the following equivalents. Much of the Greek world, including Sicily and many Aegean states, used the Attic *medimnos* as the standard dry measure. Official sub-units (*kotylai*) found in the Athenian agora show that it was equivalent to around 54 litres. In converting Roman modii to the Attic/Sicilian medimnos, Greek writers used the roughly correct ratio of 6:1, and the implied 51.72 litres seems to have become the official value of the medimnos in areas such as Sicily when they came under direct Roman rule as provinces. The most common coin standard in the Greek world, especially after it was adopted and spread by Alexander the Great, was the Attic *drachma*, which had a target weight from the fourth century on of 4.36 grammes, although in the second and first centuries BC its actual weight averaged 4.20 grammes. The standard drachma was divided into 6 (bronze) obols. To express Roman prices Greek writers simply used the drachma to stand for the denarius, and rounded sesterces and asses to the nearest obol.

To convert volumes of grain into weights we need to know the densities of ancient grains. This raises some interesting problems which are discussed in the following 'Preliminary conclusions' paper. We know the official target densities of wheat which the Roman government used in the Principate to check consignments from the main regions which supplied tax grain to Italy. They range from 74.94 to 81.49 kg/hl, in line with modern densities. For wheat sold or distributed at Rome, which will usually have come from Italy and the west Mediterranean regions under Roman control where wheats were heavier, I use as the average density the official figure for Baetican wheat, roughly 79 kg/hl (that is one modius weighed about 6.8 kg). For wheat sales in the Greek world outside Egypt I use 76 kg/hl, the official Roman density for Chersonese wheat (that is one Attic medimnos weighed about 41 kg). The density of ancient barley is even more uncertain. Fortunately there are only two barley prices from the Roman world, and for them and the Delian prices I use a guesstimate density of 60 kg/hl, at the low end of the modern range, that is one Attic medimnos of barley weighed 32.5 kg, and one modius around 5.2 kg.

Table 13.1 Grain prices from the Roman world

g silver / tonne wheat

1.	250	Rome	Pliny, *NH* 18.17 (citing Varro)

Emmer wheat (*far*) normally 1 as per modius.

2.	216	Casilinum	Strabo 5.4.10

During siege a medimnos of grain is sold for 200 dr.
[But cf. Val.Max. 7.6.3; Pliny, *NH* 8.222; Frontin., *Strat.* 4.5.20: a rat.]

3.	211/0	Rome	Polybius 9.11a.3

Shortage, wheat reaches 15 drachmas per Sicilian medimnos,
i.e. 25 asses per modius.   **1,650 g**

4.	203	Rome	Livy 30.26.5-6

Grain cheap, aediles distribute wheat from Spain at 4 asses (per
modius).   **264 g**

5.	201	Rome	Livy 31.4.6

Aediles distribute wheat from Africa at 4 asses (per modius).   **264 g**

6.	200	Rome	Livy 31.50.1

Grain very cheap, aediles distribute wheat from Africa at 2
asses per modius.   **132 g**

7.	196	Rome	Livy 33.42.8

Aediles distribute wheat from Sicily at 2 asses (per modius).   **132 g**

8.	c. 150	Gallia Cisalpina	Polybius 2.15.1

Fertile, wheat could cost as low as 4 obols per Sicilian
medimnos, i.e. (nearest Greek equivalent for) 1 as per modius.   **> 57 g**

9.	c. 150	Lusitania	Polybius 34.8.7, apud Athenaeus 8.330c

Fertile, wheat costs 9 obols 'of Alexander' (added by
Athenaeus?) per Sicilian medimnos, i.e. 2.5 asses per modius;
and barley 1 drachma per medimnos, i.e. 1.5(?) asses per
modius (**112 g** ?).   **141 g**

10a.	123-83	Rome	Livy, *Epit.* 60; *Schol. Bob.* 2.135 St.; Cic., *Sest.* 55
	& 73-59		

Subsidised price of Gracchan *frumentatio* is 6 1/3 asses per
modius, presumably meaning 5 modii (monthly ration) for 2
denarii, i.e. HS 1.6 per modius.   **226 g**

10b.	100	Rome	*Rhet. ad Herenn.* 1.21

Saturninus passes grain law 'de semissibus et trientibus' (5/6),
probably scribal error for 'de senis et trientibus' (6 1/3), i.e. re-
instating Gracchan price.

11.	c. 120-	Italy/Rome	Lucilius, *Sat.* 15.538-9
	110		(Warmington)

'Except as regards the price: the first (modius?) for a semis (0.5
as), the second for a *nummus* (HS 1, or 1 as?), the third for
more even than a whole medimnus.'

12.	late II / early I (?)	Rome In shortage (439 BC) price reaches 12 dr. (HS 48) per modius; (c. **6,800 g**) Maelius sells grain at 2 dr. (HS 8) per modius. [Prices probably drawn from by annalistic historian from Rome of his day.]	Dionys. Halic. 12.1.12	**1,131 g**

13. 74 Sicily   Cicero, *Verr.* 2.3.214-6
Wheat cheap in 76, expensive in 75 (Cicero quaestor). In 74
pre-harvest price reaches 5 denarii (= HS 20) per modius;   **2,827 g**
commutation of 'supplies' (*frumentum in cellam*) at 3 denarii
per modius is fair pre-harvest, but unfair after, i.e. price had   **< 1,696 g**
dropped below HS 12.

14. 74 Rome   Pliny, *NH* 18.16; cf. 51.2
Aedile M. Seius sells wheat at 1 as per modius.   **35 g**

15. 73-71 Sicily   Cicero, *Verr.* 2.3.72, 90,
                                                 170-4, 191, 194, 214-6,
                                                 225; *Q. Caec.* 30
Normal price in these years HS 2 per modius, sometimes HS 2.5   **283 to 424 g**
or HS 3.
lex Terentia Cassia (73 BC) and SC set compensation price for   **424 & 495 g**
second tithe (3 million modii) at HS 3 per modius and for extra
800,000 'ordered' modii at HS 3.5;
SC also authorises Verres to buy 'supplies' at HS 4 per modius   **565 g**
of wheat and HS 2 per modius of barley, (wheat) but he
enforces commutation at 3 den., i.e. HS 12 per modius of wheat.

16. 49 Spain   Caesar, *BC* 1.52.2
Caesar's army starving, wheat sells at 50 den. (HS 200) per
modius.

3. GRAIN PRICES FROM THE ROMAN WORLD

In Table 13.1 I present in chronological order all the prices of grain in the Roman world of the last three centuries BC which I have been able to find.[2] In bold type to the right I give the equivalent, where it can be calculated, of the price in terms of grammes of silver required to purchase one tonne of grain. It will be noted that all these prices come from literary sources: we have very few documents, public or private, from Republican Rome at all (excluding Cicero's correspondence), and none of the types which elsewhere provide us with prices of grain.

Of these sixteen attestations, six relate to subsidised distributions at Rome by the state or its magistrates (nos. 4–7, 10, 14), and only six of the rest seem to give what might be market prices or a possible indication of them (nos. 3, 8, 9, 12, 13, 15). The

---

[2] I have consulted and amended previous lists, of which the most recent is Szaivert and Wolters 2005. For Roman grain prices into the Principate see Rathbone 2009.

most informative of the latter group are Cicero's statements about prices in Sicily, a prime wheat-growing area, when Verres was governor (nos. 13, 15), although we may expect some manipulation to bolster his prosecution of Verres for extortion. Thus while Cicero claims that in the good years of 73 to 71 BC the normal price of wheat was HS 2 per modius, sometimes rising to HS 3, I suspect, because the senate authorised compulsory purchases at HS 3, 3.5 and 4, that the core range of prices in these years was more like HS 3 to 4 per modius (424 to 565 g / tonne). However, Cicero had no reason to exaggerate when he says that in 74 BC the pre-harvest price reached HS 20 per modius, and after the harvest only fell back to somewhere below HS 12. Rome's fiscal demands undoubtedly exacerbated local problems, but the increased demand caused by the lex Terentia Cassia of 73 BC presumably followed on indications that the harvest of that year would be good, and the main driver of high prices in Sicily was the harvest: two successive poor harvests in 75 and 74 had caused something like a fourfold rise in the price of wheat.

We have no direct evidence for the normal range of market prices of wheat in Rome and Italy of the Republic, or indeed of the Principate. It is usually supposed that the subsidised price of the Gracchan wheat distribution of 122 to 83 BC (no. 10) was about half of the normal market price, which would then have been HS 3 per modius (424 g /tonne).[3] However this is extremely unlikely in comparison with the Sicilian prices of the 70s BC. It is more plausible that the state subsidy was extremely generous, as is implied by political opposition to its high cost (see section 5 below). I suspect that the prices in the annalistic account of the supposed grain shortage in Rome in 439 BC (no. 12) reflect late Republican realities, and that HS 8 per modius would have been a fair market price, probably towards the higher end of the normal range, in Rome of around 100 BC.[4] In that case the Gracchan price was around a quarter to a fifth of the normal market range of say HS 6 to 8 per modius of wheat (990 to 1,131 g / tonne).

Nominally the Gracchan price of 6 1/3 asses (i.e. post-141/0 asses) was the same as the price of 4 asses (i.e. pre-141/0 asses) charged by aediles for ad hoc subsidised sales in 203 and 201 (nos. 4, 5), and maybe in more recent years too for which Livy's account is not extant: both were equivalent to 5 modii for 2 denarii. Granted Roman traditionalism, this may have influenced Gaius Gracchus' choice of his price. Nonetheless, I suspect that market prices at Rome were considerably lower in the early second century. In the shortage of 211/0, caused by the Hannibalic War, the high price to which wheat rose of 2.5 denarii per modius (no. 3) is only 25% higher than my suggested fair price around 100 BC of 2 denarii (HS 8) per modius. Pliny (*NH* 18.16) says that 204 BC saw a larger harvest than the preceding ten years. In 203, 201, 200 and 196 BC wheat was so abundant at Rome that the aediles sold off surplus tax wheat for 4 and even 2 asses per modius (nos. 4–7). In 202 merchants importing wheat from Sicily and Sardinia (for the state?) had to give it to the shippers to cover the transport

---

[3]   Frank 1933, 192, with many followers.
[4]   Possibly the prices are specifically those of 104 BC when the senate first appointed a special supervisor of the grain supply, one of the models for the story of 439 BC.

costs (Livy 30.38.5). Since these aediles are not presented as populists, I suspect that 4 asses represents the low end of the normal market range, and I guess that the average market price at Rome in the earlier second century was around 6 to 8 asses per modius (396 to 528 g / tonne). That would make the high price of 212/1 a plausible four times the norm, and would imply that the average wheat price at Rome had more than doubled by the later second century BC in terms of silver bullion equivalence. The apparent curiosity that these estimated normal price ranges remained the same in numbers of the contemporary unit of account, that is 6 to 8 asses and then HS 6 to 8, may be mere coincidence, but this happened to other values too, such as the minimum census levels for the first four *classes*, across the coinage reform of 141/0 BC. Possibly there had been a general rise in monetary values prior to 141/0 which was to some extent reflected in the coinage reform.

The remaining seven attestations of wheat prices are of little use to us. The two high prices caused by warfare (nos. 2, 16) are exceptional if not rhetorical; indeed most sources say that the first price was for a rat – with the moral that the profiteering seller died while the buyer who ate it survived. The price for 250 BC of 1 as per modius (no. 1) is what I have previously termed an 'iconic' price, that is a conventional symbol of happy times, here in the good old days, as emphasised by Pliny's specification of *far* (emmer wheat), the traditional grain of antique Rome.[5] This was the message in 74 BC when Seius distributed wheat at 1 as per modius (no. 14), which he might more simply have given gratis. So too Polybius' claims for the amazing fertility of the Po valley and northern Spain (nos. 8, 9) look like rhetorical figures, the first in fact the iconic 1 as per modius, the second at best perhaps representing the lowest price in good years (cf. Cicero using low prices for Sicily, no. 15). The contextless citation of Lucilius (no. 12), lastly, is opaque; at a guess it might be a jibe about some magistrate's profiteering from the requisition or sale of Sicilian wheat.

One final observation on the Roman prices: only two are for barley, and both come from provinces, Lusitania and Sicily (nos. 9, 15). The implication is that by the second century BC wheat had become the staple grain of Rome's inhabitants and soldiers, with supplies to match.

My next step is to compare the grain prices we have for this period from the old Greek world, first those for wheat and barley from Delos (Table 13.2A) and then those for wheat (all but one) from other city-states (Table 13.2B).[6] The prices are converted into equivalents, given in bold type to the right, of grammes of silver per tonne of grain. I assume throughout that medimnoi and coins are on the Attic standard; in some case this may be wrong. For the second- and first-century prices, I give the equivalents both for the target weight of the Attic drachma and its actual reduced weight.

---

[5] See Rathbone 2009 for iconic prices into the Principate.

[6] The Delian grain prices, except no. A8, are drawn from Reger 1994, 306–7 (see 289–306 for the three other commodities); I do not use the reconstructed barley-meal values criticised by Sosin 2002, 137–40, but his doubts about the unmilled grain prices seem excessive. The modern month equivalents are approximate. For the rest of the Greek world (III–I BC) I can find no systematic list of grain prices since Heichelheim 1935, which I have updated by checking the *SEG* indices.

Table 13.2a Grain purchases (and sales) on Delos

			WHEAT	BARLEY
				g silver / tonne grain
1.	282,	Jan-May, Aug-Sep Oct, Dec	Wheat at from 4 dr. 3 ob. to 10 dr. / med. Barley-meal (*alphita*) at 4 and 5 dr. / med.	479 to 1,063 g
2.	258,	Feb	Barley at 3 dr. / med.	402 g
3.	250,	Jan, May-Sep	Barley at from 2 dr. to 3 dr. 2 ob. / med.	268 to 447 g
4.	247,	Aug	Barley at 2 dr. 1.5 ob. and 2 dr. 3 ob. / med.	302 and 335 g
5.	246,	Jul	Barley at 4 dr. / med.	537 g
6.	224,	May	Barley at 2 dr. / med.	268 g
7.	190,	Dec	Wheat at 10 dr. / med.	1,063 / 1024 g
8a.	180/179,	Dec-Jan	1,484.75 med. wheat from Numidia sold for 3 dr. / med.	319 / 307 g
	179,	Mar-Apr	and 1,311.75 med. for 4 dr. / med. [*I.Délos* II 442A.100-6; the total sum banked from sale of the second lot implies an actual price of 4 dr. 1 ob., but the inscription specifies 4 dr.]	425 / 410 g
8b.	179,	Dec	Barley at 4 dr. / med.	537 / 517 g
9.	178,	Dec Dec	Wheat at 10 dr. / med. Barley at 3 dr. 4.5 ob. / med.	1,063 / 1,024 g 503 / 487 g
10.	177,	Dec	Barley at 4 dr. / med.	537 / 517 g
11.	174,	Dec Dec	Wheat at 11 dr. / med. Barley-meal (*alphita*) at 4 dr. / med.	1,170 / 1,127 g
12.	169,	Dec	Wheat at 10 dr. / med.	1,063 / 1,024 g

Twelve of the grain prices from Delos (all but no. A8a) form a set in that they all relate to purchases made by the temple officials (*hieropoioi*) who inscribed their accounts on stone. I tease out their internal implications before bringing in the other Greek prices. A first point to note is that purchases of grain are three to four times less common in the accounts than recorded purchases of firewood, olive oil and pigs. This implies that the *hieropoioi* normally had grain from temple lands to use and only purchased when that ran short, which sometimes must have reflected a more general shortage. The recorded prices fall into three groups.

First, in 282 the price of wheat started at 7 dr., fell to 4.5 dr. by April, climbed back to 7 dr. by August, and then reached 10 dr. in September; in October to December the *hieropoioi* bought barley-meal instead.[7] The pattern suggests a poor harvest in 283 followed by one which promised well but turned out worse in 282, and implies that

---

[7] If barley-meal had a similar price to grain by volume and the barley:wheat price ratio was, as in 178, around 3:8, then a price of around 13 dr. for wheat is implied.

Table 13.2b *Other grain prices from the Greek world*

				g silver / tonne grain
1.	295 BC	Athens	Plutarch, *Demetrios* 33.3	
		During siege, wheat (*puroi*) sells for 300 dr. per modius (sic).		
2.	early III BC	Ephesos	*I.Eph.* V 1455	
		When wheat (*puroi*) selling at over 6 dr. per (medimnos), honorand sells 14,000 hekteis (2,333 medimnoi) at less than the market price.		c. 638 g
3.	280s – 240s	Andros	*SEG* 44.669 (cf. 52.799)	
		Royal general acts in shortage: normal or honorand's price of wheat (*sitos*) is 5 dr. / med.; possibly he pays 20+ dr. / med. for foreign wheat. [Lacunose and uncertain text.]		532 g c. 2,500 g
4.	early 260s	Erythrai	*I.Erythr.* I 18 (Migeotte, *Emprunt* 85)	
		In serious shortage price of wheat (*puroi*) reaches 60 dr. / med.; honorand helps.		6,380 g
5.	c. 250 BC	Pergamon	*I. Perg.* I 13 (*OGIS* 266)	
		Royal edict that generals to pay for requisitioned wheat (*sitos*) at 4 dr. / med. [Presumably low end of normal range.]		> 425 g
6.	late II/early II	Olbia (Scythia)	*IosPE* I I² 32 (Migeotte, *Emprunt* 44)	
a.		In year of shortage when wheat (*sitos*) selling at 1 *chrusous* (20 dr.) per 5 med., i.e. 4 dr. / med.,		425 g
		honorand promises 2,000 med. at 1 chrus. per 10 med., i.e. 2 dr. / med.		213 g
b.		In another year of serious shortage, when wheat selling for 1 chrus. per 1 2/3 med., i.e. 12 dr. / med.,		>1,276 g
		and then rises to 1 med. for 1 2/3 chrus. [would be 3.3 dr. / med.), but just a rhetorical inversion?], honorand provides 500 med. at 1 chrus. per 4 1/6 med., i.e. 4.8 dr. / med.,		510 g
		and 2,000 med. at 1 chrus. per 2 7/12 med., i.e. 7.7 dr. / med.		819 g
	probably c. 216 or 174	Gazoros (Macedon)	*I. Philippi* 543	
		In shortage honorand promises to sell wheat (*puroi*) at 2 dr. 4 ob. / med. and barley at 1 dr. 4 ob. (**224 g**). [Possibly c. 277 BC.]		248 g
8.	early II BC	Samos	Ditt., *Syll.*³ 976 (Pouilloux, *Choix* 34)	
		Civic regulation that grain officials to pay the goddess not less than the previous 5 dr. 2 ob. / med. for wheat (*sitos*) bought from some sacred land.		> 561 / 546 g

9.	129 BC	Thessaly	*SEG* 34.558	
		Penalty of 2 stat. 9 ob. per *kophinos* on cities for non-delivery of their shares of 430,000 *kophinoi* of wheat (*sitos*) for Rome, perhaps implying 5 dr. 3 ob. / med.[1]		585 / 563 g ?
10.	129-100 BC	Priene	*I. Priene* 108	
		In shortage honorand provides 206(?) med. wheat (*sitos?*) at 4 dr. / med.		425 / 410 g
11.	late II BC	Megalopolis	*IG* V. 2 437	
		In shortage honorand sells wheat (*puroi*) at [2] stat. 9 ob. / med., i.e. 5 dr. 3 ob. [Staters in plural, more than 2 implausible.]		585 / 563 g
12.	late II/ earlier I	Arsinoe (Cyrene)	*SEG* 26.1817	
		In shortage honorand acquires wheat (*sitos*) at 30 dr. per *metron* (= medimnos ?).		3,190 / 3,073 g
13.	86 BC	Athens	Plutarch, *Sulla* 13.2	
		During siege, wheat (*puroi*) reaches 1,000 dr. / med.		
14.	74 BC	Epidauros	*SEG* 11.397 (*IG* IV².1 66)	
		In shortage exacerbated by presence of Roman fleet, wheat (*puros*) sells at 10 dr. / med.; honorand keeps price down through year to 5 or 4 dr.		1,063 / 1,024 g 425-532 / 410-512 g
15.	65 BC	Judaea	Josephus, *AJ* 14.28	
		Hurricane destroys crops, wheat (*sitos*) reaches 11 dr. / mod., i.e. say 66 dr. / med. [Conversion from local measures by Josephus, may be approximate.]		
16.	43 BC, June	Laodicea, Syria	Cicero (Cassius Parmensis), *ad Fam*.12.13.4	
		In blockade wheat (*triticum*) reaches 3 tetradrachms, i.e. probably 12 den. / mod. (rather than 12 dr. / med.), i.e. say 72 dr. / med.		
17.	36 BC	Mesopotamia	Plutarch, *M. Antonius* 45.4	
		Supply problems in army, wheat (*puroi*) reaches 50 dr. / Attic choinix, i.e. 2,400 dr. / med.		

[1] In Garnsey and Rathbone 1985 we assumed a *kophinos* equivalent to 3/16 medimnos, following Hultsch 1882, 542–4, but this produces an implausibly severe penalty of five times the normal price. More normal would be a penalty of twice or one and a half times the normal price, implying that the Thessalian *kophinos* was half or two-thirds the size of the Attic medimnos.

4.5 dr. was near the normal market price. Second, the five purchases of barley recorded in the period 258 to 224 BC range between 2 and 4 dr. Using the normal ancient price ratio of 3:5 between barley and wheat (see the following 'Preliminary conclusions' paper), an average price for wheat in these years of around 5 dr. per medimnos is implied. Third, in the period 190 to 169 BC barley was purchased twice at 4 dr. and once at slightly less, and wheat three times at 10 dr. and once at 11 dr. The prices of barley and wheat in December 178 produce an unusual ratio of 3:8, which implies that the wheat price was unusually high, as in September 282, but had not yet triggered a proportionate rise in the price of barley. The prices for 179 to 174 suggest, incidentally, that milled barley cost around the same by volume as raw barley, although its weight was roughly two-thirds that of the grain.[8] That the wheat prices of 178 to 169 were comparatively high is also suggested by the prices of 3 and 4 dr. per medimnos at which the state sold two lots of wheat gifted to it in late 180 BC by the Numidian king Masinissa (no. 8a), which were probably set at slightly below the norm to balance the financial benefit to the state and its citizens. Overall, thus, the Delian evidence seems to show a local harvest problem in 283/2, reasonably normal prices of wheat around 258 to 224 with an implied average price of about 5 dr. per medimnos, and a long phase around 190 to 169 BC of higher wheat prices, double the previous implied norm; the state sales in 180/179 BC imply belief that the norm should still be 5 dr., but higher prices may have now become usual.

The other seventeen attestations of prices from the Greek world apart from Delos all concern wheat, and only one of them (no. B7) also barley. Four of them give extreme prices in military crises (nos. B1, 13, 16, 17), of which Plutarch's three are patently rhetorical. The Judaean price after a hurricane (no. B15) is uncertain. The largest group of nine comes from inscriptions honouring benefactors for supplies in times of shortage (nos. B2, 3, 4, 6, 7, 10, 11, 12, 14), in two cases the result of the presence of troops (nos. B3, 14). Six of the nine specify the prices set by the benefactors (nos. B3, 6, 7, 10, 11, 14) while five or six give the high market prices which had provoked intervention (nos. B2, 3?, 4, 6, 12, 14); in two or three cases both low and high prices are given (nos. B3?, 6, 14). The remaining three inscriptions are state regulations (nos. B5, 8, 9). There are no direct attestations of normal market prices. However, taking the honours and regulations together, of the twelve individual prices of wheat recorded as set by the state or by benefactors, nine of varied date fall within the range of 4 to 5.5 dr. per medimnos. The eight individual high prices recorded are, ranked by size: 4, 6+, 10, 12, 20, 30, 33(?) and 60 dr. per medimnos. Because benefactors' and state prices seem typically to have been set at just under the market norm, this suggest that 5 to 5.5 dr. was a fair lowish price and 4 dr. was cheap, which implies a normal

---

[8] Hand-milling barley increases its volume by 50% according to Foxhall and Forbes 1982, 43–4, 75–8; winnowing and sifting then reduce it to 70% of its original volume, which would raise the price sharply, so *alphita*, at least here, must mean milled but unsifted barley. This supports Sosin's doubts (n. 6 above) about Reger's extrapolated prices. Note that the premium for barley-meal does not just reflect milling costs but also the higher calorific value by volume.

range in the old Greek world right through the third to first centuries BC of around 5 to 6 dr. per medimnos of wheat. The high prices are consistent with this. 10 dr. to 12 dr. per medimnos seems to have been the threshold for sparking worries and intervention; beyond that, figures could rocket in particular circumstances – or be exaggerated to magnify the honorand's benefaction. There are a couple of apparent misfits to explain. First, Olbia, where 4 dr. in a year around 200 BC is presented as a high price which the honorand halved (no. B6a), while prices in a subsequent year fit the general pattern, except that the second of the benefactor's prices of 7.7 dr. was not very generous and implies a really serious shortage (no. B6b); probably the earlier case had in fact been a dumping of surplus wheat, but was later spun as a benefaction. The drastic fluctuation in supply between years is striking for a city on the coast of the Crimean wheat fields. Second, the extraordinarily low benefactor's price of 2.67 dr. at Gazoros in roughly the same period (no. B7) may be another case of dumping, maybe from surplus royal stocks.

The normal range of 5 to 6 dr. per medimnos of wheat (532 to 638 g silver / tonne wheat) is consistent with the average of 5 dr. implied by the Delian prices. One reasonably clear and important outcome of Table 13.2B is that the reduction of the silver weight of the Attic drachma and other Greek coinages by the 170s appears to have had very little effect on wheat prices, that is the market seems to have treated the new coins as having a token value equivalent to the old one. (This means that we can ignore the bullion equivalents calculated on the low standard.) Unfortunately we have no securely dated prices from the rest of the Greek world to compare with the high prices attested on Delos in the period from 190 to 169 – although tempting, it is unsafe to assign the high prices at Olbia (no. B6b) to the 180s, and nos. B7 and B8 could be earlier – so we for now remain unsure whether they were exceptional to Delos or part of a wider, if temporary, phenomenon. Comparison of the Greek with the Roman price levels reveals some interesting differences. The normal price range of wheat at Rome at the turn of the second century of 6 to 8 asses per modius (396 to 528 g / tonne) was a band lower than the general Greek range; so too, in effect was the Sicilian range of the early first century of HS 3 to 4 (424 to 565 g / tonne), despite its marginal overlap. However the range which prices had reached at Rome by the later second century of HS 6 to 8 per modius (990 to 1131 g / tonne) was almost double the long-term Greek norm, although it is matched by the high Delian prices of the earlier second century (around 1,000 g / tonne). In section 6 I will offer a possible explanation for these differences. For the moment I note that Rome is looking to have been an oddity in the Mediterranean grain market both in terms of the normal market range of the price of wheat, and also in the generosity of the subsidy and, as we will see, the sheer scale of its civic distributions of grain through the *frumentatio* instituted in 122 BC by Gaius Gracchus.

4. THE GRAIN DEMAND OF ROME'S ARMIES

For the Middle to Late Republic we have one continuous series of annual data, albeit constructed by scholars, with implications for grain demand, which is the number of legions in service.[9] The figures are based on the record in Livy (extant in full for 218 to 167 BC only) and other literary sources, and are not entirely reliable. Uncertainties of varying import include the variable size of legions, the number of Italian allies (whose rations Rome provided free), and the lack of data for fleets and also pack animals. There is a considerable margin of error in the calculations that follow, so there is little point in spurious precision. I simplify where necessary to produce rough orders of magnitude for use in this experiment. In Section 6, furthermore, I note some problems which arise when we compare the occasional figures given by Livy for special deliveries of grain to Roman forces in the Greek world in the earlier second century BC.

My estimates in Table 13.3 below are based on the following assumptions. The target manpower of a legion – although in practice numbers were fluid – was 4,500 men in the third century; this rose to 5,500 in the Hannibalic War, say from 210 BC, and lasted, with fluctuations, until increased to 6,500 by Marius, say in 100 BC.[10] The number of Italian allies required to serve in Rome's armies was roughly equal to the number of Romans in the third century, double the number from the 190s to the 170s (say from 200 to 175), then equal again until the 120s (say 125), when it returned to double; from 90 BC the now enfranchised Italians were enrolled in the legions.[11] Throughout the period a legion contained 300 cavalry; although they may have provided proportionately more, I assume an equal proportion of cavalry in the allied contingents. For Roman and allied manpower in the fleets, I guesstimate an annual average of 3,000 in the third century, 10,000 for the 210s and 200s, 20,000 for the 190s and 180s, 12,000 for the 170s, and 25,000 thereafter.[12]

We cannot tell how much grain was actually supplied to Rome's armies, but Polybius gives us the basic planned monthly rations, which I assume held good throughout the period: for Roman and allied infantry 4 modii of wheat, for Roman cavalry 12 modii and for allied cavalry 8 modii; also 45 and 30 modii of barley to Roman and allied cavalry respectively as hard tack for their horses.[13] The rations for Roman cavalry seem to allow for two grooms and three horses, and those for allied cavalry for one groom and two horses; possibly the extra ration for Roman cavalry was just a mark

---

[9] I use Brunt 1971, 416–72, who drew on and amended earlier calculations by Toynbee and Afzelius.

[10] Following Brunt 1971, 671–6, cf. 419, 423.

[11] Again following Brunt 1971, 677–86.

[12] Brunt 1971, 423–5, covering only 200–168 BC.

[13] Polybius 6.39.13–14; I adjust his figure for the barley ration for Roman cavalrymen from 7 medimnoi (42 modii) to 45 modii (7.5 medimnoi) to keep the 3:2 ratio with the allies' wheat allowance. For wheat rations in general in the Roman world, see Rathbone 2009, 314–16.

Table 13.3 Roman military wheat and barley demand: annual averages by decades

300-221 av. 4 legions @ 4,500 men, equal allies:

infantry	33,600	x 48 mod.	1,612,800
Roman cavalry	1,200	x 144 mod.	172,800
allied cavalry	1,200	x 96 modii	115,200
fleet	3,000	x 48 mod.	144,000
total wheat			**2,044,800**
cavalry horses	*6,000*	*x 180 mod.*	*1,080,000*
pack animals	*1,700*	*x 180 mod.*	*306,000*
total barley			**1,386,000**

= 13,900 tonnes

= 7,200 tonnes

220-211 av. 17.0(?) legions @ 4,500 men, equal allies:

infantry	142,000	x 48 mod.	6,854,400
Roman cavalry	5,100	x 144 mod.	734,400
allied cavalry	5,100	x 96 mod.	489,600
fleet	10,000	x 48 mod.	480,000
total wheat			**8,558,400**
cavalry horses	*25,500*	*x 180 mod.*	*4,590,000*
pack animals	*7,100*	*x 180 mod.*	*1,278,000*
total barley			**5,868,000**

= 58,200 tonnes

= 30,500 tonnes

210-201 av. 19.3 legions @ 5,500 men, equal allies:

infantry	200,720	x 48 mod.	9,634,560
Roman cavalry	5,790	x 144 mod.	833,760
allied cavalry	5,790	x 96 modii	555,840
fleet	10,000	x 48 mod.	480,000
total wheat			**11,504,160**
cavalry horses	*28,950*	*x 180 mod.*	*5,211,000*
pack animals	*10,000*	*x 180 mod.*	*1,800,000*
total barley			**7,011,000**

= 78,200 tonnes

= 36,500 tonnes

200-191 av. 8.6 legions @ 5,500 men, double allies:

infantry	134,160	x 48 mod.	6,439,680
Roman cavalry	2,580	x 144 mod.	371,520
allied cavalry	5,160	x 96 modii	495,360
fleet	20,000	x 48 mod.	960,000
total wheat			**8,266,560**
cavalry horses	*18,060*	*x 180 mod.*	*3,250,800*
pack animals	*6,700*	*x 180 mod.*	*1,206,000*
total barley			**4,456,800**

= 56,200 tonnes

= 23,200 tonnes

190-181 av. 9.7 legions @ 5,500 men, double allies:

infantry	151,320	x 48 mod.	7,263,360
Roman cavalry	2,910	x 144 mod.	419,040
allied cavalry	5,820	x 96 modii	558,720
fleet	20,000	x 48 mod.	960,000
total wheat			**9,201,120**
cavalry horses	*20,370*	*x 180 mod.*	*3,666,600*
pack animals	*7,600*	*x 180 mod.*	*1,368,000*
total barley			**5,034,600**

= 62,600 tonnes

= 26,200 tonnes

180-171 av. 7.7 legions @ 5,500 men, av. one and a half times allies:

infantry	100,100	x 48 mod.	4,804,800
Roman cavalry	2,310	x 144 mod.	332,640
allied cavalry	3,465	x 96 modii	332,640
fleet	12,000	x 48 mod.	576,000
total wheat			**6,046,080**
cavalry horses	*13,860*	*x 180 mod.*	*2,494,800*
pack animals	*5,000*	*x 180 mod.*	*900,000*
total barley			**3,394,800**

= 41,100 tonnes

= 17,700 tonnes

170-161	av. 7.0 legions @ 5,500 men, equal allies:			
	infantry	72,800 x 48 mod.	3,494,400	
	Roman cavalry	2,100 x 144 mod.	302,400	
	allied cavalry	2,100 x 96 modii	201,600	
	fleet	25,000 x 48 mod.	1,200,000	
	total wheat		**5,198,400**	**= 35,300 tonnes**
	cavalry horses	*10,500 x 180 mod.*	*1,890,000*	
	pack animals	*3,600 x 180 mod.*	*648,000*	
	total barley		*2,538,000*	*= 13,200 tonnes*
160-151	av. 4.9 legions @ 5,500 men, equal allies:			
	infantry	50,960 x 48 mod.	2,446,080	
	Roman cavalry	1,470 x 144 mod.	211,680	
	allied cavalry	1,470 x 96 modii	141,120	
	fleet	25,500 x 48 mod.	1,200,000	
	total wheat		**3,998,880**	**= 27,200 tonnes**
	cavalry horses	*7,350 x 180 mod.*	*1,323,000*	
	pack animals	*2,500 x 180 mod.*	*450,000*	
	total barley		*1,773,000*	*= 9,200 tonnes*
150-141	av. 8.0 legions @ 5,500 men, equal allies:			
	infantry	83,200 x 48 mod.	3,993,600	
	Roman cavalry	2,400 x 144 mod.	345,600	
	allied cavalry	2,400 x 96 modii	230,400	
	fleet	25,000 x 48 mod.	1,200,000	
	total wheat		**5,769,600**	**= 39,200 tonnes**
	cavalry horses	*12,000 x 180 mod.*	*2,160,000*	
	pack animals	*4,200 x 180 mod.*	*748,800*	
	total barley		*2,908,800*	*= 15,100 tonnes*
140-131	av. 6.8 legions @ 5,500 men, equal allies:			
	infantry	70,720 x 48 mod.	3,394,560	
	Roman cavalry	2,040 x 144 mod.	293,760	
	allied cavalry	2,040 x 96 modii	195,840	
	fleet	25,000 x 48 mod.	1,200,000	
	total wheat		**5,084,160**	**= 34,600 tonnes**
	cavalry horses	*10,200 x 180 mod.*	*1,836,000*	
	pack animals	*3,500 x 180 mod.*	*630,000*	
	total barley		*2,466,000*	*= 12,800 tonnes*
130-121	av. 6.2 legions @ 5,500 men, av. one and a half times allies:			
	infantry	80,600 x 48 mod.	3,868,800	
	Roman cavalry	1,860 x 144 mod.	267,840	
	allied cavalry	2,790 x 96 modii	267,840	
	fleet	25,000 x 48 mod.	1,200,000	
	total wheat		**5,604,480**	**= 38,100 tonnes**
	cavalry horses	*11,160 x 180 mod.*	*2,008,800*	
	pack animals	*4,000 x 180 mod.*	*720,000*	
	total barley		*2,728,800*	*= 14,200 tonnes*
120-111	av. 5.6 legions @ 5,500 men, double allies:			
	infantry	87,360 x 48 mod.	4,193,280	
	Roman cavalry	1,680 x 144 mod.	241,920	
	allied cavalry	3,360 x 96 modii	322,560	
	fleet	25,000 x 48 mod.	1,200,000	
	total wheat		**5,957,760**	**= 40,500 tonnes**
	cavalry horses	*11,760 x 180 mod.*	*2,116,800*	
	pack animals	*4,400 x 180 mod.*	*792,000*	
	total barley		*2,908,800*	*= 15,100 tonnes*

110-101	av. 8.8 legions @ 5,500 men, double allies:		
	infantry	137,280 x 48 mod.	6,589,440
	Roman cavalry	2,640 x 144 mod.	380,160
	allied cavalry	5,280 x 96 modii	506,880
	fleet	25,000 x 48 mod.	1,200,000
	total wheat		**8,676,480** = 59,000 tonnes
	cavalry horses	*18,480 x 180 mod.*	*3,326,400*
	pack animals	*6,900 x 180 mod.*	*1,242,000*
	total barley		*4,568,400* = 23,800 tonnes

100-91	av. 5.2 legions @ 6,500 men, double allies:		
	infantry	96,720 x 48 mod.	4,642,560
	Roman cavalry	1,560 x 144 mod.	224,640
	allied cavalry	3,120 x 96 modii	299,520
	fleet	25,000 x 48 mod.	1,200,000
	total wheat		**6,366,720** = 43,300 tonnes
	cavalry horses	*10,920 x 180 mod.*	*1,965,600*
	pack animals	*4,800 x 180 mod.*	*864,000*
	total barley		*2,829,600* = 14,700 tonnes

90-81	av. 20.5(?) legions @ 6,500 men:		
	infantry	127,100 x 48 mod.	6,100,800
	cavalry	6,150 x 144 mod.	885,600
	fleet	25,000 x 48 mod.	1,200,000
	total wheat		**8,186,400** = 55,700 tonnes
	cavalry horses	*18,450 x 180 mod.*	*3,321,000*
	pack animals	*6,400 x 180 mod.*	*1,152,000*
	total barley		*4,473,000* = 23,300 tonnes

80-71	av. 27.7 legions @ 6,500 men:		
	infantry	171,740 x 48 mod.	8,243,520
	cavalry	8,310 x 144 mod.	1,196,640
	fleet	25,000 x 48 mod.	1,200,000
	total wheat		**10,640,160** = 72,400 tonnes
	cavalry horses	*24,930 x 180 mod.*	*4,487,400*
	pack animals	*8,600 x 180 mod.*	*1,548,000*
	total barley		*6,035,400* = 31,400 tonnes

70-61	av. 22.4 legions @ 6,500 men:		
	infantry	138,880 x 48 mod.	6,666,240
	cavalry	6,720 x 144 mod.	967,680
	fleet	25,000 x 48 mod.	1,200,000
	total wheat		**8,833,920** = 60,100 tonnes
	cavalry horses	*20,160 x 180 mod.*	*3,628,800*
	pack animals	*6,900 x 180 mod.*	*1,242,000*
	total barley		*4,870,800* = 25,300 tonnes

60-51	av. 19.3 legions @ 6,500 men:		
	infantry	119,660 x 48 mod.	5,743,680
	cavalry	5,790 x 144 mod.	833,760
	fleet	25,000 x 48 mod.	1,200,000
	total wheat		**7,777,440** = 52,900 tonnes
	cavalry horses	*17,370 x 180 mod.*	*3,126,600*
	pack animals	*6,000 x 180 mod.*	*1,080,000*
	total barley		*4,206,600* = 21,900 tonnes

of their elite status, but it was still a planned supply figure.[14] Roman armies also had pack animals, in the Principate maybe one mule per *contubernium* of eight men, but I deliberately use a low estimate of one per twenty infantry on the assumption that in the Republic much transport will have been requisitioned locally and therefore not part of planned supplies.[15] Conversely, for simplicity I assume that active service and the demand for grain lasted all year, which by the second century it usually did, and that units remained at full strength, which is presumably what the Romans assumed for logistical planning.

Although the figures in Table 13.3 are crude estimates, the chronological pattern of military demand which they present must be broadly right. Starting from the normal annual military demand for wheat in the third century of 13,900 tonnes, the Hannibalic War caused a fourfold, then over fivefold, explosion of demand, which continued afterwards so that the average annual military wheat demand over the four decades from 220 to 181 was 63,800 tonnes. From 180 to 111 annual demand averaged 36,600 tonnes of wheat, and was quite stable: if we exclude the low average for the 150s of 27,200 tonnes (still twice the pre-220 norm), the range between the highest and lowest demand was only 18% of the overall average. From 110 to 51 BC demand was both much higher, with an annual average of 57,200 tonnes, and more variable: excepting the low average for the 90s, the range of variation was 34%. Obviously the impact of Rome's military demand for grain will have depended on the availability of supplies, and on how they were obtained and distributed, to which I will return in section 6 below.

5. THE GRAIN DEMAND OF THE *FRUMENTATIO* AT ROME

Throughout the Republic the food supply of the city of Rome was mostly left to private enterprise. However, various anecdotes from the Hannibalic War on show that the inhabitants of Rome expected their magistrates and the senate to provide cheap grain when possible, probably often by selling off surplus state stocks, and to intervene to palliate shortages and high prices when they occurred. In contrast to the Hellenistic world private euergetism was unknown, in effect blocked by an unwritten rule among the elite.[16] As the city grew, these adventitious expedients proved increasingly unsatisfactory, and in 122 Gaius Gracchus established a regular state distribution of

---

[14]   Double rations were sometimes granted as a reward to infantry units. Horses doing heavy work require around 10 kg a day of hard and soft tack. The same allowance as in Polybius is found in imperial records such as *P.Oxy.* LX 4087 (mid-IV AD): 0.5 modius of barley and 20 pounds (6.5 kg) chaff a day. The Roman allowance of 2.6 kg of barley a day was low, leaving horses with less stamina. Polybius' silence on fodder implies that the Romans expected it to be found locally by foraging.

[15]   Roth 1999, 77–83 gives a useful review of the problem; he plumps for one animal per three to four men, which I think to be a high estimate more plausible for the situation in the Principate.

[16]   Cf. Table 13.1: the sales by aediles in 203, 201, 200 and 196 (nos. 4–7) were apparently of tax grain; the tale of Spurius Maelius in 439 BC (no. 12) was a warning against private euergetism.

Table 13.4a Annual wheat demand for the frumentatio by periods

period	recipients	@ 60 mod.	tonnes
122–101	60,000	3.6 million	24,500
100–82	80,000	4.8 million	32,500
81–74	none	-	-
73–63	50,000	3 million	20,500
62–59	100,000	4 million	27,000
58–50	300,000	18 million	122,500
49–45	150,000	9 million	61,000
44–3	250,000	15 million	102,000

Table 13.4b Total state demand for wheat in tonnes by decades

decades	Military demand	annona demand	total demand
122–111	40,500	24,500	63,400
110–101	59,000	24,500	83,500
100–91	43,300	32,500	75,800
90–81	55,700	32,500	88,200
80–71	72,400	-	72,400
70–61	60,100	20,500	80,600
60–51	52,900	122,500	175,400

wheat (*frumentatio*).[17] The Gracchan *frumentatio* provided its recipients with a monthly allowance of 5 modii of wheat, that is 60 modii a year – the basis for a family's subsistence diet, at a set token price (Table 13.1, no. 10a). We know that the Gracchan scheme was at some stage replaced with a more 'modest' one by the lex Octavia, which is now commonly assigned to the 90s BC although I still prefer a date before Saturninus' law in 100 BC which apparently revived the Gracchan arrangements (Table 13.1, no. 10b). In 81 Sulla abolished the *frumentatio*, but it was restored by the lex Terentia Cassia of 73 BC with the original allowance and token price. In 62 BC, in a time of upper class panic, the lex Porcia expanded the number of recipients, and in 58 the lex Clodia made the distribution free and extended entitlement again. In 49 BC Julius Caesar reduced the number of entitled recipients, as did Augustus in 2 BC.

To estimate the state's annual demand for wheat for the *frumentatio*, we need to establish the number of recipients. There are two problems: the definition of the citizens entitled and their number. On the first point, I suspect that the original requirement was to be registered in the census as domiciled in Rome, rather than to be any citizen who turned up, wherever he was domiciled. Probably citizens who migrated to Rome, even if theoretically registered elsewhere, managed to infiltrate the distributions, which will have become an increasing phenomenon after the enfranchisement of the Italian allies after 90 BC. The expansions of 62 and 58 BC may have regularised the position of such citizens. Caesar's restriction seems to have been based on a house-by-house census of residents. The demography of Rome and Italy in the Republic is currently an academic battlefield. My preferred guesstimates are

---

[17] For the establishment and history of the *frumentatio*, see Rickman 1980, 158–85, Garnsey and Rathbone 1985, and Garnsey 1988, 206–14.

around 250,000 inhabitants in the 120s rising to 1 million in the Augustan period, of whom at most a quarter were adult male citizens. We have two pairs of numbers with which any estimates must be compatible. First, Cicero claims that in the late 70s BC 200,000 modii was 'almost' enough to feed the plebs for a month, which implies a minimum of 40,000 regular recipients, and also that the senate had ordered a second tithe and some extra compulsory purchases of wheat from Sicily to a total of 3,800,000 modii, which implies a maximum of 63,000 recipients.[18] Allowing for deliberate over-supply and other uses, this suggests that the expected number of recipients was around 50,000. Second, in 49 BC Julius Caesar reduced the number of recipients from 320,000 to 150,000; it crept up through the civil wars to over 250,000 by 23 BC, until Augustus reduced the number to a fixed 200,000 in 2 BC.[19] Working back from these figures, and ignoring the lex Octavia because of its uncertain date and effect, I present my guesstimates for the annual demand in tonnes of wheat of the *frumentatio* from 122 to 51 BC in Table 13.4A, and set them beside the estimates for military demand in Table 13.4B.

If these guesstimates are roughly correct, Table 13.4B implies that in its first phase, down to Sulla's abolition, the *frumentatio* required on average 60% more wheat than Rome's armies needed. In the first decade of its revival it was equivalent to a third of military demand, but in 62 and 58 BC briefly soared to more than double it. The coincidence between the development of the *frumentatio* and the increased wheat demand from the 140s for Rome's armies meant a huge surge in the annual wheat demand of the Roman state in late second to first centuries BC. The next and final section looks at the wider effects.

6. THE IMPACT OF THE ROMAN STATE'S DEMAND FOR GRAIN ON THE MEDITERRANEAN MARKET

As mentioned in section 1, it would be a huge undertaking to collect and analyse all the miscellaneous and occasional evidence for incidents relevant to grain supply and demand in the Roman world of the last three centuries BC, and one with no guarantee of useful results. In this section I outline, necessarily without full discussion, the main regular sources of grain for the Roman Republic, and then examine in more detail two second-century periods for which there is valuable incidental information in addition to the price data collected above, in order to attempt a preliminary assessment of the impact of the Roman state on the grain market of the Mediterranean.

The Roman state acquired grain through regular taxation in kind of the provinces it created as its conquests grew, which it could supplement with extra levies or

---

[18]   Cic., *Verr.* 2.3.72, 163, 173–4.
[19]   Plut., *Div.Iul.* 41.3; Aug., *ResG* 15.4, Dio 55.10.1.

Table 13.5 Provincial tithes and state demand in wheat by periods

	tithes in modii	tithes in tonnes	demand in tonnes	
200–146	5 million	34,000	59,400	200–181
			34,500	180–151
145–130	13 million	88,400	37,300	150–121
129–74	15 million	102,000	77,300	120–61
73–	16 million	108,800	175,400	60–51

compulsory purchases.[20] The state and its magistrates could also demand or request supplies from allied states, for which it sometimes made payment. A complicating factor is that officials could demand or agree to *aestimatio*, that is commutation of grain dues into cash payments at a set supposedly fair price (or into other crops). Purchase from private suppliers was also possible. For maritime transport of grain for Rome and its armies, the state used private contractors (*publicani*), as they also did for many other public works including provision of equipment to its armies, and the collection of the tithe in the province of Asia from 122–49 BC. I note three points. First, that the Romans always provided substantial logistical support for their military expeditions so that they did not have to rely on local foraging. Second, that the supply of Rome's armies and the city required an enormous amount of shipping. For instance, the overall annual total of 80,000 tonnes of wheat guesstimated for around 100 BC will have required 1,000 trips by medium-sized ships of around 80 tonnes burden.[21] Third, that the involvement of the *publicani*, who often ran private enterprises alongside their state contracts, probably complicated the actual pattern of supply and distribution of state grain.

Cicero implies that the basic annual tithe from Sicily in the 70s BC was assessed at about three million modii of wheat, which presumably went back to Laevinus' settlement of the province in 210 BC; the tithe of western Sicily only from 241 to 211 BC may have been nearer one million modii.[22] Extrapolating from partial figures, the annual tithe of the province of Africa, created in 146 BC, may have been around eight million modii in the later second and early first centuries BC.[23] For the other provinces

---

[20]   For provincial taxation by the Roman Republic, see Frank 1933. *Aestimatio* is illustrated in Table 13.1, nos. 13 and 15.

[21]   Cf. the discussion by Tchernia 2000 of the shipping required to feed first-century AD Rome.

[22]   Cic., *Verr.* 2.3.163. The lex Rupilia of 131 BC probably formalised judicial arrangements and did not affect the tithe.

[23]   Livy 43.6.11–14 records gifts to Rome in 170 BC by Carthage and Masinissa of one million modii of wheat each, and also 500,000 modii of barley from Carthage. Plut., *Caes.* 55.1, says that Caesar claimed in 46 BC that the part of Numidia he had annexed would supply Rome annually with 200,000 Attic medimnoi (1.2 million modii) of wheat and 3 million pounds of olive oil. By the early Principate Africa was providing roughly twice as much wheat for Rome as Egypt; the annual demand of the *frumentatio* under Augustus was 12 million modii, but supplies to the *annona* in general, including the army, is probably meant, and the African tithe was probably now enormously greater.

it is pure guesswork: Sardinia and Spain, provinces since 238 and 197 BC respectively but still being pacified throughout the second century, about one million each; Asia from 129 BC, perhaps two million, and Cyrene from 73 BC, say one million. Table 13.5 gives these annual estimates in modii and tonnes of wheat and compares the average annual level of wheat demand for Rome's armies and the *frumentatio* taken from Tables 13.3 and 13.4B above.

Although the figures are all estimates, the broad pattern is not implausible. Normally the assessed tithes were more than adequate to meet average demands. The surplus produced by the annexation of Africa and then Asia in effect made feasible Gaius Gracchus' institution of the *frumentatio* in 122 BC. Two periods stand out when tax wheat was seriously inadequate: the 190s and 180s because of heavy military activity, and the 50s after the enormous expansion of the *frumentatio*. Plutarch says that after the lex Porcia of 62 BC the *frumentatio* cost the state 7.5 million denarii per annum, part of which was presumably transport, storage and distribution costs, but half or more must represent purchases, whether through requisition or on the free market.[24] Even in the times of theoretical sufficiency tithes will have tended to produce less than was assessed and demands to exceed theoretical needs, and the business of applying supplies to needs will have meant extra consumption and waste itself. I look now in more detail at the period c. 192–169 BC and then the 130s and 120s to try to trace what effect Rome's increasing control of grain-producing regions and its vast annual state movements of grain had on the Greek world.

For most of the Republic the bulk of Rome's military effort, in terms of legions deployed, was in the western Mediterranean. Although the evidence is very thin, most of the wheat supplies for these campaigns must have come from Sicily and Sardinia, and later Spain. Hannibal's invasion of Italy disrupted supplies for over ten years; hence the crisis price in 210 BC and request to Ptolemy IV of Egypt for wheat.[25] However by 204 BC production in central Italy was recovering and there were surpluses from abroad at least down to 196 BC.[26] This is somewhat surprising in that in 200–198 BC the Romans were campaigning in Greece against Philip V, but may be explained by a combination of second tithes, requisitions from allies and release of stockpiles from the end of the Hannibalic War.[27] However, we do have evidence for problems caused by the Roman campaigns in the Greek world from 192 to 168 BC.

For the war against Antiochos III (192–189 BC) the Romans fielded two legions in 191 and four in 190–188, and probably double the number of Italian allied troops. Using the same procedure as in Table 13.3 above, the annual grain demand of these

---

[24] Plut., *Cato min.* 26.1, *Caes.* 8.4.

[25] Table 13.1, no. 3; Polybius 9.11a.1–3; cf. Livy 27.4.10.

[26] Pliny, *NH* 18.6: harvest of 204 BC the best for ten years. Abroad: Table 13.1, nos. 4–7; also Livy 30.38.5: in 202 BC merchants (*mercatores*) importing wheat from Sicily and Sardinia had to give it to the shippers to cover the transport costs.

[27] Gifts from Carthage and Numidia are attested in 200 and 198, and use of tax-grain from Sicily and Sardinia in 198 BC: Livy 31.50.1, 32.27.2.

forces (allowing for 10,000 naval personnel) can be estimated at 3.9 million modii of wheat (26,400 tonnes) and 2 million modii of barley (10,800 tonnes) in 190–188, and half that in 191. In 191 Rome levied double tithes from Sicily and Sardinia, of which the second Sardinian tithe was shipped to Rome and the rest, say 7 million modii of wheat, to the army in Greece; in addition Carthage and Numidia provided at no cost one million modii of wheat and 800,000 modii of barley for those forces, as well as 550,000 modii of wheat and 500,000 modii of barley for the city of Rome.[28] Double tithes of wheat were again raised in Sicily and Sardinia in 190 and 189 and all, except the second Sardinian tithe in 190, sent to the armies in the east.[29] In 191 to 189 some 157,000 tonnes of wheat are recorded as being dispatched as against an estimated military need over the full four years of 92,400 tonnes of wheat and 37,800 tonnes of barley. The apparent over-supply of wheat was massive, and our record of supplies is probably incomplete.

For the Third Macedonian War (171–168 BC) the Romans fielded two legions in 171–169 and four in 168, probably with equal numbers of Italian allies. On the same assumptions as for 200–198 BC, the annual grain demand of these forces will have been 11,000 tonnes of wheat and 3,800 tonnes of barley in 171–169, and double that in 168. In 171 double tithes were raised in Sicily and Sardinia and sent to the army, that is eight million modii of wheat; in addition a month's grain supply was levied at Aquileia and 100,000 modii of wheat from Athens, and the army harvested crops in Thessaly.[30] In 170 the army received two million modii of wheat and 500,000 modii of barley from Carthage and Masinissa; it had also requisitioned 20,000 modii of wheat and 10,000 modii of barley from the Epirotes, and was foraging in Macedon.[31] These recorded supplies total 69,400 tonnes of wheat and 2,600 tonnes of barley. The record looks to be incomplete, yet even if we allow for some commutation from wheat to barley, again there seems to have been a massive over-supply of wheat.

We might expect any state-organised levying and distribution of grain to have involved commutation and losses. However the scale of over-supply of Rome's armies in Greece on these two campaigns suggests that Roman warfare caused massive disruption and losses. I would guess that much of this was due to the *publicani* profiting through commutation, re-sale and so on. The extraordinary logistical efforts for these campaigns affected Rome itself where in 189 the aediles fined grain merchants (*frumentarii*) for profiteering, the one and only time in the Republic such action is recorded, while in 170 the senate banned governors in Spain from imposing *aestimatio* on the wheat tithe.[32] We are so ignorant of the normal pattern of grain flows in the ancient Mediterranean that it is difficult to estimate the effect on the Greek world of Rome's increased control of Sicilian and African supplies. By chance we know that in

---

[28] Livy 36.2.10–13, 4.5–9 (text as in OCT).

[29] Livy 37.2.12, 37.50.9–10.

[30] Livy 42.31.8; 43.1.8, 6.3; 42.64.2–3, cf. Appian, *Mac.* fr. 8.3.

[31] Livy 43.6.11–14; 44.16.2–4. Note that Livy 42.29.8 implies that Masinissa had already sent wheat in 171 BC.

[32] Livy 38.35.5–6; 43.2.12.

180 BC Masinissa king of Numidia donated almost 3,000 medimnoi (some 120 tonnes) of wheat to Delos which the state sold at lowish prices to its citizens, and it is unlikely that prior to the Hannibalic War the Greek world had not been drawing on wheat from Syracuse and Carthage.[33] War made the situation worse. Athenian envoys to Rome complained of the levy in 171 from their infertile land whose farmers lived off imported grain (the old story), and the Rhodians in 169 BC had to ask the senate to allow them to buy and export 100,000 medimnoi (600,000 modii) of grain from Sicily.[34] Roman warfare in the area is probably the best explanation for the high wheat prices attested on Delos in 190, 178, 174 and 169 BC, because the *publicani*, who made it their base, stayed there between the wars.[35]

After 167 BC Livy's history is not extant, so we have no more even partial records of grain supplies for Roman campaigns. However the various sources we have suggest a particular phase of more general problems in the 130s and 120s BC. We are told that grain was short or prices high at Rome in 138, 129 and 125–123 BC.[36] Supplies from Sicily were disrupted by the slave revolt of 135–132 BC, while Africa was hit in 125/4 by a plague of locusts whose destructive trail now leads to Babylon in late July 124.[37] Indeed a spate of locust invasions of Babylonia are attested in 142, 136, 132, 130, 124 and 122 BC, which suggests that north Africa too may have been more frequently plagued in this period than the one extant reference attests. Resistance to Roman annexation of the Attalid kingdom (Asia) in 131–129 and the troubles in Egypt in 130–127 BC will have disrupted those sources of supply. The institution of the *frumentatio* at Rome in 122 BC significantly increased the regular grain demand of the Roman state. In the following decades to the fall of the Republic, despite occasional lulls, the Greek world experienced increasingly frequent and increasingly large-scale military interventions by Rome.

By the late second century the price of wheat at Rome had doubled. Probably the price been rising through the second century, maybe with a spurt due to the coinage reform of 141/0 BC. Its basic cause was probably the massively increased monetary wealth of Rome and Italy from the profits of imperial expansion and also increased monetisation.

---

[33] Table 13.2A, no. 8a. The curious total of 2,796.5 medimnoi suggests conversion into Attic medimnoi at their real value (54 l) of a consignment reckoned by Masinissa in modii, that is 17,500 modii. The two lots in which the wheat was sold may represent two shiploads, the first of 9,300 modii (63 tonnes), the second of 8,200 modii (56 tonnes). At least two statues to Masinissa were erected on Delos, *I.Délos* II 1115 and 1116, the first by one of the officials involved in the gift of 180 BC, the other by a Rhodian.

[34] Athens: Livy 43.6.3; they were probably claiming payment, like the Epirotes in 170. Rhodes: Polybius 28.2, only mentioned because of Roman duplicity; the episode is not recorded by Livy, illustrating the randomness of the record.

[35] Note that there were grain shortages in Rome and Italy in 181–180 and maybe 175: Livy 40.19.3, 29.12, 36.14; 41.21.5–7; cf. Plut., *Cato maior* 8.1.

[36] Val.Max. 3.7.3; *SEG* 34.558 (Table 13.2B, no. 9); Plut., *Gaius Gracch.* 2.3, 6.2.

[37] Livy, *Per.* 60. For the Babylonian evidence, see Pirngruber's paper in this volume.

When the data are so few and often of uncertain date, interpretation is hazardous and provisional. The Delian evidence, and the experience of Epidauros in 74 BC (Table 13.2B, no. 14), suggest that close contact with Rome as an expanding military power meant high wheat prices. But the crises were normally short-lived and when they passed prices in the Greek world seem to have returned to their traditional normal level. A new world system was emerging, in which Rome was the dominant anomaly. With peace and Principate the grain supply of the Greek world may have become more adequate than before: the single useable attestation of normal prices in the area in that period, from Pisidian Antioch in AD 93, sets them at equivalent to 3 to 4 drachmas per medimnos.[38]

REFERENCES

Abbreviations for ancient sources are given as in *The Oxford Classical Dictionary* (3rd edition 1996, revised 2003).

Brunt, P. A. (1971) *Italian Manpower 225 B.C.-A.D. 14*. Oxford: Clarendon Press.

Foxhall, L. and Forbes, H. (1982) Σιτομετρεία: the role of grain as a staple food in classical antiquity. *Chiron* 12, 41–90.

Frank, T. (1933) *Rome and Italy of the Republic. Economic Survey of Ancient Rome*, Vol. I. Baltimore/London: Johns Hopkins Press/Oxford University Press.

Garnsey, P. (1988) *Famine and Food Supply in the Graeco-Roman World*. Cambridge: Cambridge University Press.

Garnsey, P. and Rathbone, D. W. (1985) The background to the grain law of Gaius Gracchus. *Journal of Roman Studies* 75, 20–25.

Heichelheim, F. (1935) Sitos. In Pauly-Wissowa (ed.), *Real-Encyclopädie,* suppl. VI, 819–992.

Hultsch, F. (1882) *Griechische und römische Metrologie*. 2nd edn. Berlin: Weidmann.

Rathbone, D. W. (2009) Earnings and costs: living standards and the Roman economy (first to third centuries AD). In A. Bowman and A. Wilson (eds), *Quantifying the Roman Economy. Methods and Problems*, 299–326. Oxford: Oxford University Press.

Reger, G. (1994) *Regionalism and Change in the Economy of Independent Delos*. Berkeley: University of California Press.

Rickman, G. (1980) *The Corn Supply of Ancient Rome*. Oxford: Clarendon Press.

Roth, J. P. (1999) *The Logistics of the Roman Army at War (264 B.C. - A.D. 235)*. Leiden: Brill.

Sosin, J. D. (2002) Grain for Andros. *Hermes* 30, 131–145.

Szaivert, W. and Wolters, R. (2005) *Löhne, Preise, Werte. Quellen zur römischen Geldwirtschaft*. Darmstadt: Wissenschaftliche Buchgesellschaft.

Tchernia, A. (2000) Subsistances à Rome: problèmes de quantification. In C. Nicolet (ed.), *Mégapoles méditerranéennes: géographie urbaine retrospective*, 751–760. Paris: Maisonneuve et Larose.

---

[38] *AE* 1925.126b: normal price was HS 2 to 2.5 per modius; in a shortage, the governor ordered landowners to release stocks at HS 4 per modius.

Mediterranean and Near Eastern Grain Prices c. 300 to 31 BC: Some Preliminary Conclusions[1]

Dominic Rathbone

1. AIMS

Long-period and wide-area economic analysis, statistical where possible or at least based on large data-sets, has always interested economists, for instance Goldsmith's 1987 comparative study of a number of pre-modern societies and, most recently and ambitiously, Maddison's 2007 survey of world economic developments over the last two millennia. It has also interested mediaeval and early modern historians, for example McCormick's 2001 study of trade in the European economy of AD 300–900 and Braudel's 1979 survey of the Mediterranean economy of the fifteenth to eighteenth centuries. However, although Goldsmith and Maddison both start with the Roman world of the early Principate (Maddison by re-working Goldsmith's figures), only one ancient historian has attempted such a grand survey for Graeco-Roman antiquity, Fritz Heichelheim in his 1930 study of economic cycles (*Wirtschaftliche Schwankungen*) from Alexander to Augustus, extended by his paper of 1954/5 on price trends from the sixth century BC to the seventh century AD. Heichelheim seems to have expected his work to interest economic historians more than ancient historians, and in effect abetted this, for he published his book in a series for studies of the circumstances of economic change and his article in *Finanzarchiv*, a journal of economic history. Although it was reprinted in 1979, the *Wirtschaftliche Schwankungen* has never been translated, unlike

---

[1] This is a brief attempt to explain the context and draw out the main principal conclusions of the preceding three papers. My two collaborators (van der Spek and von Reden) have contributed input and comments but are not responsible for the deficiencies of this part of our project.

his 1938 general study of the economy of the ancient world (*Wirtschaftsgeschichte*) which has English and Italian translations.

It is not that all ancient historians avoid economic history or think they lack adequate data to make its study worthwhile. Although the Graeco-Roman world has not produced any series of data remotely comparable to the prices in the Babylonian astronomical diaries, prices and earnings form one of the largest categories of numerical data (alongside ages) which survive to us, and a new phase of interest in collecting this data began in the late twentieth century with the spread of personal computing. For the Greek world, to give a few examples, we have Loomis 1998 on wages in classical Athens and Reger 1994 on the prices in the temple accounts of Hellenistic Delos.[2] For the Roman world we have the empire-wide survey edited by Frank (1933–40), Duncan-Jones (1974/1982) on various costs mainly on Italy and Africa, Drexhage (1991) on prices and earnings in Roman Egypt and Bagnall (1985) on fourth-century Egypt, Sperber (1974/1991) on later Roman Palestine, and the collection by Szaivert and Wolters (2005) of all figures in literary sources.[3] The problem with much of this data, however, is that it is sparse, random and extremely heterogeneous. One late fifth-century BC price for a trumpet is a curiosity of minimal significance; nine scattered prices for ivory are little better.[4] Even for commodities such as wheat and wine with a fair spread of data, synthesis is difficult because of the variety of measures and coinages used (see further Section 2 below). This is one reason why collection and analysis of the data have usually been restricted to particular areas and periods, and grander projects thought suspect. However, there is another important reason, which is theoretical.

Heichelheim's *Wirtschaftliche Schwankungen*, published a year after the Wall Street crash, is permeated by the economic concerns and thought of that time. In a little under a hundred and fifty pages Heichelheim attempted to plot the changing health of the ancient economy, covering the Mediterranean and Near East, over three centuries, primarily through a chart of its temperature expressed in price-changes, although he also brought in wages, rents and interest rates. Like Rostovtzeff (1935–36), he believed that the similar economic demands and productive strategies of the Hellenistic monarchies and their elites created a 'world' economy of interconnected price-setting markets of goods and services. He went further, however, in seeking evidence in the data for economic cycles, and came up with two main conclusions: that in the third century monarchic support for production and trade had caused a general fall in commodity prices, and that a combination of adverse factors in the late second century had led to a sharp and enduring general rise in prices which caused

---

[2]   Note also the Bremen database (incomplete) at: http://nomisma.geschichte.uni-bremen.de. For study of Ptolemaic data see the paper of von Reden in this volume.

[3]   Also in an online version at: http://www.stanford.edu/~scheidel/NumIntro.htm.

[4]   Trumpet: Aristoph., *Peace* 1240-1. Ivory: c. 370 BC (two cases without quantities) at Epidauros; 334, 276, 269 and 250 BC on Delos; AD 48 at Puteoli; c. 150 at Alexandria; AD 301 in Diocletian's Maximum Price Edict (without quantity).

a serious general recession.[5] Such unquestioning use of neoclassical economic concepts has been anathema to most ancient historians since the appearance in 1973 of Finley's *The Ancient Economy*. In practice that has not stopped the continuing fascination, prompted by late twentieth-century experience, with cases of price inflation in the ancient world, particularly the later Roman Empire, and more recently there has been some grudging acceptance that neoclassical economic theories can be useful if used with attention to the problems of context, especially if coated with the sugar of the New Institutionalism.[6] There have, for example, been attempts to compare prices and earnings to estimate ancient living standards, and to explore the formation of prices, that is the extent to which they were conventional or administered, or the result of free market supply and demand.[7] However, such studies have been few, and also mostly regional with an inevitable tendency to eschew broad explanations. Thus Reger's 1994 monograph on the Delian prices, one of the few studies to respond explicitly to Heichelheim, rejects a pan-Mediterranean or even pan-Aegean picture in favour of explanations based on local particularities.

In our three papers we make a first experiment, confined to grain prices in the last three centuries BC, in reviving Heichelheim's project of comparing prices, earnings and related data across a large geographical area and period of time. Rather, however, than starting with the assumption of a 'world' market straightforwardly suitable for neoclassical economic analysis, we are interested in exploring whether, to what extent and how contact between localities and regions led to the emergence of regional or 'world' market frameworks which had a general overarching influence on the fundamental local factors of production, consumption and exchange. More specifically we are interested in whether the creation of the Hellenistic kingdoms and then the Roman empire led to greater market integration of their constituent zones and, prospectively, higher levels of exchange and productivity. Another part of this experiment is to develop a more robust methodology for dealing with the uncertainties and deficiencies of the ancient data.

2. SOME METHODOLOGICAL OBSERVATIONS

The basic problem of comparing prices and earnings over large areas and long periods is regional and chronological variation in the measures and units of value (coinages) used. A subsidiary problem for the ancient world is that sometimes we are not certain of these values. While the modern equivalents of Roman measures and coinage are as certain as can be (even if old inaccurate values are still often cited), and the Ptolemaic coinage systems are now quite well understood, there are still uncertainties such as

---

[5]   Reprised in apocalyptic terms in Heichelheim 1938/1970, 37–41.

[6]   See further Scheidel and Von Reden 2002, introduction.

[7]   E.g. Andreau, Briant and Descat 1997; Bowman and Wilson 2009. In contrast, there are only a few passing allusions to prices and earnings in Scheidel, Morris and Saller 2007, and the brief index entries for 'prices' and 'wages' both have the sub-entry 'shortage of data'!

the extent of use of non-Attic medimnoi and the capacity of the *kophinos* in the Greek world, and the value of the artaba, or perhaps different artabas, in Ptolemaic Egypt, and how exchanges between the coinages of different states were calculated. Heichelheim's solution to these problems was to create baselines for indexing prices from different systems by selecting pairs of more or less contemporary prices as equivalents, for instance the later second-century BC wheat prices of 6 1/3 asses per modius for the Gracchan *frumentatio* at Rome and 2 3/8 drachmai per artaba in Egypt.[8] This procedure was arbitrary and unsafe: picking the extremely low Gracchan administered price, for example, as his baseline for Rome artificially inflated the other Roman prices. It also produced a complicated graph comparing levels of change rather than levels of prices which is unnecessarily difficult to read and comprehend. Our choice instead has been to convert all prices into grammes of silver per tonne of grain. This has its own problems, as we now recognise more clearly through writing these papers, and while we would stick to using silver bullion as the best, or least bad, common measure of value, we would in future quantify grain by volume rather than weight.

All our states used silver coinages, almost all of an extremely high purity, and our knowledge, from numismatic studies, of the target weight to which coins were minted is fairly good, which facilitates conversion of values, even when expressed in related bronze coins, into weights of silver bullion. Of course there were events which may have affected the purchasing power of these coinages. There were variations, sometimes sharp if brief, in the free market value of silver bullion. Alexander the Great's dispersal of the Persian royal treasures, for instance, must have caused a fall in the value of precious metals. Sometimes the weight or purity of silver coinages were reduced without alteration to the official tariff, as apparently happened to the Attic drachma and some other Greek coinages in the early second century BC, raising the question of whether prices then reflected these changes or the coins held their value as a token coinage. This is not really a problem as long as it is recognised. The real values of any commodity may have altered, and there is no obviously preferable common alternative: wheat and grape wine, for instance, do not feature in the Babylonian diaries, and pig prices are generally very variable and too few. Ideally, in a fuller study, we would check variances over time between coin values and a basket of other goods and earnings to look for changes in the purchasing power of our coinages.

Grain prices have two big advantages but a problem of comparability. Grain prices are one of the best, perhaps the best, in terms of number of attestations in the ancient world. Grain was the most important component of most ancient diets, making its price a privileged indicator of living standards (allowing, of course, for the level of earnings). However consumption of grains was variable by region and perhaps status. Wheat was the preferred grain of the Graeco-Roman world, even if barley was still often consumed, while barley was the dominant grain of Babylonia. Egyptian *olyra*

---

[8]   Heichelheim 1930, 74; cf. 1954/5, 501 n.1.

and Roman *far*, both forms of emmer wheat, seem to have been rural subsistence staples, little traded. Although there is evidence that the prices of wheat and barley in the Graeco-Roman world were often related in a fairly stable ratio, that leaves open the question of the relationship, if any, to them of Babylonian barley prices and the effect on some wheat and barley markets of rural consumption of other grains, for example *olyra* in Ptolemaic Egypt.

For these papers we chose to quantify wheat prices by weight, that is grammes of silver per tonne of wheat, mainly because this is how costs are commonly reckoned and compared by economic historians (and it also facilitates calculating calorific value). Unfortunately, the issue of the density of ancient grains has proved more awkward, and interesting, than we anticipated. Densities of grains vary by type, region and stage of processing, for barley much more so than wheat because it is more varied in type and has more husk to lose. The density of modern European wheats lies around 75–80 kg/hl and of barleys around 58–70 kg/hl.[9] Writing a decade or so before AD 79, the elder Pliny lists the target weights per modius used by the Roman state to check consignments of wheat from the principal areas where it raised tithes: these range from 75 to 81.5 kg/hl, in line with the modern range. The official nature of Pliny's figures is confirmed by the recurrence of the value for Egyptian wheat (78 kg/hl) in two late Roman papyri, one of which also gives target weights for Egyptian barley and *olyra* (emmer wheat) equivalent to 62.5 kg/hl and 36.5 kg/hl respectively; the barley fits the modern scale, and is in the common 5:6 ratio with the wheat density. However, a recently published Athenian regulation of 374/3 BC sets target weights for checking deliveries of state grain from the northern Aegean equivalent to just over 50 kg/hl for barley and 60 kg/hl for wheat, in the usual 5:6 ratio but with extraordinarily low values, especially for wheat.[10] We may suspect a particular reason here for specifying an artificially low density, perhaps to give the contractors a larger safety and profit margin. However, Pliny too gives two problematic other 'private' figures: that the density of barley rarely exceeds 56 kg/hl, which seems too low, while the best Italian *far* (emmer wheat) reaches 94 kg/hl and more, which seems very high.[11] Clearly more study of the nature and processing of ancient grains would be useful, including consideration of *alphita*, a semi-processed form in which barley was sometimes sold in the Greek world, and might resolve some of the conundrums these figures pose.

In our three papers we admit to some metrological differences which we were not able to resolve before publication. The densities we use for barley are all close enough: 62 kg/hl by van der Spek, 69.4 (Egypt, rather high, but only four cases) and 57.8 kg/hl (Athens) by von Reden, 60 kg/hl by Rathbone. For wheat Rathbone uses 79 kg/hl for Rome and the west and 76 kg/hl for the Greek world, while von Reden uses 75 kg/

---

[9]   For this and the following references see Rathbone 1983.

[10]   *SEG* 48.96; Rhodes and Osborne 2003, no. 26, who note that the implied improvement to Roman densities from this low density is implausible, and suggest that it was to benefit the contractors.

[11]   Pliny, *NH* 18.62: barley not over 15 pounds / modius; 18.66: *far* to 25 or even 26 pounds / modius.

hl for Egypt but, following the Attic law of 374/3 BC, 60 kg/hl for Delos and Athens. Hence the conversions into silver values of the Delian and other Greek prices of wheat by von Reden and Rathbone diverge, with von Reden's equivalents being some 35% higher.[12] To avoid these sorts of problems, we now advocate calculating the equivalent silver values of ancient wheat prices by volume (per hl) rather than weight. Indeed, this would in any case be better because, although the Greeks and Romans were clearly well aware of regional variations in grain density and used that knowledge to check official consignments by weighing, presumably, a sample number of units delivered, they consistently used measures of volume when dealing with yields, rations, prices and so on of grain.[13] Only when comparing grain prices with those from other periods which have been calculated by weight is it necessary to convert values by volume into values by weight, and for this, pending further study, the Roman weights seem more plausible than the Attic ones.

3. PATTERNS IN THE GRAIN PRICES

One of the most striking features of the grain prices we have collected from the Mediterranean and Near East in the period 300–31 BC is their normal long-term stability. The normal range of Babylonian barley prices was broadly stable from 230 to 140 BC, and the same is true for wheat in Egypt in the second to first century. In the Greek world the normal 'fair' price of wheat was 5–6 drachmas per medimnos right through the period, even after the reduction in weight of the Attic drachma at the start of the second century; indeed this price-level is also found in late-fifth- and fourth-century Athens. This suggests, incidentally, that the Attic drachma was so well established among the Greeks that it was able to retain its value as a token coinage after the weight reduction. Across the Mediterranean a price ratio of 3:5 between barley and wheat was the norm: in Egypt, reinforced by official prescription for penalty prices, in late-fourth-century Athens, in Macedon around 200 BC, in Lusitania in the mid-second century. This suggests a broadly common pattern of production and consumption of these two grains.

Deviations from the normal range of prices were often caused by local shortfalls in production and were usually short-term. In Egypt, perhaps because of the tradition of state storage and control of grain, price rises were limited compared to small Greek states where the search for extra outside supplies could be difficult. The Babylonian and Roman data illustrate well the dramatic impact on grain prices of major military campaigns, but also that normal prices returned quickly – within a year – with peace.

---

[12]   Von Reden tables 12.3 and 12.6; Rathbone tables 13.2A and 13.2B. The difference is greater than that between the densities used because von Reden also takes the medimnos as equivalent to 50 litres, Rathbone to 54 litres.

[13]   We do not have the depth of data to investigate whether heavier wheats (with greater calorific value) had any price premium on, for instance, the market in Rome, or were perhaps preferred given a choice.

Some longer-term trends emerge from the data. In Babylonia barley prices were relatively low in the 180s to 160s and then peaked sharply around 125 BC, after which there were several decades of unusual volatility. Egypt saw a 25% price increase by the end of the third century, and much greater variation in the price range in the second century. At Rome prices seem to have more than doubled by the end of the second century; also, in Sicily of the 70s BC, the price ratio between barley and wheat was 1:2 rather than 3:5, perhaps implying a decline in consumption of barley as an alternative to wheat.

At first sight, the normal ranges of grain values seem to show little market integration between the zones examined. Throughout the period the normal range for wheat in the Greek world was 530–640 grammes of silver per tonne, while in Egypt it was two to three times lower at 180–310 g, a level which is confirmed by the double-rate penalty prices equivalent to 400–600 g. Wheat in Italy in the earlier second century was somewhat cheaper than in the Greek world at 400–500 g, but by the late Republic was twice as expensive at 1,000–1,100 g, although in Sicily in the 70s the range was around 420–560 g, the same as the previous Italian norm. The normal range of barley prices in Babylon altered significantly from around 90–290 g for most of the third century to around 80–150 g in the period 230–140, and to around 190–380 g thereafter. The four Egyptian barley prices, at 150–170 g, compare best with the Babylonian prices before 230. On a 3:5 ratio the hypothetical wheat equivalents for the three periods of Babylonian barley prices would be around 150–480 g, 130–250 g and 300–600 g respectively.[14] The first two are not incompatible with Egyptian wheat prices; in the third period they are more expensive, comparable to Greek and Sicilian wheat prices.

Of course the processed data we present are of varying validity: the Babylonian data, for instance, are robust, but the Roman early second-century prices are an estimated extrapolation. Nonetheless some glimmers of a history of growing integration emerge (in addition to the common barley-wheat price ratio). In times of relative stability, grains were generally cheaper in major areas of production with state storage systems (which at the least reduced vulnerability to private hoarding) and limited geographical links to the Mediterranean world, that is the Egyptian *chora* and Babylonia in the period 230–140 BC. Differences were less if contacts were easier: thus the Italian prices of the earlier second century, drawing on western supplies, and Sicilian prices in the 70s were only a band below prices in the Greek world. The two wheat prices we have from Alexandria are equivalent to 6.5 and 6 drachmas per medimnos, at the top of the normal range of wheat prices in the Greek world.[15] This suggests that the

---

[14]   The hypothetical wheat equivalent is just a tool to compare Babylonian barley prices with Egyptian wheat prices, irrespective of whether there was a wheat market in Babylon. However, I would be surprised if the Greek settlers in Hellenistic Babylonia had not tried to cultivate or import wheat (as the Greeks did in Egypt); of course the Diaries would have ignored this untraditional commodity.

[15]   Von Reden, table 12.1, nos. 2 and 12 (270 and 249 BC). I convert the prices assuming an artaba of 40 l and a medimnos of 54 l.

pricing of wheat in the Egyptian *chora* was consciously less than in the Greek world, and also that Alexandria, as the largest and probably wealthiest metropolis of the Hellenistic world, was in itself an anomalous centre of demand with its own high price range, as Rome was to become, but on a far greater scale by the end of the second century. We seem to be dealing with a world where regional factors of production and consumption set normal ranges of grain prices but there was sufficient overarching market integration to link these ranges in patterns of fairly stable relationships. That does imply that major change in one area might be expected to produce effects in others, of varying scale depending on the strength of the market contact. Although when we began this project we were sceptical of Heichelheim's theory of a general economic crisis in the later second century BC, we now have to admit that this is what the evidence seems to suggest. Wheat prices in Rome and Italy had more than doubled, and so too barley prices in Babylonia. The Babylonian and Egyptian data show much greater price volatility. Only the Greek world seems relatively untroubled but simply through lack of evidence.[16] What may have caused this is difficult to say. Across the whole area we have a spate of attestations of natural disasters affecting production, also of social unrest which probably exacerbated problems; another factor may have been the knock-on effects of the development of Rome as an imperial capital with a huge grain demand for its armies and new civic distribution scheme (*frumentatio*) and an extraordinarily high purchasing power from its imperial incomes.

To take this study forward there is much we would need to do. Greater certainty on metrological issues would help. We need to consider regional changes to the purchasing power of silver, for example whether the huge booty, indemnities and then cash taxes sucked by Rome from the Hellenistic world over the last two centuries BC made silver sufficiently scarcer in the east to increase its purchasing power as the inflow of wealth to Rome seems to have raised grain prices there. Indeed movements of capital (money and bullion, people too) through Roman imperialism may have been the main driver towards market integration, albeit of an asymmetric type.[17] We need to compare the price behaviour of wheat against other commodities, as van der Spek does in his paper with the Babylonian prices of dates, and also against earnings, as von Reden does briefly, to estimate living standards and changes in them as price structures changed. This experiment with grain prices has shown that it will not be easy but has convinced us that it will be worth it, and that there is a story of changing patterns of overarching integration as well as of underlying regionalism to be found and told.

---

[16]   The four benefactions of the time, or a bit later, are not good evidence for normal prices, but may by their concentration, imply a period of difficulties.

[17]   Cf., for the Roman empire of the Principate, von Freyberg 1998.

REFERENCES

Abbreviations for ancient sources are given as in *The Oxford Classical Dictionary* (Third edition 1996, revised 2003).

Andreau, J., Briant, P. and Descat, R. (eds) (1997) *Prix et formation des prix dans les économies antiques.* Saint-Bertrand-de-Comminges: Musée archéologique départemental de Saint-Bertrand-de-Comminges.

Bagnall, R. (1985) *Currency and Inflation in Fourth Century Egypt.* Chico: Scholars Press.

Bowman, A. and Wilson, A. (eds) (2009) *Quantifying the Roman Economy.* Oxford: Oxford University Press.

Braudel, F. (1979) *Les structures du quotidien: le possible et l'impossible.* Paris. (Transl. *Civilization and Capitalism, 15th-18th Centuries.* 1981–84. London: Collins.)

Drexhage, H.-J. (1991) *Preise, Mieten / Pachten, Kosten und Löhne im römischen Ägypten bis zum Regierungsantritt Diokletians.* St. Katharinen: Scripta Mercaturae Verlag.

Duncan-Jones, R. P. (1982) *The Economy of the Roman Empire. Quantitative Studies.* 2nd edition. Cambridge (1st edition 1974): Cambridge University Press.

Finley, M. I. (1973) *The Ancient Economy.* London (2nd edition 1985): Hogarth Press.

Frank, T. (ed.) (1933–40) *Economic Survey of Ancient Rome,* 6 vols. Baltimore: Johns Hopkins Press.

Goldsmith, R. W. (1987) *Premodern Financial Systems. A Historical Comparative Study.* Cambridge: Cambridge University Press.

Heichelheim, F. (1930) *Wirtschaftliche Schwankungen der Zeit von Alexander bis Augustus. Beiträge zur Erforschung der wirtschaftlichen Wechsellagen. Aufschwung, Krise, Stockung,* vol. 3. Jena: G. Fischer. Repr. New York 1979, Arno Press.

Heichelheim, F. (1938) *Wirtschaftsgeschichte des Altertums: vom Paläolithikum bis zur Völkerwanderung der Garmanen, Slaven und Araber.* 2 vols. Leiden. 2nd edn. 3 vols. 1969. Transl. and rev. *An Ancient Economic History: from the Palaeolithic Age to the Migrations of the Germanic, Slavic and Arabic Nations.* 3 vols. 1958, 1964, 1970. Leiden. Transl. *Storia economica del mondo antico.* 1972. Bari: Laterza.

Heichelheim, F. (1954/5) On ancient price trends from the early first millennium B.C. to Heraclius I. *Finanzarchiv* 15, 498–511.

Loomis, W. (1998) *Wages, Welfare Costs and Inflation in Classical Athens.* Ann Arbor: University of Michigan Press.

McCormick, M. (2001) *Origins of the European Economy. Communications and Commerce AD 300-900.* Cambridge: Cambridge University Press.

Maddison, A. (2007) *Contours of the World Economy 1-2030 AD. Essays in Macro-Economic History.* Oxford: Oxford University Press.

Rathbone, D. W. (1983) The weight and measurement of Egyptian grains. *Zeitschrift für Papyrologie und Epigraphik* 53, 265–275.

Reger, G. (1994) *Regionalism and Change in the Economy of Independent Delos.* Berkeley: University of California Press.

Rhodes, P. and Osborne, R. (2003) *Greek Historical Inscriptions, 404 - 323 BC.* Oxford: Oxford University Press.

Rostovtzeff, M. (1935–36) The Hellenistic World and its economic development. *Ancient History Review* 41, 231–252.

Scheidel, W., Morris, I. and Saller, R. (eds) (2007) *The Cambridge Economic History of the Greco-Roman World.* Cambridge: Cambridge University Press.

Scheidel, W. and Von Reden, S. (eds) (2002) *The Ancient Economy.* Edinburgh: Edinburgh University Press.

Sperber, D. (1991) *Roman Palestine, 200-400: Money and Prices*. 2nd edition. Ramat-Gan (1st edition 1974): Bar-Ilan University Press.

Szaivert, W. and Wolters, R. (2005) *Löhne, Preise, Werte. Quellen zur römischen Geldwirtschaft*. Darmstadt: Wissenschaftliche Buchgesellschaft.

Von Freyberg, H.-U. (1998) *Kapitalverkehr und Handel im römischen Kaiserreich (27 v. Chr. – 235 n. Chr.)*. Freiburg im Breisgau: Haufe.

Index

GEOGRAPHICAL NAMES

TEXTUAL SOURCES (CUNEIFORM)

TEXTUAL SOURCES (GREEK AND LATIN)